LOCKE, BERKELEY, HUME

Locke, Berkeley Hume

CENTRAL THEMES

BY

JONATHAN BENNETT

CLARENDON PRESS · OXFORD

Oxford University Press, Ely House, London W.1

GLASGOW NEW YORK TORONTO MELBOURNE WELLINGTON
CAPE TOWN IBADAN NAIROBI DAR ES SALAAM LUSAKA ADDIS ABABA
DELHI BOMBAY CALCUTTA MADRAS KARACHI LAHORE DACCA
KUALA LUMPUR SINGAPORE HONG KONG TOKYO

First published 1971
Reprinted in Great Britain
at the University Press, Oxford
by Vivian Ridler
Printer to the University
1972

PREFACE

THIS book discusses three topics, in the company of three philosophers: meaning, causality, objectivity; Locke, Berkeley, Hume. These 'central themes' are the only large philosophical areas on which each of these philosophers had a good deal to say. Berkeley says almost nothing about innate ideas, or about personal identity, but my real reason for omitting these empiricist themes is that I have nothing worthwhile to say about them.

I do not aim to be scholarly, except in the limited sense that I sometimes attend closely to textual details. Nor are my concerns historical: they relate primarily to three topics, and only secondarily to three philosophers. I hope to contribute to the understanding of the latter, not by presenting an amply rounded picture of their thought (even on the central themes), but by making it easier to get a firm hold on the logic of some of what they wrote. By focusing on just these philosophers, I do not imply an historical judgement. I need not care, for instance, whether Hume read Berkeley. All I need is the assumption, for which I hope my own book is evidence, that the work of each of the three can be usefully related to the work of the others.

The book grew out of lectures given in Cambridge in 1958–60 and 1962–4. More recently, I have conducted courses on the British empiricists while visiting Cornell University, the University of Michigan, and Princeton University: I am deeply grateful to these universities for their hospitality, and to the students whom I taught there for all that they taught me. I have been helped by more people than I can name here, but I do wish to express especial gratitude to Robert M. Adams, John Gates Bennett, Malcolm Budd, E. J. Furlong, Arnold Herschorn, Anne Wilbur MacKenzie, George Pitcher, H. H. Price, Richard Sorabji, and Michael Tanner.

A dozen sections of the book are versions of material which has appeared before—§§ 11, 14–16, 20, 24–25 in the *American Philosophical Quarterly,* and §§ 35–9 in *Philosophy*. I am indebted to the editors for their permission to reprint.

Readers are advised to glance over the Bibliography before trying to cope with the footnotes.

University of British Columbia   J. F. B.

CONTENTS

V. BERKELEY ON REALITY: AGAINST LOCKE

VI. BERKELEY ON REALITY: IDEALISM

VII. BERKELEY ON GOD AND SCEPTICISM

VIII. ACTIVITY AND CAUSALITY

IX. EMPIRICISM ABOUT MEANINGS

CONTENTS

I

IDEAS AND MEANINGS: LOCKE

1. *Meaning and understanding*

SOMEONE may utter words and mean nothing by them, or hear words and understand nothing by them: communication involves not just uttering and hearing, but also meaning and understanding. What is it to attach a meaning to an utterance? Or, to take plainly related questions, what is it for a type of utterance to have a meaning, or for a system of such types to constitute a language? I intend these as questions about the meaning of 'mean', 'language' and so on, not about what else goes on when someone speaks with meaning, hears with understanding or the like.

One kind of theory about this has been widely accepted across the centuries. Locke and Hume were devotees of it, and Berkeley was a fellow-traveller. I want to examine it both for its own sake and because a grasp of it is essential to an understanding of all three of these philosophers. Let us examine the theory in Locke's version of it. Because God wanted us to be able to communicate with one another in language, Locke says:

Man, therefore, had by nature his organs so fashioned, as to be fit to frame articulate sounds, which we call words. But this was not enough to produce language; for parrots ... make articulate sounds distinct enough, which yet by no means are capable of language. Besides articulate sounds, therefore, it was further necessary that he should be able to use these sounds as signs of internal conceptions; and to make them stand as marks for the ideas within his own mind, whereby they might be made known to others, and the thoughts of men's minds be conveyed from one to another.[1]

To attach meaning to an utterance, then, is to make it 'stand as a mark' for one or more 'internal conceptions' or 'ideas' in one's own mind, and language's main task is to transfer ideas from one mind to another. This is the translation view of language: wishing to share with you something in my mind, I translate it

[1] *Essay* III. i. 1–2.

into the public medium of articulate sounds; you hear the objective, interpersonal noises that I make, and re-translate them back into something in your mind; and so communication is complete. Thus Locke, explicitly:

Man, though he have great variety of thoughts, and such from which others as well as himself might receive profit and delight; yet they are all within his own breast, invisible and hidden from others, nor can of themselves be made to appear. The comfort and advantage of society not being to be had without communication of thoughts, it was necessary that man should find out some external sensible signs, whereof those invisible ideas, which his thoughts are made up of, might be made known to others. . . . Thus we may conceive how *words*, which were by nature so well adapted to that purpose, came to be made use of by men as the signs of their ideas.[2]

This surely has truth in it. We do have private thoughts which we communicate through language, and when communication succeeds—when you and I attach the same meaning to my words —it is reasonable to say that I, through my words, transmit my thought to you.

An important detail: as sentences are built out of words, Locke implies, so 'thoughts' are built of 'ideas'; an idea is an atom of meaning, expressible by a word which is an atom of language. This deserves tolerance too, for is it not natural to say 'His idea of communism is different from mine', for example, meaning 'He does not mean by "communism" what I do'?

Many familiar distinctions can be expressed in terms of Locke's theory: between what I usually mean by a given word and what I mean by it on one occasion, between its standard or normal meaning and what Smith means by it, between misunderstanding it and attaching no meaning to it, and so on. For example, Locke can equate *the meaning of the sentence S* with *the kind of thought people usually associate with S*. This is too simple (we still do not know just how 'the meaning of S' relates to 'what x means by S'), but it goes in the right direction. Locke's theory does, in a way, work.

But here tolerance stops. Those virtues in the theory are superficial ones without which it could hardly have tempted anyone. When the theory is probed, fatal defects come to light. I shall expound two of these: each depends only upon the theory's

<hr>

[2] *Essay* III. ii. 1.

general structure and not its special details, and the two together point towards an alternative kind of theory which is much more promising.

According to Locke, if I say 'Pass the sugar' and give this sentence its normal meaning, then I must have in my mind an 'idea of sugar'—that is, I must be thinking about sugar. What about the converse of this? If I think about sugar while using the word 'sugar', does it follow that I am giving 'sugar' its standard meaning? (1) If Locke said 'Yes', he would be wrong. Obviously, someone could brood over his need for sugar while uttering the sentence 'Pass the sugar' without meaning by that sentence that the sugar was to be passed, and indeed without meaning by it anything at all. For example, he might know no English and, in the course of experimentally trying to make English-sounding noises, happen to produce that sentence while wishing that someone would pass him the sugar. (2) In fact, Locke would answer 'No': for a speaker to mean something by his words, he must not merely have ideas in his mind but must use his words to 'stand as marks for' his ideas. Locke usually includes this extra condition, and most clearly here (my emphasis):

So far as words are of use and signification, so far is there a constant connexion between the sound and the idea, *and a designation that the one stands for the other*; without which application of them, they are nothing but so much insignificant noise.[3]

It is implausible to say that words, when used meaningfully, always stand for ideas in the speaker's mind; but never mind that.[4] My complaint is that Locke offers to explain 'meaning' yet helps himself to 'stand for', as though this needed no explanation. The two are not equivalent, for plenty of meaningful words, such as 'when', do not straightforwardly 'stand for' anything; but still they are much too closely connected to be split apart as Locke splits them. Someone who asks 'What is it for a word to be uttered and meant?' will surely also think it worthwhile to ask the slightly less general question 'What is it for a word to be used to stand for something?' Locke's only answer to the latter is the answer generated by his analysis of 'meaning' generally: 'To use the word "sugar" [say] to stand for sugar is to use it to

---

[3] *Essay* III. ii. 7.
[4] See Kretzmann, 'The Main Thesis of Locke's Semantic Theory'.

stand for the idea of sugar in one's mind'—which is no answer at all.

This difficulty about 'speaker's meaning' also infects 'hearer's meaning'—i.e. understanding. To count as understanding what one hears, it is not enough that while hearing it one also has a certain thought. Nor is it enough, as Locke perhaps thinks, that the thought be caused or 'excited' by what one hears:[5] your words might excite a thought in me through a psychological mechanism of which I knew nothing; in which case I might wrongly think that they had nothing to do with the advent of the thought, and *rightly* think that I understood nothing by them. Locke might strengthen the conditions for understanding thus: I understand something by your words if they excite in me a thought which I take to be like the one you used your words to 'stand for'. That would be a move in the right direction, since, broadly speaking, what I understand by your words is what I take you to mean by them. But just because the concept of 'hearer's meaning' is in this way dependent upon that of 'speaker's meaning', Locke's failure with the latter is also a failure with the former.

My second criticism of Locke's theory is addressed to a single aspect of it, namely its implying that meaning is something which one does or undergoes while uttering.

Because one can utter words without meaning anything by them, 'He uttered S and meant something by it' says more than 'He uttered S'. It does not follow, though, that the former statement conjoins a report on one thing he did (uttering) with a report on another thing he did at the same time (meaning). If it did follow, we should have to say that two synchronous activities are reported by 'He criticized Kant and thereby made a fool of himself' or by 'He gave John ten dollars and thereby discharged his debt'—and that would clearly be wrong. So the conclusion that to utter-and-mean is to do two things at once is not adequately supported by the true premiss that one can utter without meaning.

The conclusion is not just inadequately supported, but is false. I proceed to argue this by reductio ad absurdum.

If meaning something by what you utter involves uttering while doing or undergoing something else, then the 'something else' must be an *inner* activity or process. That is, it cannot be anything like an overt, casually observable, physical gesture or

[5] *Essay* III. ii. 6.

expression. This is because, as we all know, two people may utter a sentence, only one of them meaning something by it, without there being any outward, observable, behavioural difference between them at the time; whence it follows that if one of them performs an 'act of meaning' and the other does not, it must be an inner act.

An 'inner act', in my sense, need not be a mental act and need not be essentially private. It could be the pushing around of electrons in one's brain. Locke does represent the act of meaning (or process of understanding) as a kind of mental happening, and he may be committed—by that together with other aspects of his philosophy—to saying that one *could* not discover whether anyone else ever performed such an act or underwent such a process. And—to take another way in which he makes himself unnecessarily vulnerable[6]—he commits himself to the view that acts of meaning and understanding are open to introspection, and that one could not perform such an act without being aware of it. But I shall appeal to no such relatively detailed points in Locke's theory. Just by having a synchronous-act theory of meaning, Locke commits himself to the act's being 'inner' in my weak sense, i.e. to its being one that does not meet the eye of the unskilled though alert bystander; and this suffices to refute the theory. For, even if we could come to know whether our fellow-humans perform inner acts of the relevant kind (whatever that may be), we have not yet gained such knowledge: what most of us *do* know about one another is restricted to what can be learned from passive, unexperimental, hands-off observation; and so we do not in fact know what inner acts, if any, they perform. So, if an inner-act theory of meaning is correct, we do not yet know that people sometimes do, and that other animals sometimes do not, mean something by what they utter, and *a fortiori* we do not yet know *what* anyone means by what he utters. Since we clearly do have knowledge of this kind, that refutes every inner-act theory of meaning, and thus every synchronous-act theory of meaning.

For example, Locke could not comfortably explain how he knows that 'parrots make articulate sounds yet by no means are capable of language'. According to his kind of theory, the parrot's cries are 'insignificant noise' rather than meaningful

6 See J. J. Katz, *The Philosophy of Language* (New York, 1966), pp. 176–85.

language because a requisite inner activity or process is not going on in the parrot—but how does Locke know that it isn't going on? Again, he is not entitled to his confidence that people often mean something, and his frequent confidence about what they mean, by the words they utter. For years now Smith's use of English has been normal and socially acceptable; but we have not checked on what has been happening inside Smith's body or 'inside' his mind; and so we do not—according to Locke's theory—know that he has ever understood or meant anything.

Locke seldom mentions this agnostic conclusion, though in one place he seems to accept it with some complacency.[7] Elsewhere he sees it as a prima facie difficulty which he undertakes, a good deal too blandly, to dispatch. Admitting that two people might use a word in the same way in the same circumstances and yet give it different meanings, he airily brushes this possibility aside because (1) we could not know whether it was realized, (2) it is probably not realized, and (3) even if it were realized it would not be useful to know this! The incoherence of this shows Locke's failure to see the depth of his difficulty:

Neither would it [matter if] *the same object should produce in several men's minds different ideas* at the same time; v.g. if the idea that a violet produced in one man's mind by his eyes were the same that a marigold produced in another man's, and vice versa. For, [1] since this could never be known, ... neither the ideas hereby, nor the names, would be at all confounded, or any falsehood be in either ... [2] I am nevertheless very apt to think that the sensible ideas produced by any object in different men's minds, are most commonly very near and undiscernibly alike. For which opinion, I think, there might be many reasons offered: but that being besides my present business, I shall not trouble my reader with them; but only mind him, that [3] the contrary supposition, if it could be proved, is of little use, either for the improvement of our knowledge, or conveniency of life, and so we need not trouble ourselves to examine it.[8]

I have treated that passage as an episode in Locke's theory of meaning, but does it not look more like philosophy of perception? It is in fact both at once, and this is explained by a special feature of Locke's theory which will loom larger as we proceed—namely the use of 'idea' to refer to a mental item which could endow a

[7] *Essay* III. ii. 4.   [8] *Essay* II. xxxii. 15.

word with a meaning and to refer to a sense-impression or sense-datum. For Locke, this is not an ambiguity in 'idea'. The two questions 'Do you mean by "violet" what I do?' and 'Do violet things sensorily affect you as they do me?' are doubtless closely related; but Locke genuinely does not distinguish them, taking them to be two versions of the single, univocal question 'Are your ideas of violet the same as mine?' I shall return to this point later.

The second objection I have brought against Locke's theory raises a problem. If 'He uttered S at time *t* and meant something by it' does not conjoin two reports on things he did at *t*, what does it do? What sort of addition does it make to the simple 'He uttered S at *t*'? Wittgenstein has helped us to see how to answer this without representing meaning as an act or process.[9] The question of what someone means by S when he utters it at *t* could, Wittgenstein suggests, be equivalent to one or more questions of the form 'What would he have said or done at *t* if . . .?' together perhaps with questions about his sayings or doings at other times. So, two speakers who don't differ outwardly at *t* may both utter S at *t* with only one of them meaning something by it, for two reasons. Firstly, they may differ in their dispositions at *t*; that is, questions of the form 'What would he have said or done at *t* if . . . ?' may have different answers for each. Secondly, they may differ in their actual behaviour, linguistic and otherwise, at times other than *t*. Both sorts of difference are available to the casual observer, because the second sort gives evidence for the first.

As well as dispositional differences at *t* and episodic differences at other times, there may well be episodic differences at *t*—perhaps physiological ones which would causally explain the differing behavioural dispositions, or differences in the mental imagery of the two speakers. But inner accompaniments—whether physiological, imaginative, or what you will—are not constitutive of meaning. They may have a role in the scientific explanation or the natural history of meaning phenomena, but they do not figure in the analysis of the concept of meaning: when we say 'One of them means something by S and the other does not' we are not saying that there is an inner episodic difference between them.

To take a closely related point: it may be true that no human

<hr>

[9] L. Wittgenstein, *The Blue and Brown Books* (Oxford, 1958), pp. 37–44.

can perform well enough to count as knowing a language unless he has acquired a certain inner structure, e.g. by having unconsciously constructed a generative grammar of the language in question. But could it be maintained with any plausibility that when we say that someone 'knows English' we *mean* something about the generative grammar which he has unconsciously constructed? Chomsky apparently thinks so:

Suppose that we were to propose that to know a language is to have constructed, to be sure unconsciously, a specific generative grammar. A familiar argument against this proposal is that I can tell whether someone knows English, but I know nothing of the internal workings of his mind. The argument seems to me weak, because it begs a question rather like the one under discussion. If we are prepared to admit that the mind can incorporate unconscious theories, systems of principles and rules that we might describe as unconscious knowledge, then it is at least conceivable that I have an unconscious theory that attributes to other persons minds of a certain character, and that assigns to them mental states by virtue of certain actions that they perform. Suppose, furthermore, that this theory relates to my unconscious theory of English in such a way that I believe someone to know English when I attribute to him the mental state described by (or incorporating) the rules and principles of English grammar, arriving at this conclusion on the basis of his behaviour. I see no incoherence in this formulation, which would lead to the conclusion that my concept 'knowledge of a language' is directly related to the concept 'internalization of the rules of grammar'.[10]

The suggestion seems to be that there might be a specific mental structure M, which 'incorporates' an adequate generative grammar for English, such that we unconsciously accept *both* a theory of the form 'If x's behaviour is . . ., then x has M' *and* the theory that if x has M then x knows English. I shall not object to the former of these. If there is a mental structure M which I *have*, and which underlies my own linguistic competence, then indeed I might unconsciously relate your linguistic performances to your having M, even though I have absolutely no conscious knowledge of what M is. But what of the other 'unconscious theory'— the one by virtue of which I am supposed to move from 'x has M' to 'x knows English'? This so-called 'theory' is supposed to relate my concept of M to my concept of knowing-English; and

[10] N. Chomsky, 'Knowledge of Language', *Times Literary Supplement*, 15 May 1969, p. 524.

so my having this 'theory' must really be my *meaning* by 'knows English' something which involves the meaning of 'has M'. Furthermore, I am supposed to mean this 'unconsciously'—being unable to mean it consciously until grammatical or neurophysiological research discovers what M *is*. This is just Chomsky's suggestion with the wraps off, and I submit that it is obviously untenable. His phrase 'unconscious theory of English' is misleading: it suggests that what Chomsky is supposing is indeed 'rather like' the sort of unconscious mental structure to which he alludes at the start of the quoted passage; but really it is not like that to any significant extent.

I am not here objecting to anything in Chomsky's suggestion about what is involved in knowing English: for purposes of my present argument I do 'admit that the mind can incorporate unconscious theories' etc. But I deny that it is therefore 'conceivable' that what we mean by some expression should vastly outrun the limits of our conscious knowledge.

Of course, Chomsky's suggestion might be plausible if it were watered down to this: we unconsciously accept a theory of the form 'If x's behaviour is . . ., then x has whatever mental structure would account for this behaviour', and we mean by 'x knows English' something of the form 'x has whatever mental structure would account for his behaviour's being . . .'. I am not sure that this differs significantly from the Wittgensteinian thesis that what we mean by 'x knows English' is just something about how x does behave and how x would behave if. . . . In any case, the watered-down version cannot be what Chomsky wants to defend: if it were, then the 'familiar argument' could obviously be rebutted without appealing to a further double dose of unconscious theory.

Let us now return to my first criticism of Locke's theory. It amounted to this: the theory makes no satisfactory provision for the notion of what is meant or understood *by* an utterance; to escape connecting the utterance to the meaning far too loosely, it has to invoke a connexion ('standing for') which begs too much of the question. So that criticism, like the other one, locates a problem, namely that of giving a proper account of 'meaning *by*'.

The concept of *intending* presents a glittering prospect. If meaning were a kind of intending, then 'meaning something *by* what one utters' could be elucidated in terms of the more general 'intending something *by* what one does': even if meaning were a very special case of intending, relatable to it only through a very complex analysis, one might expect the notion of '. . . -ing *by*' to carry through from general to special, from intending to meaning.

It is easy to think that 'meaning' can be elucidated in terms of 'intending', and indeed without much complexity: to mean something by what you utter is just to intend by your uttering to produce in your hearers a certain result—a belief if you mean a statement, an action if you mean a command, an utterance if you mean a question, and so on. Minor details apart, haven't we here the essentials of a satisfactory analysis of 'mean' in terms of 'intend'? Notoriously, we have not. There are innumerable cases where 'He intended by uttering S to produce in his hearers . . .' is true although the corresponding statement of the form 'What he meant by S was . . .' is false; and attempts to deal with these cases by piecemeal repairs to the analysis have regularly failed.

Still, intending is not yet out of the running, for a remarkable paper by H. P. Grice contains a fresh and highly promising suggestion as to how meaning might be a special case of intending.[11] Grice's work needs—in addition to minor corrections —major expansion and elaboration.[12] As it stands, it is much less than a full-fledged analysis of the concept of meaning. But in my judgement, which I shall not defend here, it is a thoroughly promising starting-point for such an analysis.

The threads can now be drawn together.

There is a growing consensus among philosophers that a statement of the form 'By doing A at *t*, he intended . . .' does not report a process or activity of intending which occurred at *t*, but rather says something about what he would have done at *t* if . . ., and perhaps also about what he did or will or would do at other times. If this general view about intending is correct, and if meaning is a kind of intending, then we reach Wittgenstein's view that what someone means at *t* is a matter of how he behaves at other times and about how he would behave—at *t* or at other times—if circumstances were different in various ways. And this was the view I advocated in connexion with my *second* criticism of Locke's theory.

[11] H. P. Grice, 'Meaning', *Philosophical Review*, vol. 66 (1957).
[12] See H. P. Grice, 'Utterer's Meaning and Intentions', *Philosophical Review*, vol. 78 (1969).

So the problem of 'meaning something *by* . . .' points to the notion of intending, and Grice's work makes it possible to follow the pointer; and then a certain plausible view about intending has implications which solve our other problem, namely the one about how to represent meaning as publicly accessible and therefore as something other than an activity which is synchronous with uttering. Grice's work, then, promises to add depth and exactness to Wittgenstein's suggestions about meaning, and also relates them to neighbouring conceptual areas. To be fair, I should add that it does this only with the help of a general view about intending which itself owes much to Wittgenstein.[13]

2. *Classifying*

How does one recognize distinct particular things as being of the same kind, and thus know to apply a single classificatory word to each of them? Locke sought to answer this, apparently, by describing a rule or technique or general method for classifying —a method which requires that each word shall be associated with a kind of idea. This 'theory of classification' of Locke's is not often separated as sharply as it should be from his theory of word-meaning.[14] I shall discuss the relations between them at the end of this section, but in the meantime I take the former theory severely on its own.

Before expounding the theory, I shall argue that it fails, that it must fail because it attempts the impossible. The argument can be stated briefly, since the line of thought it involves has its own literature and is now fairly familiar.[15]

A comprehensive rule or technique for doing D must be statable as instructions to a novice—that is, instructions which someone who cannot yet do D could in principle follow and thereby be enabled to do D. But a novice at classification—someone who does not yet know how to assign any particulars to a

[13] On the theme of this entire section, see Flew, *Hume's Philosophy of Belief*, ch. 2.
[14] But see W. Doney, 'Locke's Abstract Ideas', *Philosophy and Phenomenological Research*, vol. 16 (1956), pp. 407–8.
[15] I. Kant, *Critique of Pure Reason* A 132–4 = B 171–4. L. Wittgenstein, *The Blue and Brown Books* (Oxford, 1958), pp. 1–19; *Philosophical Investigations* (Oxford, 1953), Pt. I, §§ 189–90; *Remarks on the Foundations of Mathematics* (Oxford, 1956), Pt. I, §§ 1–4. D. F. Pears, 'Universals', in A. Flew (ed.), *Logic and Language*, second series (Oxford, 1953). A. M. Quinton, 'Properties and Classes', *Proceedings of the Aristotelian Society*, vol. 58 (1957–8).

kind—cannot follow any rules or instructions. The instructions must take the form: 'Classify x in such and such a way if and only if Fx'; and the novice can follow them only if he already knows how to determine whether Fx. But if he can establish some truth, no matter what, about x, then he is not a novice of the kind we want, for he can already classify without the aid of the proffered rule. A rule for classifying as such, then, could be followed only by someone who did not need it; any such rule must be competence-presupposing.

The crucial statement about x which the rule or instructions embodied might be a relational one, but the argument still stands. A relation is just a property of pairs, trios, etc., and so someone who can determine whether Gxy or whether $Hxyz$ is someone who can classify and is therefore not our novice. This use of 'classify' might be arbitrary or wrong in some contexts, but not here. There are no grounds for demanding a technique for monadic classifications—the kind involved in applying adjectives and general nouns to individuals—while assuming that no such aid is needed for dyadic, triadic, etc., classifications of the kind involved in relational statements about pairs, trios, etc., of individuals.

The foregoing argument predicts that any supposed rule or technique for classifying will be in some specific way competence-presupposing. This prediction is certainly fulfilled by what I shall call 'universalism', i.e. the theory that we classify particulars by attending to the *universals* which they instantiate.[16] I want to know whether a given particular, x, is of the same kind as certain others, because I want to know whether to describe x as 'green', say. Universalism tells me to call to mind the universal which all those others instantiated, and which I associate with 'green', and to note whether x instantiates it too. If it does, then call x 'green'; otherwise don't. This could not help a novice, for it presupposes the ability (*a*) to re-identify the appropriate universal and (*b*) to recognize a case of instantiation, i.e. to tell that *that* is how x relates to the universal. As regards (*a*): for present purposes, I contend, re-identifying the very same universal is on a par with classifying. This is not obvious, but I shall defend it soon. As regards (*b*): it might be replied that there is no relation of instantiation—that to say 'x instantiates the universal of

[16] See B. Russell, *The Problems of Philosophy* (London, 1912), chapters 9 and 10.

greenness' is not to relate x to something else but is merely to say that x has the property of greenness, i.e. that x is green. That defence, though, renders the whole theory nugatory, for now its instructions say: 'Classify x as green if and only if it is green'. Versions of universalism do characteristically waver between the mysterious and covertly competence-presupposing, and the clear but explicitly competence-presupposing.

Locke rejected universalism: not because it is competence-presupposing, still less because it is bound to be so, but for the bad reason that 'All things that exist are only particulars',[17] and so there are no universals, and so universalism is just false. Locke had no inhibitions about trying to produce a rival theory which would succeed in universalism's impossible task. He saw the essential rivalry as consisting in his replacement of non-particular or universal items in the objective realm by 'general ideas' in our minds:

General and universal belong not to the real existence of things; but are the inventions and creatures of the understanding, made by it for its own use, and concern only signs, whether words or ideas. Words are general . . . when used for signs of general ideas.[18]

That, however, is tremendously misleading, and we shall see that it threw Berkeley right off the scent. Let us come down to details, patiently.

(Locke focuses on language-embodied classifications—on 'Shall I describe x as "green"?' rather than 'Shall I classify x as green?' When the two questions are expressed in words their differences are negligible; but a creature with no language may nevertheless classify, and so Locke's approach does narrow the area. Still, the narrowing makes for brevity and does no real harm: all my arguments could, though laboriously, be generalized into objections to Locke's theory considered as offering a technique not just for describing but for classifying generally.)

I want to know whether to describe x as 'green'. Locke tells me to bring to mind a 'general idea' of the kind associated with the word 'green', and to check this against x: if they 'agree', I may call x 'green'; if they do not, I may not. In his own words:

The mind makes the particular ideas received from particular objects to become general; which is done by considering them as they are in

17 Essay III. iii. 6.   18 Essay III. iii. 11.

the mind, . . . separate from all other existences, and the circumstances of real existence, as time, place, or any other concomitant ideas. . . . Such precise, naked appearances in the mind, without considering how, whence, or with what others they came there, the understanding lays up (with names commonly annexed to them) as the standards to rank real existences into sorts, as they agree with these patterns, and to denominate them accordingly.[19]

This technique for classifying is, like universalism, doubly competence-presupposing. To 'rank real existences into sorts' by Locke's method, one must already be able (a) to recognize a given 'general idea' as being of the appropriate kind, and (b) to recognize cases of 'agreement' between general ideas and particulars. Each point needs elaboration.

(a) Locke might be—and by Berkeley he was—thought to agree with universalism that there are inherently general or universal items, and to part company with it only in 'locating' these items in the mind rather than out there in the rest of the world. This would be a misinterpretation, for Locke insists that a 'general idea' is a mental *particular* which is 'general' only in the sense that it is used in a certain way:

Words are general . . . when used for signs of general ideas, and so are applicable indifferently to many particular things; and ideas are general when they are set up as the representatives of many particular things: but universality belongs not to things themselves, which are all of them particular in their existence, even those words and ideas which in their signification are general . . . [General ideas] are only creatures of our own making; their general nature being nothing but the capacity they are put into, by the understanding, of signifying or representing many particulars. For the signification they have is nothing but a relation that, by the mind of man, is added to them.[20]

The notion of a mental particular is unclear and suspect (see § 5 below); but Locke's stress on the particularity of all ideas has some fairly clear implications, e.g. that a single idea—as distinct from a pair of similar ones—cannot occur in two minds. Another consequence, one would think, is that one cannot have the very same idea in one's mind on separate occasions, and that Locke ought not to say that the mind 'lays up' ideas as though they were durable objects being stored for occasional use. In one rather inconclusive passage he does half-concede this,[21] and I think that

[19] *Essay* II. xi. 9.   [20] *Essay* III. iii. 11.   [21] *Essay* II. x. 2.

if pressed he would have agreed that a single idea cannot occur at separate times in someone's mind.

But then his technique for classifying is obviously competence-presupposing. It orders me, when I am wondering whether to call *x* 'green', to form in my mind an idea of the kind associated with 'green', and I cannot obey unless I can already classify ideas. In short, Locke presents ideas as 'standards' to be used in all classifications of particulars, but ideas are themselves particulars and cannot serve as standards until they have themselves been classified.

Of the suggestion that I obey the order 'Fetch me something red' by imagining something red and then looking for an object to match the image, Wittgenstein says:

Consider the order *'imagine* a red patch'. You are not tempted in this case to think that *before* obeying you must have imagined a red patch to serve you as a pattern for the red patch which you were ordered to imagine.[22]

This puts a precise finger on one circularity in Locke's kind of theory.

Locke probably overlooked the need to classify ideas because they are in the mind and, as Wittgenstein remarks, 'the mind' often serves as a haven for the not-to-be-explained. Suppose that in Locke's theory we replace mental images by physical ones such as paintings. The theory that images are all-purpose aids to classification is, now that the image is a physical one and has thus lost its 'occult' character, obviously worthless. 'It was in fact', Wittgenstein adds, 'just the occult character of the mental [image] which you needed for your purposes.'[23] This seems a not unfair comment on Locke's statement: 'The mind has a power in many cases to revive perceptions which it has once had, with this additional perception annexed to them, that *it has had them before*',[24] which occurs, without defence or explanation, in the chapter on 'Retention' which immediately *precedes* Locke's first sketch of his theory of classification.

I have construed Locke's technique as saying: 'Form in your mind *an* idea of the "green"-associated *kind* . . .'. But even if the identity of ideas were like that of universals, or alternatively

[22] L. Wittgenstein, *The Blue and Brown Books*, p. 3; see also p. 12.
[23] Ibid. p. 5.   [24] *Essay* II. x. 2.

like that of durable particular objects, so that the very same idea
could recur on separate occasions, the objection would still go
through. For the technique would still require one to re-identify
an individual idea on distinct occasions, and to re-identify *is* to
classify: re-identifying any enduring item A is classifying occasions
as A-encounters. This is why the universalist technique for classifying, in requiring one to identify a given universal as the one
instantiated in the past by such and such particulars or as the
one customarily associated with such and such a word, presupposes classificatory ability.

(*b*) Given that I somehow know that I have a 'green'-
associated idea in my mind, Locke's technique now requires me
to determine whether this idea 'agrees' with or is 'conformable'
to *x*. But this is to determine whether a certain relation holds
between *x* and the idea, which is another exercise in classifying.

Locke uses 'agree with' to mean 'resemble'. I deny that an idea
or mental image can resemble an extra-mental object (see § 5
below), but even if it can the present criticism still stands. To
discover that *x* resembles *y* is to discover that *x-y* is a resembling
pair, which is logically on a par with discovering that John holds
hands with Mary, i.e. that John-Mary is a hand-holding pair.

This is sometimes denied. Price, for example, in a context
closely related to our present theme, says that resemblance 'is too
fundamental to be called a relation at all, in the ordinary sense of
the word "relation".' [25] Locke himself may have some sympathy
with this view: there are pointers in that direction in his peculiar
theory that relations are 'not contained in the real existence of
things, but [are] something extraneous and superinduced',[26] and
in what he says about *comparison* as the basis for all our relational
statements.[27] But this is too complex a matter to be explored here,
and I can only say that *if* Locke did not count resemblance as a
relation I do not know why.

There is, however, another reason why he might have overlooked the second failure of his technique. He may have intended
the technique to demand a resemblance between *x* and the idea,
and have assumed that resemblance, even if it is a relation, is
somehow so special, so ultimate, that no question could arise

[25] H. H. Price, *Thinking and Experience* (London, 1953), p. 26.
[26] *Essay* II. xxv. 8.
[27] *Essay* II. xii. 7; xxv. 9; xxviii. 1-2.

about how one knows whether one thing resembles another. For an oblique but penetrating criticism of this assumption, I refer the reader to Wittgenstein.[28]

A technique for classifications of a given kind need not presuppose an ability to make classifications of that kind. For example, instructions for applying terms in diagnostic medicine can be followed by someone who cannot yet apply any of *those* terms. So Locke might say: 'We find it easier to classify ideas than to classify extra-mental objects ("real existences"), and easier to discover resemblances than other relations. My theory describes the technique whereby, starting with a command of the easier tasks, we advance to a command of the harder ones.' This would clear him of both my criticisms, but only by laying him open to another, namely that the theory is refuted by empirical evidence. Of course, even in its unrestricted form the theory conflicts with the empirical evidence, but a proponent of it might say 'Well, we must accept this theory if we can't find an alternative to it: there has to be some technique which, whether or not we are conscious of it, we employ in classifying; for otherwise our ability to classify is just an intolerable mystery.' But the theory in its restricted form cannot be backed up with any such plea. Support for it must take the form: 'One can classify without employing anything like a rule or general technique; but in fact some of our classificatory activities do depend upon a technique of comparing objects with already-classified ideas.' It would be absurd to accept *this* without empirical evidence in its favour, but in fact the empirical evidence goes strenuously against it.

So Locke's purported technique will not stand, whether it is intended as fully comprehensive or only as a technique for making some classifications given the prior ability to handle others. Which way *did* Locke want his technique to be understood? There is probably no right answer. Indeed, Locke would probably have rejected each alternative if it had been presented to him clearly and explicitly, but that conjecture is not a defence of him. As Gibson says in a different connexion:

In attacking a position the practical strength of which depends upon an absence of clear definition, it is necessary to place the alternative interpretations of which it is susceptible in as searching a light as

[28] L. Wittgenstein, *Remarks on the Foundations of Mathematics* (Oxford, 1956), Pt. I, § 3.

possible; and the enterprise cannot be held to have failed of its object, if the result is to show that even in the opinion of its defenders no part of the ground is tenable.[29]

There are countless possible theories of classification against which my arguments do not have, and are not intended to have, any power at all. Among these are indefinitely many theories of the form 'In making F classifications we utilize our prior ability to make G classifications, in the following way ...'. Some such theories will be true, others false; but I have argued against only one of them, namely the theory that we classify extra-mental things on the basis of a prior ability to classify ideas and to spot resemblances. Clearly, if Locke is advancing a theory of this general sort it must be that one in particular.

I should mention a kind of theory which, though covering all classifications, nevertheless escapes my arguments in this section. In criticizing attempts to base classifications on an all-purpose technique, I have taken a 'technique' to be something expressible in the form 'If ..., do A' which comes into play only if someone's doing A arises from his *accepting* the conditional and *knowing* (or thinking, or seeing, etc.) that its antecedent fits his given situation. It was of the essence of my argument that something like knowledge had to be brought to bear upon the antecedent. But there can also be conditionals of the form 'If ..., then x does A', not embodying techniques or rules or recipes for doing A, but offering causal explanations of doings of A. A conditional of this sort bears upon my doing A just so long as the conditional is true and its antecedent fits my situation—I needn't accept the conditional or be in any way cognitively or intellectually involved with its antecedent. So a theory might, without circularity, explain every human achievement of classifying or recognizing. In explaining any intellectual feat of someone's, one must start from some fact about him; but this may be a fact about his brain or his bloodstream or his eyes, and need not be a fact about some preliminary intellectual feat which has helped him to the one being explained.

Even a theory of this sort might come under fire from someone whose interest is not in human functions but in the Nature of Generality. Some philosophers—probably including Locke—have been inclined to ask 'What makes it possible for generality to be

[29] Gibson, *Locke's Theory of Knowledge*, p. 40.

imposed upon a world of particulars?' This seems to demand that our ability to classify be explained, and yet it is plausible to say that even a causal-explanatory theory of classification would subtly beg this question, or pseudo-question. But the detailed development of this point would take me too far afield.

Anyway, we cannot attribute a causal type of theory to Locke. Admittedly, he does not describe classifying as a long-drawn-out procedure in the way I have implied, and I have done less than justice to his preparedness sometimes to view 'the understanding' not as an agent but as a receptacle for mental happenings.[30] So he may well see the classifying procedure thus: the pattern-idea just comes into one's mind, unbidden, at the moment one perceives the item to be classified; and the two are instantly checked off against one another; so that the question is answered before it can be asked. But if Locke is to escape from my main criticism, he needs more than this. Specifically, he has to say that in classifying one need neither *recognize* the pattern-idea nor *see that* it matches or resembles the item to be classified. I cannot—though I should like to—believe this account of his intentions.[31]

In my first section I accepted a broadly Wittgensteinian approach to questions about meaning. One aspect of this approach could be summed up in the statement that what someone (usually) means by a given word W is determined by how he (usually) does or would use W. This links meaning with classifying, since, for many values of W, how W is used is largely a matter of what particular things it is applied to. For example, the question of how someone uses 'elastic', and thus of what he means by that word, involves the question of whether he would apply it to such things as a brick, an ocean, a rubber band.

That is not all it involves, though. A full grasp of the meaning of 'elastic' includes, as well as the ability to pick out elastic things and describe them alone as elastic, also the ability to use the word properly in general statements, conditionals, questions, and so on. Furthermore, words like 'if' and 'perhaps' and 'is' and 'yesterday' have meanings which cannot be described even partly in these terms. We cannot even start to discover that someone uses 'if' correctly by considering what particular things he applies it to.

[30] *Essay* II. i. 22, 25; x. 7–8.   [31] *Essay* III. iii. 13, 20.

So any theory about the application of classificatory words to particulars would fall doubly short of being a comprehensive theory of word-meaning: it would be silent on many aspects of the meanings of classificatory words, and on all aspects of the hosts of words which are not classificatory.[32] Locke, however, was not apt to see this. He tends to write as though our only use of classificatory words were to apply or withhold them, like labels; and, though he acknowledges the existence of 'particles' such as 'is' and 'if', his very cursory treatment of them amounts to a depiction of them as classificatory after all—specifically, as words for classifying 'the several postures of [the] mind in discoursing'.[33] So I think Locke would tend to exaggerate the proportion of the total area of 'meaning' which is also covered by 'classifying'.

If he did, then he could summon one of his theories to the aid of the other, particularly in trying to deal with my charge in § 1 that he makes meanings inaccessible to the casual observer. (1) He might stick by his theory of meaning, and say that I can know that my neighbour means what I do by 'green' through a reliable symptom, namely his calling 'green' the things that I do. That this is a reliable symptom follows from the theory of classifying, which says that *how my neighbour applies* 'green' to things in the world depends (causally) upon *what ideas he associates with* that word, and by Locke's theory of meaning this is equivalent (analytically) to *what he means by* the word. (2) Alternatively, Locke might relinquish his theory of meaning as formulated, admitting that what constitutes the meaning one gives to a word is how one uses it in the public domain; yet go on to maintain that he was right, at least, in giving ideas a central role in meaning-theory even if they are not definitive of 'meaning'. For, he might say, meaning is constituted (analytically) by use, but the theory of classifying shows that disciplined use is made (causally) possible only by associating words with ideas.

Locke was too unaware of his own difficulties to be able to adopt either of these approaches, but the fact that each was prima facie open to him, I suggest, helps to explain the confidence with which he connects meaning with ideas.

---

[32] See P. T. Geach, *Mental Acts* (London, 1957), § 11; also Zabeeh, *Hume*, pp. 78–80.

[33] *Essay* III. vii. 3.

3. *Abstract ideas*

The ideas figuring in Locke's theories of meaning and classification were supposed to be 'abstract' in a sense which must now
be partially explained. Let us start here:

> The mind having got an an idea which it thinks it may have use of
> either in contemplation or discourse, the first thing it does is to abstract
> it, and then get a name to it; and so lay it up in its storehouse, the
> memory, as containing the essence of a sort of things, of which that
> name is always to be the mark.[34]

So, we have to *abstract* an idea in order to make it usable. The
process is essentially one of neglecting, omitting, setting aside:

> The mind makes the particular ideas received from particular objects
> to become general; which is done by considering them as they are in
> the mind . . . separate from all other existences, and the circumstances
> of real existence, as time, place, or any other concomitant ideas. This
> is called ABSTRACTION, whereby ideas taken from particular beings
> become general representatives of all of the same kind.[35]

Abstraction, though, involves somehow stripping an idea not
just of the 'circumstances' in which its like originally came into
one's mind, but also of some of its internal detail:

> When [children learn] that there are a great many other things in the
> world, that in some [respects] resemble their father and mother, and
> those persons they have been used to, they frame an idea, which they
> find those many particulars do partake in; and to that they give, with
> others, the name *man*, for example. And thus they come to have a
> general name, and a general idea. Wherein they make nothing new;
> but only leave out of the complex idea they had of Peter and James,
> Mary and Jane, that which is peculiar to each, and retain only what is
> common to them all.[36]

This procedure can be repeated to yield, for example, the still
more abstract idea of *animal*:

> which new idea is made, not by any new addition, but only as before,
> by leaving out the shape, and some other properties signified by the
> name man, and retaining only a body, with life, sense, and spontaneous
> motion, comprehended under the name animal.[37]

---

[34] *Essay* II. xxxii. 7. The main texts are II. xi. 8–10 and III. iii. 6–9.
[35] *Essay* II. xi. 9   [36] *Essay* III. iii. 7.   [37] *Essay* III. iii. 8.

In the next section the term 'abstract' is re-introduced, and the notion of omission is further stressed. So much for the textual basis.

I have already noted that Locke takes all 'ideas' to be something in the nature of sense-data—either as acquired in ordinary perception, hallucinations etc., or as imaginatively conjured up at will. This fact—which now shifts towards the centre of our concerns—shows in his saying, above, that the 'ideas' involved in meaning and classifying are developed by abstraction from 'particular ideas received from particular objects'. The latter are certainly meant to be the sense-data acquired in ordinary perception; and the ideas which figure in meaning and classifying— the ones that may be abstract, and that can be called to mind at will and are 'excited' in us when we understand—are supposed to be copies of them. You have a copy-idea in your mind when, for example, you see a face in your mind's eye or have a tune running through your head.

So an 'abstract' idea is a copy-idea, an idea such as one might have in imagining something, which is in some way sketchy or undetailed. Problems about just what this means will be discussed in §§ 6–7 in connexion with Berkeley's view that there cannot be abstract ideas. At the present stage, I am prepared to say confidently that something like a Lockean abstract idea can occur, on the grounds that someone can close his eyes and picture a woman's face, neither 'seeing' her as smiling nor 'seeing' her as unsmiling— which I take to imply that he has a somewhat abstract idea or image of her. Having a poor visual imagination, I prefer an example like this: I play a tune in my head, and I 'hear' it as orchestrated, which is different from 'hearing' it as played on a tin whistle; yet I do not 'hear' it as orchestrated in any completely specific fashion, neither as involving at least three oboes nor as involving fewer than three oboes; and so my auditory idea or image is abstract. Most people agree that they can do something of the sort I have here roughly and metaphorically described. Whether images can be sketchy to the same degree that word-meanings can be general is, of course, another question.

As that remark implies, the theory of abstractness is required by Locke's view that the meaning of a word is determined by the idea (or class of similar ideas) associated with it. Here is the reason. If I say of something 'That is an animal', giving this its ordinary meaning, I say nothing about what sort of animal it is; and so the 'idea of animal' in my mind must not be the idea of a vertebrate animal, nor may it be the idea of an invertebrate animal; since an idea of either of these kinds would endow my utterance with a stronger meaning than is ordinarily carried by 'That is an animal'. In short, if meanings are determined by ideas, then the fact that meanings can be more or less informative or specific implies that ideas must be able to be more or less saturated with detail. To mean what is ordinarily meant by 'animal', I must make it 'stand for' an idea which has enough detail to count decisively as an idea of an animal but isn't detailed enough to count as an idea of an F animal, for any non-vacuous F. Clearly, the theory of meaning subjects the theory of abstractness to some strenuous demands.

Berkeley, we may note in passing, gives a quite different account of 'the source of this prevailing notion' that there are abstract ideas.[38] Obscure as this account is, I am fairly sure that its main thrust—if it has one—is correctly described by Warnock.[39] According to Warnock's Berkeley, Locke thought of general words as proper names, each referring to some one entity; and he postulated abstract ideas because they were needed to play the role of such entities—so that 'green', for instance, is the proper name of the abstract idea of green. Now, someone *might* arrive at the theory of abstract ideas by this route, but is there any evidence that Locke *did*? I have no reason to think that Locke regarded general words as proper names,[40] or that he thought that corresponding to every general word there is just one abstract idea rather than different abstract ideas in the minds of different people and at different times. And evidence is needed, for Berkeley's explanation cannot be forced onto us as the only possible one.

The theory of abstract ideas can also be seen as an aid to, or incident in, Locke's theory of classification. If I am to discover whether *x* is a man by checking *x* against a 'man'-associated idea, it may help if I have an idea which 'agrees' as closely with any man as with any other man; an idea lacking the sort of detail which usually informs the ideas (= sense-data) I have when sensorily confronted by real men; an idea, that is, which is abstract. The

---

[38] *Principles*, Introduction § 18.   [39] Warnock, *Berkeley*, pp. 72–3.
[40] See *Essay* III. iii. 12.

theory of abstractness, then, has a role to play in Locke's account of classification, and this is the role that Lockean commentators usually stress, in the belief that it is a leading one. 'How, in a nutshell, did Locke try to solve the "problem" of explaining our ability to classify particulars?' Most commentators, and indeed Locke himself, would answer: 'By means of his theory about *abstract* ideas.' This answer is misleading.

The crucial point is that Locke's abstractness doctrine goes no way towards meeting the charge that his theory of classification presupposes competence in two distinct ways. The questions 'How do I know that this idea is a "man"-linked one?' and 'How do I know that the relation between x and this idea is one of agreement?' are not made one whit more answerable by the stipulation that the idea in question is an abstract one. The irrelevance of the abstractness doctrine to the objections which kill the theory of classification implies that the former is not a large or vital part of the latter. In fact, the abstractness doctrine is not even prima facie a solution of the 'problem' of how we can apply one word to many particulars, but only of the following tiny part of it.

If we classify things by checking them against 'patterns' or samples, how do we know which features of a given sample are relevant? Someone wonders whether to describe x as 'red', and he has established, somehow, that S is a sample of red and that S resembles x. But the resemblance is not total: in fact (though *he* is not in a position to say this), S is red, square, made of tweed, rough to the touch, and smelling faintly of lavender; while x is red, round, made of silk . . . etc. How can he select from among all the features of S the ones which are relevant to his problem of whether to describe x as 'red'?[41]

The theory of abstractness is, at least prima facie, a solution of this 'problem'. It says that the sample is always an idea which is sketchy or abstract to such a degree that it simply doesn't have any features which are irrelevant to the classification in question, so that the problem of 'how to select the relevant features' does not arise.

So if we could render credible the thesis that we always classify things by comparing them with samples, while leaving shrouded in mystery the question of how we manage to select the relevant

[41] See L. Wittgenstein, *Philosophical Investigations* (Oxford, 1953), Pt. I, § 73.

feature(s) of any given sample, *then* we should have a problem to which the theory of abstractness might be the solution. But in relation to the large 'problem' of how we are able to classify particulars, abstractness as such is peripheral. As some of the quoted passages show, Locke did not see this. He saw his theory of ideas as a rival to universalism in explaining how we classify, and thought that the crux of his theory—the feature of it which fitted it to do universalism's work without invoking universals—was precisely its saying that the ideas we use as patterns are abstract. In this he erred.

4. *The double use of 'idea'*

Locke's thought is dominated by his attempt to use 'idea' univocally as a key term in his accounts of perception and of meaning—or, in short-hand, his use of 'idea' to cover both sense-data and concepts. Passages already quoted show this use at work, but not sharply enough.

Here is Locke's initial explanation of the word 'idea':

I must here . . . beg pardon of my reader for the frequent use of the word *idea*, which he will find in the following treatise. It being that term which, I think, serves best to stand for whatsoever is the *object* of the understanding when a man thinks, I have used it to express . . . *whatever it is which the mind can be employed about in thinking.*[42]

Then later he says: 'To ask, at what *time* a man has first any ideas, is to ask, when he begins to perceive; *having ideas*, and *perception*, being the same thing'.[43] If the two passages seem to conflict violently, recall that Descartes, by whom Locke was much influenced, was prepared to use 'think' to cover mental goings-on of any sort at all. Taken together, these two passages have the effect of stretching 'think' in one direction and 'perceive' in the other; and Locke's willingness to make these stretches is fundamental to his thought.

His double use of 'idea', then, is not a mere terminological nuisance: it embodies his substantive mistake, shared with Berkeley and Hume and others in the empiricist tradition, of assimilating the sensory far too closely to the intellectual. Having made some general remarks about this mistake elsewhere, I shall

---

[42] *Essay*, Introduction § 8.   [43] *Essay* II. i. 9.

here confine myself to presenting detailed instances of it.[44] To understand the empiricists' writings one must be able to handle their assimilations of the sensory to the intellectual: to recognize them, correct them, salvage sense from passages infected by them, trace their influence, and so on. I can offer no clear rules or reliable techniques for doing this; but examples may help, and the main purpose of this section is to provide some.

(1) Locke was an empiricist about meanings: he held that no classificatory word makes sense to us unless either (a) we have sensorily encountered things to which it applies, or (b) we can define it in terms of words which satisfy (a). I shall discuss this theory, in Hume's version of it, more fully in chapter IX; just now, one aspect of it will serve to illustrate the sensory-intellectual assimilation. According to Locke, one makes sense of a word by associating it with a kind of idea, and ideas are also the items one has in ordinary perception; and so he can drastically over-simplify meaning-empiricism by taking it to say merely that one cannot have ideas in one way without first having them in another. A doctrine which is so complex that no one has yet stated it adequately thus appears to Locke to have the same logical form as the *simple* untruth: 'You cannot see a play without first reading it.'

This spurious simplicity of meaning-empiricism probably also increases Locke's confidence in its truth. Any kind of idea must have entered my mind in the first place—*ex nihilo nihil fit*—which is just to say that it must have entered from the outside, i.e. have first been had in sensory encounters with things. So we find Locke saying:

If it shall be demanded then, *when* a man *begins* to have any ideas, I think the true answer is,—*when he first has any sensation*. For, since there appear not to be any ideas in the mind before the senses have con-veyed any in, I conceive that ideas in the understanding are coeval with *sensation*.[45]

The words 'there appear not to be' suggest that Locke is offering a tentative empirical conjecture (see § 47 below). But doesn't he also seem inclined to think that it stands to reason that ideas must enter the mind *from* somewhere, and thus to regard his meaning-empiricism as a simple, obvious, inevitable truth?

[44] J. Bennett, *Kant's Analytic* (Cambridge, 1966), § 17.   [45] *Essay* II. i. 23.

For a further illustration of how the double use of 'idea' simplifies meaning-empiricism, look back at the 'violet/marigold' passage discussed in § 1 above.

(2) Locke avoids a certain difficulty in his theory of meaning by saying that words 'stand for' the ideas with which they are associated, which seems to imply—implausibly—that a word stands for its meaning. Remember, though, that for Locke 'ideas' are also sense-data. He is given to saying that in our experience of the objective world all we are directly confronted with are our own 'ideas' or sensory states; and this allows him to think that in everything we say our most immediate and intimate sub-ject-matter consists of our own *ideas*, the reference to *things* being a secondary one. This is a thesis about 'ideas' not as meanings but as sense-data, but it can also be expressed in the words 'Our words stand for our ideas'.

I do not defend 'Our words stand for our ideas' on either in-terpretation of it, but merely note that Locke's double use of 'idea' makes both interpretations available to him. I further suggest that his acceptance of a statement which seems to imply 'I use the word "sugar" to stand for its own meaning' may be partly explained by his construing it so as to imply 'I use the word "sugar" to stand for sugar-as-I-experience-it, or for the sense-data I have when I see or taste or touch sugar'.

(3) I shall introduce more striking consequences of the double use of 'idea' in §§ 52, 62 below; but I now restrict myself to one further example, not of what Locke is led into by this mistake, but rather of the way in which its presence in his work can enrich and complicate our exegesis.

The example concerns Locke's use of 'idea' to mean 'quality'. He tries to keep the words apart, and tells us how to construe his failures to do so:

Whatsoever the mind perceives *in itself*, or is the immediate object of perception, thought, or understanding, that I call *idea*; and the power to produce any idea in our mind, I call *quality* of the subject wherein that power is. Thus a snowball having the power to produce in us the ideas of white, cold, and round,—the power to produce those ideas in us, as they are in the snowball, I call qualities; and as they are sensations or perceptions in our understandings, I call them ideas; which *ideas*, if I speak of sometimes as in the things themselves, I would be understood to mean those qualities in the objects which produce them in us.[46]

'That last explanation must be unnecessary. Surely no-one would slip into the practice of speaking of ideas "as in the things themselves".' On the contrary, Locke unwittingly adopts the practice in this very passage! The crucial words are: 'the power to produce those ideas in us, as *they* are in the snowball', where 'they' must refer back to 'ideas' and not to the singular 'power'. We might conjecture that Locke meant to write 'power*s*'; but then, apparently, he would be referring to the powers of a snowball as 'sensations or perceptions in our understandings', which won't do either.

Anyway, Locke often speaks of ideas as in the things themselves. Here is one of the more glaring examples: 'We cannot observe any alteration to be made in . . . anything, but by the observable change of its sensible ideas; nor conceive any alteration to be made, but by conceiving a change of some of its ideas.'[47] This passage can be unpacked according to Locke's instructions, and so perhaps can every other use of 'idea' to mean 'quality'. But why should he adopt this peculiar usage in the first place? I have two suggestions, one corresponding to each basic function of the word 'idea'.

(*a*) It is plausible to say that the meaning of any classificatory word W is determined solely by the qualities a thing must have if W is to apply to it; so statements about meanings are precisely correlated with statements about qualities;[48] and so the work done by 'quality' can as well be done by 'idea' (= meaning).

(*b*) Sense-data are our only source of information about the qualities of things; so when we speak of things' qualities our immediate subject-matter consists in the sense-data things cause in us; and so the work done by 'quality' can as well be done by 'idea' (= sense-datum).

Of these, (*b*) is the likelier explanation of the 'snowball' passage, but is the availability of (*a*) a sheer coincidence? I submit that Locke's tendency to use 'idea' to mean 'quality' is fed by both these sources.

Berkeley said that qualities *are* ideas: for him this was not an

---

[46] *Essay* II. viii. 8.
[47] *Essay* II. xxi. 1.
[48] Cf. G. Ryle, 'John Locke on the Human Understanding', pp. 18–19.

ellipsis to be unpacked (see § 14 below). In his case the explanation lies in (*b*), of which he accepted a very strong form; and (*a*)
probably has little to do with it. But even if (*a*) were a substantial
part of the explanation in Berkeley's case too, it would be wrong
to say, as I once did, that Berkeley was led to use 'idea' to cover
qualities by his having the double use of 'idea' which is my main
theme in this section, i.e. its use to cover both meanings and
sense-data.[49] My mistake was not exegetical but philosophical. A
philosopher who did not use 'idea' to cover sense-data could still
come by route (*a*) to use it to cover qualities; and one who did
not use 'idea' to cover meanings could still come by route (*b*) to
use it to cover qualities. Conversely, a philosopher might use
'idea' for both meanings and sense-data yet decline to use it for
qualities because he rejected both (*a*) and (*b*). In short, the meaning/
sense-datum equivocation does not of itself lead to speaking of
'the ideas of things' meaning 'the qualities of things'; all it yields
is the possibility of someone's coming to speak in this way for
two distinct reasons, one having to do with meanings and the
other with sense-data.

It is dangerous to speak as I have done of Locke's 'double use
of "idea" ', for this suggests that we are here confronted with a
case of simple ambiguity. The misleadingness of that account of
the situation can be seen by considering the common view that
Lockean 'abstract ideas' are not supposed to be sketchy images,
as Berkeley unfairly supposed, but rather to be general meanings.[50]
That complaint against Berkeley assumes that Locke's use of
'idea' is straightforwardly ambiguous: it alleges that in some of
his uses of 'idea'—and always in the phrase 'abstract idea'—Locke
simply uses the word 'idea' to mean 'meaning'.[51] But then his
theory of abstract ideas is just the thesis that there are general
meanings, which is boring, uncontroversial, and not even prima
facie explanatory. Locke thought he was explaining how there
can be general meanings, and to do justice to this aspect of his

---

[49] J. Bennett, 'Substance, Reality and Primary Qualities', Martin p. 94 (also in
Engle).

[50] Thus C. R. Morris, *Locke, Berkeley, Hume* (Oxford, 1931), pp. 72–3. Against this
mistake, see Warnock, *Berkeley*, p. 68; and J. Linnell, 'Locke's Abstract Ideas',
Philosophy and Phenomenological Research, vol. 16 (1956).

[51] C. Maund, *Hume's Theory of Knowledge* (London, 1937), pp. 67, 166–7; D.
Greenlee, 'Locke's Idea of "Idea"', *Theoria*, vol. 33 (1967). For a much better
account, see Flew, *Hume's Philosophy of Belief*, p. 22.

intentions we must construe his theory as saying that words get general meanings by being associated with quasi-sensory images of a certain sort, these latter being known as 'abstract ideas'.

I have no brief, satisfactory way of saying what the situation is regarding the use of the word 'idea' by Locke or Berkeley or Hume.

II

IDEAS AND MEANINGS: BERKELEY

5. How not to reify sense-data

I HAVE said vaguely that Locke's 'ideas' are, first and foremost, sense-data. A little more carefully: 'ideas of sensation' are sense-data; these are the ideas one has in perceiving the objective realm, in hallucinations, and so on. 'Ideas of reflection', on the other hand, are supposed to occur when we reflect or introspect, and to explain our understanding of words like 'pain', 'thought', 'puzzlement', etc.[1] This is part of Locke's account of self-knowledge as, almost literally, a kind of peering inwards. I agree with the currently popular view that the account is interesting but untenable, and my only reason for side-stepping it—and the associated problems about Berkeley's attitude to it[2]—is that I know I have nothing worthwhile to say on these topics.

Reverting now to the ideas (of sensation) which are sense-data: in giving them a role in his theory of meaning, Locke does not say that someone who hears and understands the sentence 'The house is on fire' has ideas *exactly* like those he would have if he saw or felt or heard the fire; for he would allow a difference of detailedness and perhaps also of intensity. Still, to explain what Locke supposes an 'idea' to be in any of its philosophical roles, we must begin by saying: ideas are sense-data.

Are there such things as sense-data? When I see a tree, do I immediately apprehend a visual sense-datum—an 'idea of sensation'—through or by means of which I see the tree? Many philosophers now reject this apparent reduplication of the objects of experience, thus condemning both Locke and my way of explaining him. In self-defence, and also in preparation for some Berkeleian themes, I must explain why and how I think it legitimate to use the term 'sense-datum'. My main task will be to criticize an improper way of using it—one of which Locke and

[1] See *Essay* II. i. 4, 7–8; vi. Also Gibson, *Locke's Theory of Knowledge*, pp. 56–7, 89–90.

[2] E. J. Furlong, 'An Ambiguity in Berkeley's Principles', *Hermathena*, vol. 94 (1960); G. A. Johnston, *The Development of Berkeley's Philosophy* (London, 1923), pp. 142–7.

Berkeley were both guilty, though it did not contribute much to any of the mistakes of Locke's which I have discussed so far. It is a misuse which looms large in most twentieth-century defences of, and attacks on, the 'sense-datum' terminology.

The question about sense-data, and the answer to it which I shall defend, involve a certain logical structure which should perhaps first be displayed in a less controversial application. So I shall first consider the question 'Are there such things as moods?', in the hope that this will clarify—*not support*—what I have to say about the question 'Are there such things as sense-data?' In stressing the logical similarity between the two questions, and between their respective answers, I deliberately snub a popular point which seems to me to have no philosophical significance—namely that 'sense-datum' does not (as 'mood' does) belong to vernacular English.

Of course there are moods. I was in a bad mood this morning, and my mood changed around noon. Still, one hesitates to say that there are such *things* as moods—it seems wrong to reify moods. To clarify 'It is wrong to reify moods' I offer the following two-part justification of it. Firstly, the only intelligible statements about moods are statements—which may be negative, general, conditional, etc.—about people's being *in* moods. I take this to be obviously true. Secondly, any statement about someone's being in a mood is equivalent to an explicitly non-relational statement about that person. I base that upon the availability of translations like these:

He is in a good mood = He is cheerful and friendly
He is in a bad mood   = He is gloomy and irritable
His mood has changed = He doesn't feel as he did.

If both points are right, then all statements about moods can be expressed wholly as non-relational statements about people, and this fact, I suggest, primarily explains our conviction that moods are radically un-thing-like. Moods are not things but emotional states.

Does it follow that we cannot say about moods anything of the sort we can say about things? It does not. Moods are states; and states, like things, can be owned and clocked and compared with one another; so we have at least the following three ways of talking about moods without reifying them. (i) Moods, like gramophones and handkerchiefs, can be owned. The person who is in, or has, a mood is just the subject of the corresponding non-relational statement: a mood of depression is mine if and only if it is I who am depressed. (ii) Moods, like objects, can be clocked—can come into and go out of existence at stated times. This is because we can say when something started or finished being in a given state, e.g. when it became true, or when it became false, of me that I was depressed. (iii) Moods can be compared and contrasted with one another, as objects can, and may be classified and described on the basis of such comparisons. Your mood is like mine because, so far as our present emotional states go, you are like me; and my present mood is unlike my mood of last night because I don't feel the way I did last night.

So we may say of a mood, as of a cigarette, that it was mine, that it did not last for long, and that it was unlike several others I have had. But we may not ask whether a mood was literally blacker than pitch; or think that a vacant mood is an uninhabited one, a mood with nobody in it; or wonder, when someone is in blue velvet and a filthy mood, whether the mood is inside the velvet. Above all, we may not speculate about the niceties of 'the relation of in-ness' which a man has to his mood. Because a mood's existing is its having this one unique 'relation' to some person, the 'relation' is not a relation at all.

To reify moods—on that account of what is involved—would obviously be preposterous, and nobody needs to be convinced of this. That is why I choose moods as an example.

Are there such things as sense-data? Yes and no: there are sense-data but it is wrong to reify them. In elaborating this I shall keep parallel to the discussion of moods. Firstly, then, the only intelligible statements about sense-data are statements about their being had, apprehended, perceived etc. by sentient beings ('people', for short). And, secondly, any statement about someone's having etc. a sense-datum is equivalent to an explicitly non-relational statement about that person, attributing to him a certain sensory state, saying how he sensorily is. I base this second point on the availability of equations of the form:

He has a ϕ sense-datum $=$ It is with him as though he were perceiving a. . . .

$=$ He is sensorily affected in the way he usually is when he perceives a. . . .

If both points are right, then all statements about sense-data can be expressed wholly as non-relational statements about people; and this is why it is wrong to reify sense-data, for my two points imply that sense-data are not things but sensory states.

Like moods, sense-data may be brought under personal possessives, may be clocked, and may be compared and contrasted with one another. What else can be said about them? The answer is: anything that can be re-expressed in non-relational statements about people, using no such noun as 'sense-datum'. There does not seem to be much else that passes this test.[3] For example, adjectives of shape, colour, size, pitch etc. seem to be applicable only in metaphors, to be cashed through the equations above, so that 'He has a red sense-datum' becomes 'It is with him as though he were seeing something red'. (That is why I disagreed in § 2 with Locke's view that an 'idea' can resemble an extra-mental thing in respect of shape, colour, etc.) Furthermore, we ought not to debate whether a man's relationship to his sense-datum is one of possession, awareness, apprehension, perception etc.; for there is no more a *relation* between a man and his sense-datum than between a man and his mood or his size.

Before proceeding, I turn aside briefly to stress a distinction. I have contended (a) that if we are to apply physical-object language to sense-data we must use the as-though-one-were-perceiving device. I also agree with those who say (b) that if we are to describe sense-data in publicly intelligible ways we must avail ourselves of physical-object language.[4] But these are distinct theses. Someone might accept (a) and yet, being in error about what is needed for communication, reject (b); or accept (b) and yet, wrongly reifying sense-data, reject (a). It is because both are true that I do not try to describe sense-data except by the 'as-though-one-were-perceiving' device. Even if I had a private vocabulary for describing my sense-data, a vocabulary which was not semantically linked with any public language, I could have no reason to parade it in a published book. (Whether such a vocabulary is even possible is a tangled question on which I here express no opinion.) Someone who understands that this is why descriptions of sense-data always seem relational, or oblique, or indirect, will presumably not be tempted to infer that sense-data

[3] See B. Mates, 'Berkeley was Right', Pepper, pp. 164–5.
[4] G. Ryle, *The Concept of Mind* (London, 1949), pp. 201–3.

must in some mysterious way be 'diaphanous' or lacking in properties of their own.

I have done more to explain than to defend the thesis that one ought not to reify sense-data. Rather than defending it directly, I shall adopt it as an hypothesis and, at intervals throughout this book, test it by putting it to work. Its power to solve problems will recommend it more highly than could any direct argument.

The anti-reification thesis also abolishes pseudo-problems. To many readers, writings in the philosophy of perception seem to be addressed partly to (a) genuine and interesting philosophical problems and partly to (b) mildly lunatic conundrums which one would ignore if they did not seem to be forced upon us by theories adduced to solve (a).[5] Among the questions which many would include in class (b), on their own inherent demerits, are these: 'Can there be an unapprehended sense-datum?'; 'Are sense-data perceived in the same way, or in the same sense of "perceive", as are physical things?'; 'Do apprehended sense-data exist in the same sense of "exist" as do unobserved things?'; 'Is the visual sense-datum I have just after blinking the very same one that I had just before?'; 'How do visual sense-data relate to the surfaces of physical objects?' These 'problems' constitute a good part of the class (b) of topics in the philosophy of perception which no intelligent adult would put up with if he could see how to disentangle them from (a) the worthwhile topics; and every single one of them is visibly dissolved by the anti-reification thesis, for if the latter is correct in any form of it then each of those questions is abolished by the basic logic of the term 'sense-datum'.

Taking the classes (a) and (b) to be defined by responses which I have observed in myself and a good many others, long before thinking about reification as such, I am prepared to say that I do not know of anything in class (b) which is not, or anything in class (a) which is, condemned by the thesis that it is wrong to reify sense-data. This is presumably evidence that the thesis is true.

6. *Against abstractness*

Berkeley was sure that the theory of abstract ideas is false:

[5] See, for example, G. E. Moore, *Philosophical Studies* (London, 1922), pp. 189 ff.; *Some Main Problems of Philosophy* (London, 1953), pp. 34 ff.; *Commonplace Book* (London, 1962), pp. 119–20.

Whether others have this wonderful faculty of *abstracting their ideas*, they best can tell: for my self I find indeed I have a faculty of imagining, or representing to my self the ideas of those particular things I have perceived and of variously compounding and dividing them. I can imagine a man with two heads or the upper parts of a man joined to the body of a horse. I can consider the hand, the eye, the nose, each by it self abstracted or separated from the rest of the body. But then whatever hand or eye I imagine, it must have some particular shape and colour. Likewise the idea of man that I frame to my self, must be either of a white, or a black, or a tawny, a straight, or a crooked, a tall, or a low, or a middle-sized man. I cannot by any effort of thought conceive the abstract idea above described [i.e. the one 'retaining only what is common to all' men].[6]

The formation of abstract or sketchy ideas, then, is a psychological impossibility for Berkeley and, he thinks, for everyone else too: 'If any man has the faculty of framing in his mind such an idea of a triangle as is here described, it is in vain to pretend to dispute him out of it, nor would I go about it.'[7] He clearly expects no such challenge from anyone who tries to form abstract ideas and honestly reports the outcome.

The challenge is forthcoming, all the same. Of those who can picture things imaginatively, most are compelled to leave out details. Someone who can hear a tune 'in his head', and indeed hear it as orchestrated, is unlikely to be able to hear it as orchestrated in any highly specific fashion: only a gifted few can 'realize' a score fully in the imagination.

On the other hand, no one would claim to have formed an abstract 'idea of animal' or an 'abstract idea of motion distinct from the body moving'. Berkeley is right to deny that ideas can be abstract to that extent.[8]

It is not too surprising that Locke implies the contrary. His whole theory of meaning and classification is, if 'ideas' are images or sense-data, obviously empirically false; to persist with it at all Locke must frequently forget his basic explanation of what an 'idea' is; and this will enable him to overlook his obligation to test the theory—including the part about abstractness—against the facts of imagination. But Berkeley's denial that ideas can be abstract at all is just as blatantly at odds with the facts, and is

---

[6] *Principles*, Introduction § 10.   [7] *Principles*, Introduction § 13.
[8] *Principles*, Introduction §§ 9–10.

more puzzling. The explanation of it, I think, is that without quite realizing it Berkeley objected to the theory of abstract ideas not on psychological but on logical grounds. For a definite, wrong reason, he thought it logically impossible that there should be an abstract idea.

We can come at this reason through a passage of Locke's. In the course of arguing that abstract ideas 'do not so easily offer themselves as we are apt to imagine', Locke cites, as an example of an idea which it demands 'some pains and skill to form',

the general idea of a triangle, [which] must be neither oblique nor rectangle, neither equilateral, equicrural, nor scalenon; but all and none of these at once. In effect, it is something imperfect, that cannot exist; an idea wherein some parts of several different and inconsistent ideas are put together.[9]

One can understand Berkeley's gleefully taking this to concede almost his whole case against abstract ideas; but the passage merits closer scrutiny than he gave it.

What is it that 'cannot exist'? Not the idea, but a triangle which answers to or 'agrees with' the idea. When Locke says 'something imperfect, that cannot exist', we must take him to mean 'something imperfect which cannot be realized, cannot have anything corresponding to it, in the objective realm'. This concession is damaging enough, but Locke ought not to have made it. Of the two things he says which might be thought to support it, one does imply the concession but is false, while the other is true but does not imply the concession.

(1) Locke lists a set of mutually exclusive properties, and implies that only a triangle having 'all of these' would answer to the abstract idea of a triangle. Admittedly, no such triangle could exist. But Locke's 'all of these' is just a mistake: to abstract is to omit detail, not to pile on detail to the point of inconsistency.[10] The reference to 'some parts of several . . . inconsistent ideas' is also wrong or irrelevant.

(2) The crux is not 'all of these' but 'none of these': if the abstraction doctrine calls in question any logical law, it is that of excluded middle and not non-contradiction. Locke rightly

[9] *Essay* IV. vii. 9.
[10] See Craig, 'Berkeley's Attack on Abstract Ideas', p. 436.

thinks that an abstract idea of a triangle must be neither an idea of an equilateral triangle nor an idea of an equicrural triangle nor an idea of a scalenon triangle; and from this he infers, apparently, that a triangle answering to such an idea must lack all three of these properties—cannot have three sides of the same length, or two the same and one different, or all three different. And certainly no such triangle can exist.

The inference, however, is invalid. From the fact that an abstract idea of a triangle is (in short-hand) neither an idea of an F triangle nor an idea of a G triangle nor an idea of an H triangle it does not follow that an actual triangle corresponding to the idea must be neither F nor G nor H. Compare a triangle's corresponding to an abstract idea with its answering to an incomplete description. The description 'triangular, but neither F nor G nor H' could fit only a triangle which was neither F nor G nor H, and so no triangle can answer to or 'agree with' that description; but the description 'triangular', which contains nothing about F- or G- or H-ness, fits every triangle. Might not an abstract idea have the logical properties of 'triangular' rather than of 'triangular, but neither F nor G nor H'? Yes, it might. In § 7 I shall show how an abstract idea can share with an incomplete description the privilege of remaining silent, as it were, about details. But first I have to explain Berkeley's puzzling mistake.

If it were legitimate to reify ideas, it might be true that an idea of a triangle must itself be triangular, that an idea of an equilateral triangle must be equilateral as well as triangular, and so on. In that case an abstract idea of a triangle might itself have to be *triangular but neither F nor G nor H*; and, since nothing can answer to that description, there could not be any such idea. Locke was a confident reifier of ideas, and often implies that an idea of K-ness must itself be K. This probably explains his seeming to say in the quoted passage that the abstract idea itself 'cannot exist'; though this, being a total retraction of the whole theory of abstract ideas, cannot be his consciously considered view.

I suggest that this is Berkeley's half-considered view. Although he does not reify ideas, he does assume that an idea of K-ness must be K, and thus that an abstract idea of a triangle must break the law of excluded middle. I think that this line of thought inclined him to the view that abstract ideas of the kind demanded by Locke's theory are logically impossible. This would explain his confidence that the candid reader will agree that he cannot form any abstract ideas; and I know of no other explanation.[11]

The anti-reification thesis of § 5 implies that someone who has an image or idea of a triangle does not 'perceive' or 'apprehend' a triangular image. The statement 'He has an image of a triangle' is equivalent to 'He is in a visual state like the ones he is ordinarily in when seeing triangular things', which does not imply that while he has the image there is anything—mental or extramental—which is itself triangular. We still have a problem, however, about the statement 'Smith has an abstract idea [image] of a triangle'. We have to equate this with some non-relational statement about Smith, and some ways of doing this would still imply that abstract ideas are impossible. For example, if 'Smith has an abstract image of a triangle' means 'Smith is in a visual state like the ones he is ordinarily in when seeing things which are triangular but neither F nor G nor H', then we must still come to Berkeley's conclusion even if not for his reason. So there is a challenge here to anyone who thinks he can see a face in his mind's eye and truthfully answer 'No' both to 'Did you see her as smiling?' and to 'Did you see her as unsmiling?' Abstract ideas will not do what Locke asks of them; but those of us who think that there are abstract ideas are under pressure to show how they are possible. I now try to meet that challenge.

7. Abstract ideas: a positive account

The problem is to show how an abstract idea can, as it were, have the logic of 'triangular' rather than of 'triangular but neither F nor G nor H'. We have to put the exact shape of the imaged triangle on a par with the exact number of Lady Macbeth's children. As a first step, we need to clarify the notion of 'seeing in the mind's eye', 'hearing in the mind's ear (or in one's head)', and so on. In what ways is a conjured-up image of a ϕ different from, and in what ways is it similar to, the sense-data one has when perceiving a real ϕ? This is to ask what the differences and likenesses are between a person's state when he imagines something and his state when he actually perceives it.

[11] For confirmation see Berkeley, *Alciphron* VII, § 6 in the first two editions (*The Works of George Berkeley*, vol. 3, pp. 333–4). See also Hume, *Treatise*, pp. 19–20; J. Laird, *Hume's Philosophy of Human Nature* (London, 1932), ch. 2, § 4.

We can understand one another's uses of 'I played the slow movement over in my head' only because we can agree on this much: a person can sometimes induce in himself a state which is *significantly like* that of perceiving a ϕ—by which I mean a state which is somewhat like perceiving a ϕ and is more like that than like perceiving anything else. This, thin as it is, suffices to underpin such expressions as 'see in the mind's eye, as from the main entrance' and 'hear in the mind's ear, as played by a brass band'. But it *is* thin. These induced quasi-sensory states, and similar uninduced ones, are partly unlike the sensory states we have in actual perception; and one would like to be able to say more about the dissimilarities, i.e. to improve upon 'significantly like' as an account of the similarities. Attempts to do this have always failed. Hume, for example, says that the only difference is one of intensity, which he calls 'strength', 'liveliness', 'vivacity'. But auditory intensity is just volume; and hearing a tune in the mind's ear is not, for me at least, exactly like hearing it played extremely quietly. Nor, for many people, is seeing something in the mind's eye just like actually seeing it in conditions which give the colours a washed-out appearance. Proposals other than Hume's seem likely to meet the same fate, namely challenge by someone who says 'That is not what the difference is in my case'.

The question 'How does one's state when forming an image of a ϕ differ from one's state when perceiving a ϕ?' may not admit of a general answer. The differences may vary from person to person, or from sense to sense for a single person, or even from time to time with respect to one sense of one person—so that his 'mind's-eye' visual images differ from his visual sense-data sometimes in one way and sometimes in another. Any or all of these possibilities would be consistent with our having a public use for 'see in the mind's eye' and the like, and they would explain our failure to agree on any general account of how the images of imagination differ from those of perception.

Anyway, I shall leave it at this: when someone voluntarily forms an image of a ϕ he is significantly like the way he is when he perceives a ϕ. I suspect that the 'significantly like' cannot be replaced by any one more specific expression; but even if it can—even if it serves merely to hold the place open for a still-undiscovered empirical or analytic theory—still we can advance from this point to a better grasp of what it is to form an abstract or undetailed image.

How much detail can be omitted from an image of a ϕ? The following suggestion (made to me by Michael Tanner) seems right: one can omit from an induced image of a ϕ only such details as one could fail to *notice* when actually perceiving a ϕ and noticing that it was a ϕ. This suggests an answer to the deeper question of what it is to form an undetailed image of something, i.e. the question of how the third of these relates to the first two:

(1) I have an image of a face
(2) I have an image of a smiling face
(3) I have an image of a face, but not one of a smiling or of an unsmiling face.

If we want to translate these in accordance with the anti-reification thesis, while also employing the notion of noticing, the following look plausible:

(1) I am significantly like the way I am when I see a face and notice that it is a face.
(2) I am significantly like the way I am when I see a smiling face and notice that it is a smiling face.
(3) I am significantly like the way I am when I see a face and notice that it is a face but do not notice whether or not it is smiling.

I offer those as instances of a general analysis of the notion of abstractness or undetailedness as applied to images. The use of 'significantly like' may represent an incompleteness in the analysis; and 'notice' may need to be replaced by something more careful—I have not attended to differences between noticing, being aware of, taking in, etc. But I submit that the analysis solves in principle the problem of what it is for an image to be abstract; that it shows how imagined things, like fictional things, can break the law of excluded middle. (Soberly speaking, no thing breaks that law: 'imagined things' and 'fictional things' ought not to be reified, are not things.)

The analysis helps to explain why some details cannot be omitted from an image of a ϕ. Locke postulates an abstract idea corresponding to the word 'large', but there cannot be such an image because one could not perceive something large and notice nothing about it except that it was large. Nor, to take another example, could one notice that a surface was equilateral while noticing nothing else about it—having to answer 'Perhaps' when asked 'Ten sides?' and when asked 'A thousand sides?' On the other hand, one might see something red and notice only its colour: there are special reasons, adumbrated in § 20 below, why Locke's theory is at its most plausible when applied to secondary qualities.

The limits on omittable detail probably can't be captured in any general, interpersonally valid rule, because people will vary in their capacities for selective noticing. Still, certain general considerations do rule out multitudes of the 'abstract ideas' postulated by Locke's theory.

(1) Locke's catalogue of abstract ideas includes such ideas as those of existence and unity.[12] There could not be such ideas as these, not because in noticing a thing's existence or its unity one would have to notice other features of it as well, but rather because a thing's existence and its unity are not features of it at all. A proper description of something cannot begin 'Existent and . . .' or 'One and . . .'.

(2) Consider an abstract visual idea of a dog. Being only visual, it would not be sufficient to guarantee that any object 'agreeing' with it was a dog; for a picture of a dog might 'agree' with it but would not 'agree' with a fully-fledged abstract idea of a dog which would presumably comprise tactual and auditory ideas as well as a visual idea. Locke is not in trouble yet. But, now, any dog can be recognized, just from how it looks, as a dog rather than any other kind of animal; a single glance leaves open the possibility that it is an artful model or a *trompe-l'oeil* painting, but it can settle decisively that if the thing is an animal it is a dog rather than, say, a fox or a ferret; and Locke must postulate an abstract visual idea of a dog which does justice to this fact. This would have to be a visual idea which was of a dog though not of any specific kind of dog, but which at the same time was decisively not an idea of any other kind of animal. This is impossible, because one could not notice purely visually that something was a dog (and not a fox or a ferret) while noticing nothing about what kind of dog it was. I base this on facts not about selective noticing but about the visual appearances of various kinds of dogs and of

[12] *Essay* II. vii. 7.

foxes and ferrets. To notice enough about an animal's visual appearance to see that it is not a fox *is* to notice enough to see either that it is not a Chihuahua or to see that it is not an Afghan wolf-hound. This example is one of many that could be given.

(3) This is the place to raise a difficulty which does not concern abstractness as such but which questions the spirit of Locke's whole enterprise. Let us waive the difficulty in (2), and ask Locke to describe an idea 'agreement' with which is *sufficient* for something to count as a dog. By not insisting that 'agreement' with it also be *necessary* for doghood, we free Locke from the burdens of abstractness and allow him to present an extremely specific visual idea combined with tactual and auditory and perhaps also olfactory ideas which can also be as specific as he likes. But however specific and unabstract he makes it, 'agreement' with it won't guarantee doghood. A thing's being a dog has to do not only with how it looks and feels and sounds and smells at a given moment, but also with how it was born, how it behaves, what it is like inside, and so on. There is no chance of embodying all that in a complex idea or image. Here again, examples could be multiplied: try to describe an idea or image such that anything 'agreeing' with it must be a king, or a philosopher, or a neurotic.

This point is important. It is easy, even while rejecting Locke's over-all theory, to accept too much of his picture of the meaning-structure of our language: the picture of language as consisting of words with 'simple' meanings which can be defined only ostensively, and of words with 'complex' meanings which are defined out of the former *per genus et differentiam*. Underlying this picture is the assumption that I can decide whether W applies to *x* merely by noting what my sensory state is when I confront *x*. If W is a secondary-quality word—a word with a 'simple' meaning —this assumption crudely approximates to the truth; but for the remaining 99·9 per cent of the words in the language it is thoroughly false.

8. *Abstraction's consequences*

Berkeley regarded the doctrine of abstract ideas as not just false but pernicious, productive of error which—he sometimes seems to think—is worse than that of abstractionism itself. Most commentators easily agree with him about this, but really this is a complex and difficult matter.

Some of Berkeley's most casual jibes at abstractionism, in which 'abstract' functions as little more than a substitute for 'unintelligible', may reflect a specific complaint which is certainly voiced by some commentators,[13] namely that the abstraction doctrine departs from meaning-empiricism and licenses the use of idle words which cannot be cashed in experience.[14] If this is Berkeley's complaint, he does not voice it explicitly, nor does he ever try to justify it. Had he tried he would have failed, for this accusation against Locke's theory cannot be sustained.

The theory of abstract ideas, so far from deserting Locke's meaning-empiricism, contains it.[15] Any general term which has meaning according to Locke's abstraction theory must stand for some aspect of experience—some feature which is abstracted from, and was therefore present in, unabstract ideas which were had in ordinary sense-experience. Locke, notoriously, countenances many terms which his meaning-empiricism does not permit him, and says that there are abstract ideas corresponding to them. But in so doing he sins against both meaning-empiricism and the theory of abstract ideas, and so these lapses provide no backing for Berkeley's implied claim that the abstraction theory encourages its adherents to adopt meaningless terminology. In fact, if it were properly applied it would allow its adherents almost no terminology of any sort (see § 7 above). If this seems a rather back-handed defence of Locke, then I should explain that I have no interest in defending Locke but a great interest in understanding his theory of abstract ideas.

There is a different fault which Berkeley seems to find with the theory of abstract ideas, namely that it implies, or at least encourages, the view that 'sensible things' can exist at times when they are not being perceived. This view, and Berkeley's rejection of it, will be extensively discussed in later chapters; at present I shall merely label the view 'materialism', and say that according to Berkeley the existence of a 'sensible thing' logically implies its being perceived.

[13] E.g. Warnock, *Berkeley*, pp. 80–2.
[14] *Principles*, Introduction § 17; *Principles* §§ 13, 68, 74, 81, 143; *Dialogues*, pp. 248, 256, 258; *Philosophical Commentaries*, entry 779.
[15] Thus D. Odegard, 'Locke as an Empiricist', *Philosophy*, vol. 40 (1965), p. 187.

I align myself with those who have trouble finding the supposed link between the theory of abstract ideas and materialism.[16] The crucial passage is one where, having alluded to the 'opinion strangely prevailing' that 'sensible objects have an existence . . . distinct from their being perceived by the understanding', Berkeley says:

If we thoroughly examine this tenet, it will, perhaps, be found at bottom to depend on the doctrine of *abstract ideas*. For can there be a nicer strain of abstraction than to distinguish the existence of sensible objects from their being perceived, so as to conceive them existing unperceived?[17]

There are also some other passages which seem to have the same line of thought underlying them.[18] But what line of thought is it? The best answer I can find is as follows.

The materialist will affirm both *There is now a K sensible thing* and *Nobody now perceives a K sensible thing*, which is, in Berkeley's view, to affirm (P & ~Q) in a case where (P→Q). For Berkeley, that is, the materialist is an entailment-breaker. Now I have argued that Berkeley sees the doctrine of abstract ideas as flouting the law of excluded middle or something like it: he sees it as affirming of something both that *It is triangular* and that *It is neither F nor G nor H*, even though in fact *x is triangular* entails *x is F or G or H*. An adherent of the abstraction theory, on this view of him, is also an entailment-breaker. So Berkeley can see materialism and abstractionism as connected to the extent that they share a common logical fault—entailment-breaking.

So thin a connexion hardly deserves to be mentioned. Certainly it does not support the suggestion that one doctrine 'depends' upon the other, and only one writer that I know of has seriously tried to argue that it does.[19] But is there, in fact or in Berkeleian theory, any more substantial connexion than this?

We might improve the story slightly by noting that Berkeley sees the abstraction doctrine as guilty of entailment-breaking in more than one way. I have stressed the logically special case, where P entails (Q or R or S) and someone affirms P and denies

[16] M. C. Beardsley, 'Berkeley on "Abstract Ideas"', Martin p. 413 (also in Engle); Thomson, 'G. J. Warnock's *Berkeley*', p. 432.

[17] *Principles* § 5.

[18] *Principles* §§ 10, 11, 99; *Dialogues*, pp. 177, 192–4, 222, 225, 230; *De Motu* § 47.

[19] G. D. Hicks, *Berkeley* (London, 1932), p. 80.

each of Q, R, S, because it is this kind of entailment-breach
which seems to lie at the heart of Berkeley's rejection of abstract
ideas. But he does apparently think of abstraction as violating
logic in another way also, as when he connects 'abstract ideas'
with the difficulties we incur 'if *time* be taken, exclusive of all
those particular actions and ideas that diversify the day, merely
for the continuation of existence, or duration in abstract.'[20]
The passage containing this is very obscure, but the point could
be that the concept of time logically involves the concept of
happenings, and that the doctrine of abstract ideas contradicts
this—or incites its adherents to deny it. Berkeley does seem to
picture the abstraction theory not only as involving a kind of
abstraction which is absolutely wrong, but also as involving an
excess of some sort of logical operation which, within limits,
is legitimate. But what exactly this operation is, and why the
theory of abstract ideas might be thought to encourage it, I
have not been able to discover. Certainly, what Berkeley says about
'time' is not significantly different from some remarks of Locke's.[21]

So I have to conclude that even if materialism and the theory
of abstract ideas are both taken at Berkeley's valuation of them,
the connexion between them remains embarrassingly tenuous.

Berkeley repeatedly displays hostility to the asking of certain
kinds of philosophical questions 'in the abstract', as it were.[22]
This attitude, which is displayed in the 'time' passage and elsewhere, arises from one or more of the following theses. (*a*) It is
often hard to explain the meaning of a word which one is nevertheless able to use competently. (*b*) The meaning of a general
word—even an unambiguous one—often has to be stated in a
piecemeal rather than a unitary fashion. (*c*) Fully to appreciate
the utility of certain words (such as 'force') one must see what
roles they play in theories. (*d*) There are certain useful general
words (such as 'force') which do not stand for anything in the
world.[23]

Is any of this directly relevant to the theory of abstract ideas?
I think not, except to this very limited extent:—The abstraction
theory presupposes a certain broad picture of what sort of meaning a respectable, unambiguous general word must have, and

---

[20] *Principles* § 97.   [21] *Essay* II. xiv. 3-4.
[22] *Principles* §§ 97-8, 100, 111; *Alciphron* VII, § 6; *De Motu* §§ 4, 39, 43.
[23] See C. M. Turbayne, 'Berkeley's Two Concepts of Mind', Engle.

this picture conflicts with some or perhaps all of (*a*) to (*d*). If that is right, then (*a*) to (*d*) could yield part of the case against the abstraction theory, by generating an attack on one of its pre-suppositions. Berkeley, however, repeatedly implies that there is a closer relevance than that, and in this I think he is simply wrong. Thesis (*c*), incidentally, is part of Berkeley's significant contribution to the philosophy of science.[24] I do not minimize that contribution by remarking that Berkeley was not clear enough about how (*c*) relates to the abstraction doctrine. His tendency to conflate (*c*) with (*b*) and with (*d*) is perhaps more serious, but it lies well beyond my present scope.

9. *Berkeley on classifying*

Berkeley is sometimes credited with having soundly and incisively criticized not just Locke's abstraction doctrine but also the larger theory of classification within which it is nested. I disagree: Berkeley's treatment of this matter is seriously flawed, exegetically and philosophically.

Firstly, he misunderstood Locke. He thought that Locke sought to include inherently general items in his ontology, and that he dissented from universalism only in 'locating' them in the mind rather than outside it. This misrepresentation produces some curious shadow-boxing. For example, there is the passage where Berkeley, having allowed that there are 'general ideas' or 'universal notions', goes on to insist that these ideas are themselves mental particulars,

universality, so far as I can comprehend not consisting in the absolute, positive nature or conception of any thing, but in the relation it bears to the particulars signified or represented by it: by virtue whereof it is that things, names, or notions, being in their own nature *particular*, are rendered *universal*.[25]

The phrase 'being in their own nature particular' is, one can hardly doubt, supposed to be part of the thrust at Locke. Yet here is what Locke says:

Universality belongs not to things themselves, which are all of them particular in their existence, even those words and ideas which in their signification are general.[26]

[24] See Popper, 'A Note on Berkeley'.   [25] *Principles*, Introduction § 15.
[26] *Essay* III. iii. 11.

The immediate object of all our reasoning and knowledge, is nothing but particulars. Every man's reasoning and knowledge is only about the ideas existing in his own mind; which are truly, every one of them, particular existences. . . . Universality is but accidental to [knowledge], and consists only in this, that the particular ideas about which [knowledge] is are such as more than one particular thing can correspond with and be represented by.[27]

In insisting that ideas are 'in their own nature particular', and that an idea's generality consists only in 'the relation it bears to the particulars signified by it', Berkeley is not disagreeing with Locke at all.

One can see why he thinks that he is. In Locke's theory, an idea which is general (i.e. used as an aid to classifying) will be internally different from some non-general ideas because it will be abstract (i.e. deprived of some detail); and its abstractness is a fact about what it is like, not merely about how it is or might be used—it is, in Berkeley's words, a fact about its 'positive nature' and not about any 'relation it bears' to things it signifies. But this inherent property of Lockean general ideas—this abstractness—simply is not the inherent universality Berkeley sometimes implies it to be. Locke can easily allow that any given abstract idea is a mental particular which can occur only once in a single mind.

As one piece of evidence that Berkeley is involved in this mistake, consider his reference to the 'incomprehensible idea of Man which shall have nothing particular in it'. If his concern here is with abstractness, the phrase should be rather '. . . nothing specific in it'; and I conjecture that Berkeley used 'particular' because he was not clear in his mind about the distinction between abstract/specific on the one hand and universal/particular on the other. Also, he says this: 'I do not deny absolutely there are general ideas, but only that there are any *abstract general ideas*.'[28] If 'abstract' is used properly, i.e. in Locke's sense, that remark is simply false: Berkeley denies not only that there are any abstract general ideas, but also that there are ideas whose generality is somehow built into them, ideas which are general or universal in the sense that one of them could recur in different minds or at different times, ideas whose generality consists in something more than the use to which they are put. In suppressing this second

[27] *Essay* IV. xvii. 8.   [28] *Principles*, Introduction § 12.

denial, Berkeley shows that he has not properly distinguished it from the first denial.[29]

I remarked in § 3 that in Locke's theory of classification the bit about abstractness bears only on the sub-'problem' about selecting the relevant features of the mental sample. Berkeley did not see this. He shared Locke's picture of the abstraction doctrine as central to Locke's whole account of how we classify; and so of course he saw himself as rejecting Locke's theory of classification *in toto*. Interestingly, he did not try to put any rival theory in its place. This is strikingly shown in parts of the first draft of the Introduction—parts which did not survive in the published version. For example:

When I say the word Socrates is a proper . . . name, and the word Man [a] general name, I mean no more than . . . that the one is peculiar & appropriated to one particular person, the other common to a great many particular persons, each whereof has an equall right to be called by the name Man. This, I say, is the whole truth of the matter. . . .[30]

I would fain know, why a word may not be made to comprehend a great number of particular things in its signification, without the interposition of a general idea. Is it not possible to give the name Man to Peter, James, & John, without having first made that strange &, to me, incomprehensible idea of Man which shall have nothing of particular in it?[31]

What, I pray, are words but signs of our thoughts? & how are signs of any sort render'd universal, otherwise than by being made to signify, or represent indifferently, a multitude of particular things?[32]

Did Berkeley grasp the fundamental defect of Locke's theory of classification? Did he see that the theory was foredoomed because nothing could count as a technique or all-purpose rule for classifying? Perhaps he did. When he says 'This is the whole truth of the matter', one can take him to be implying something like this: 'The basic fact is that we *do* classify particulars in disciplined and agreed ways, and it is just no use looking for a comprehensive account of how we do this, or for a comprehensive explanation of our being able to do it.' (Or: '. . . that we *do* classify things correctly, and . . .'—the relationship between the two formulations

---

[29] See Gibson, *Locke's Theory of Knowledge*, pp. 68–70.
[30] A. A. Luce and T. E. Jessop (eds.), *The Works of George Berkeley*, vol. 2 (London 1949), p. 127. [31] Ibid. [32] Ibid. p. 128.

is, I believe, a deep and dark philosophical matter about which I dare not say anything.) This would credit Berkeley with an important insight which did not become common property until it was expressed and defended by Wittgenstein.

There is, however, another explanation of Berkeley's not trying to revise or to replace Locke's theory, namely that he did not properly see what the theory was trying to do in the first place. The theory sought to solve the ancient 'problem of the One and the Many', which can be expressed in the question: 'What enables us to impose generality upon a world of particulars, as we do in applying general words?' On the basis of their attitude to this, philosophers could be sorted into three groups. (a) Some, such as Locke and the universalists, think that the 'problem' is a genuine one and seek to solve it. (b) Some, like Wittgenstein, see that the 'problem' admits of no solution. They feel the force of the question 'We uniformly apply one word to many things—how is the trick worked?', and perhaps even regard it as showing great insight on the part of the questioner, but they reject the question nonetheless: just because the 'trick' is involved in all our intellectual activities, there cannot be a technique for it or a comprehensive account of how it is worked. (c) Some fail to locate the 'problem' in the first place. They do not stand far enough back from the familiar to see it as strange and in need of explanation; they do not enter into the frame of mind of someone who can ask, even of such an omnipresent and fundamental activity as generalizing or classifying, 'How is it done?' Berkeley, I suggest, belongs not to (b) but to (c).

His being content to reject Locke's 'solution' of the 'problem' of classification, without offering an alternative solution, would be explained by his being in (b) or in (c). But the conjecture that (b) he had the Wittgensteinian insight is in great tension with facts which present no problems for the conjecture that (c) he didn't ever see what the fuss was about. For example, there is the fact that Berkeley did not ever explicitly say that Locke's theory was attempting an impossible task, and hardly even hinted at such a view except in passages which he did not publish. Furthermore, those passages, although they give the best available support for a Wittgensteinian reading of Berkeley's position on classifying, also contain details which make such a reading virtually impossible. Consider this one:

Suppose I have the idea of some one particular dog to which I give
the name Melampus and then frame this proposition Melampus is an
animal, where 'tis evident the name Melampus denotes one particular
idea. And as for the other name [in] the proposition there are a sort of
philosophers will tell you thereby is meant not only a universal conception but also corresponding thereto a universal nature or essence
really existing without the mind whereof Melampus doth partake. But
this with reason is exploded as nonsensical and absurd. But then those
men who have [exploded it] are themselves to me equally unintelligible.
For they will have it that . . . I must make the name animal stand for
an abstract, generical idea which agrees to and corresponds with the
particular idea marked by the name Melampus. But . . . I do declare
that in my thoughts the word animal is neither supposed to stand for an
universal nature nor yet for an abstract idea which to me is at least as
absurd and incomprehensible as the other.   Nor does it indeed in that
proposition stand for any idea at all. All that I intend to signify thereby
being only this, that the particular thing I call Melampus has a right
to be called by the name animal.[33]

The words 'has a *right* to be called by the name animal', which
echo the earlier 'has an equal right to be called by the name Man',
show that Berkeley is wandering in the dark. What is it for something to 'have a right' to be described as 'an animal'? Well, it is
to *be* an animal, i.e. to be properly co-classifiable with other
animals or with other things called 'animal'. Having sorted out
Berkeley's obscure phrase thus far, we have reached the point
where the Lockean and universalist theories *start*.[34] Berkeley
merely helps himself to the expression 'has a right to be called...',
implying that there is no problem about it, and claiming thereby
to dispose of the 'problem' which was bothering Locke and the
universalists; whereas the expression is prima facie problematic,
precisely because it contains within itself the whole 'problem'
which theories of classification were supposed to solve. There
could hardly be clearer evidence that Berkeley, rather than
advancing beyond Locke on classifying, stops short of him.

Berkeley, like Wittgenstein, is innocent of any purported
theory of classification-as-such. But the comparison stops right
there. Berkeley had none of Wittgenstein's grasp of what Locke
and others were trying to do—none of his sharply focused intellectual sympathy for the position which was to be destroyed.

---

[33] A. A. Luce and T. E. Jessop (eds.), *The Works of George Berkeley*, vol. 2 (London
1949), p. 136.   [34] See *Essay* III. iii. 12.

Lingering doubts about this should be dispelled by reading the 'Melampus' passage immediately after reading the opening pages of the *Blue Book*.

10. *Berkeley on meaning and understanding*

Since Berkeley did not feel the force of the 'problem' about classification, he lacked one motive for thinking that (some) words owe their meanings to associated ideas. Still, he might have accepted Locke's theory of meaning on other grounds.

In fact, he did not accept it completely, for he says that a word can be meaningful even when not associated with an idea of any kind. This is not just about abstract or inherently general ideas, and so it is a rejection of Locke's theory of meaning which is independent of Berkeley's views on abstraction and classification. Here is a sample:

A little attention will discover, that it is not necessary (even in the strictest reasonings) significant names which stand for ideas should, every time they are used, excite in the understanding the ideas they are made to stand for: in reading and discoursing, names being for the most part used as letters are in *algebra*, in which though a particular quantity be marked by each letter, yet to proceed right it is not requisite that in every step each letter suggest to your thoughts, that particular quantity it was appointed to stand for.[35]

This revives the hope that Berkeley is anticipating Wittgenstein, this time about meaning rather than about classification. As well as denying that a word's meaning is a mental correlate of it, Berkeley implies that the crux of our understanding of a word is our ability to 'proceed right' in handling it; and this is a positive step towards the broadly Wittgensteinian view that to know what a word means is to know how to use it properly.

There is much more to the same effect in Berkeley's writings—including some in passages which I should take as directly bearing on the classification theme (the line between meaning-theory and classification-theory is peculiarly hard to draw in Berkeley's texts). Several recent writers—especially Warnock[36]—have made it unnecessary for me to emphasize Berkeley's reservations about the core of Locke's theory of meaning. What is necessary is to

---

[35] *Principles*, Introduction § 19.   [36] Warnock, *Berkeley*, pp. 69-76.

bring out how incomplete his rejection of that theory was; and this is my topic in the present section.

In the passage just quoted, Berkeley says that a meaningful word need not be idea-linked every time it is used. He does not deny, and seems to assume, that if I understand a word of the relevant kind I must *sometimes* allow it to 'excite in my understanding' an appropriate idea; and to that extent his view of meaning is still Lockean. On the other hand, Berkeley's reference in that passage to words which 'stand for ideas' is not in itself clear evidence of Lockean tendencies in his views about meaning; for those ideas may be ones which, in Berkeley's ontology, are physical objects and the like.

In the very next section, Berkeley says:

The communicating of ideas marked by words is not the chief and only end of language, as is commonly supposed. There are other ends, as the raising of some passion, the exciting to, or deterring from an action, the putting the mind in some particular disposition; to which the former is in many cases barely subservient, and sometimes entirely omitted. . . . May we not, for example, be affected with the promise of a *good thing*, though we have not an idea of what it is? [As with 'general names', so also with proper names.] For example, when a Schoolman tells me *Aristotle hath said it*, all I conceive he means by it, is to dispose me to embrace his opinion with the deference and submission which custom has annexed to that name.[37]

In similar vein, in the first draft of the Introduction, Berkeley discusses the statement 'The good things which God hath prepared for them that love him are such as eye hath not seen nor ear heard nor hath it enter'd into the heart of man to conceive'. Although we cannot form the corresponding ideas, Berkeley says, this 'saying' is not meaningless, because:

The saying is very weighty and carrys with it a great design, but it is not to raise in the minds of men the abstract ideas of thing or good nor yet the particular ideas of the joys of the blessed. The design is to make them more cheerfull and fervent in their duty.[38]

Perhaps this goes against Locke,[39] but it does not go against the core of his position. Berkeley is right to stress that words may be

---

[37] *Principles*, Introduction § 20.
[38] *The Works of George Berkeley*, vol. 2, p. 137.
[39] But see *Essay* II. xxi. 29 in the first edition (in Fraser's edition at pp. 375–6).

used 'in propriety of language' for purposes other than *theoretical* ones of stating or mis-stating what is the case about some factual matter, e.g. that one may speak in order to 'raise some passion' in the hearer. But if Berkeley is saying that words can be used meaningfully in the absence of ideas *only* because words can be used non-theoretically, then he is divorcing meaning from ideas only in respect of the periphery of language; he is a long way from Wittgenstein's position; and he has not touched the central error in Locke's position.

Flew speaks of Berkeley's 'revolutionary and historically premature insight' in the theory of meaning, and cites in evidence for this a passage from one of Berkeley's later works:

The algebraic mark, which denotes the root of a negative square, hath its use in logistic operations, although it be impossible to form an idea of any such quantity. And what is true of algebraic signs is also true of words or language, modern algebra being in fact a more short, apposite, and artificial sort of language, and it being possible to express by words at length, though less conveniently, all the steps of an algebraical process.[40]

Berkeley here chooses an 'algebraic mark' of which one *cannot* form a corresponding idea, and seems to say that 'algebraic signs' are not, in the relevant respect, a special case: 'what is true of [them] is true also of words or language'. Isn't this impressive evidence that he thoroughly and radically rejects Locke's theory of meaning?

Surprisingly, it is not. When the passage is read in context it can be seen to connect not only with the first theme introduced in the present section ('letters in algebra' etc.) but also with the second ('the raising of some passion' etc.); and when these connexions are sorted out, the fragment quoted by Flew changes colour—subtly and surprisingly but, I contend, quite decisively.

In the section from which the quoted bit is drawn, Berkeley is concerned with non-theoretical or practical uses of language. He thinks that mathematics is best considered not as a set of theoretical truths but rather as a practical instrument, as something which can help us build bridges and the like:

Even the mathematical sciences themselves, . . . if they are considered, not as instruments to direct our practice, but as speculations to employ

[40] *Alciphron* VII, § 14, quoted in Flew, *Hume's Philosophy of Belief*, p. 262.

our curiosity, will be found to fall short in many instances of those clear and distinct ideas which, it seems, the minute philosophers of this age, whether knowingly or ignorantly, expect and insist upon in the mysteries of religion.[41]

Berkeley objected to mathematics as theory, or as a body of 'speculations' about what is mathematically the case, because he saw the incoherence of the explanations currently being given of such mathematical terms as 'infinitesimal'.[42] His view that mathematics is nevertheless acceptable as an 'instrument to direct our practice' is supposed to invoke his usual theoretical/practical distinction. Presumably the idea is that, just as 'The good things which God hath prepared ... etc.' has the practical force of 'Cheer up and do better', so Pythagoras' Theorem has the practical force of 'If you want such and such a structure, cut your materials thus and so'. Even if it isn't helpful to bracket these together, treating them as instances of a single kind of phenomenon which might be called 'practical meaning', Berkeley thinks that it is. And in this section—which is simply an exercise in Christian apologetics—he is directly comparing them. Faced with the accusation that the 'mysteries of religion' cannot be presented as clean, clear theory, Berkeley is replying that the same is true of mathematics, and that the kind of intellectual respectability that mathematics *can* have is also available to the mysteries of religion. The section is a rather well-controlled *ad hominem* argument, directed against the 'minute philosophers'—the minutely carping critics for whom mathematics, and sciences which are mathematically expressible, were paradigms of what is intellectually acceptable. It is the essence of this argument of Berkeley's that it divorces meaningfulness from ideas only in respect of practical mathematics and practical uses of language; and so it does not advance significantly beyond the limited anti-Lockean positions which I have already attributed to Berkeley. The argument as a whole does not support the view that Berkeley had a 'revolutionary insight' into what it is for language—including theoretical language—to be meaningful.

Passages where Berkeley accuses Locke of radical error about meaning are less important than what Berkeley says when he is off his guard, i.e. when he is not self-consciously discussing the

[41] *Alciphron* VII, § 14.
[42] *Philosophical Commentaries*, entries 351–6, 368–75, 759–68.

concept of meaning but rather employing it in the discussion of other topics. Passages of the latter kind, as well as bearing somewhat on the question of whether Berkeley ever achieved a really clear view of Locke's central error about meaning, are decisive on the question of whether he cleansed his own thinking of that error. That is really my main concern. Even if Berkeley knew exactly what to say *about* Locke's theory of meaning (which I deny), there is much in his writings which can be understood only on the hypothesis that Berkeley's usual assumptions about meaning were highly Lockean. Important examples will be discussed in their proper places; but in the rest of this section I present, just to be going on with, a few relevant passages where Berkeley is off his guard.

To begin with, the closing words of the Introduction:

Whoever therefore designs to read the following sheets, I entreat him to make my words the occasion of his own thinking, and endeavour to attain the same train of thoughts in reading, that I had in writing them. By this means it will be easy for him to discover the truth or falsity of what I say. He will be out of all danger of being deceived by my words, and I do not see how he can be led into an error by considering his own naked, undisguised ideas.[43]

Compare that, as an example of emancipation from the associated-idea theory of meaning, with Locke's explanation of why nearly one-fifth of his *Essay* is about words:

When I first began this Discourse of the Understanding, and a good while after, I had not the least thought that any consideration of words was at all necessary to it. But when . . . I began to examine the extent and certainty of our knowledge, I found it had so near a connexion with words, that, unless their force and manner of signification were first well observed, there could be very little said clearly and pertinently concerning knowledge: which being conversant about truth, had constantly to do with propositions. And though it terminated in things, yet it was for the most part so much by the intervention of words, that they seemed scarce separable from our general knowledge. At least they interpose themselves so much between our understanding, and the truth which it would contemplate and apprehend, that, like the medium through which visible objects pass, the obscurity and disorder do not seldom cast a mist before our eyes, and impose upon our understandings.[44]

[43] *Principles*, Introduction § 25.   [44] *Essay* III. ix. 21. See also II. xxxiii. 19.

In calling words a 'disguise' or a 'mist', both concede too much
to the Lockean view of language as merely a public vehicle for
activities which have a self-sufficient life of their own independently of language. But it is Locke who escapes the worst consequences of this mistake by resolving therefore to take words
seriously as objects of study, whereas Berkeley compounds the
error by saying that since words are a snare they should be
virtually disregarded so that we may 'clear the first principles of
knowledge, from the embarras and delusion of words'.[45]

Even more illuminating is Berkeley's way of discussing the
meanings of particular expressions—not what he says but how
he expresses or defends what he says.

Here, for example, is an episode from the first Dialogue:

PHILONOUS: Try if you can frame the idea of any figure, abstracted
from all particularities of size, or even from other sensible qualities.
HYLAS: Let me think a little—I do not find that I can. PHILONOUS: And
can you think it possible, that should really exist in Nature, which
implies a repugnancy in its conception?[46]

Berkeley's spokesman Philonous here declares something to be
'repugnant', meaning self-contradictory or at least logically in-
admissible, on the basis of an imaginative try-out: Hylas's *de
facto* failure to 'frame the idea' is supposed to prove that the
relevant expression is defective in meaning. It might be argued
that here, as in a funny exchange later on in the Dialogues,[47]
Philonous is using Lockean modes of argument merely *ad hominem*,
against a Lockean opponent. But other parts of the *Three Dialogues*
will not bear this interpretation.

Nor could such a defence apply to the many similar examples
in the *Principles*. For example, of a supposed key phrase in Locke's
metaphysics Berkeley says:

To me it is evident those words mark out either a direct contradiction,
or else nothing at all. And to convince others of this, I know no readier
or fairer way, than to entreat they would calmly attend to their own
thoughts: and if by this attention, the emptiness or repugnancy of
those expressions does appear, surely nothing more is requisite for
their conviction.[48]

[45] *Principles*, Introduction § 25.   [46] *First Dialogue*, p. 194.
[47] *Second Dialogue*, p. 222.   [48] *Principles* § 24.

There, in the context of a ground-floor philosophical argument, Berkeley makes an explicit methodological remark betraying wholly Lockean assumptions about meaning. Also here:

It is but looking into your own thoughts, and so trying whether you can conceive it possible for a sound, or figure . . . to exist without the mind, or unperceived. This easy trial may make you see, that what you contend for, is a downright contradiction.[49]

Nothing would be known about public meanings if Locke were right about them, and so Berkeley cannot actually apply the inaccessible criteria laid down by Locke's theory. Like everyone else[50] he must base his specific judgements about meanings on criteria which are available to him, i.e. the ones highlighted by Wittgenstein, and this fact naturally shows up in some things he says. But he does not make anything of these passing non-Lockean remarks: he does not see as a live possibility the replacement of an associated-idea theory of meaning by a comprehensive theory which relates meaning to use. In response to a suggested definition of 'matter', for example, Berkeley says:

I answer, you may, if so it shall seem good, use the word *matter* in the same sense, that other men use *nothing*, and so make those terms convertible in your style. For after all, this is what appears to me to be the result of that definition, the parts whereof when I consider with attention, either collectively, or separate from each other, I do not find that there is any kind of effect or impression made on my mind, different from what is excited by the term *nothing*.[51]

We have there a sentence which (because of 'use' and 'convertible in your style') smacks strongly of Wittgenstein, followed immediately by one which is purest Locke.

[49] *Principles* § 22.   [50] e.g. Locke, *Essay* II. xxvii. 9–10.   [51] *Principles* § 80.

III

SUBSTANCE AND REALITY

11. *Substance*

BERKELEY attacked Locke's doctrine of material substance, as everyone knows. But Locke had no doctrine of material substance: he was the victim of exegetical and philosophical mistakes initiated by Berkeley and inherited by many later writers. Locke did discuss the concept of substance, and he had a theory of reality. These two bits of work contributed to the hybrid which Berkeley called his theory of 'material substance'; and in this chapter I shall expound them, stressing the issues raised by Berkeley's mistake. In Chapter IV I shall consider the third ingredient in the doctrine of 'material substance', namely Locke's theory about primary and secondary qualities. Only then will it be possible, in Chapters V and VI, to focus on the work of Berkeley's which most interests us today, namely his dislodgement of Locke's theory of reality.

First, then, the concept of substance. Locke entertained—I would not say adopted—a certain line of thought about substance, which runs as follows.[1]

What concepts are involved in the subject of the statement that *The pen in my hand is valuable*? Certainly, the concepts of being a pen and of being in my hand; but these are not all, for the statement is about a *thing which* falls under these two concepts. What thing is this? It is the purple thing which I now see; but when I say that the purple thing I now see is a pen and is in my hand, I speak of a *thing which* is purple etc., and so I have still failed to capture the whole concept of the subject in my original statement. Any further expansion along these lines can only be a delaying action, for it must omit an essential element from the concept of the pen in my hand. What will be missing from any list of descriptive concepts is the concept of a 'thing which . . .': this is an *ingredient* in the concept of a 'thing which is F' for each value of F, and so it cannot be *identical* with the concept of a 'thing which is F' for any value of F. This constituent of every subject-concept is

---

[1] *Essay* II. xiii. 17–20; xxiii. 1–6, 15, 37.

the concept of a property-bearer, or of a possible subject of pre-
dication—let us call it the concept of a *substance*. So, if any existential or subject-predicate statement is true, then there are two sorts
of item—substances, and properties or qualities. The former have
the privilege of bearing or supporting the latter without themselves being in the same way borne by anything. We imply the
existence of 'substances' in this sense every time we imply that
some property is instantiated.

The idea ... we have, to which we give the *general* name substance,
being nothing but the supposed, but unknown, support of those
qualities we find existing, which we imagine cannot subsist ...
without something to support them, we call that support *substantia*;
which, according to the true import of the word, is, in plain English,
standing under or upholding.[2]

Note the stress on 'general': Locke is describing the entirely
general concept of a thing which ... According to a certain
theory, our concepts of particular substances or specific kinds of
substance *include* this concept of substance-in-general; but one
may speak of gold as a kind of substance, or complain of the
sticky substance on the kitchen floor, without being committed
to this theory about the analysis of what one is saying. In Locke's
words:

An obscure and relative idea of *substance in general* being thus made we
come to have the ideas of *particular sorts of substances*, by collecting
such combinations of simple ideas as are ... taken notice of to exist
together ... Thus we come to have the ideas of a man, horse, gold,
water, &c.; of which substances, whether any one has any other *clear*
idea, further than of certain simple ideas co-existent together, I appeal
to every one's own experience. It is the ordinary qualities observable
in iron, or a diamond, put together, that make the true complex idea
of those substances, which a smith or a jeweller commonly knows
better than a philosopher; who, whatever *substantial forms* he may talk
of, has no other idea of those substances, than what is framed by a
collection of those simple ideas which are to be found in them: only
we must take notice, that our complex ideas of substances, besides
all those simple ideas they are made up of, have always the confused
idea of something to which they belong, and in which they subsist: and
therefore when we speak of any sort of substance, we say it is a thing
having such or such qualities; as body is a thing that is extended,
figured, and capable of motion; spirit, a thing capable of thinking. ...[3]

[2] *Essay* II. xxiii. 2.   [3] *Essay* II. xxiii. 3.

Besides showing how 'substance in general' relates to 'particular sorts of substances', that passage shows Locke's ambivalent attitude to the former. He says we have 'no other idea' of gold etc. than one composed wholly of certain 'simple ideas', and then proceeds to 'take notice' that there is after all a further ingredient in our ideas of gold etc. This wavering reflects his lack of enthusiasm for 'the idea of substance in general'. Sometimes he abuses it in the act of giving it primacy:

The ideas of *substances* are such combinations of simple ideas as are taken to represent distinct *particular* things subsisting by themselves; in which the supposed or confused idea of substance, such as it is, is always the first and chief.[4]

Elsewhere he just abuses it:

We have no idea of what [substance in general] is, but only a confused, obscure one of what it does. . . . Were the Latin words, *inhaerentia* and *substantia*, put into the plain English ones that answer them, and were called *sticking on* and *under-propping*, they would better discover to us the very great clearness there is in the doctrine of substance and accidents, and show of what use they are in deciding of questions in philosophy.[5]

I think that Locke's treatment of 'substance in general' was mainly sceptical in content and ironical in form. This is not true of the Stillingfleet correspondence, but is Locke likely to have been less clear and candid in his magnum opus than in his letters to a touchy and not very intelligent bishop? I shall not defend this minority opinion at length, however, and am content to call the substratum analysis of the concept of substance 'Lockean', meaning, at least, that Locke said a good deal about it. I want to consider the analysis itself, starting from R. I. Aaron's discussion of it.

Aaron credits Locke with the view that we have no experience of substance-in-general, and therefore no *idea* of substance-in-general.[6] Thus far, I agree with him: but two aspects of the following require comment:

Locke certainly 'bantered the idea of substance', to use Berkeley's phrase. He showed that the traditional view could not stand examination. He did not deny the being of substance, and he did not deny the

---

[4] *Essay* II. xii. 6.   [5] *Essay* II. xiii. 19–20.
[6] R. I. Aaron, *John Locke* (Oxford, 1955), pp. 174–5.

need of a support to qualities. But he denied that we have knowledge of this substance. Experience itself suggests its existence, but it does not reveal its nature. It is hidden from us and will remain hidden from us, until we gain faculties, which we do not now possess, whereby the inner nature of the being of things will be revealed.[7]

First, a general point. Someone who says 'We have no idea of substratum-substance', meaning that the expression 'substratum-substance' has no meaning for us, cannot properly go on to say '... but still there may *be* substratum-substances' or to say '... and I don't think there *are* any substratum-substances'. If an expression is meaningless then we may not use it, however humbly, agnostically, or subjunctively. Perhaps Locke did take the position Aaron describes, but its incoherence should be pointed out.

It could arise, incidentally, from a mistake of which Locke is sometimes guilty,[8] namely that of making a point about meaning, expressing it in terms of 'ideas', and then treating it as only a point about knowledge. Such a sentence as 'We have no ideas of substratum-substance' has an ambiguity generated by the double use of 'idea' discussed in § 4 above.

Secondly, there is something wrong with: 'Experience ... does not reveal [substance's] nature. It ... will remain hidden from us until we gain faculties ... etc.' The Lockean analysis implies that nothing could count as experience of substratum-substance, but there is also a deeper objection, namely that Lockean substratum-substance *cannot have a 'nature' at all*.[9] Locke himself speaks of 'the secret abstract nature of substance in general',[10] but on this point Leibniz saw more clearly:

In distinguishing two things in [any] substance, the attributes or predicates, and the common subject of these predicates, it is no wonder that we can conceive nothing particular in this subject. It must be so, indeed, since we have already separated from it all the attributes in which we could conceive any detail.[11]

Leibniz's insight can be generalized into the following argument, which exposes the vital defect in the substratum theory. Is there a property S-ness which defines substantiality—a value of S

---

[7] R. I. Aaron, *John Locke* (Oxford, 1955), pp. 178–9.   [8] *Essay* II. xxiii. 29–30.
[9] See Gibson, *Locke's Theory of Knowledge*, ch. 5, § 6.
[10] *Essay* II. xxiii. 6.   [11] Leibniz, *New Essays* II. xxiii. 2.

such that *x* is a substance if and only if S*x*? (*a*) If a proponent of the Lockean theory says 'Yes', then his account of what it is for a property to be instantiated, viz. that P is instantiated if and only if some substance bears P, says merely that P is instantiated if and only if some item is both S and P. His analysis of a statement about the instantiation of one property thus yields, uselessly, a statement about the joint instantiation of two properties. (*b*) So he must say 'No'. That is, he must deny that substances are items of a certain kind: to be of a kind is to have the properties which define the kind, and there cannot be properties which items must have in order to qualify as substances. But the claim that substances are items of a certain kind *is* the Lockean theory of property-instantiation. The theory's whole point and interest lies in its claim that every subject-concept includes the concept of a kind of item whose special right and duty it is to bear properties.

The theory's crucial error is the move from 'There is a concept of a *thing which* . . .', which enters into every subject-concept' to 'There is a kind of item about which nothing can be said except that such items bear properties'. There are many kinds of things, but *things* do not constitute a kind. There is, perhaps, a 'concept of a subject in general'; but it is to be elucidated in terms of the ways in which more special concepts function in certain kinds of statements, and is not to be regarded as a concept which picks out a class of items.

12. *Reality*

Locke's theory of reality is a view about the nature of the distinction between the subjective and objective, inner and outer, appearance and reality; the distinction between there being sensory evidence for something's being the case, and its really being the case.

The words 'appearance' and 'reality' do not, as they stand, mark the distinction I want. In the statement 'John appeared to be ill— he was white-faced and trembling', John's pallor and tremors are represented as appearances of the reality which is his illness; but colour, movement, etc., are objective, inter-personal facts which Locke and I want to put on the 'reality' side of the appearance/reality distinction. Any statement at all may provide evidence for something's being the case, and in that sense may report what 'appears' to be the case; but I use 'appearance'/'reality' to refer to the distinction which has facts about sensory states on one side of it and everything else on the other.

This terminological choice does not matter in itself, but the reason for it does. I attend to what I call 'the distinction between appearance and reality', and I choose that label for it, because I share with Locke and Berkeley and Hume the belief that one's evidence for what is objectively the case consists in or rests ultimately upon facts about one's own sensory states. For example, even if I offer 'John was white-faced and trembling' in explanation of my saying 'John appeared to be ill', the former statement will in its turn rest upon something in the realm of 'appearance' in my specialized sense—e.g. it will rest upon the evidence of my eyes. The evidence of someone else's eyes might be relevant, of course; but only if he tells me what he saw, so that my belief about John's condition rests partly upon the evidence of my ears. For this reason, the 'distinction between appearance and reality' (in my sense) goes deeper than the sliding, vernacular distinction involved in such statements as 'He appeared to be ill—he was white-faced and trembling'.

The distinction to which I am calling attention is one which we do often enough employ. It is involved in much of our knowledge that things which appear to be *thus* are really *so*: I have been working with royal blue so that the eggshell-blue wall now looks green to me; the circular saw sounded like a child screaming; a drunken fight looked like a street-accident; they were mussels, but they smelled like squid. When a question of this kind arises, we can check whether what appears to be so is really so. I may compare the wall with the sample labelled 'eggshell blue', or ask my wife whether the things in the tin look to her like mussels. These checks introduce further sensory evidence, the reliability of which may in its turn be supported by further checks. But although we can check anything, we cannot check everything. To assess any item of sensory evidence, it seems, we must simply accept some other such item.

Consider now the question 'Is anything in the objective realm really in any way as it appears to be?'—which turns into the question 'Is there really an objective realm at all?' We cannot tackle this question, all in a lump, by any of the methods we

ordinarily use to check on the evidence of our senses; for those
methods involve assessing some bits of sensory evidence by
trusting others, whereas our present question forbids us to trust
our senses at all until after the question has been answered. The
conjecture 'Perhaps there is no objective realm' is not a mere
expansion of 'Perhaps the wall is not really green', any more than
'Teach me how to apply classificatory words' is a mere expansion
of 'Teach me how to apply the word "neurotic" '.

So someone who conjectures that perhaps there is really no
objective world 'out there' is either misusing the ordinary distinction between what is really the case and what (going by what
we see, feel, etc.) appears to be the case, or else he is employing
some unordinary distinction which could be expressed in the
same words. In the latter case, of course, he owes us an explanation of what unordinary distinction he has in mind.

Locke addresses himself to such conjectures several times, and
always fumbles them.[12] He does not criticize the question 'Is
anything really as it appears to be?'—or, in his words, 'How
shall the mind, when it perceives nothing but its own ideas,
know that they agree with things themselves?'[13]—on the grounds
that it precludes any use of the ordinary appearance/reality distinction without introducing and explaining an unordinary
alternative to it. Rather, he seeks to answer the question just as
it stands:

Whether we can . . . certainly infer the existence of anything without
us, which corresponds to [our ideas], is that whereof some men think
there may be a question made. . . . But yet here I think we are provided
with an evidence that puts us past doubting. For I ask any one, Whether
he be not invincibly conscious to himself of a different perception,
when he looks on the sun by day, and thinks on it by night; when he
actually tastes wormwood, or smells a rose, or only thinks on that
savour or odour?[14]

But the questioner, once started, will rightly refuse to be fobbed
off with this; for he is asking, among other things, whether we
do ever really look on the sun or taste wormwood. He will say:
'The mere fact that what is commonly called "imagining the sun"
differs markedly from what is commonly called "seeing the sun"

[12] *Essay* IV. ii. 14; iv. 4–5; xi. 2–10.
[13] *Essay* IV. iv. 3. See also Locke, *Examination of Malebranche* § 51.
[14] *Essay* IV. ii. 14.

does not imply that the latter kind of experience really is, at least sometimes, a seeing of a real sun.' In giving him that reply, I am not guessing as to his probable character, but merely following out the logic of his original question. The same point arises when Locke says:

Many of those ideas are *produced in us with pain*, which afterwards we remember without the least offence. . . . We remember the pains of hunger, thirst, or the headache, without any pain at all; which would either never disturb us, or else constantly do it, as often as we thought of it, were there nothing more but ideas floating in our minds, and appearances entertaining our fancies, without the real existence of things affecting us from abroad. The same may be said of *pleasure*, accompanying several actual sensations.[15]

Again, why? What reason can Locke give, without begging the question at issue, for saying that if there were no 'things affecting us from abroad' any given kind of 'idea' would be either always or never accompanied by pain?

Some of his arguments explicitly beg the question: 'It is plain those perceptions are produced in us by exterior causes affecting our senses: because those that want the *organs* of any sense, never can have the ideas belonging to that sense produced in their minds.'[16] This argument for the conclusion that 'our senses . . . do not err in the information they give us of the existence of things without us'[17] has a premiss about sense-organs, including those of other people. But sense-organs are among the 'things without us' whose reality is in question.

Locke has another argument whose premiss was also the cornerstone of Berkeley's metaphysics and theology:

Sometimes I find that *I cannot avoid the having those ideas produced in my mind*. For though, when my eyes are shut, . . . I can at pleasure recall to my mind the ideas of light, or the sun, which former sensations had lodged in my memory; . . . if I turn my eyes at noon towards the sun, I cannot avoid the ideas which the light or sun then produces in me. So that there is a manifest difference between the ideas laid up in my memory . . . and those which force themselves upon me . . . And therefore it must needs be some exterior cause, and the brisk acting of some objects without me, whose efficacy I cannot resist, that produces those ideas in my mind, whether I will or no.[18]

15 *Essay* IV. xi. 6.   16 *Essay* IV. xi. 4.
17 *Essay* IV. xi. 3.   18 *Essay* IV. xi. 5.

There is indeed this 'manifest difference', but why 'needs must' it be explained in that way? Locke cannot reply without begging the original question.

What is wrong with the question is, precisely, that nothing could count as a legitimate argument for an affirmative answer to it.

Locke's trouble is not that he is too patient with the question, but that he is impatient with it in the wrong way and for wrong reasons. He says (emphases mine) that we have 'the greatest assurance *we are capable of* concerning the existence of material beings', that 'God has given me *assurance enough* of the existence of things without me', and, combining both points, that 'The certainty of things existing in *rerum natura* when we have the testimony of our senses for it is *not only as great as our frame can attain to, but as our condition needs*'.[19] All this suggests that there is room left for residual doubt, and if that is conceded then everything is conceded.

Also, Locke thinks it relevant to criticize the questioner's character.[20] He says: 'I think nobody can, in earnest, be so sceptical...', and speaks of the sceptic's desire 'to surmount every the least (I will not say reason, but) pretence of doubting'. He snaps that it is 'foolish and vain ... to expect demonstration [= rigorous proof] and certainty in things not capable of it'. And he makes the debating point that the sceptic 'will never have any controversy with me; since he can never be sure I say anything contrary to his own opinion'. Locke's tormentor, however, can evade this onslaught by a 'retreat' which yields no ground at all. For he can say: 'I agree that I neither need nor could be entitled to have greater assurance than I do have as to the reality of things outside me. All I want to know is what entitles me to this great assurance which I have.' This raises the old embarrassing question, and Locke's replies are fatally flawed—not by falling short of 'demonstration' but by having no force at all except on assumptions which include the whole conclusion.

Empirical arguments, just because they must make assumptions about the objective or 'real' in Locke's sense, must move from limited premises about sensory states to *limited* conclusions about the objective realm. Any such argument turns on the fulcrum of an unquestioned acceptance of the existence of an objective world about which we know a good deal. If we stand back and try to

[19] *Essay* IV. xi. 3, 8.   [20] *Essay* IV. xi. 3, 10.

focus on the relation between sensory states as a whole and the objective realm as a whole, asking *en bloc* whether the former are ever reliable guides to the latter, empirical arguments cannot get a grip; and the 'cannot' is a logical one.

That is our clue. There is a connexion between 'sensory states as a whole' and 'the objective realm as a whole', or between the concepts of appearance and reality, of such a kind that the question 'Is appearance ever a reliable guide to reality?' should be answered 'Yes' on *logical* grounds. (Or of such a kind that the question is logically improper—depending on how the questioner takes it. Analogously, if someone asked 'Are facts about actual plumbers ever a guide to facts about the average plumber?' we might answer 'Yes' on logical grounds; but if the questioner expected us to base our answer on facts about actual or average plumbers, or to be embarrassed because we couldn't, we might say that his question involved a logical mistake.) Using a familiar short-hand which will later be explained and defended: reality is a logical construction out of appearances.

This will be called phenomenalism, and so indeed it is. Though disinclined to apologize, I wish at this stage to be placatory. All I need now is agreement, which may be given even by those who have been swayed by the anti-phenomenalist literature, that Locke did mis-handle the general question 'Is appearance a reliable guide to reality?' and its immediate offspring 'Is there really an objective realm?';[21] that he went wrong not in detail but in principle; and that the following are important parts, causes or symptoms of his mistake. (*a*) He tended to view the general sceptical question as just the sum of all limited sceptical questions. (*b*) He thought that the question needed to be answered rather than criticized. (*c*) He did not think it relevant to inquire into the meanings of such expressions as 'real things without us'. (*d*) He thought that empirical arguments could support an affirmative answer to the general sceptical question.

Agreement on those points will suffice for the purposes of the rest of this chapter and the next.

13. *The 'veil-of-perception' doctrine*

Locke represents the difference between (*a*) seeing a tree and (*b*) being in a visual state as of seeing a tree though there is no

[21] See Gibson, *Locke's Theory of Knowledge*, ch. 7 § 16.

tree there to be seen, as the difference between (*a*) having a visual 'idea' while in the presence of a corresponding 'real thing' and (*b*) having such an 'idea' while not confronted by any such 'real thing'. This is harmless in itself. It becomes noxious only if 'real things' are logically divorced from 'ideas', so that an empirical basis is sought for a rebuttal of total scepticism about the objective realm. I speak of Locke's 'theory of reality', referring mainly to his fumbling of the issues associated with the general sceptical question; and so the word 'theory' is just a convenient misnomer. Berkeley has popularized the opinion that Locke's thought on these issues had the weight and deliberateness ordinarily associated with a 'theory' or 'doctrine', but the opinion is false.

Locke puts the objective world, the world of 'real things', beyond our reach on the other side of the veil of perception; so I call this aspect of his thought his 'veil-of-perception doctrine'. The more usual label, 'representative theory of perception', is unsatisfactory because it does not express what is wrong with the theory. There is nothing wrong with saying that when I see a tree my visual field 'represents' a real thing with which I am confronted. Nor is it objectionable to say that I see the tree by the mediation of my ideas or visual sense-data, if this means that without the sense-data I should not see the tree, or that my having those sense-data is part but not the whole of my seeing of the tree. 'But isn't it objectionable if it means that your seeing of the tree is only indirect?' I do not know, because I cannot find clear meaning in the uses philosophers of perception make of 'direct' and its cognates.

Locke often speaks of a 'correspondence', 'agreement' or 'conformity' between my visual field and the tree, suggesting that the two resemble one another. This is indeed objectionable (see § 5 above), but it is independent of the essential error in Locke's theory of reality,[22] namely his setting the entire range of facts about sensory states over against the entire range of facts about the objective realm and then looking for empirical links between them. The blanket question 'Do sensory states ever represent the objective realm?' is indeed a bad one—not because of what 'represent' means, but just because the question is a blanket one. The phrase 'representative theory of perception' does not capture this fact.

[22] Contrast P. D. Cummins, 'Berkeley's Likeness Principle', Martin pp. 353–5.

Perhaps Locke also has a causal theory of perception. He does say that when I see a tree there is a real thing causing me to have a certain visual 'idea'. But this too is in itself harmless, for there may in any given case be such a causal connexion as Locke postulates. To know that there was, however, we should need independent access to empirical facts about the objective realm, and so the reference to causal connexions ought not to take the blanket form: 'The fundamental relation between the whole range of subjective facts and the whole range of objective facts is a causal one.' I have elaborated this point elsewhere.[23]

In short, whether we say that ideas represent or are caused by real things, there is serious error only if the thesis is expressed in an all-at-once way, purporting to relate sensory states *en bloc* to objective states of affairs *en bloc*. The fact that Locke erred in that way is expressed, fairly satisfactorily, by calling his position 'the veil-of-perception doctrine'.

14. *The two doctrines in Berkeley*

The Lockean theory of substance (§ 11) is utterly distinct from the veil-of-perception doctrine which I have excogitated from Locke's handling of scepticism (§§ 12–13). The former tries to say what concepts we use when we say *Something is F*, while the latter has to do with the difference between *I see a tree* and *It is as though I were seeing a tree*. Although these two concerns are as different as chalk from cheese, the Lockean treatments of them have been confidently identified by Berkeley and many others.

Sometimes Berkeley does isolate one or other of the doctrines. He discusses the substratum theory, without introducing the veil-of-perception doctrine, in just two passages of which this is one:

In this proposition, a die is hard, extended and square, they will have it that the word *die* denotes a subject or substance, distinct from the hardness, extension and figure, which are predicated of it, and in which they exist. This I cannot comprehend: to me a die seems to be nothing distinct from those things which are termed its modes or accidents. And to say a die is hard, extended and square, is not to attribute those qualities to a subject distinct from and supporting them, but only an explication of the meaning of the word *die*.[24]

[23] J. Bennett, *Kant's Analytic* (Cambridge, 1966), § 7.
[24] *Principles* § 49. See also *First Dialogue*, pp. 197–9.

Elsewhere, much of the case against the veil-of-perception doctrine can be found unmixed with polemic against substrata.[25]

Nearly always, though, Berkeley welds the two doctrines together to form a single view about 'material substance'. He uses the word 'matter' and its cognates to refer to Locke's purported 'real things' which lie beyond the veil of perception. (He also, with more warrant from Locke's text, associates 'matter' with Locke's views about primary qualities; but that must wait until Chapter IV.) His use of the word 'substance', on the other hand, connects with Locke only in respect of the substratum theory about what it is for a property to be instantiated: the other contexts where Locke uses it lie outside Berkeley's purview. The phrase 'material substance', then, which Berkeley uses so lavishly and which hardly occurs in Locke, gives any discussion of one of the doctrines a good chance of becoming entangled with a discussion of the other.

Sometimes the mixture is fairly innocent. For example, one of Berkeley's attacks on the substratum theory, although ostensibly concerned with 'matter', is not seriously infected by anything which is appropriate to the veil-of-perception doctrine rather than the substance doctrine.[26]

Often, though, the mixture is lethal: 'It is said extension is a mode or accident of matter, and that matter is the *substratum* that supports it. Now I desire that you would explain what is meant by matter's *supporting* extension.'[27] Berkeley wants to make a point about substratum-substance. Not only does he distractingly call it 'matter', but he also drags 'extension' into the limelight. In Locke, 'extension' has much to do with primary qualities and a little to do with the real things beyond the veil of perception, but it has no special role in the substratum theory. Locke clearly regarded the latter as equally relevant or irrelevant to every sort of item—whether creaturely or divine, extended or unextended—that can instantiate or 'support' a quality.[28]

Here is Berkeley's next attempt to locate the target:

If we inquire into what the most accurate philosophers declare themselves to mean by *material substance*; we shall find them acknowledge, they have no other meaning annexed to those sounds, but the idea of

---

[25] *Principles* §§ 18–20, 86–8.
[27] *Principles* § 16.
[26] *Principles* § 68, first half.
[28] *Essay* II. xiii. 18.

being in general, together with the relative motion of its supporting accidents.[29]

This fairly enough reports the Lockean theory not of 'material substance' but of 'substance'. The adjective is important, for Berkeley adds that he does not understand the proffered account of the 'meaning annexed to those sounds', and continues:

But why should we trouble ourselves any farther, in discussing this material *substratum* or support of figure and motion, and other sensible qualities? Does it not suppose they have an existence without the mind? And is not this a direct repugnancy, and altogether inconceivable?[30]

Then, with the phrase 'existence without the mind' as his pivot, he modulates into an attack on the veil-of-perception doctrine! A complaint against a wrong analysis of subject-concepts is thus jumbled with a complaint against Locke's insufficiently idealist analysis of the concept of reality.

Some of Berkeley's turns of phrase could, without much strain, be construed in either way:

If the word *substance* be taken in the vulgar sense, for a combination of sensible qualities, such as extension, solidity, weight, and the like; this we cannot be accused of taking away. But if it be taken in a philosophic sense, for the support of accidents or qualities without the mind: then indeed I acknowledge that we take it away, if one may be said to take away that which never had any existence, not even in the imagination.[31]

This might mean 'Of course there are things with properties, but in saying this we do not employ a concept of naked thinghood'; or it might mean 'Of course there are real objects, but that statement can be analysed purely in terms of mental states'. There is no basis for preferring either reading: 'support' tends one way, but then 'without the mind' tends the other way.

Here are just two more examples:

But though it be allowed by the *materialists* themselves, that matter was thought of only for the sake of supporting accidents . . .[32]

If you stick to the notion of an unthinking substance, or support of extension, motion, and other sensible qualities, then to me it is most

[29] *Principles* § 17.   [30] Ibid.
[31] *Principles* § 37.   [32] *Principles* § 74.

evidently impossible there should be any such thing. Since it is a plain repugnancy, that those qualities should exist in or be supported by an unperceiving substance.[33]

There are many other examples of Berkeley's conflating or identifying the two doctrines. Some of the clearest cases also introduce Locke's view about primary qualities, and will be quoted later.

This calamitous mistake of Berkeley's can be explained. His philosophy put intellectual and linguistic pressures on him to make it—pressures transmitted almost wholly by his use of the word 'idea'. I shall try to explain how.

In § 4 above I noted Locke's preparedness to use 'idea of *x*' to mean 'quality of *x* by virtue of which *x* causes an idea in a percipient', and I suggested that his contentment with this curious ellipsis might be partially explained thus: 'Ideas (= sense-data) give us all our data about the qualities of things, and so what we have to say about things' qualities might as well be expressed in terms of the ideas which things cause in us.' Now, Berkeley's alternative to the veil-of-perception doctrine is a strong form of idealism: the real things in the objective realm *are* just collections of sensory states—the sensory states which, for Locke, are just symptoms and effects of the presence of real things. So Berkeley could replace the line of thought which explains Locke's idea/ quality ellipsis by something like this: 'Real things are sets of ideas (= sense-data), and so statements about the qualities of things *are* statements about ideas.' Thus, for Berkeley the use of 'idea' to mean 'quality of a thing' is simply, literally correct: 'Qualities, as hath been shewn, are nothing else but *sensations* or *ideas*, which exist only in a *mind* perceiving them.'[34] And the identification of qualities with ideas is also highlighted by this statement of Berkeley's idealist rival to the veil-of-perception doctrine:

By matter therefore we are to understand an inert, senseless substance, in which extension, figure, and motion, do actually subsist. But it is evident from what we have already shewn, that extension, figure and motion are only ideas existing in the mind, and that an idea can be like nothing but another idea, and that consequently neither they nor their archetypes can exist in an unperceiving substance.[35]

[33] *Principles* § 76. See also *First Dialogue*, p. 197.
[34] *Principles* § 78.
[35] *Principles* § 9.

(I suggested in § 4 that Locke's ellipsis was also encouraged by the role of 'ideas' as meanings. This could apply to Berkeley too, perhaps, but there is no need of it: the above account of why Berkeley identifies ideas with qualities, involving only ideas considered as sense-data, is quite sufficient. My earlier published attempt to involve both the primary roles of 'idea' in a single explanation is, as I indicated in § 4 above, an embarrassing muddle.)

Given this fact about Berkeley's use of 'idea', it is natural that he should conflate the two Lockean doctrines; for each purports to offer an anchor for free-floating 'ideas'—one tying sensory states to objects, the other tying qualities to substrata—and of each doctrine Berkeley can say that it over-populates the world by postulating something unknowable when known 'ideas' would suffice. The rather Berkeleian sentence 'Things are just collections of ideas, not something over and above them' can be interpreted, taking ideas to be sensory states, as denying the veil-of-perception doctrine; or, taking ideas to be qualities, as denying the substratum theory.

I am not saying that Berkeley, given his idealism and his resultant identification of ideas with qualities, was entitled to identify the two Lockean doctrines. He should have seen that he was confronted by what looked like two doctrines, and then perhaps argued *from* idealism to the conclusion that the pair were really just two versions of a single thesis. No such argument occurs in Berkeley's pages. So far from saying 'That looks like a gap, but I shall use idealism to show that it isn't', Berkeley did not even see that there might be thought to be a gap, and ran the two doctrines together even in his arguments *for* idealism.

15. *The two doctrines in Locke*

The Lockean theories of substance and reality are distinct in fact, but are they also distinct in Locke? One might expect not, given Locke's tendency to use 'idea' to mean 'quality'. Lacking Berkeley's reason for treating this as more than a mere ellipsis, he nevertheless has the other reason mentioned in § 4 above: the set of *qualities* a thing must have for W to apply to it uniquely determines the *meaning* of W, and thus the *ideas* associated with W; but ideas are indisputably *sense-data* as well; and so 'idea of *x*' can univocally mean both 'quality of x' and 'appearance of x'. With this conclusion flowering from roots which run fairly deep in his thought, Locke might well have identified the substratum and veil-of-perception doctrines.

Yet my citations on substance in § 11 above contain not a word about 'real things' or 'things without us'; nor, in all the anti-sceptical polemic quoted in § 12, does 'substance' occur even once. This is not because of bias in my selection of passages to quote; no bias was needed. In the relevant parts of the *Essay*, Locke simply does not make the wrong identification which subsequently loomed so large in Berkeley's exegesis of him. (Berkeley notwithstanding, these parts are not extensive. Locke says little about 'the idea of substance in general', I think because he regards it as embarrassing and trivial; and little about 'real things', perhaps because he does not see the depth of his problem about them.)

'Locke simply does not make . . .'—or rather he *complicatedly* does not make the identification. Without intending to identify the substratum and veil-of-perception doctrines, Locke cannot help expounding the former, and some of its relatives, in ways appropriate to the latter. The two drift towards one another of their own accord, drawn by forces inherent in Locke's basic assumptions and choice of language. In this section I present some examples.

First, Locke's substance/mode polarity needs to be explained:

Modes I call such complex ideas which, however compounded, contain not in them the supposition of subsisting by themselves, but are considered as dependences on, or affections of substances;—such as are the ideas signified by the words triangle, gratitude, murder, &c.[36]

I think that modes are just (ideas of) properties or qualities, and that Locke's peculiar choice of examples is to be explained by his distaste for overtly universalist language.[37] The geometrical study of 'triangles' is really a study of triangularity; yet a sturdy anti-universalist, who will not want 'triangularity' in his inventory of the world's contents, may feel that he can safely include 'triangles (of the sort studied in geometry)'. Again, although he regards redness and validity and manhood as parts of the universalist mythology, he may feel safe in admitting such apparently

[36] *Essay* II. xii. 4.   [37] *Essay* II. xxii. 3–10; III. v. 3–6.

down-to-earth, unabstract, observable items as gratitude and
murder. In short, modes are properties or qualities or universals;
and Locke, wanting to allow such items while still maintaining
that 'All things that exist are only particulars', has to select
examples of modes which do not give the game away by their
verbal form—e.g. has to select 'incest' rather than 'incestuousness'.

The other side of the polarity is presented thus:

The ideas of *substances* are such combinations of simple ideas as are
taken to represent distinct *particular* things subsisting by themselves;
in which the supposed or confused idea of substance, such as it is, is
always the first and chief.[38]

Something 'subsists by itself' if it is a thing and not a quality,
not an 'affection' of something else, not logically dependent on
anything else as a mode is on a substance, e.g. as a murder is on
a murderer.

The substance/mode distinction, then, draws the line between
particulars and properties. It is a purely logical distinction, whose
left-hand side is not restricted to particulars of some special kind,
e.g. to 'material substances' or to 'real things without me'. So
the substratum theory, which offers an analysis of the distinction,
is a piece of wholly general philosophical logic: it implies something about what there is, but not specially about what there is
in the objective realm or the world 'without me'. As even
Berkeley sometimes sees,[39] the analysis purports to deal with 'I
am unhappy' as well as with 'That is square'. That Locke credits
the substratum theory with this degree of generality is shown by
his way of introducing the substance/mode distinction; and there
is other evidence too. For example, when he suggests that the
belief in substrata arose from the quasi-reifying of qualities or
'accidents': 'They who first ran into the notion of *accidents*, as a
sort of real beings that needed something to inhere in, were
forced to find out the word *substance* to support them',[40] there is
no hint that substances are confined to 'real things without us'.
In the preceding section he teasingly asks the substratum theorists
whether God and finite minds and bodies are all 'substances' in
the same sense; which presupposes that the substratum theory is
intended to have full generality.[41]

---

[38] *Essay* II. xii. 6.   [39] *Philosophical Commentaries*, entry 785.
[40] *Essay* II. xiii. 19.   [41] See also *Essay* II. xxiii. 5, 15.

So much for the apartness of the substance and reality doctrines in the *Essay*. I now turn to the other half of the story.

(1) When Locke explains 'substances' as things 'subsisting by themselves', the self-subsistence in question is clearly meant to be logical; but the phrase could mean 'existing independently of any percipient', and so could link the substance doctrine with the theory of reality—'Are there substances, i.e. things subsisting by themselves, i.e. real things without us?' A shift of this kind does occur in Locke's writings. He maintains that in constructing complex ideas of modes we are subject only to the laws of logic: 'There is nothing more required to this kind of ideas to make them real, but that they be so framed, that there be a possibility of existing conformable to them',[42] whereas our ideas of substance are subject to a more stringent requirement:

Our complex ideas of *substances*, being made all of them in reference to things existing without us, and intended to be representations of substances as they really are, are no further real than as they are such combinations of simple ideas as are really united, and co-exist in things without us.[43]

If these passages are stipulatively defining 'real' as applied to ideas, then what they say cannot be false. But if, as seems likely, Locke thinks that an idea (or the expression which 'signifies' it) is legitimate only if the idea is 'real', then what he says about the 'reality' of ideas of substances is surely wrong. If 'gratitude' is all right in a world where no-one is ever grateful, why may we not have 'horse' in a world devoid of horses? All that, though, is by the way. My main point is that in making this mistake Locke explicitly connects 'ideas of substances' with 'things without us', which threatens to infect the substratum theory with the veil-of-perception doctrine. But he does not carry out the threat: in this passage, where ideas of *substances* are so overtly connected with 'things without us', there is no mention of the supposed idea of *substance*.

(2) Some of Locke's versions of the substratum doctrine have a feature which quietly nudges it over towards the appearance/reality area. The general theory of substratum-substance, I have maintained, is addressed to the question 'What is it for a quality to be instantiated by a particular?' Locke, however, says that 'we

[42] *Essay* II. xxx. 4.　　　　[43] *Essay* II. xxx. 5.

accustom ourselves to suppose some *substratum* as a support for
'a certain number of simple ideas [which] go constantly together';[44]
and this seems to narrow the doctrine's scope (*a*) to the species
of cases where several qualities are jointly instantiated by one
particular, and (*b*) to the sub-species where the qualities in question
'go constantly together'. (*a*) does not matter, for Locke could
argue that since we have no room for the notion of a thing with
only one quality, the question of a quality's being 'had' by something does not arise unless other qualities are also 'had' by that
same thing. But (*b*) is puzzling: why does Locke confine himself
to cases where the qualities all 'go constantly together', and
what does he mean by that anyway?

I have, of course, been construing 'idea' to mean 'quality',
for only thus does the passage under discussion bear on the substance doctrine at all. Our puzzle about 'ideas which go constantly
together', however, is solved if we take these 'ideas' to be not
qualities but sensory states. For then the puzzling phrase refers
to cases where one's sensory history manifests certain kinds of
pattern or order—the kinds, in fact, which are our basis for
thinking that there are 'things without us'. So instead of expressing
a queerly restricted version of the substratum doctrine, the passage
on this reading of it gestures towards the province of the veil-of-
perception doctrine.

Locke makes nothing of this opportunity for error. Indeed, a
mere four sections later he uses arguments which, in effect, positively insist that the whole point of the substratum theory is its
being applied to particulars of every kind and not just 'real
things without us'. Still, it is worth noting that a basis for linking
'substance' with 'real thing' is laid down in the connexion of the
former with 'ideas which go constantly together'.

(3) The passage in which that phrase occurs, like some others
in the *Essay*, contains something else which drags the substratum
doctrine off towards the veil-of-perception doctrine. When we
notice several ideas which 'go constantly together', Locke says,
'not imagining how these simple ideas *can* subsist by themselves,
we accustom ourselves to suppose some *substratum* wherein they
do subsist, and from which they do result, which therefore we
call *substance*'.[45] If this concerns the substratum doctrine at all,
the 'ideas' in question must again be qualities; but in that case

---

[44] *Essay* II. xxiii. 1. [45] Ibid.

Locke is saying that substances are supposed to *cause* their qualities; and one wonders why he should think that anyone has ever supposed this. This puzzle too is removed when we recall that 'ideas' can also be sensory states; for then the clause 'from which [ideas] do result' echoes the causal aspect of Locke's theory of reality.

Still Locke does not cash in on the unhappy verbal overlap between the two doctrines. On the contrary, he proceeds immediately to drag 'idea' apart from 'quality', and thus to cleanse the substance doctrine from any causal element by saying that substrata *support* qualities and that qualities *cause* ideas:

If any one will examine himself concerning his notion of pure substance in general, he will find he has no other idea of it at all, but only a supposition of he knows not what *support* of such qualities which are capable of producing simple ideas in us.[46]

Observe that Locke is no more explicit or deliberate in separating the two doctrines, and the two relevant senses of 'idea', than he is in running them together. He sometimes nearly commits Berkeley's outright identification of them, and sometimes implicitly resists it; but at no stage does he seem to be aware of what is going on.

16. *The two doctrines in the 20th century*

So much for Berkeley and Locke; but what of those philosophers who, unaided by the conviction that 'Qualities are nothing else but sensations or ideas', have nevertheless collapsed the substratum theory into the veil-of-perception doctrine?

I cannot fully explain why Berkeley's problems are so often taken at his own valuation; but the following hypothesis may have some force. Someone might follow in Berkeley's footsteps by illustrating the distinction between appearance and reality by the question 'It seems to me that I see something square, but is there really something square which I see?', and equating this with 'I am in the presence of an instance, in my visual field, of squareness; but am I in the presence of something which is square?' A question about appearance and reality would thus be quietly transmuted into a question about property-instantiation. And someone who noticed that each question could wrongly

[46] *Essay* II. xxiii. 2.

though plausibly be analysed in terms of an elusive 'something we know not what', might be further encouraged to view them as two versions of a single question to which Locke gave a single wrong analysis.

The train of thought I have sketched is invalid, for the question 'Given that I seem to see something square, is there really something square that I see?' is not about the instantiation of a presented property, and the substratum doctrine is irrelevant to it. I prove this by a dilemma, with one horn for those who reify sense-data and another for those who don't.

(*a*) If it is all right to reify sense-data, then we can say that I have or apprehend a square sense-datum; or that some part of my visual field is square. But in that case the sense-datum *is* the 'thing which' is square, i.e. it bears the property of squareness with which I am now presented. A Lockean substratum-substance need not be physical or objective or extra-mental: the whole point of the doctrine, as is often remarked even by victims of Berkeley's muddle, is that it separates the substance from *all* its properties, claiming that properties are borne by items of which nothing can be said except that they bear properties. So: *if I have a square sense-datum, I am not in the presence of a property for which I am seeking a bearer*, for the property in whose presence I am already has a bearer.

(*b*) If it is wrong to reify sense-data, then I don't have a square sense-datum but am in a state like those I am ordinarily in when seeing square things. But then my question as to whether there is something square which I see implies agnosticism about whether I am presented with an instance of squareness at all. My question 'Is the world at this point really as it appears to be?' is therefore not of the form 'Is there a bearer for this property?' So: *if I do not have a square sense-datum, I am not in the presence of a property for which I am seeking a bearer*, for I am not, in the required sense, 'in the presence of a property' at all.

(My treatment of (*a*) implies that if it is right to reify ideas then they are substances.[47] Locke would not have drawn such a conclusion, but he was committed to it for all that, and his failure to see the commitment had less to do with unthoroughness about 'substance' than with unclarity about the status of 'ideas'.)

[47] Cf. H. H. Price, 'Appearing and Appearances', *American Philosophical Quarterly*, vol. 1 (1964).

The foregoing dilemma is conclusive, but I do not know whether anyone has adopted the line of thought it attacks. The nearest thing to it that I have found is in Berkeley himself, who shifts from 'Does something real correspond to this sensory state?' to 'Does something have this property?' in something like the way I have described:

It is worth while to reflect a little on the motives which induced men to suppose the existence of material substance. . . . First therefore, it was thought that colour, figure, motion, and the rest of the sensible qualities or accidents, did really exist without the mind; and for this reason, it seemed needful to suppose some unthinking *substratum* or *substance* wherein they did exist, since they could not be conceived to exist by themselves. . . .[48]

As for our contemporaries, I can only show that they do, for whatever reason, make Berkeley's mistake. I select examples which help to expose the mistake's logical structure.

O'Connor sees that there is *a* doctrine about substance of a purely logical kind. But he brings it in as an afterthought, and dismisses it, without argument, as an impossible reading of 'the substratum theory':

It is certainly not . . . true that colours, for instance, cannot occur except as properties of a coloured something. If I stare at a light for a few seconds and then turn my gaze away, I shall see an 'after-image' in the form of a coloured patch which certainly does not inhere in any substance. The supporter of the substratum theory of substance has either to claim that (i) the after-image is itself a substance or (ii) that it inheres in my visual field. (i) is a *reductio ad absurdum* of the substratum theory, though a sense-datum would qualify as a substance in the *logical* sense of the word: it has properties without being itself a property of anything.[49]

With satisfying explicitness, Morris presents Berkeley's idealism as contradicting something said 'on the credit of Aristotle's logic':

Philosophers had always taken it for granted, largely on the credit of Aristotle's logic, that qualities must be supported by some underlying permanent self-subsistent substance. . . . Berkeley [argues against this] that throughout our whole experience of the physical world, we never

---

[48] *Principles* § 73.
[49] D. J. O'Connor, *John Locke* (Pelican Books, 1952), pp. 80-1.

apprehend anything but sensible qualities and collections of sensible qualities. All we know of things or can know of them is what we perceive by sense; if there were more in things than this, we could not know it. . . . This doctrine is evidently based on the argument that whenever we are aware of a physical object, introspective analysis shows that there is nothing present in our mind but a number or collection of simple ideas of qualities; and it is taken by Berkeley to prove that knowledge simply consists in the awareness of sensible qualities.[50]

Warnock mixes the substratum and veil-of-perception doctrines by sliding smoothly from 'matter' to 'the essential "support" of qualities'.[51] Also, and more interestingly, he says that according to Locke: 'There is a world of physical ("external") objects [which within certain limits] actually have the qualities which our ideas incline us to assign to them',[52] and also that: 'Locke had asserted the existence of "matter", "material substance", a *something* of which nothing could be either said or known.'[53] Warnock purports to be describing a single Lockean doctrine in these two passages. Yet the two are inconsistent: items which 'actually have the qualities . . .' cannot be ones about which 'nothing could be said'. Of course the inconsistency is not Locke's (for him it is 'real things' which 'actually have the qualities . . .', and substrata of which 'nothing could be said'), but results from the Berkeleian exegesis. Of all the writers who credit Locke with thinking that the essentially unqualified items which support qualities may also resemble our ideas, I have not found one who calls attention to the inconsistency.

The error of Berkeley's that I have been discussing does not occur in Gibson's masterly work on Locke; and Armstrong and Broad have both rejected it—fairly explicitly though without detailed diagnosis.[54] With those three exceptions, Berkeley's error seems to run untrammelled through the entire literature of Locke-Berkeley commentary.

Nor are 'historical' writings the only source of the mistake. It is in the course of a piece of straight philosophy that Ayer uses the phrase 'sensible properties' in high Berkeleian fashion to

[50] C. R. Morris, *Locke, Berkeley, Hume* (Oxford, 1931), pp. 74–5.
[51] Warnock, *Berkeley*, p. 103.
[52] Ibid. pp. 95–6.   [53] Ibid. p. 109.
[54] D. M. Armstrong, Introduction to *Berkeley's Philosophical Writings* (New York, 1965), pp. 15–16; Broad, 'Berkeley's Denial of Material Substance', p. 174.

effect a slide from 'the thing itself as opposed to anything which may be said about it' to 'the thing itself [as opposed to] its appearances':

It happens to be the case that we cannot, in our language, refer to the sensible properties of a thing without introducing a word or phrase which appears to stand for the thing itself as opposed to anything which may be said about it. And, as a result of this, those who are infected by the primitive superstition that to every name a single real entity must correspond assume that it is necessary to distinguish logically between the thing itself and any, or all, of its sensible properties. And so they employ the term 'substance' to refer to the thing itself. But from the fact that we happen to employ a single word to refer to a thing, and make that word the grammatical subject of the sentences in which we refer to the sensible appearances of the thing, it does not by any means follow that the thing itself is a 'simple entity', or that it cannot be defined in terms of the totality of its appearances. It is true that in talking of 'its' appearances we appear to distinguish the thing from the appearances, but that is simply an accident of linguistic usage. Logical analysis shows that what makes these 'appearances' the 'appearances of' the same thing is not their relationship to an entity other than themselves, but their relationship to one another.[55]

17. *Connecting substance with reality*

Despite my arguments in this chapter, there is a connexion between the reality issue and a certain issue about substance. It certainly does not legitimize Berkeley's proven tendency to *identify* the reality and substance questions, but it may provide a sound basis—to which Berkeley could have appealed though in fact he didn't—for partly expressing idealism in the sentence 'There are no material substances'. In explaining this connexion between the two issues, I shall be repairing a serious gap in my published paper on this topic—a gap made clear to me by Robert M. Adams, to whom I am much indebted.

The substratum analysis of property-instantiation, or of the concept of substance, is a bad attempt to answer a serious question, namely: 'What is it for an item to be a thing rather than a property or attribute of a thing or a process which a thing undergoes?' This can be expressed in the form: 'What is the difference between substances and properties?' or 'What are the criteria

---

[55] A. J. Ayer, *Language, Truth and Logic* (London, 1964), p. 42.

governing the substance/property distinction?' One may dismiss the 'substratum' answer without objecting to the question itself.

Nevertheless, the question is hard, if not impossible, to answer at that level of generality. I can make no headway with the concept of substance except within some area which, even if extremely large, excludes some possible topics of discourse. One such area is that of what I call the objective realm. Within this, we can ask and at least partly answer the question: 'What are the criteria for the distinction between something's being an object or objective substance and its being a property of an object or a process which objects undergo?' Consider, for example, the borderline case of a magnetic field. This can be regarded as an object which is created by electric currents etc., and whose presence causes compasses etc. to behave in certain ways; but it is also plausible to say that the existence of the magnetic field *consists in* facts about the presence of electric currents, the behaviour of compasses etc. The former way of thinking of the magnetic field views it as substantial, the latter as non-substantial or attributive. A consideration of the choice between them might help us to see what is going on in clearer cases, such as the substantiality of my hand and the non-substantiality of the whiteness of my hand.

The magnetic field example, as well as suggesting what a serious question of the form 'Are . . . substantial?' might be like, points the way to how such questions should be answered. The inclination to refuse a thing-like status to magnetic fields connects essentially, I suggest, with the belief that we do not need any such substantival expression as 'magnetic field'; that the facts we can report by means of it can also be expressed in statements whose substantival expressions refer only to wires, dynamos, compasses and so on; that magnetic fields, in short, can be fully accommodated in a language which handles them adjectivally rather than substantivally. On this criterion for substantiality, a house is substantial while a fight is not, because what we say with the substantive 'fight' can easily be said without it. We can replace 'The fight was a fierce one' by something like 'The men fought fiercely', and so on; whereas no such replacements seem to be available for everything we might say using 'the house'.

The suggested criterion for substantiality leaves a question open: is an item to be deemed non-substantial if the facts about it *can*, never mind how, be expressed without a substantival expression referring to that item? Or is to count as non-substantial only if we cannot easily or economically handle it adjectivally while still covering all the facts? The latter alternative still leaves questions open (how easily? with what sorts of economy?), but my concern is with the former alternative. That is, I am concerned with the idea that an item counts as substantial, or as a substance, only if we must handle it substantivally in our language —only if we *cannot* express the facts about it without availing ourselves of a substantival expression referring to it.

This rather strong requirement for substantiality has found favour with some philosophers, e.g. with Spinoza, Leibniz and Kant.[56] It goes with thinking of substances as the basic and fundamental and irreducible stuff of reality, as for example in this: 'The only substances are physical atoms. The basic facts about the universe are all facts about what atoms there are and about their various properties and relations; and the things we say using substantival expressions like "house" and "dust-storm" are really just complex facts about the qualities and relations and dispositions of atoms. Given substantives referring to atoms, and an unrestricted range of non-substantival expressions, I could in principle say all that there is to be said about reality.' This line of thought illustrates a sense of 'substance' which is not absurd, which has had a good deal of currency in the philosophical tradition, and which we may conjecture to have exerted some influence, whether recognized or not, upon Berkeley's uses of the word 'substance'.

Now Berkeley's idealism entails that facts about material objects are, or boil down to, facts about 'ideas'. Furthermore, he usually thinks that any statement about someone's having an idea is a fact about the state the person is in, a fact expressible in a one-noun statement whose subject-term refers to a particular person or mind or 'spirit'. (That is, he accepts the anti-reification thesis of § 5, though he certainly does not see all its implications. In § 6 I accused Berkeley of thinking, like a reifier, that an idea of a triangle must be triangular; and so he does. But he does not reify ideas—rather, he idealizes *things*.) Given these two views of Berkeley's, he could, using 'substance' according to the strong criterion I have sketched, say that the only substances are minds

[56] Spinoza, *Ethics*, Pt. I, definition 3 and propositions 8, 12; Leibniz, *Monadology* §§ 1–7; Kant, *Critique of Pure Reason* A 242–3 = B 300–1.

or spirits. He could say that although there are chairs and tables and houses, such items as these—items including all material 'things'—are not *substances*; they are not part of the basic story of what there is; for the basic story can be told in a language which refers only to 'spirits' and their sensory states, and then statements about 'chairs' and 'houses' can be introduced later as *façons de parler*—as convenient ways of expressing the basic facts rather than as introducing a new range of facts.

So there is a connexion between substance and reality after all. For there is a reasonable sense of 'substance' in which Berkeley can express a large part of his claim about reality—or about why the veil-of-perception doctrine is wrong—by saying 'There are no material substances'. It is important that the word 'substances' is doing real work here. The position is not that Berkeley can say 'There are no material items of any kind' and thence draw trivial corollaries of the form 'There are no material Fs' where 'F' could stand for 'ducks' or 'substances' or any idle word at all. On the contrary, Berkeley says that there *are* material items, including chairs and ducks and houses; and much of the force of his opposition to Locke's view about *reality* can be brought out by his adding '. . . but these material items are not *substances*.'

If Berkeley appreciated, at some level of his mind, the possibility of using 'substance' in the way I have described,[57] that would help to explain his saying some of the things he does say—and especially his thinking that 'substance' has a central role to play in his denial of Locke's theory of reality. But this explanation has nothing to do with the supposed notion of a substratum. The legitimate way in which Berkeley could have used 'There are no material *substances*' does not equate this with 'There are no material substrata'; and, indeed, it requires an understanding of the term 'substance' which has no coherent and straightforward connexion with the substratum analysis. *A fortiori*, nothing in the foregoing pages has the slightest tendency to justify Berkeley and many commentators in confusing the question about ideas/objects with the question about properties/substrata.

(When Berkeley addresses himself to the sort of substances which he thinks do exist, namely mental or spiritual ones, he does accept a thoroughly substratum-type analysis of the concept of substance [see § 45 below]. This suggests that he ties 'There are

[57] See *Principles* § 91.

no material substances' to 'There are no material substrata' simply because he takes them to be synonymous—because he cannot see how to avoid a substratum analysis of the concept of a substance. This would imply, ironically, that passages in which Berkeley is thought to attack the veil-of-perception doctrine and the substratum analysis are really attacks on the former in terms of Berkeley's whole-hearted *acceptance* of the latter. The irony is pleasing, but the interpretation which implies it is wrong: the two clean-cut thrusts at the substratum analysis are there, and cannot be ignored. It can indeed be argued that Berkeley cared very much about the veil-of-perception theory, and very little about the substratum analysis; but I think we have to see him as trying to attack both these Lockean doctrines, and as confusing them with one another in the ways I have described.)

I have tried to present a link between the concepts of substance and reality—a link which may be relevant to Berkeley's procedures even if he did not explicitly avail himself of it. It is relevant at all, as I noted earlier, only if Berkeley does regard ideas as adjectival on minds or spirits; and some writers have said that he does not, and that Berkeleian ideas are radically other than spirits, are not mental, are 'perceived' in a genuinely relational way, are 'immaterial' *only* in the sense that they are not Lockean· 'real things'. This interpretation creates a sensible, cheerful, likeable Berkeley, who 'restores our native confidence in our senses'[58] (supposing that we had ever lost it), but who has no claim on our attention as philosophers. As well as flattening out the depths and complexities in Berkeley's metaphysics, the disputed interpretation puts its adherents to some desperate shifts on matters of relative detail: they have to construe 'ideas are in the mind' as meaning 'ideas are perceived' and nothing more; since Berkeley equates 'idea' with 'sensation' they have to say that 'A *sensation* in Berkeley's usage is . . . an object sensed';[59] and they cannot explain why Berkeley should say that 'unperceived idea' is a 'contradiction'. This last point is rightly treated as crucial in Pitcher's definitive treatment of this matter,[60] to which the reader is referred for—among many things—a discussion of the two main passages in Berkeley which do favour the disputed

---

[58] A. A. Luce, 'Berkeley's Existence in the Mind', Martin p. 289.
[59] A. A. Luce, *The Dialectic of Immaterialism* (London, 1963), p. 191.
[60] Pitcher, 'Minds and Ideas in Berkeley'.

interpretation.[61] I ought to mention an entry in the *Philosophical Commentaries* which has been adduced in support of the disputed interpretation: 'Nothing properly but persons i.e. conscious things do exist, all other things are not so much existences as manners of ye existence of persons.' [62] Against this entry, which clearly implies that ideas are states of minds, Berkeley later put a sign which means 'Reject' or 'False' or the like; and this has been adduced as powerful evidence of his having finally come to the view credited to him by the disputed interpretation.[63] Even if he did arrive at that view firmly enough to put a 'Reject' sign in a notebook, the fact remains that all the significant structure of his thought requires the assumption that ideas are indeed states of mind. And in any case, the 'Reject' sign means many things:[64] that Berkeley has come to think that the entry is false, or that he no longer approves of its wording, or that he has decided for some other reason not to use it in his published work. The quoted entry's use of 'existence' as a non-abstract noun is quite untypical of the published writings; and the word 'persons' is one which Berkeley later decided to avoid as far as possible,[65] and which in fact occurs nowhere in the *Principles*. It is likely enough that Berkeley marked the entry as not to be used, for those two quasi-stylistic reasons.[66]

[61] *Principles* § 49; *Third Dialogue*, p. 237. See Pitcher, op. cit. pp. 201–3.

[62] *Philosophical Commentaries*, entry 24.

[63] A. A. Luce, *The Dialectic of Immaterialism*, p. 82.

[64] Thus Luce, in his Introduction to the *Commentaries*. See *The Works of George Berkeley*, vol. 2, p. 4.

[65] *Commentaries,* entry 713.

[66] For an indignant rejection of my earlier piece, see M. R. Ayers, 'Substance, Reality, and the Great, Dead Philosophers', *American Philosophical Quarterly*, vol. 7 (1970). One major point in this is met in the present section.

IV

PRIMARY AND SECONDARY
QUALITIES

18. *Primary qualities and 'body'*

LOCKE inherited from Descartes, or borrowed from Newton and Boyle, a distinction between 'primary' and 'secondary' qualities.[1] His attempts to define it in general terms are unsatisfactory, and for now a pair of lists must suffice. A thing's primary qualities are its 'solidity, extension, figure, motion or rest, and number';[2] and its secondary qualities are its colour, temperature, smell, taste and sound.

It is often thought that this distinction is a shaky one, that Locke certainly did not put it to good use, and that we owe these two insights to Berkeley. I shall argue that the distinction is well-grounded and interesting, that Locke had grasped an important truth about it, and that Berkeley's treatment of this matter is impercipient and unhelpful. Berkeley assimilated the primary/secondary distinction to that monolithic 'theory of material substance' which he thought he detected in Locke's writings; and I shall argue that that is the dominating fact about his failure to deal competently with the distinction between primary and secondary qualities.

Locke has two general, true things to say about the primary/secondary distinction. One of them is his thesis that primary qualities are

such as are utterly inseparable from the body, in what state soever it be; and such as in all the alterations and changes it suffers, all the force can be used upon it, it constantly keeps; and such as sense constantly finds in every particle of matter which has bulk enough to be perceived.[3]

In most of Locke's theorizing, a thing's primary qualities are taken to consist in its being (say) spherical, two feet across, and

---

[1] *Essay* II. viii. 9–26; xxiii. 9–11; IV. iii. 11–13, 28.
[2] *Essay* II. viii. 9.
[3] Ibid.

falling rapidly;[4] but here they are thought of rather as a thing's being shaped, of some size, mobile, etc. That is, in the thesis that primary qualities are ones which a body cannot lose, it is determinable qualities which are in question and not determinate ones. Locke's example reinforces this reading: 'Take a grain of wheat, divide it into two parts; each part has still solidity, extension, figure, and mobility: divide it again, and it retains still the same qualities.'[5] It is not clear that 'solidity' is a determinable, either in its normal meaning or in Locke's specialized sense in which 'solid' means 'impenetrable'. In this respect, as in others which we shall meet later in this section, solidity is a special case.[6]

Locke has a good point here, but he ought not to express it as though it were a prediction about the outcome of an experiment, for really it is a point about the meaning of the word 'body', or about the concept of a body or a physical thing. He does in fact know this: 'People [mean] by *body* something that is solid and extended, whose parts are separable and movable different ways.'[7] Indeed the word 'primary' for Locke partly means that these are qualities a thing must have to count as a 'body'. (His other account of what 'primary' means is indefensible.[8])

Locke's discussions of the concept of body involve detailed points (e.g. against Descartes) which are of some interest but which lie beyond my present scope. His general thesis that the raw materials which constitute the concept of body are to be found within the realm of primary qualities, and that secondary qualities are conceptually inessential, seems safe enough. Yet Berkeley apparently denies it: 'It is not in my power to frame an idea of a body extended and moved, but I must withal give it some colour or other sensible quality . . . In short, extension, figure, and motion, abstracted from all other qualities, are inconceivable.'[9] There is an uncertainty of interpretation here, which is also suspiciously present in the corresponding passage in the *Dialogues*.[10] The quoted passage is, as it stands, true: a thing's being extended, or its taking up space, must involve some

---

[4] See Jackson, 'Locke's Distinction between Primary and Secondary Qualities', pp. 60–5.

[5] *Essay* II. viii. 9.

[6] See C. J. F. Williams, 'Are Primary Qualities Qualities?', *Philosophical Quarterly*, vol. 19 (1969), pp. 314–18.

[7] *Essay* II. xiii. 11.

[9] *Principles* § 10.

[8] *Essay* II. viii. 23.

[10] *First Dialogue*, p. 193.

spatial region's being occupied *by* something—some quality must be manifested in that region other than mere extension. But the quality could be solidity, which is on Locke's list of primary qualities.[11] If Berkeley really is saying only that 'body' could not be defined out of extension, figure and motion, without recourse to solidity, then his point is correct but it does not count against Locke, or help Berkeley with the larger claim for which he is arguing, or justify his claim to be discussing 'figure, motion, *and the rest of the primary or original qualities*' (my italics). It is, indeed, a point which Locke himself makes and insists upon, in criticism of Descartes' account of the concept of body.[12]

But perhaps Berkeley is, as he is sometimes thought to be, making a stronger claim to the effect that secondary qualities are essential to the concept of body: he may be saying, a little carelessly, that nothing could count as experience of a world of bodies which had primary but not secondary qualities. What he says, on that reading of it, is certainly relevant to Locke's thesis; but it is also a manifest falsehood which could be believed, I think, only by someone who had lapsed into thinking of perception too exclusively in terms of sight. Granted that we could not see things to have sizes and shapes without seeing them to have (not necessarily chromatic) colours, the crucial point is that we could perceive objects to have sizes and shapes without ever seeing them—and, it can be added, without ever hearing or tasting or smelling them either.

That Berkeley discusses this view of Locke's is not due to his having sharply separated it from Locke's other claims about primary and secondary qualities. On the contrary: it is little more than an accident that we can find in Berkeley an argument which goes against this Lockean thesis in particular, and the passages containing it are jammed into discussions of entirely different matters (see § 24 below). In contrast with that, Hume's section 'Of the Modern Philosophy' is devoted almost exclusively to expounding and criticizing the view that the concept of a body can be adequately based upon primary qualities alone. One notable fact about Hume's treatment is its emphasis upon the primary

---

[11] *Essay* II. viii. 9. See also A. M. Quinton, 'Matter and Space', *Mind*, vol. 73 (1964); N. Fleming, 'The Idea of a Solid', *Australasian Journal of Philosophy*, vol. 43 (1965); D. Sanford, 'Volume and Solidity', Ibid. vol. 45 (1967).

[12] *Essay* II. xiii. 11–15.

quality so conspicuously ignored by Berkeley—namely solidity. (Berkeley's passing remark that solidity is 'plainly relative to our senses', though it bears on a certain view he attributed to Locke, has nothing to do with the thesis we are now considering.[13])

Hume says explicitly that the primary qualities other than solidity are an inadequate foundation for the concept of body, and then argues separately that the addition of solidity still does not save the day for Locke's thesis. The argument about solidity starts like this:

The idea of solidity is that of two objects, which being impell'd by the utmost force, cannot penetrate each other; but still maintain a separate and distinct existence. Solidity, therefore, is perfectly incomprehensible alone, and without the conception of some bodies, which are solid, and maintain this separate and distinct existence. Now what idea have we of these bodies?[14]

Hume then proceeds to argue that the 'idea' needed to supplement and give content to that of solidity cannot be a primary-quality one, for it has already been shown that all the other primary qualities need supplementation themselves; and so it must be a secondary-quality one, specifically it must be an idea of colour; and so Locke's thesis is wrong. As Hume expresses it a little later:

What idea do we form of these bodies or objects, to which we suppose solidity to belong? To say, that we conceive them merely as solid, is to run on *in infinitum*. To affirm, that we paint them out to ourselves as extended, either resolves all into a false idea, or returns in a circle. Extension must necessarily be consider'd either as colour'd, which is a false idea [according to Hume's understanding of Locke]; or as solid, which brings us back to the first question.[15]

Hume is surely right that the notion of impenetrability needs to be supplemented, in the same way and for the same reason as does the notion of extension. The difficulty about getting 'occupant of region x' to stand on its own feet is equally a difficulty about 'occupant of x to the exclusion from x of everything else'. Yet Hume's claim that the supplementation must involve colour is obviously wrong, since it implies that the congenitally blind cannot, without borrowing from the rest of us, have any workable, contentful concept of body or of occupant-of-space.

---

[13] *First Dialogue*, p. 191.   [14] *Treatise*, pp. 228–9.
[15] *Treatise*, p. 229.

To see where Hume has gone wrong, consider what the congenitally blind have at their disposal which he implicitly denies them—namely, the sense of touch. A little more adequately: a blind person can build up an account of what bodies there are, what their shapes and sizes and positions are, and so on, by means which fundamentally consist in his knowing what impediments there are to specific movements of (parts of) his own body. This requires him to have independent knowledge of how his own body moves, but that is all right: he can know where his body is and how it moves because he moves it and does not merely observe its movements.[16] So, I contend, an adequate basis for a knowledge of bodies can be provided by sensory means in which the sense of touch plays a large part and which need not involve any perception of things' secondary qualities.

Hume denies this, on the basis of a very peculiar argument. He seems to take it that what he has to deny is a view which we tend 'naturally' to accept, namely that 'we feel the solidity of bodies, and need but touch any object in order to perceive this quality'. He denies this on the grounds that 'tho' bodies are felt by means of their solidity, yet the feeling is a quite different thing from the solidity; and . . . they have not the least resemblance to each other'.[17] This obscure utterance does not, as it stands, give us any help at all, simply because there is not 'the least resemblance' between *any* feeling and *any* quality. Still, one gets some idea of what Hume means by this denial from looking at his reason for it: 'A man, who has the palsey in one hand, has as perfect an idea of impenetrability, when he observes that hand to be supported by the table, as when he feels the same table with the other hand.'[18] Apparently Hume wants to deny that tactual feelings relate to solidity as visual sense-data do to colours. Not only do we see colours, but—Hume will say—the notion of colour is purely visual in its sensory basis; there is a biconditional relationship, a two-way flow, between facts about visual sense-data and facts about sense-based colour-judgements. By way of contrast, Hume is saying, judgements about solidity can have either a visual or a tactual basis, as witness the man who has palsy. So tactual feelings are 'different from' solidity; we do not 'feel the solidity of

---

[16] See S. Hampshire, *Thought and Action* (London, 1959), pp. 47–55.
[17] *Treatise*, p. 230.
[18] Ibid.

bodies'; and so Locke's thesis cannot be rescued by invoking the sense of touch.

This argument completely fails. From the premiss about the man with palsy, Hume can reach his lemma that tactual feelings are unlike solidity only if he construes 'Tactual feelings resemble solidity' as entailing 'Tactual feelings are *required* as a sensory basis for solidity-judgements'. But the denial of this does not entail Hume's conclusion, which is a denial of 'Tactual feelings *suffice* as a sensory basis for solidity-judgements'. Hume has moved from the premiss that T is not necessary for S to the conclusion that T is not sufficient for S, through a cloudy lemma expressed in such words as that T 'has not the least resemblance' to S.

19. *The Analytic Thesis*

Locke's other general claim about the distinction between primary and secondary qualities is more interesting, though also the source of more problems, than is the meaning-of-'body' thesis.

Briefly, and in Locke's words, it is the claim that secondary qualities 'are nothing in the objects themselves but powers to produce various sensations in us',[19] or that 'when truly considered [they] are only *powers*, however we are apt to take them for positive qualities'.[20]

To say that x has a power to produce S in me is to say, among other things, that if x were related to me in a certain way then S would occur in me. If that were all it meant, then Locke would be saying just that any statement attributing a secondary quality to a thing is equivalent to a counterfactual conditional of the form:

> If x stood in relation R to a normal human, the human would have a sensory idea of such and such a kind.

For example, the claim would be that 'x is green' means roughly the same as 'If x were sunlit and were in the line of vision of a normal open-eyed human, he would have a visual field of such and such a kind' (Locke would describe the visual field as 'green', no doubt; but never mind that).

[19] *Essay* II. viii. 10.   [20] *Essay* II. xxiii. 37.

But the notion of a 'power to produce', and thus Locke's central claim about the primary/secondary distinction, have more content than that. Locke's claim has in fact two components—the *Analytic Thesis* sketched above, and what I shall call the *Causal Thesis*, which is a view about what causes us to have the secondary-quality ideas that we do have. Since these are philosophically linked in a certain way, and are so interwoven in Locke's text that I cannot cite any passage expressing one but not the other, I present them as components of a single 'central claim' of Locke's about primary and secondary qualities. Still, they need to be examined separately, and my present concern is with the *Analytic Thesis*.

Is the Analytic Thesis true? More precisely, does it express a truth about secondary qualities *which is not equally a truth about primary qualities*? The italicized clause is vital. Locke wanted to *contrast* the two sorts of quality, and Berkeley's main criticism was that no contrast was effectively drawn—that anything true that Locke said about secondary qualities is equally true of primary. There is some excuse for Berkeley, in that Locke's arguments are all rather poor and some of his formulations are downright misleading. Still, there is a legitimate contrast between primary and secondary qualities, and I contend that it is one which Locke noticed and tried to formulate and defend.

In his arguments for the Analytic Thesis, Locke repeatedly stresses the fact that one's perceptions of secondary qualities may vary greatly according to the state of one's body and environment.[21] Berkeley replied that that is equally true of primary qualities.[22] On the face of it, Berkeley seems to be right; but let us suspend judgement until we have considered, more carefully than Berkeley did, what might be thought to follow from Locke's perceptual-variation point. Never mind whether it yields a contrast between two sorts of qualities—what does it show about any sort of quality for which it does hold? As to that, I conjecture that Locke had half-grasped, and was moving towards expressing, something like the following point. We are all familiar with the way in which something which tastes sweet to most people may taste bitter to a sick person. Now, if we reflect on this phenomenon, and on similar ones involving other secondary-quality

[21] *Essay* II. viii. 21; xxiii. 11.
[22] *Principles* § 15; *First Dialogue*, pp. 188–91.

perceptions, we shall see how thoroughly contingent it is that we are in a position to say of anything that it is bitter or green or noisy or the like. The occasional failures of agreement bring home to us how dependent our public secondary-quality terminology is upon the fact that we usually *do* agree in our secondary-quality discriminations—the failures help us to realize that our notion of two things' having the same colour, say, is only as secure as our ability to muster an overwhelming majority who see them as having the same colour.

Perhaps Locke was nowhere near having such thoughts as these. Anyway, they yield an argument for his Analytic Thesis; they embody a truth about secondary qualities which does not hold equally for primary qualities, and so they provide a basis for the contrast that Locke thought he could establish between primary and secondary qualities. The section that follows is a defence of all this.[23]

20. *In defence of a distinction*

I want to contrast two kinds of sensory aberration: in one, someone (C) sees two things as having the same colour when in fact they haven't, and in the other someone (S) sees and feels two things as having the same size when in fact they haven't.

C is confronted by a red thing and a white thing, and satisfies us that he sees them as having exactly the same colour. He believes our claim that they have different colours; and, since they differ in no other way, we could if necessary prove to him that we can see a difference between them which he cannot. Also, C could discover that the two objects reflect light of different wave-lengths, and might know that wave-lengths usually correlate with seen colours. But if he ignores what others say about the two objects, and ignores esoteric facts of optics, he may never learn that he has a sensory defect. A failure in secondary-quality discrimination, in one who is otherwise sensorily normal, can and sometimes does persist unsuspected through any variations in distance or angle of view, light-conditions, and so on.

Contrast this with the case of S who, going by what he sees and feels, judges a certain jug to have the same size as a certain

[23] For a somewhat similar defence, see A. Sloman, 'Primary and Secondary Qualities', *Mind*, vol. 73 (1964).

glass which is in fact shorter and narrower than the jug. (Grice has discussed the case where what he sees supports one judgement and what he feels supports another.[24]) In this case, we can place the glass inside the jug; or fill the jug with water, and then fill the glass from it and throw away the remaining water; or place both vessels on a table and draw S's hand across the top of the glass until it is stopped by the jug; and so on. What are we to suppose happens when S is confronted by these manipulations of the two objects? There are just two relevant possibilities. (a) When we manipulate the glass and jug, S takes in what is happening and thus quickly realizes that he was wrong about their relative sizes. (b) Each time we contrive a happening with the glass and the jug, S mis-perceives it so that what he sees and feels still fits in smoothly with his original judgement about their sizes.

To adopt (a) is just to abandon the attempt to put size-'blindness' on a level with colour-blindness. If the point of the latter were just that secondary-quality perceptions can err, then we could say the same of primary-quality ones. What gives relevance and bite to colour-blindness, and to its analogues for tastes etc., is the fact that any such abnormality can persist indefinitely without the victim's getting any clue to it from his other, normal sensory responses. The tricks with the glass and jug could be performed by S himself; they involve ordinary commerce with familiar domestic objects; and they are in a very different case from C's attention to wave-lengths or to what other people say about things' colours.

To get an analogy between size-'blindness' and colour-blindness, then, we must adopt supposition (b). This requires us to credit S with such inabilities as the following. He cannot see or feel that the glass is inside the jug (or that the jug has not stretched or the glass contracted); he cannot see or feel that the glass is full of water (or that water remains in the jug after the glass has been filled from it); he cannot see or feel that his hand is touching the rim of the glass (or that his hand is stopped by the side of the jug). It will not do to suppose that as each trick is performed S sees and feels nothing: the analogy with colour-blindness requires that he shall have no reason to suspect that

[24] H. P. Grice, 'Some Remarks about the Senses', in R. J. Butler (ed.), *Analytical Philosophy* (Oxford, 1962), pp. 149–51.

there is anything wrong with him, and so his visual and tactual states throughout must present no challenge to his belief that he is handling an ordinary pair of vessels which are of the same size. This is bad enough, but there is worse to follow. S must not only fail to see or feel the water left in the jug after the glass has been filled from it, but he must also have compensating sensory aberrations when the water is used to douse a candle or to dissolve sugar, or when it is thrown in S's face. Similarly with any of the other sensory aberrations with which we prop up the initial one: each requires further props which demand others in their turn, and so on indefinitely.

The analogy has collapsed again. C's colour-blindness was not clued by his other sensory responses although these were normal; but to keep S in ignorance of his initial sensory failure we have had to surround it with ever-widening circles of further abnormalities.

Strictly speaking, it is not quite true that C's single failure of colour-discrimination could remain unclued by his other, normal sensory responses. If he sees no difference between R which is red and W which is white, how does he see a third thing R* which is in fact red? If his only sensory failure concerns R and W, then we must suppose that he efficiently sees R and R* as having the same colour and sees a *large* difference of colour between W and R*. Since *ex hypothesi* he sees R and W as having the same colour, this is impossible; and to salvage the story we must suppose C to be blind to colour-differences between red things and white things generally. This still does not restore the analogy with size-'blindness', however. C's single red/white failure spreads only into other red/white failures; whereas S's initial failure to discriminate sizes had to be backed by failures also of shape-discrimination, movement-detection, sensitivity to heat, etc., ramifying out endlessly into virtually all his perceptions of his environment.

We have lost our analogy beyond recall; and we are losing our grip on an initial datum of the size-'blindness' case, namely that we can agree with S about the identity of a certain glass and jug, while silently noting his error about their relative sizes. For now we find that S disagrees with us about countless visible and tangible aspects of our environment, so that it is no longer clear that we share with him a sensory awareness of a single objective world.

From the foregoing discussion there emerge two closely related contrasts between primary and secondary qualities.

(1) There are countless exoteric general facts about how a thing's primary qualities connect with its ways of interacting with other things: of two rigid things, the smaller cannot contain the larger; one thing cannot block another's fall without touching it; a cube cannot roll smoothly on a flat surface; a circular disc's imprint on wax will be circular; and so on, indefinitely. It is true that a thing's colour, say, may also connect with its behaviour in relation to other things: brown apples are usually more squashable than green ones, blue flames boil water faster than yellow ones, a red surface reflects lightwaves of different lengths from those reflected by a blue surface, and so on. But for colours and other secondary qualities we cannot make, as we can for primary qualities, a long tally of obvious, familiar, inescapable connexions of the relevant kind.

(2) Just because a thing's primary qualities correlate in so many obvious ways with its modes of interaction with other things, we cannot intelligibly suppose that these correlations might persistently fail. There could be no point in crediting something with a shape, say, which was belied by enough of its interactions with other things.

As against this, there could be a point in calling a thing red even if this were belied by the wave-lengths of the light reflected from it, or by its flavour, hardness or chemical composition. If something's colour were in sunlight indistinguishable from that of things agreed to be red, this fact could reasonably be reported in the words 'That thing is red', even if we had to add riders such as 'though its light-reflecting properties are atypical for red', or '. . . though its taste is atypical for red wine', or '. . . though its temperature is atypical for red iron'. Since wave-lengths of reflected light (within the range to which humans are sensitive) do correlate with the colours seen by most people in sunlight, we do not need to decide for or against defining colour words in terms of how things look and treating associated wave-lengths as mere empirical correlates of colours. But if we had to decide, we could choose to give our colour terminology a purely visual basis and still have it doing most of the work it does for us now. Analogous remarks apply to the other secondary qualities.

Not so, however, for primary qualities. The inter-relations between things in respect of their primary qualities are many and varied and tightly interlocked, so that we cannot isolate a subset of them and suppose that *just those* might continue to hold while all the rest failed. *A fortiori*, we cannot describe a partial breakdown, the survivors of which would support a working vocabulary of primary qualities. The only kind of breakdown we could hope to describe without losing control would be one involving the collapse of all but one of the normal correlates of some primary quality: for example, a world in which 'the size of x' had to be defined solely in terms of the visual field presented by x to an observer ten yards away, with none of the other actual correlates of size continuing to hold. This supposition is clearly self-defeating; for it bases 'size' on 'distance' while making it impossible to measure distance. That special feature apart, however, it is clear that no supposition of this general sort can preserve a minimal sense of 'size' analogous to the purely visual sense of 'colour'. Any such supposition, in cutting away so much of what ordinarily goes with size, leaves no basis for a language of physical objects. Offering us a minimal sense of 'size', it robs us of everything that could have a size.

21. *Corollaries*

We are now in a position to see that Locke's Analytic Thesis does express a truth about secondary qualities which is decisively not true of primary qualities.

Part of the point is that the Analytic Thesis equates x's being green, say, with the truth of a conditional stating that under certain circumstances a specific, characteristic kind of sensory state would occur. Now, it may be true that x will be deemed square, say, if and only if our sensory states in respect of it are such as to warrant its being described as square, but this fact cannot be expressed by picking on some specific kind of sensory state and saying that the occurrence of *that* in specified conditions is more or less definitive of a thing's squareness. The reason why this is so is brought out, I believe, by my analysis in the preceding section. It is just that a thing's being square, or having any other specific primary quality, consists in its relating to many other kinds of things in specific ways, and all of these are comprised in the notion of our sensory states' being such as to warrant our describing the thing as square.

But my analysis is also relevant in a different way. The Analytic Thesis says that a thing's having a given secondary quality is *its having* a certain power; and just this, prescinded from any question of what sort of power, is inapplicable to the primary qualities of things. We can identify a glass, say, while remaining ignorant of or in disagreement over its secondary qualities; and so we have the notion of *the glass* as an object which, among other facts about it, has certain 'powers' to affect us in ways which are our basis for crediting it with colour, taste etc. But we cannot identify a glass independently of all its primary qualities such as location, size, shape, etc.; and so we cannot have the notion of *the glass* as an object which, among other facts about it, affects us in ways which are our basis for crediting it with primary qualities. Granted that everything we say about the glass is based on sensory states it causes us to have, it is still misleading to speak of *its* power to make us perceive it as having a certain shape, size, etc.; for that way of speaking suggests that we have some notion of *it*—some way of identifying and studying the glass—independently of, and as a preliminary to, discovering what its primary qualities are. My analysis shows why we cannot have this.

There is another point on which a little light can now be thrown. It is often thought that whatever significant differences there are between primary and secondary qualities are in some way due to an underlying difference expressed by this:

(A) Each kind of secondary quality is associated with just one of our senses, whereas each kind of primary quality is associated with two—sight and touch in every case.[25]

There is presumably a truth lurking behind this, but (A) as stated does not capture it; for one can know that the starter's gun is making a noise because one sees the smoke, and discover that the apple is green by tasting it, and so on. No doubt (A) can be modified so as to cope with these cases, but just what modifications are needed in order to turn (A) into something precise and true, and how interesting it would then be, I do not know.

[25] See R. Sartorius, 'A Neglected Aspect of the Relationship between Berkeley's Theory of Vision and his Immaterialism', *American Philosophical Quarterly*, vol. 6 (1969). See also *Philosophical Commentaries*, entry 57.

My main point, however, is that neither (A) nor anything like it can explain the differences between primary and secondary qualities which came to light through my contrast between size-'blindness' and colour-blindness. For these differences would have emerged just as easily if the size-'blind' man had been *blind*. Depriving him of sight altogether would not have helped us to entertain the hypothesis that he mistook the relative sizes of the jug and the glass and maintained that mistake through a series of down-to-earth transactions with the two objects in question. That hypothesis would, indeed, be blocked by every one of the sample obstacles presented in the original story. So the facts about primary qualities to which I was calling attention cannot be linked with any facts about vision in relation to primary qualities; whence it follows *a fortiori* that the contrast I was drawing between primary and secondary qualities does not arise from anything expressed by the thesis (A) or any modified version of it.

If one could explain the differences between primary and secondary qualities by adducing facts about their respective sensory bases or correlates, I suspect that the crux of the explanation would turn out to be the fact that the sense of touch—or rather of touch-and-movement—is involved in all the primary qualities in a way in which it isn't with any of the secondary. But that is only a suspicion. Someone should write a book on the epistemology of the sense of touch.

22. *The Causal Thesis*

The Causal Thesis about primary and secondary qualities is this: in a perfected and completed science, all our secondary-quality perceptions would be causally explained in terms of the primary qualities of the things we perceive. For example, our colour-discriminations would be explained by a theory relating the colour aspects of visual sense-data to the sub-microscopic *textures* of seen surfaces. While admitting that we do not in fact have the theory, or set of theories, which would yield these explanations, Locke is immensely sure that this is only because of our ignorance. He does not doubt that some theory of this kind is true.

This confidence is prima facie puzzling. The state of seventeenth-century physiology surely did not warrant it. The success of

Newtonian physics in other areas might, of course, have induced an optimism about its chances of eventually explaining everything. Consider, for example, this argument of Locke's for his central claim about secondary qualities:

Pound an almond, and the clear white colour will be altered into a dirty one, and the sweet taste into an oily one. What real alteration can the beating of the pestle make in any body, but an alteration of the texture of it?[26]

This argues that an almond's colour and taste are mere upshots or symptoms of its primary-quality 'texture', since the latter is all that can be altered by pounding. It is invalid: the assumption that pounding can cause only primary-quality changes in the object pounded is false, as is shown by what happens when an almond is pounded with a pestle. Still, Locke's using the argument does suggest that he was encouraged in maintaining the Causal Thesis by a general faith in the power and comprehensiveness of a purely primary-quality physics.

But that is not all. Locke's advocacy of the Causal Thesis can be partly explained on the basis of his acceptance—for good, fumbled reasons—of the Analytic Thesis. There is a very natural intellectual route from one to the other, and Locke comes into sharper focus if we suppose that he followed it.

By way of introduction, I call attention to three features of the Analytic Thesis. (1) According to it, secondary qualities are *dispositional*: '*x* is green' is equivalent to a counterfactual conditional. (2) It represents secondary qualities as *relational*: '*x* is green' means something about items (people) other than *x*, and could become false just because of a monadic change in those other things. (3) It represents secondary qualities as involving something *mental*: '*x* is green' means something about the occurrence of a certain kind of idea. Putting these three features in a nutshell: according to the Analytic Thesis a secondary quality of a thing is its *power* to induce in *something else* an *idea*. The three features are quite distinct. They generate eight possible kinds of property, which are exemplified by the following eight adjectives: green (1,2,3), poisonous (1,2), depressive (1,3), explosive (1), stinging (2,3), indebted (2), worried (3), square. One notes with pleasure that of the three features credited to the secondary quality greenness, none is credited to the primary quality square-ness.

Each of these features of secondary qualities will help to explain certain aspects of Locke's handling of the Analytic Thesis. I start with the first of them, i.e. with the fact that secondary qualities are dispositional, which is just to say that secondary-quality attributions are equivalent to counterfactual conditionals.

It is sometimes said that anything of this form:

(1) If x were F, it would be H

means the same as, or should be analysed into, something of this form:

(2) There is some non-dispositional ϕ such that: x is ϕ, and it is a causal law that if anything is both ϕ and F then it is H.

I believe that (2) does more than bring out the meaning of (1). Still, western science has for centuries proceeded on the assumption that wherever (1) is true (2) will be true also; and this assumption—or regulative principle—has clearly been instrumental in scientific advance, e.g. by implying that if something is soluble in water it has a chemical, structural property which *explains* its solubility. It would be astonishing if Locke, with his feeling for and understanding of the western scientific tradition, had not assumed that dispositions are always causally rooted in non-dispositional properties.

If he did, then he would think that whenever something of this form is true:

(1′) If x were faced in sunlight by a normal human, the human would have a G idea,

then the corresponding statement of this form will also be true:

(2′) For some non-dispositional ϕ: x is ϕ, and it is a causal law that if anything which is ϕ is faced in sunlight by a normal human, the human has a G idea.

This comes close enough to saying that x, by virtue of some non-dispositional property that it has, will cause a G idea in . . . etc. We have nearly got Locke as far as the Causal Thesis.

Not quite, though, for the Causal Thesis says that our

secondary-quality perceptions are to be explained through the *primary* qualities of the perceived objects. To express this, we must replace 'For some non-dispositional ϕ . . .' by the stronger 'For some primary-quality ϕ . . .'. But of course that strengthening will be acceptable to Locke: of the two sorts of qualities-of-objects at his disposal, one sort, secondary qualities, have already been declared by the Analytic Thesis to be dispositional; and so the only candidates he has for the role of non-dispositional properties are primary qualities. And so we have arrived at the full-strength Causal Thesis.

Notice that the only grounds I can give Locke for saying that our secondary-quality perceptions are to be explained in terms of things' *primary* qualities is just the *de facto* absence of any other suitable candidate. So if my conjecture about the movement of his thought is right, he ought to concede that the true causal explanations might turn out to involve not primary qualities but qualities of some now unknown kind. And so he does: 'Secondary qualities . . . depend . . . upon the primary qualities of [objects'] minute and insensible parts; or, if not upon them, upon something yet more remote from our comprehension.'[27]

I have remarked that Locke argues poorly for his view about primary and secondary qualities. This fact can be explained. The trouble is that Locke had a false belief about what *sorts* of considerations were needed to support his central claim. Kneale says: 'The distinction between primary and secondary qualities was a philosophical discovery, and Locke was mistaken when he wrote of it as though it had been established by experiments unfamiliar to plain men.'[28] Kneale presumably thinks of the distinction as 'established' by whatever supports the Analytic Thesis; and I agree with him that this is a philosophical thesis whose support involves no recherché scientific information, no appeals to microscopy or the like, but only to the unexciting kind of empirical material to be found in § 20 above—reminders assembled for a purpose. The further move to the Causal Thesis does not need strenuous argument: it is really just a matter of combining the Analytic Thesis with a highly respectable regulative principle or scientific working assumption. But Locke, having failed to distinguish the Analytic from the Causal Thesis, sees the latter as

[27] *Essay* IV. iii. 11.
[28] W. C. Kneale, *On Having a Mind* (Cambridge, 1962), p. 38.

needing argumentative support; and, since it has implications for science's future, Locke naturally thinks that its support must come from science's past and present.

23. *The other versions*

Locke has two other contrasts—or ways of drawing the contrast—between primary and secondary qualities. I shall argue, with regard to each of these, that it is intelligible only if regarded as a fumbled attempt to express the central claim with which I have already credited Locke.

The first of the two is fairly plain sailing. Here is a typical expression of it:

The ideas of primary qualities of bodies are resemblances of them, and their patterns do really exist in the bodies themselves, but the ideas produced in us by these secondary qualities have no resemblance of them at all. There is nothing like our [secondary-quality] ideas, existing in the bodies themselves.[29]

Since ideas cannot resemble either bodies or qualities of bodies, this must be either discarded or transformed. The only plausible transformation is into something like the following: in causally explaining ideas of primary qualities, one uses the same words in describing the causes as in describing the effects (shape-ideas etc. are caused by shapes etc.); whereas in causally explaining ideas of secondary qualities one must describe the causes in one vocabulary and the effects in another (colour-ideas etc. are caused by shapes etc.). If this is not what Locke's 'resemblance' formulations of the primary/secondary contrast mean, then I can find no meaning in them.

Suppose that they do mean what I have suggested. Someone might challenge Locke: 'Why should we not explain colour-ideas etc. in terms of the *colours* of the objects which are seen?' He would have to reply: 'We could, but that would not be to give the most basic kind of causal explanation of secondary-quality ideas.' In saying this, he would be reiterating the Causal Thesis. And that makes my main point about these 'resemblance' formulations: if they present us with anything we can get our teeth into, it is the Causal Thesis. There seems to be no other reading of

[29] *Essay* II. viii. 15.

them, no other way of representing them as more than mere paragraphs, inert word-sequences with which we can do nothing.

The one remaining kind of thing Locke often says about the primary/secondary distinction is to the effect that secondary qualities are not 'really in' the bodies to which we thoughtlessly attribute them. His remarks in this vein have three separate sources, corresponding to the three things the Analytic Thesis says about secondary qualities—that they are dispositional, relational, and mind-involving.

The first of these is not very important, but there is at least one example of it: 'Yellowness is not actually in gold, but is a power in gold to produce that idea in us by our eyes, when placed in a due light...'[30] This use of 'idea' is unsatisfactory: the phrase 'that idea' seems to refer back to yellowness, but yellowness is a quality and not an idea! Locke is in a difficulty here which I shall discuss shortly. My present concern is with the first dozen words in the quoted passage. If they don't express a crude inconsistency (yellowness is not in gold but is in gold), then I think they must involve the actual/potential distinction. I suggest, that is, that Locke wants to say that yellowness is only a disposition or 'power' of the gold and not a non-dispositional or 'actual' property of it. On that reading, the remark primarily expresses one aspect of the Analytic Thesis, and does not introduce any new line of thought which needs separate consideration.

The second of the three features looms larger. That is, Locke's tendency to speak of secondary qualities as 'not in the object' seems to be in good measure due to his preoccupation with the fact that according to the Analytic Thesis secondary qualities are relational. Consider this passage:

...all which ideas are nothing else but so many relations to other substances; and are not really in the gold, considered barely in itself, though they depend on those real and primary qualities of its internal constitution, whereby it has a fitness differently to operate, and be operated on by several other substances.[31]

Again the use of 'idea' is sloppy. The vital phrase, however, is 'not really in the gold, *considered barely in itself*': Locke's point is that the gold's being yellow depends not just upon it but also

[30] *Essay* II. xxiii. 10.   [31] *Essay* II. xxiii. 37.

upon other things (people), so that yellowness, rather than being 'in' the gold, is in a manner of speaking *between* the gold and the class of normal, sighted humans. Locke, I suggest, goes too far here. The notion of 'where' a secondary quality is, is metaphorical and so perhaps harmless in itself; but Locke seems to be cashing this metaphor, and going too far, when he says that secondary qualities are called 'qualities' only 'to comply with the common way of speaking'.[32]

I think he would be prepared to argue somewhat as follows: a given kind of substance might be bitter at one time and tasteless at another, simply because in the interim there had been a suitable change in the taste-buds of humans. In such an eventuality, the substance would have lost its bitterness *without changing in itself*; but to change *is* simply to undergo some turnover in the qualities that one has; and so it follows that the substance would have lost its bitterness without losing any of its qualities. So bitterness is not a quality—and similarly, *mutatis mutandis*, for other secondary 'qualities' and indeed for relational 'qualities' generally.

That argument is not valid. For in the situation envisaged, the substance *would* have undergone a change, namely a change in its taste. It is natural to protest that for a substance to lose its bitterness in that way is not for it to change *in itself*; but the force of that is just that bitterness is a relational property—which is the point from which we started.

The third source of Locke's 'not in the object' remarks about secondary qualities is by far the most important. Here are two examples:

The same water, at the same time, may produce the idea of cold by one hand and of heat by the other: whereas it is impossible that the same water, if those ideas were really in it, should at the same time be both hot and cold.[33]

The sensible secondary qualities, which, depending on [the primary], are nothing but the powers those substances have to produce several ideas in us by our senses; which ideas are not in the things themselves, otherwise than as anything is in its cause.[34]

Notice that in these passages what Locke says is not that *secondary qualities* are 'not in' the objects, but rather that *secondary-quality*

---

[32] *Essay* II. viii. 10.   [33] *Essay* II. viii. 21.
[34] *Essay* II. xxiii. 9. See also viii. 24.

ideas are not in the objects. How then does this mark a contrast between secondary and primary? There are only two assumptions on which it can do so.

(*a*) Primary-quality ideas are, literally, in the objects to which primary qualities are attributed. If this were so, then the claim that secondary-quality ideas are not in objects would indeed distinguish primary- from secondary-quality ideas and to that extent mark a distinction between the two sorts of quality.

(*b*) There is no distinction between secondary qualities and secondary-quality ideas. If that were so, then the denial that secondary-quality ideas are in objects would imply a denial that secondary qualities are in objects; and, since primary qualities are really in the objects to which they are attributed, this would mark a distinction between primary and secondary qualities.

Of these two quite different possibilities, (*a*) seems to me the more obviously untenable as an interpretation of Locke's thought. We have seen that his elliptic use of 'idea' to mean 'quality' does sometimes run away with him; and it has been pointed out to me that Locke sometimes uses 'sensation' instead of 'idea', but never when primary-quality ideas are in question—a fascinating fact which is prima facie evidence of his wanting to get primary-quality 'ideas' out of the mind and into the object. But I just do not see how to carry this interpretation through, and I am content to jettison it since there is a much more plausible alternative.

For (*b*) is a thoroughly plausible reading of the 'not in the object' remarks which I have just quoted. Sometimes, it seems, we must admit that Locke tends to identify secondary qualities with ideas of them, as when he says of porphyry that 'it is plain it has no colour in the dark'.[35] Consider also this passage:

Sweetness and whiteness are not really in manna; [for they] are but the effects of the operations of manna, by the motion, size, and figure of its particles, on the eyes and palate: as the pain and sickness caused by manna are confessedly nothing but the effects of its operations on the stomach and guts, by the size, motion, and figure of its insensible parts . . .[36]

Having just remarked that 'every one readily agrees' that 'these ideas of sickness and pain are *not* in the manna', Locke now argues that we ought to say the same about taste and colour; and his

[35] *Essay* II. viii. 19.   [36] *Essay* II. viii. 18.

wording forces us to construe him as identifying secondary qualities ('sweetness and whiteness') with secondary-quality ideas ('the effects').

In thus identifying secondary qualities with ideas of them, Locke sins *both* against his clearly announced distinction between qualities of both sorts and ideas, *and* against his central claim that secondary qualities are powers to cause ideas. How did he get himself into this self-contradictory situation? Why, when he was possessed of the truth that secondary qualities are powers to cause ideas in humans, should Locke give countenance to the conflicting and false thesis that secondary qualities are ideas in humans?

His drift from truth into error can be explained as arising from three distinct mis-handlings of the truth.

The first of them consists in moving from 'not in the object' to 'in the mind'. Of course this move is invalid if secondary qualities' being 'not [actually] in the object' is so understood that it follows from their being dispositional or from their being relational; but I suggest that Locke may have been inclined to make it, and that this helps to explain his sometimes implying that secondary qualities are ideas.

The second explanation can be approached through Locke's comparison of secondary qualities with pains, sickness, etc. This whole line of argument arose, I submit, because Locke saw that he had flushed out a problem but then proceeded to misidentify it. The problem arises thus: we can report a thing's power to cause certain states in us by calling it 'sweet', 'white', 'warm', etc., while its powers to cause other states in us are not reportable in single adjectives except clumsy (and explicitly causal) compounds like 'sick-making' and 'pain-causing'. Why do we draw that line between the two classes of states of ourselves, and thus between the two classes of powers? Locke assumes, far too boldly, that we cannot have a good reason for drawing the line just there; and his conjecture about our bad reason for the line's location really will not bear scrutiny.[37] But his real trouble is that he has misunderstood what sort of line it is. Seeing that his Analytic Thesis about secondary qualities raises a question about how secondary qualities relate to pains and sickness, he has completely misunderstood *what* question of this sort it raises. The Analytic

[37] *Essay* II. viii. 25.

Thesis implies that 'green' means 'apt to cause G ideas', which is structurally like 'apt to cause sickness'. But that does not even prima facie threaten to put 'green' on a par with 'sick', or greenness with sickness. It puts 'green' on a par with 'sick-making', and what it puts on a par with 'sick' is 'having a G idea'. The Analytic Thesis about secondary qualities, when properly stated, does not pose any problem of the form 'Why do we treat greenness differently from pain in the respect that . . . ?', and so it does not raise the question to which Locke addressed himself, namely 'Why do we regard greenness but not pain as in the object?' Still, it is not bewildering that Locke should think that he is confronted by this question; for the Analytic Thesis does raise a genuine problem which, being of the form 'Why do we draw the line just there?' and also involving pains and secondary qualities, could fairly easily be mistaken for the pseudo-problem which Locke raises.

The third mistake which may contribute to Locke's tendency to assimilate secondary qualities to ideas of them is as follows. His Causal Thesis implies that a secondary quality of x is a power which x has because of its primary qualities—as a thing may *be soluble because of* its chemical composition. Also, in seeing x as green one has an idea which occurs because of x's primary qualities—as a thing may *dissolve because of* its chemical composition. These are different types of dependence; but the fact that they can be expressed in the same words may have helped Locke not to notice when he was slipping from one sort of dependent to the other.

Recall once more the three features which I stressed in § 22: secondary qualities are *dispositional*, *relational*, and involved with something *mental*. In the present section I have argued that Locke's remarks about secondary qualities as 'not in the object' are fed by each of these sources. Because a secondary quality is dispositional it is only a power, and is therefore not an actuality in the object, and is therefore 'not actually in the object'. Because it is relational it is 'not in the object considered barely in itself'. And (though here I compress the argument) because it is obliquely mental it is 'not in the object' because it is in the mind. These uses of the 'not in the object' language are all deplorable, but their inter-relations are part of the structure of Locke's thought.

24. *Berkeley's conflation*

Berkeley's attack on this part of Locke's work was addressed to the worst of all Locke's formulations. What Berkeley attacked was the thesis that, while primary qualities are in objects, secondary qualities are not because they are ideas and are therefore in the mind. In this two-part thesis, what he dissented from was the part about primary qualities: Locke's mistake, according to Berkeley, lay in his not saying about primary qualities what he did say about secondary, namely that they are ideas in the mind.

Berkeley did not—as I once inexplicably alleged[38]—endorse Locke's arguments for the mental nature of secondary qualities; but he used them *ad hominem* against Locke, and thought that *he* had valid arguments for the same conclusion. Remarking that Locke's arguments 'may with equal force, be brought to prove the same thing of extension, figure, and motion' as they purport to prove about secondary qualities, Berkeley adds a disclaimer:

Though it must be confessed this method of arguing doth not so much prove that there is no extension or colour in an outward object, as that we do not know by sense which is the true extension or colour of the object. But [my own] arguments plainly shew it to be impossible that any colour or extension at all . . . should exist in an unthinking subject without the mind, or in truth, that there should be any such thing as an outward object.[39]

This does not adequately describe the short-comings of Locke's arguments in this vein—e.g. the argument that water could not feel warm to one hand and cold to the other if 'those ideas' were really in the water, and the argument about sweetness and whiteness in relation to sickness and pain. Berkeley, however, does not care to examine those arguments thoroughly because he so likes their conclusion: he agrees with what he thinks Locke is saying about secondary qualities, and complains only over Locke's failure to say it about primary qualities also.

I should mention in passing Berkeley's treatment of *number*.[40] This, though I have carefully neglected it, does occur on Locke's list of primary qualities; and Berkeley deals with it through a

---

[38] J. Bennett, 'Substance, Reality and Primary Qualities', Martin p. 109.
[39] *Principles* § 15.
[40] *Principles* § 12.

special argument which does not follow the general pattern outlined above. We owe to Frege an important insight about the concept of number, namely that given any stretch of reality there is no number-expression which is absolutely the right one to apply to it.[41] It may, for example, be *one* book, or *sixty* pages, or *millions* of molecules. Berkeley had some understanding of this, but he mis-handled it. He said: 'The same thing bears a different denomination of number, as the mind views it with different respects', from which he inferred that 'number is entirely the creature of the mind'. But this is wrong. The item objectively is one book, and objectively is sixty pages, and nobody's mind has anything to do with it. If someone asks of some part of the world 'What number?', the question cannot be answered: it must be replaced by a question of the form 'What number of Fs?' But Berkeley implies that the original question can be answered in more than one way, and that we cannot know which answer to give until we know something about the questioner's frame of mind. In short, he thinks that the question requires psychological rather than logical completion. Frege's point disinclines one to classify number as a primary quality, but not for any reason that supports Berkeleian idealism.

Berkeley's treatment of number, although special in its argumentative tactics, is in its conclusion just like his handling of the other members of Locke's list of primary qualities. The point, Berkeley thinks, is that all of these qualities share the feature of secondary qualities stressed by Locke—namely, they are in the mind rather than in the object. How can we assess the adequacy, exegetical or philosophical, of this part of Berkeley's work? Locke's 'not in the object' remarks about secondary qualities are, as we have seen, flimsy and unstructured and inconsiderable; we cannot explain them except through his having somehow drifted from his central insight, the Analytic Thesis; and really that is all that can be said about them. If they include stray sentences which Berkeley can adopt as expressing (part of) a genuine philosophical view of his own, that is just a typographical accident. When one has seen what the provenance is of the 'not in the object' remarks within Locke's thinking about primary and secondary qualities, one will not regard them as expressions of *any* solid philosophical position.

[41] G. Frege, *The Foundations of Arithmetic* (New York, 1953), §§ 45–54.

In thinking otherwise, Berkeley erred. The error, however, is not in itself an interesting one. Is there nothing else we can say? Well, there is a point of some importance, arising from this:

HYLAS: I wonder, Philonous, if what you say be true, why those philosophers who deny the secondary qualities any real existence, should yet attribute it to the primary. If there is no difference between them, how can this be accounted for? PHILONOUS: It is not my business to account for every opinion of the philosophers. But among other reasons which may be assigned for this, it seems probable, that pleasure and pain being rather annexed to the former than the latter, may be one.[42]

Philonous is here challenged to explain the mistake, supposedly made by some philosophers, of distinguishing secondary qualities from primary in respect of the possession of 'real existence' (as distinct from 'ideal existence', i.e. existence in the mind). He rightly assumes that to explain this one must point to some genuine differences between primary and secondary qualities—but then look at what he actually offers! As well as being far from the centre of the primary/secondary distinction, it is not even true. In support of it Berkeley might point out that 'hot' is usually more relevant to pain than 'round' is, but what about 'sweet' as compared with 'sharp' or 'hard' or 'large' or 'rapid'?

Berkeley hints that he could say more ('among other reasons'), but this dismally inadequate offering is all that he actually produces. Apparently he could not find in Locke's work the makings of any legitimate contrast between primary and secondary qualities. So he can and should be criticized not just for over-dignifying the 'not in the object' remarks, but also for over-looking or mis-estimating the other, better parts of Locke's discussions of the primary/secondary distinction.

There is a further point about Berkeley's procedures which is essential for an understanding of Locke and of the truth, if not of Berkeley himself. When Berkeley approves Locke's saying that secondary qualities are in the mind, and deplores his refusal to say the same of primary qualities, he is thinking about the conflict between his and Locke's theories of reality. In Berkeley's view, Locke's doctrine on secondary qualities is the thin edge of a wedge which can be used to dislodge the entire veil-of-perception doctrine. When Philonous has coaxed Hylas out of a pre-

---

[42] *First Dialogue*, p. 191. See also *Philosophical Commentaries*, entry 692.

Lockean position and into agreeing that 'all sensible qualities beside the primary ... are only so many sensations or ideas existing no where but in the mind', he sketches the next part of his strategy as follows:

PHILONOUS: You are still then of opinion, that extension and figures are inherent in external unthinking substances. HYLAS: I am. PHILONOUS: But what if the same arguments which are brought against secondary qualities, will hold good against these also? HYLAS: Why then I shall be obliged to think, they too exist only in the mind.[43]

Berkeley, then, sees Locke as having a view about secondary qualities which restricts or partly retracts the veil-of-perception doctrine, and a thesis about primary qualities which affirms a restricted version of the veil-of-perception doctrine.

This is a gravely wrong picture of how Locke's *central* claim about primary and secondary qualities relates to his veil-of-perception doctrine, as I shall try to show. 'But Berkeley didn't intend it as a picture of Locke's central claim—only of his peripheral "not in the object" version'—that defence of Berkeley is an over-simplification, but even if it were perfectly valid my points would still need to be made. I contend that Locke's central claim, which is made up of the Analytic and Causal Theses fused together, has *nothing* to do with the veil-of-perception doctrine: it does not embody a version of that doctrine, or a qualification of or rival to it. The doctrine is just Locke's mis-handling of the sceptical question about whether the objective realm is in any way at all as it appears to be; and I contend that this question must be answered affirmatively, on the basis of routine trust in the senses, before one can begin to expound and defend Locke's central claim about the primary/secondary distinction. These contentions are non-trivial, in that their falsity is implied in virtually every commentary on this part of Berkeley's work. This can be so only because most commentators do at least partly grasp Locke's central claim, and are not completely in thrall to the language of 'not in the object, because in the mind'. I believe that they have been led astray because the central claim itself, even if not expressed in the 'not in the object' form, can seem to be connected with the veil-of-perception doctrine. This pseudo-connexion is my main present concern.

One last reminder: the Analytic Thesis represents secondary

[43] *First Dialogue*, p. 188.

qualities as *dispositional*, as *relational*, and as logically connected with something *mental*. Of these three features, it is the third which now assumes a major explanatory role. Because of that third feature, the following picture is plausible: the veil-of-perception doctrine says that statements about objects are logically dissociated from statements about ideas, and the Analytic Thesis re-affirms this for primary-quality attributions but concedes that it does not hold for statements purporting to attribute secondary qualities to things. If this were right, it would fully justify Berkeley's tactics against Locke; but it is in fact wholly wrong.

If it were right, the Analytic Thesis would be a bore. *Obviously* some predicates of objects are logically connected with mental predicates: no one would doubt that we imply something about states of minds when we say that castor oil is nasty or that warm baths are soothing. If the Analytic Thesis were significant only as conceding that some predicates of objects are logically connected with mental predicates, it would have no significance at all. What gives it interest is not its saying (*a*) 'Some predicates of objects have *some* logical connexions with mental predicates', but rather its saying (*b*) 'Secondary-quality predicates have *these* logical connexions with mental predicates'. Now, (*b*) does not tend to support the view that all predicates of objects are logically connected with mental predicates: Locke's view about the status of secondary qualities is no more a step towards idealism or phenomenalism than is the Nazi valuation of Aryans a step towards a belief in the worth and dignity of all men.

Just as Locke's claim about secondary qualities is not a significant *restriction*, so his claim about primary qualities is not a restricted *version*, of the veil-of-perception doctrine. If to (*a*) 'Some predicates of objects have some logical connexions with mental predicates' we add the rider 'but primary-quality predicates don't', the result is indeed a form of the veil-of-perception doctrine, and does contradict idealism and phenomenalism. But if to (*b*) 'Secondary-quality predicates have *these* logical connexions with mental predicates' we add the rider 'but primary-quality predicates don't', the result says only that primary-quality predicates are not connected with mental predicates *in the way* secondary-quality ones are. This does not challenge Berkeley or any competent phenomenalist: my defence of it in § 20 conceded nothing to the veil-of-perception doctrine.

Even those who reject Berkeley's idealism, and phenomenalism as well, agree that his principal service to philosophy lay in his criticisms of Locke's account of reality—his insight into what goes wrong if the distinction between appearance and reality is mishandled in certain ways. So it is lamentable that he should have muddied these waters by stirring in materials drawn not just from the substratum theory but also from Locke's views about primary qualities. Here, for example, all three ingredients are present in concentrated form:

In process of time, men being convinced that . . . secondary qualities had no existence without the mind, they stripped this *substratum* or material substance of those qualities, leaving only the primary ones, . . . which they still conceived to exist without the mind, and consequently to stand in need of a material support.[44]

The mix-up does lead to positive error, of which I cite just one example. It is common ground among all philosophers who attach value to the primary/secondary distinction that objects do have primary qualities; the veil-of-perception doctrine allows that, just conceivably, 'real things' may have none of the properties we attribute to them; and substrata as such cannot have any properties at all. So Berkeley is prepared to say: 'By matter . . . we are to understand an inert, senseless substance, in which extension, figure, and motion, do actually subsist,'[45] and also: 'The matter philosophers contend for, is an incomprehensible somewhat which hath none of those particular qualities, whereby the bodies falling under our senses are distinguished one from another.'[46] Berkeley is not here pin-pointing an inconsistency in Locke, but rather committing an inconsistency of his own which is generated by his misunderstanding of Locke's problems.

The commentaries do not yield the same rich harvest of thorough, glad commissions of this mistake as they do of the one discussed in Chapter III.[47] Most commentators (again Armstrong is an exception) merely take Berkeley's word for it that the veil-of-perception doctrine is integrally connected with the primary-quality thesis, and slide quickly over the gap where the connexion is supposed to be.

[44] *Principles* § 73.   [45] *Principles* § 9.   [46] *Principles* § 47.
[47] But see A. C. Fraser, *Berkeley* (Edinburgh, 1909), p. 54; G. D. Hicks, *Berkeley* (London, 1932), p. 104; C. R. Morris, *Locke, Berkeley, Hume* (Oxford, 1931), pp. 34-5, 38-40; J. Collins, *The British Empiricists* (Milwaukee, 1967), pp. 18-21.

25. *The conflation's sources in Locke*

I can find no evidence that Locke saw his theory, or theories, about primary and secondary qualities as on the same level as the veil-of-perception doctrine. Positive evidence the other way occurs when he interrupts his discussion of primary and secondary qualities in order to say:

I have in what just goes before been engaged in physical inquiries a little further than perhaps I intended. . . . I hope I shall be pardoned this little excursion into natural philosophy; it being necessary in our present inquiry to distinguish the *primary* and *real* qualities of bodies, which are always in them . . . etc.[48]

In a later passage he denies that any 'correspondence or connexion' can be found between our secondary-quality ideas 'and those primary qualities which (experience shows us) produce them in us'.[49] It is true that Locke tries to confute the sceptic by covert appeals to empirical evidence; but even he would see that in the context of the anti-sceptical debate—the veil-of-perception doctrine—open references to 'physical inquiries' and to what 'experience shows us' would be merely grotesque.

Nor does Locke confound his primary/secondary views with the issue about substratum-substance. In his principal exposition of the former, the word 'substance' does not occur once.[50]

Still, some aspects of Locke's writings serve to explain, if not to excuse, the conflation by Berkeley and others of the primary-quality theory with the theory of reality.

One of these is the part played in Locke's discussions of primary and secondary qualities by the notion of an idea's *resembling* an object or a quality of an object. He sometimes says that there is such a resemblance in the case of primary-quality ideas but not secondary-quality ones; and this could tempt Berkeley to see the primary/secondary thesis as asserting the veil-of-perception doctrine for primary qualities while denying it for secondary.

But 'resemblance' plays only a minor role in Locke's formulations of the primary/secondary thesis; and his standard way of presenting the veil-of-perception doctrine, or the issue over

---

[48] *Essay* II. viii. 22.   [49] *Essay* IV. iii. 28.
[50] *Essay* II. viii. 9–26.

scepticism, is not in terms of resemblance between ideas and real things. The arguments I have quoted in § 12, indeed, prove that Locke sees the sceptical question to be neutral as between primary and secondary qualities. The sceptical question asks: 'Are all our ideas just hallucinations or dream-states or the like?', and the Berkeleian exegesis would have Locke reply: 'Not all our ideas—only the secondary-quality ones.' But in two of Locke's most considerable discussions of scepticism he defends the veridicality of our ideas against the sceptic in terms of just four examples—the taste of wormwood, the smell of a rose, the heat of a fire, and the whiteness of a page![51]

That alone makes Berkeley's exegesis inexcusable. Still, perhaps we should hunt out some more of its possible sources in Locke's text.

Locke's unsatisfactory classification of ideas into 'real' and 'fantastical' might entice one into Berkeleian errors.[52] He says that 'real' ideas do, while 'fantastical' ones do not, 'have a conformity with the real being and existence of things, or with their archetypes'.[53] This might lie within the area of the veil-of-perception doctrine, e.g. by being connected with Locke's notion of 'real knowledge'.[54] Yet it is not clear that that is right. The ideas Locke calls 'fantastical' are ones 'made up of such collections of simple ideas as were really never united, never were found together in any substance: v.g. a rational creature, consisting of a horse's head, joined to a body of human shape . . .'[55] That is, they are ideas which fail in an ordinary everyday way to 'conform' to 'reality'. Is there room here for even the prima facie possibility that all our ideas might be 'fantastical'? The real/fantastical distinction is in fact a rather muddled piece of philosophical logic, concerning ideas in their role as meanings rather than as sense-data, so that its relations with the veil-of-perception doctrine are bound to be cloudy.

Even if the two were tightly linked, though, the real/fantastical distinction would support Berkeley's exegesis only if Locke also said that primary-quality ideas are 'real' while secondary-quality ones are 'fantastical'. But this second step is explicitly ruled out:

---

[51] *Essay* IV. ii. 14; xi. 2.
[52] See Gibson, *Locke's Theory of Knowledge*, ch. 6 §§ 6–8.
[53] *Essay* II. xxx. 1.   [54] *Essay* IV. iv. 4–5.
[55] *Essay* II. xxx. 5.

'Our *simple ideas* are all real, all agree to the reality of things: not that they are all of them the images or representations of what does exist; the contrary whereof, in all but the primary qualities of bodies, hath been already shown ... [The] ideas of whiteness and coldness ... are real ideas in us, ... the reality lying in that steady correspondence they have with the distinct constitutions of real beings. But whether they answer to those constitutions, as to causes or patterns, it matters not; it suffices that they are constantly produced by them.[56]

There is, then, no support for Berkeley in the distinction between real and fantastical ideas.

Locke's theory about *real essences* could also lead to misunderstanding. While pouring scorn on 'those who [use] the word essence for they know not what',[57] Locke gives to the phrase 'real essence' a sense which he believes to be legitimate:

The other and more rational opinion is of those who look on all natural things to have [a 'real essence' in the sense of] a real, but unknown, constitution of their insensible parts; from which flow those sensible qualities which serve us to distinguish them one from another, according as we have occasion to rank them into sorts, under common denominations.[58]

From now on I shall use 'real essence' to mean 'real essence of the kind Locke approves', i.e. the microphysical primary-quality constitution of a thing from which flow all its large-scale qualities, primary and secondary. The theory of real essences is, then, integrally bound up with Locke's Causal Thesis about primary and secondary qualities.

Locke's notion of real essence is one of the finest things in the *Essay*, and he handles it almost flawlessly. Yet a careless reader might assimilate it to the theory of reality, or to that of substance, because of Locke's insistence on how little we know about real essences:

Though the familiar use of things about us take off our wonder, yet it cures not our ignorance. When we come to examine the stones we tread on, or the iron we daily handle, we presently find we know not their make; and can give no reason of the different qualities we find in them. ... What is that texture of parts, that real essence, that makes lead and antimony fusible, wood and stones not? What makes lead and iron malleable, antimony and stones not?[59]

[56] *Essay* II. xxx. 2.   [57] *Essay* III. iii. 15–17; vi. 1–13, 35–40.
[58] *Essay* III. iii. 17.   [59] *Essay* III. vi. 9.

Here he is preparing to argue that real essences are not in fact our basis for classification: they cannot be, since we know so little about them.[60] But the passage has a larger purpose which should also be mentioned. With characteristic intelligence, insight and humility, Locke took every possible chance—of which the quoted passage is one—to stress the gap between the intellectual control which we do impose on the world and the science-plus-conceptual-scheme which we might find appropriate if we 'cured our ignorance'.

Sometimes, however, he gives the impression of thinking that real essences are not just mainly unknown but in principle unknowable. For example, he says that 'we are so far from being admitted into the secrets of nature, that we scarce so much as ever approach the first entrance towards them', and defends this in a fine passage which starts thus:

We are wont to consider the substances we meet with, each of them, as an entire thing by itself, having all its qualities in itself, and independent of other things; overlooking, for the most part, the operations of those invisible fluids they are encompassed with, and upon whose motions and operations depend the greatest part of those qualities which are taken notice of in them.[61]

Against this common assumption, Locke maintains that individual things are continually propped up, so to speak, by their causal relations with other things:

Take the air but for a minute from the greatest part of living creatures, and they presently lose sense, life, and motion. This the necessity of breathing has forced into our knowledge. But how many other extrinsical and possibly very remote bodies do the springs of these admirable machines depend on, which are not vulgarly observed, or so much as thought on; and how many are there which the severest inquiry can never discover?[62]

He concludes in his next section that, as well as the difficulty of discovering the 'size, figure and texture' of the 'minute and active parts' of bodies, there is the problem of finding 'the different motions and impulses made in and upon them by bodies from without'; but these motions and impulses are also part of the real essences of bodies, for upon them 'depends . . . the greatest and

---

[60] See also *Essay* III. vi. 2.   [61] *Essay* IV. vi. 11.
[62] Ibid.

most remarkable part of those qualities we observe' in bodies; and so 'this consideration alone is enough to put an end to all our hopes of ever having the ideas of [bodies'] real essences'.[63]

Is Locke here presenting real essences as necessarily unknowable—as a 'something we know not what' or a something beyond the veil? If so, that might link the notion of a real essence, and thus the primary/secondary theory containing it, with either substrata or the 'real things' of the veil-of-perception doctrine. The answer to the question is 'No'. Even when Locke is at his most pessimistic about our prospects of discovering the real essences of things, his pessimism is reasonable, argued, and unabsolute.[64] What he says is not that real essences are in principle unknowable, but only that there are reasons for suspecting that full knowledge of them would require scientific inquiries of a depth and scope that lie beyond our capacities.

It would be in the spirit of Locke's theory of essences to suggest that we might, as scientific knowledge increases, eventually give up all our present ways of describing and classifying physical things. This suggestion could, unhappily, be expressed by saying 'Perhaps nothing in the physical world is in any respect what it seems to be'; but this sentence, when it carries that meaning, has nothing to do with the veil-of-perception doctrine. Berkeley notwithstanding, it does not express a 'sceptical' position, nor does it in any significant sense 'depreciate our faculties, and make mankind appear ignorant and low'.[65] Berkeley's inability to do justice to this aspect of Locke's thought seems to have been a matter of temperament as much as of intellect—apparently he could not get himself into the frame of mind of someone who, without jeering at the ignorance of others or bewailing his own, thinks it likely that science has so far barely scratched the surface of the real.

Another aspect of the theory of real essences could, at a hasty glance, seem to connect it with the substratum doctrine in particular. What Locke stresses is the difficulty of discovering the real essences of *substances*; and someone might infer from this that real essences are supposed to be unknowable in the same way, and perhaps for the same reason, that the 'nature' of substratum-

---

[63] *Essay* IV. vi. 12.
[64] See Gibson, *Locke's Theory of Knowledge*, ch. 7 § 12.
[65] *Principles* § 101. Cf. *Essay* II. xxiii. 12.

substance is unknowable. This too would be a misunderstanding. Locke is interested in the distinction between real and 'nominal' essences, and this distinction works only in application to substances—a fact which Locke records, not very satisfactorily, by saying that the nominal essence of a property or mode is also its real essence.[66] The basic point underlying this dark saying is, I think, as follows..

The nominal essence of a red thing (*qua* red) is just the meaning of 'red' or the idea we associate with that word. The real essence of a red thing (*qua* red) is that primary-quality texture of it which causes it to look as it does and thus qualify for the description 'red'. To discover a real essence, then, we must start with a meaning or an 'idea', and then dig for certain empirical facts about the items—the substances—which correspond to it. Consider now the property of redness. Its nominal essence is just the same as that of any red thing (*qua* red), that is, it is determined wholly by the meaning of the word 'red'. And that is all there is to be said about the property itself, as distinct from the things that have it. The only way of going beyond what we mean by 'red' or by 'redness'—the only way of filling in relevant empirical facts—is by going from redness to red things, from properties to substances. (Locke's own account of the matter is clouded by his speaking not of 'properties' but of 'simple ideas and modes', and by his implicitly contrasting 'triangles [of the sort studied in geometry]' with triangular things or substances. If I was right in § 15 about why he chooses geometrical 'triangles' as paradigm modes, then we can take him to be contrasting the property of triangularity with actual triangular things or substances; and then his basic point is as I have expounded it.)

Locke's point, on this reading of it, is perfectly correct; there is no mystery about it; and it has nothing to do with substrata. For example, when he refers to 'the unknown essence of that substance',[67] all he means is 'the microphysical constitution of that lump of stuff' or '. . . of that kind of stuff'. He is, quite harmlessly, using the language of his excellent theory of real essences.

[66] *Essay* II. xxxi. 11, 14; III. iii. 18.   [67] *Essay* II. xxiii. 3.

V

BERKELEY ON REALITY: AGAINST LOCKE

26. *Two specific arguments*

BERKELEY'S attack on the veil-of perception doctrine raises methodological issues which are worth a short chapter. It is interwoven with his attacks on the substratum and primary/secondary theories, but each passage I shall cite can be read, with the aid of § 14 and § 24 above, as a clean-cut thrust at the veil-of-perception doctrine alone.

Philosophers in the empiricist tradition often disclaim any intention of theorizing, preferring plain common sense to the perversely intricate theories of their opponents. Thus Berkeley has Philonous say: 'I do not pretend to frame any hypothesis at all. I am of a vulgar cast, simple enough to believe my senses, and leave things as I find them.'[1] Berkeley does have a theory, though. He defends a general, controversial thesis—usually called *idealism*—about the nature of objectivity-concepts, the meanings of statements about the real or external world. Much of his attack on Locke stems directly from idealism, but my present concern is with two valid arguments in which idealism is not presupposed.

The first rebuts Locke's claim that ideas *resemble* real things. Against this, Berkeley objects that 'an idea can be like nothing but an idea', so that our ideas could be 'the pictures or representations' of Lockean real things only if the latter were themselves ideas, in which case Locke's doctrine would collapse.[2]

This argument, as well as going against something Locke says about primary qualities, also refutes the veil-of-perception doctrine in so far as the latter claims that ideas 'resemble' real things. We have seen, though, that this claim is neither a weighty nor a central part of the doctrine; it is not required for the thesis that ideas 'represent' real things; so that this argument of Berkeley's has a severely limited scope.

---

[1] *Third Dialogue*, p. 229.   [2] *Principles* § 8.

Its premiss—that an idea can be like nothing but another idea—
is true. Since it is wrong to reify sense-data (see § 5 above), a
visual sense-datum cannot have shape, colour, etc., and so cannot
resemble a physical thing in shape, colour, etc. The sentence 'I
have (apprehend, perceive) a square sense-datum' can only be a
bad short-hand for 'It is with me as though I were seeing something square', which does not imply that there is anything square.
Berkeley, however, stands this point on its head. To the reasonable
view that only perceivable items can have empirical properties,
he adds the idealist thesis that only ideas are perceivable (see § 30
below), and thence infers that only ideas or sense-data can have
such empirical properties as squareness. This gives an odd twist
to his handling of the truth that only ideas can resemble ideas:

But how can that which is sensible be like that which is insensible? Can
a real thing in itself *invisible* be like a *colour*; or a real thing which is
not *audible*, be like a *sound*? In a word, can any thing be like a sensation
or idea, but another sensation or idea?[3]

Perhaps Lockean 'real things' are invisible; but not for the reason
that they don't resemble colours or—a different point which
Berkeley takes to be the same one—that they don't resemble
ideas.

Berkeley's other substantial argument tells against the veil-of-
perception doctrine itself, not just against one version of it. He
deploys this argument, too, in the light of a theory of his own,
but perhaps less damagingly than in the previous case.

Locke defends his doctrine as a reasonable explanatory hypothesis: many of my sensory states are forced in on me, in orderly
and dependable ways, and this fact can be explained only by 'the
brisk acting of some objects without me'.[4] Berkeley rightly
objects.[5] The 'explanatory hypothesis' defence of the doctrine
treats 'objects without me' as causes, whereas Berkeley has a theory
that only a mind can be a cause (see § 42 below). This is implausible, but Berkeley also has a sounder basis for his attack. Consider
how we do discover what we ordinarily call 'causal' connexions
and what Berkeley, refusing them that label, calls 'laws of nature':
'The *Laws of Nature* . . . we learn by experience, which teaches

---

[3] *First Dialogue*, p. 206. See also *Principles* § 8.
[4] *Essay* IV. xi. 5.
[5] *Principles* §§ 18–20, 30–32, 51–53, 86–87; *Dialogues*, pp. 216–20, 242–3.

us that such and such ideas are attended with such and such other ideas, in the ordinary course of things.'[6] That is the crucial point. We have to look for 'causal' explanations on this side of the veil of perception, seeking to connect appearances with other appearances. Such a search could not reveal any link between appearance as a whole and a supposed realm of 'real things' to which we have no direct access.

This mode of attack, which underlies § 12 above and which runs through much of Berkeley's polemic against the veil-of-perception doctrine, is the vital core of his negative position. It can be generalized into the claim that no empirical evidence could bear on the existence of Lockean real things: 'As for all that *compages* of external bodies which you contend for, . . . you cannot either give me any reason why you believe it exists, or assign any use to it when it is supposed to exist.'[7] This may imply that the thesis that there are Lockean real things is meaningless. It certainly implies that that thesis is empty, dead, negligible.

A theory which lacks empirical content should not be attacked on empirical grounds. Berkeley seems to do just that:

It is granted on all hands (and what happens in dreams, phrensies, and the like, puts it beyond dispute) that it is possible we might be affected with all the ideas we have now, though no bodies existed without, resembling them. Hence it is evident the supposition of external bodies is not necessary for the producing our ideas: since it is granted they are produced sometimes, and might possibly be produced always in the same order we see them in at present, without their [sc. bodies'] concurrence.[8]

This argument looks vulnerable to the following dilemma. The argument takes dreams to be idea-sequences with no corresponding 'bodies': if 'bodies' *does* mean 'Lockean real things' then Berkeley cannot know that bodies are absent in dreaming, and if it *doesn't* then the argument is irrelevant to the veil-of-perception doctrine. Berkeley, however, might rebut the first horn of this dilemma. He might say that the premiss 'In dreams there are no bodies or "real things" corresponding to one's ideas' is not something he asserts, but merely something he uses *ad hominem* because it is 'granted on all hands' by the Lockeans. As for his saying that it is 'beyond dispute': he can defend that too, on the grounds that if the veil-of-perception doctrine is to be even

---

[6] *Principles* § 30.   [7] *Principles* § 22.   [8] *Principles* § 18.

remotely plausible it must, at the very least, be offered as explaining the difference between dreaming and normal waking experience.

In fact, if dreams seem to be relevant to the dispute it is as part of the case *for* Locke's position, because 'real things' may seem to explain or elucidate the manifest difference between dreams and normal perceptions. This apparent relevance is illusory, of course. The distinction between dreams and waking experience, just because there are empirical criteria for its application, cannot bear either way on Locke's empty theory. In the Third Dialogue Berkeley handles this point impeccably. He introduces dreams as prima facie favouring Locke, and then makes Philonous say:

There is ... no danger of confounding [waking experience] with the visions of a dream, which are dim, irregular, and confused. And though they should happen to be never so lively and natural, yet by their not being connected, and of a piece with the preceding and subsequent transactions of our lives, they might easily be distinguished from realities. In short, by whatever method you distinguish *things* from *chimeras* on your own scheme, the same, it is evident, will hold also upon mine. For it must be, I presume, by some perceived difference, and I am not for depriving you of any one thing that you perceive.[9]

Here, as elsewhere, Berkeley's rejection of the 'explanatory hypothesis' defence of Locke's doctrine hints at the stronger claim that the doctrine has no empirical content.

One episode in Berkeley's attack requires comment: 'What reason can induce us to believe the existence of bodies without the mind, from what we perceive, since the very patrons of matter themselves do not pretend, there is any necessary connexion betwixt them and our ideas?'[10] This presumably takes up Locke's point that things' primary qualities do not necessitate the ideas they cause in us—that the correlations between quality and idea are God-ordained, and do not 'stand to reason'. (Locke says this of *all* our ideas. In my published article I restricted the point to ideas of secondary qualities, having misunderstood a Lockean subtlety.[11]) When thinking about 'real things' rather than about primary qualities, Locke would probably have said the same thing: 'real things' cause our ideas but do not necessitate them in

---

[9] *Third Dialogue*, p. 235. [10] *Principles* § 18.
[11] J. Bennett, 'Substance, Reality and Primary Qualities', Martin p. 107; *Essay* IV. iii. 13.

a strong, logical sense of 'necessitate'. But this does not provide Berkeley with an argument he can fairly use. *He* does not think that causes 'necessitate' either, and so he is not entitled to treat the fact that 'the patrons of matter do not pretend . . . etc.' as in any way weakening their position.

27. *'Meaningless' and 'contradictory'*

Idealism implies that qualities are ideas; and ideas must be in minds; whence it follows that the veil-of-perception doctrine is downright self-contradictory or logically false:

The sensible qualities are colour, figure, motion, smell, taste, and such like, that is, the ideas perceived by sense. Now for an idea to exist in an unperceiving thing, is a manifest contradiction; for to have an idea is all one as to perceive . . .[12]

Berkeley often infers from idealism that Locke's doctrine involves 'a contradiction' or—meaning the same thing—'a repugnancy'.[13] This presupposes that he knows what the doctrine means—but does he? I suggested in § 12 that the doctrine avails itself of a distinction between appearance and reality which cannot be our ordinary one, yet does not explain what unordinary one it is; and this sounds like the charge that the doctrine is too unclear to be assessed for truth, or perhaps even that it is meaningless. Berkeley sometimes says this too, as when he speaks of 'the vague and indeterminate description of . . . corporeal substance, which the modern philosophers are run into by their own principles',[14] or remarks that 'the words *material substance* [have] no distinct meaning annexed to them'.[15]

In this vein, he typically gives the doctrine as much elbow-room as possible, inviting Locke to explain the unusual but legitimate sense in which his key terms are being used:

I would fain know how any thing can be present to us, which is neither perceivable by sense nor reflexion, nor [etc., etc.] The words *to be present*, when thus applied, must needs be taken in some abstract and strange meaning, and which I am not able to comprehend.[16]

---

[12] *Principles* § 7.
[13] e.g. in *Principles* §§ 4, 17, 76.
[14] *Principles* § 11.
[15] *Principles* § 17.
[16] *Principles* § 68.

What therefore can be meant by calling matter an *occasion* [of our ideas]? This term is either used in no sense at all, or else in some sense very distant from its received signification.[17]

Even more explicitly, against the substratum theory:

HYLAS: You still take things in a strict literal sense: that is not fair, Philonous. PHILONOUS: I am not for imposing any sense on your words: you are at liberty to explain them as you please. Only I beseech you, make me understand something by them. You tell me, matter supports or stands under accidents. How! is it as your legs support your body? HYLAS: No; that is the literal sense. PHILONOUS: Pray let me know any sense, literal or not literal, that you understand it in.[18]

This tactic, though admirably deployed, does not square with the charge of inconsistency. In particular, there is something wrong here:

As for all that *compages* of external bodies which you contend for, I shall grant you its existence, though you cannot either give me any reason why you believe it exists, or assign any use to it when it is supposed to exist. I say, the bare possibility of your opinion's being true, shall pass for an argument that it is so.[19]

Locke cannot 'give any reason . . . or assign any use . . .' precisely because his doctrine has cut itself loose from the ordinary appearance/reality distinction; that condemns it as meaningless, or at least as fatally 'vague and indeterminate'; which in turn protects it from the charge of inconsistency. Berkeley hopes to base that charge on idealism, but the latter, even if it were true, could hardly turn a meaningless doctrine into a logically false one.

Usually, though, Berkeley does better. He knows that a charge of contradiction presupposes a grasp of meaning:

When words are used without a meaning, you may put them together as you please, without danger of running into a contradiction. You may say, for example, that *twice two* is equal to *seven*, so long as you declare you do not take the words of that proposition in their usual acceptation, but for marks of you know not what.[20]

---

[17] *Principles* § 69.
[18] *First Dialogue*, p. 199. See also *Principles* §§ 16–17.
[19] *Principles* § 22; see also § 20.
[20] *Principles* § 79. See also *Second Dialogue*, pp. 225–6.

And his arguments, when they do not depend directly on idealism, have the form: if Locke's doctrine uses words in their ordinary senses it is self-contradictory; no unordinary senses are offered, and apparently none could be which would save the doctrine; and so the latter is an array of words which 'mark out *either* a direct contradiction, *or else* nothing at all'.[21] This disjunction does not reflect indecisiveness. Rather, it shows that Berkeley is launching a creative attack. Instead of merely saying 'Well, *I* do not understand Locke's doctrine', he meets it half-way, tries to put it to work, and condemns it because its structure renders it obstinately idle.

One might think that no logical operations can be performed on something which is eventually declared to be meaningless. That would be a mistake, but not an obvious one, so the point deserves expansion.

When Philonous is asked why he disbelieves in 'matter', he replies:

It is to me a sufficient reason not to believe the existence of any thing, if I see no reason for believing it. But not to insist on reasons for believing, you will not so much as let me know what it is you would have me believe, since you say you have no manner of notion of it. After all, let me entreat you to consider whether it be like a philosopher, or even like a man of common sense, to pretend to believe you know not what, and you know not why.[22]

This seems right: until the doctrine's meaning is established we cannot consider whether or not to believe it, for there is no *it* to believe. Yet elsewhere Berkeley seems to belie this: 'But though it were possible that solid, figured, moveable substances may exist without the mind, corresponding to the ideas we have of bodies, yet how is it possible for us to know this?'[23] If Locke's theory really is meaningless, what right has Berkeley to say that even if it were true we could not know that it was?

Perhaps he is here thinking of the theory not as meaningless but as logically false. But even if he is regarding it as meaningless he can be entitled to say that if it were true we could not know that it was. This is because the doctrine, even if meaningless, is not unconstruable gibberish: it has a logical structure, is supposed

---

[21] *Principles* § 24, my italics.
[22] *Second Dialogue*, p. 218. See also *Principles* § 45.
[23] *Principles* § 18.

to do certain work, is claimed to have certain logical relations with other statements; and so one may be in a position to say that its author, on his own showing, must admit that even if it were true there could be no evidence for it.

The point goes far beyond Berkeley. Consider, for example, how one can apply to a sentence S the claim that *whatever is not empirically verifiable is therefore meaningless*. Does one take S to express some proposition P, then discover that P is unverifiable, and thence conclude that S is meaningless and thus does not express P (or anything else) after all? That is quite incoherent, which is presumably why Ayer resorts to the notion of what S 'purports' to express:

A sentence is factually significant to any given person, if, and only if, he knows how to verify the proposition which it purports to express— that is, if he knows what observations would lead him, under certain conditions, to accept the proposition as being true, or reject it as being false.[24]

This is still unsatisfactory, for it implies that S may be uniquely associated with P, by the purporting-to-express relation, though without succeeding in actually expressing it.

Still, it is a serious attempt to solve a real problem, namely the problem of avoiding a purely passive handling of the verifiability (or any other) criterion of meaningfulness. If Ayer applied the criterion in the form: 'S is not significant, because I cannot construe it so that it expresses something verifiable', he would be using it passively rather than creatively—saying something which would apply equally to Locke's veil-of-perception doctrine and to such gibberish as 'Fridays are as complex as mountains are soulless'. But a sentence expressing Locke's doctrine is not mere gibberish: there is more to be said about it than 'I don't understand it, and no one else will either'; for it admits of logical operations which are warranted by the normal meanings of some of the constituent words, or by what the author of the sentence claims for it, or both.

For example, the substratum theory is defective as to meaning, but we can still say with confidence that substrata as such cannot have a 'nature', i.e. that there can be no F such that necessarily x is a substratum-substance if and only if Fx. It will not do to say

[24] A. J. Ayer, *Language, Truth and Logic* (London, 1949), p. 35.

that we discover this by examining the proposition which the theory 'purports' to express; but the language of 'purporting to express' does at least register the fact that when philosophers speak of meaninglessness—in the way in which it is natural to level the charge at a 'theory' or 'thesis' rather than at a 'sentence' or 'paragraph'—they are not merely reporting a *de facto* failure to construe.

Berkeley does not theorize about these matters, but in practice his handling of them is impressively sound. In at least one passage he uses both 'It is meaningless' and 'If it were true we could not know it', and holds them in a delicate and satisfactory relation with one another.[25]

28. *Meaningless beliefs*

In one place Berkeley fumbles the notion of meaninglessness in an interesting way. Accused of denying what 'the whole world' believes, he replies:

Upon a narrow inquiry, it will not perhaps be found, so many as is imagined do really believe the existence of matter or things without the mind. Strictly speaking, to believe that which involves a contradiction, or has no meaning in it, is impossible: and whether the foregoing expressions are not of that sort, I refer it to the impartial examination of the reader. In one sense indeed, men may be said to believe that matter exists, that is, they act as if the immediate cause of their sensations, which affects them every moment and is so nearly present to them, were some senseless unthinking being. But that they should clearly apprehend any meaning marked by those words, and form thereof a settled speculative opinion, is what I am not able to conceive. This is not the only instance wherein men impose upon themselves, by imagining they believe those propositions they have often heard, though at bottom they have no meaning in them.[26]

I shall ignore the phrase 'involves a contradiction', and shall pursue this passage on the assumption that Berkeley really does regard Locke's doctrine—abbreviated to 'Matter exists'—as meaningless. Can Berkeley consistently say this, and also say that men act as though it were true that matter exists?

On the face of it, he cannot. Someone who says 'Men act as though it were true that matter exists' is not discussing the sentence 'Matter exists' but is using it; and if it is meaningless then so is what he says using it. A sentence which is unintelligible considered as expressing a 'speculative opinion' does not gain meaning just by being relegated to a subordinate clause.

A statement like 'He acts as though I were his enemy' would ordinarily mean 'He acts as though he believed I were his enemy'; and we probably ought to construe Berkeley's 'Men act as though . . .' analogously, if only because the passage as a whole centres on *belief*. But even if we take Berkeley to be saying that men act as though they believed that matter exists, he is still in trouble. If men act as though they believe that P, it must be possible for someone actually to believe that P; and Berkeley himself says that 'strictly speaking, to believe that which has no meaning in it is impossible'. And isn't he right about that? It is peculiar to say 'Smith believes that . . .' with a completion which one regards as meaningless, as though—to repeat my earlier point—nonsense could become intelligible just by occurring in a subordinate clause.

Still, one might 'unstrictly speaking' say 'Smith believes that...' with a meaningless completion. One might say 'Smith believes that matter exists', meaning that Smith believes that 'Matter exists' expresses something true; or meaning that there is some sentence which holds the same position in its language as 'Matter exists' does in English, and which Smith believes to express something true. This 'unstrict' use of 'believes that' can be criticized for masking the fact that Smith's belief is about a sentence. Still, it is a possible sense—and apparently the only one—for the form '*x* believes that . . .' with a meaningless completion. So let us construe Berkeley accordingly.

Now we have him saying that men act as though they believed that 'Matter exists' expressed something true. To act like that, though, would be to produce arguments with 'Matter exists' as premiss or conclusion, to utter 'Matter exists' assertively, to buy Locke's books and burn Berkeley's, and so on. This cannot be what Berkeley means, for these would be the actions of someone with a theoretical interest in certain philosophical issues, not of the common man of whom Berkeley is speaking. Furthermore, if someone did act in those ways we should have no reason to say merely that he acted *as though* he believed that 'Matter exists' expressed something true.

So Berkeley's 'Men act as though . . .' makes sense only when so construed that it says something false which isn't what Berkeley wants to say. There are two possible accounts of what he does want to say. (1) When Berkeley says that men 'act as if [they believed that] the immediate cause of their sensations . . . were some senseless unthinking being', he means that they act as though they did not believe that God causes their sensations. On that reading, we can see how Berkeley thinks action fits into the picture: 'It is downright impossible, that a soul pierced and enlightened with a thorough sense of the omnipresence, holiness, and justice of that *Almighty Spirit*, should persist in a remorseless violation of his laws.'[27] But then the passage under discussion must be judged as ill-written and badly thought out, if only because Berkeley *does* see how someone can hold the non-existence of God as a 'settled speculative opinion'. (2) I am inclined to think that Berkeley has slipped into conceding that, theology apart, there are ordinary modes of conduct which reflect Lockean assumptions. If this were even possible, his main case against the veil-of-perception doctrine would fail. He argues that nothing in experience could count for or against the doctrine; which implies that there cannot be ways of handling the empirical world which are more appropriate to the doctrine's truth than to its falsity, or, therefore, ways of handling the empirical world which are 'as if' one accepted rather than rejected the doctrine.[28]

[27] *Principles* § 155.
[28] See R. H. Popkin, 'David Hume: his Pyrrhonism and his Critique of Pyrrhonism', Chappell, pp. 84–9.

VI

BERKELEY ON REALITY: IDEALISM

29. *Idealism and phenomenalism*

I SHALL introduce Berkeley's idealism by contrasting it with what I call phenomenalism. The latter answers the same questions as do Locke's and Berkeley's theories of reality; and, though it is distinct from both, it is a natural development out of idealism and an improvement on it. Phenomenalism, if not true, lies between idealism and the truth. I maintain this judgement even when 'phenomenalism' is defined by the theories so called in the twentieth century.[1] The chief defects of those theories consist in lingering remnants of Berkeleian idealism, while their best merits clearly constitute advances on Berkeley. When they are cleansed of their idealist mistakes there is a residue of truth which, I think, still warrants the name 'phenomenalism'. The label itself does not matter; but it is important to distinguish the several strands in the theories in question, so that we can assess and sift the arguments which purport to 'refute phenomenalism'.

Idealism and phenomenalism agree that the veil-of-perception doctrine is wrong. Denying that there is a gap between appearance (in general) and reality (in general) which can be crossed by empirical arguments, they reject Locke's grounds for confidence that there are 'real things without us'; and denying that there is an unbridgeable gap between appearance and reality, they reject also the sceptical conclusion which Locke sought to avoid. Both of them affirm that the 'gap' can be bridged by logical or *a priori* means; by attention to meanings or concepts; by getting clear about what it means to say that something is objectively the case. I give no primacy to any one of these formulations, nor do I stress any distinctions there may be amongst them. Things like this are sometimes said: 'A competent grasp of objectivity-concepts involves a readiness to base statements about what is objectively the case on truths about what appears to be the case, but the latter can never *entail* the former.' Or: 'The relationship

---

[1] See Davis, 'Berkeley and Phenomenalism'.

between appearance and reality is *a priori* but not *logical*' or
'. . . but not *analytic*.' Such remarks presuppose distinctions which
we do not have in a sufficiently clear-cut form to justify this
high-theoretical use of them.

Idealism, then, shares with phenomenalism a view about the
nature of objectivity-concepts, or about the meanings of statements about the objective realm. Underlying this view is a
general empiricism about all meanings: to understand any statement, I must be able to connect the difference between its truth
and its falsity with some difference it could make to me—some
difference in the data, the raw chunks of reality, with which I am
confronted, i.e. in the sensory states which I have or, as Berkeley
would say, in the ideas I perceive. If this is even roughly correct,
then Locke's problem about 'real things without us' should not
arise. Someone who says: 'Whatever I know about my sensory
states, there remains the further question of whether there is
really a world of things outside me' has misunderstood the
question 'Is there really a world of things outside me?'

Sketchy as this is, it exhausts the overlap between phenomenalism and idealism. The overlap-thesis, as one might call it, could
be expressed thus: any statement about the objective realm has a
meaning which could be expressed in statements about 'ideas' or
appearances or sense-data. There would be some historical
warrant for saying that the overlap-thesis defines 'phenomenalism';
but then Berkeley's theory would be one form of 'phenomenalism',
and it doesn't suit me to use the label in that way. I want to contrast Berkeley's idealism with a rival theory which adds to the
overlap-thesis a little that Berkeley does not add, and which
omits a great deal which is included in Berkeley's theory. I
reserve the title 'phenomenalism' for this rival theory—mainly
as an expository convenience, though there is historical warrant
for this usage too.

Phenomenalism says that any statement about the objective
realm has a meaning which could be expressed in some set (not
necessarily a conjunction) of statements about sense-data, and it
adds that any such set will be long and complex and will contain
members of the form 'If it were the case that . . ., then such-and-
such sense-data would be had'. One short way of saying that any
objectivity-statement is equivalent to a set of statements, including
counterfactual conditionals, about sense-data, is to say that

Objects are logical constructions out of sense-data. According to Berkeley's idealism, on the other hand, objects are *collections* of sense-data:

As several [ideas] are observed to accompany each other, they come to be marked by one name, and so to be reputed as one thing. Thus, for example, a certain colour, taste, smell, figure and consistence having been observed to go together, are accounted one distinct thing, signified by the name *apple*. Other collections of ideas constitute a stone, a tree, a book, and the like sensible things.[2]

The difference between collections and logical constructions, as expressed in the contrast between that passage and phenomenalism, makes itself felt throughout Berkeley's thought.[3] My present concern is to contrast the two in as abstract and structural a way as possible.

Before proceeding with that, I should point out that I assume nothing about what 'logical construction' has meant in the twentieth-century philosophical literature. My uses of the phrase will be based solely upon the stipulative definition I have given. My uses of 'collection', on the other hand, are answerable to the word's normal English meaning.

Someone who says that Fs are logical constructions out of Gs implies that any given statement about an F is equivalent to some set of statements about Gs; but all he commits himself to, regarding this set, is its being long and complex and its including counter-factual conditionals. But the statement that Fs are collections of Gs, as well as implying that any given F-statement is equivalent to some G-statement(s), sets quite severe limits on what G-statements can be equivalent to a given F-statement. The word 'collection' is too wide and vague for these limits to be stated precisely, and we must not exaggerate their severity. It is not implied, for example, that if S asserts that a given F is ϕ then S is equivalent to $(S_1 \ \& \ S_2 \ \& \ ...)$ where each conjunct asserts that a given G is ϕ; for a football team, which is a collection of players, may be unbeatable even though no one of its members is unbeatable. Still, some limits clearly do obtain.

Notably, the thesis that Fs are collections of Gs, if 'collections' is taken seriously, implies that F-statements relate to G-statements in such a way that *There are Fs* entails *There are Gs*. (For example,

---

[2] *Principles* § 1.   [3] See Day, 'George Berkeley', pp. 270–1.

There are football teams entails *There are football players*, and the reason why this entailment holds is just that it is a fact about the meaning of 'team' that a team is a collection of players.) And from this it follows by elementary logic that, for any given proposition P, *If there are Gs then P* entails *If there are Fs then P.* Neither of these entailments follows from the claim that Fs are—in my stipulated sense—'logical constructions' out of Gs.

Let us apply these points to Berkeley. His idealist thesis that *Objects are collections of ideas*, together with the premiss that *If there are ideas then someone is in a sensory state*, implies that *If there are objects then someone is in a sensory state*. He could avoid this conclusion only by rejecting the second premiss and thus allowing that there can be ideas which no one has. The premiss in question is entailed by the anti-reification thesis of § 5 above, and Berkeley accepts it, more or less for that reason. So he will say not only that if there are ideas then someone is in a sensory state, but further that *No idea can exist unless someone has it*; which yields the further conclusion that *No object can exist unless each of its member-ideas is had by someone.*

Now, one of the mainsprings of Berkeley's idealism is the desire to connect 'what there is' with 'what is perceived'. So it is natural and inevitable that he should equate *x has an idea belonging to object O* with *x perceives O*. This equation, together with the final conclusion of the preceding paragraph, yields Berkeley's most famous conclusion, namely that *No object can exist unless it is perceived by someone*:

It is indeed an opinion strangely prevailing amongst men, that houses, mountains, rivers, and in a word all sensible objects have an existence natural or real, distinct from their being perceived by the understanding. [But this opinion involves] a manifest contradiction. For what are the forementioned objects but . . . ideas or sensations; and is it not plainly repugnant that any one of these or any combination of them should exist unperceived?[4]

The thesis that there cannot be unperceived objects will be fully discussed in Chapter VII. My aim here has been merely to show that Berkeley is committed to this thesis just by the truth that there cannot be unowned ideas, together with 'Objects are collections of ideas' and the natural corollary that to perceive an object is to have one of its member-ideas. If 'collections of' were replaced by 'logical constructions out of', the argument would not go through.

The logical-construction/collection line does not correspond to the analytic/synthetic line or anything like it. A 'logical constructions' statement must be about meanings or concepts, while a 'collections' one need not be ('Veterans' associations are collections of reactionaries'). But a 'collections' statement *may* be offered as a claim about meanings, or as a necessary truth warranted by meanings ('Football teams are collections of players'). Berkeley certainly saw idealism as a conceptual theory: he says that it will be accepted by 'any one that shall attend to what is meant by the term *exist* when applied to sensible things',[5] and often characterizes the denial of it as 'repugnant' or as 'a contradiction'. There have been theories which, though they interest us as conceptual analyses, were thought by their authors to be something else, something more like news about what the world contains; but Berkeley's idealism is not one of them.[6]

30. *'Only ideas are perceived'*

Why does Berkeley say that objects are collections of ideas? Here is a possible argument: (*a*) objects are collections of qualities, and (*b*) qualities are ideas, therefore (*c*) objects are collections of ideas. Although (*a*) connects with the substratum issue, I still maintain that the latter is irrelevant to our present concerns;[7] for the above argument does not explain Berkeley's position. If we ask why he accepts (*b*), the answer is that he derived it from idealism—and his idealism is just what we are trying to explain.

A non-circular explanation is hinted at in a passage to which I alluded earlier. I quoted Berkeley as saying 'What are objects but . . . ideas or sensations?', but here is the clause with the gap filled: 'What are objects but the things we perceive by sense, and what do we perceive besides our own ideas or sensations'?[8] It is fundamental to his thought that Berkeley repeatedly explains 'sensible things' or 'objects' as things which can be perceived, and contends that *nothing can be perceived except ideas*.

[5] *Principles* § 3.

[6] See A. R. White, 'A Linguistic Approach to Berkeley's Philosophy', *Philosophy and Phenomenological Research*, vol. 16 (1955–6).

[7] For a vigorously argued opposing view, see E. B. Allaire, 'Berkeley's Idealism', *Theoria*, vol. 29 (1963).   [8] *Principles* § 4.

This contention of Berkeley's needs to be explained, and, since he argues for it at length, there is no shortage of raw materials for an explanation. Let us start here:

PHILONOUS: In reading a book, what I immediately perceive are the letters, but mediately, or by means of these, are suggested to my mind the notions of God, virtue, truth, &c. Now, that the letters are truly sensible things, or perceived by sense, there is no doubt: but I would know whether you take the things suggested by them to be so too. HYLAS: No certainly, it were absurd to think *God* or *Virtue* sensible things, though they may be signified and suggested to the mind by sensible marks, with which they have an arbitrary connexion. PHILONOUS: It seems then, that by *sensible things* you mean [as I do] those only which can be perceived immediately by sense. HYLAS: Right. [9]

Certainly, I may be put in mind of something by reading about it—whether it be God or virtue or a 'sensible thing' like the Pentagon—without perceiving it immediately or in any other way. We can also grant part of Berkeley's next step, in which Philonous gets Hylas to agree that:

By *sensible things* I mean those only which are perceived by sense, and... the senses perceive nothing which they do not perceive immediately: for they make no inferences. The deducing therefore of causes or occasions from effects and appearances, which alone are perceived by sense, entirely relates to reason. [10]

I may indeed perceive something without perceiving its causes, as when I see a book without seeing the press it was printed on. Perhaps I 'deduce' by 'reason' that it was printed on a press, but that inference forms no part of my present perception.

In agreeing with Berkeley on the strength of my examples, I am misrepresenting the much more constricting line which *he* wants to draw around what is 'immediately perceived'. Just after the passage last quoted, it is further agreed that: '[We do not] immediately perceive by sight any thing beside light, and colours, and figures: or by hearing, any thing but sounds: by the palate, any thing beside tastes: by the smell, beside odours: or by the touch, more than tangible qualities.' [11] These immediately-perceivable items are all supposed to be qualities, and shortly thereafter the equation of qualities with ideas comes into play;

[9] *First Dialogue*, p. 174.   [10] *First Dialogue*, pp. 174–5.
[11] *First Dialogue*, p. 175.

but that line of argument, we have seen, does not illuminate the structure of Berkeley's thought. A more promising passage occurs when Hylas, after being hustled into accepting idealism, recants:

HYLAS: I did not sufficiently distinguish the *object* from the *sensation.* Now though this latter may not exist without the mind, yet it will not thence follow that the former cannot. PHILONOUS: What object do you mean? the object of the senses? HYLAS: The same. PHILONOUS: It is then immediately perceived. HYLAS: Right. PHILONOUS: Make me to understand the difference between what is immediately perceived, and a sensation.[12]

Hylas fails, of course, and his attempt is rather unhelpful: he allows that the object in question is an 'unthinking substance'; and Philonous' objections to that partly concern the substratum theory and are thus irrelevant, and partly rest on general idealist considerations and thus beg our question.

We are still looking for an argument from uncontroversial premisses to the conclusion that only ideas can be perceived, or to the double conclusion that only ideas can be immediately perceived and that all (genuine) perception is immediate. We begin to get it a few pages further on, when Philonous says (omitting Hylas' limp affirmatives):

When you behold the picture of Julius Caesar, do you see with your eyes any more than some colours and figures with a certain symmetry and composition of the whole? . . . And would not a man, who had never known any thing of Julius Caesar, see as much? . . . Consequently he hath his sight, and the use of it, in as perfect a degree as you. . . . Whence comes it then that your thoughts are directed to the Roman Emperor, and his are not? This cannot proceed from the sensations or ideas of sense by you then perceived; since you acknowledge you have no advantage over him in that respect. It should seem therefore to proceed from reason and memory: should it not?[13]

Knowing that one is confronted by *a picture of Julius Caesar,* then, involves not just visual intake but also 'reason and memory', i.e. background knowledge and the ability to relate it to the sensory present. But these are also involved in knowing that one is confronted by *a picture*—that is, by a physical object which can be touched and moved around, which would look different in various lights, and so on. Berkeley explicitly says this, not about the picture but about a similar example which—at last—gives us the explanation we have been looking for:

I grant we may in one acceptation be said to perceive sensible things mediately by sense: that is, when from a frequently perceived connexion, the immediate perception of ideas by one sense suggests to the mind others perhaps belonging to another sense, which are wont to be connected with them. For instance, when I hear a coach drive along the streets, immediately I perceive only the sound; but from the experience I have had that such a sound is connected with a coach, I am said to hear the coach. It is nevertheless evident, that in truth and strictness, nothing can be *heard* but *sound*: and the coach is not then properly perceived by sense, but suggested from experience. So likewise when we are said to see a red-hot bar of iron; the solidity and heat of the iron are not the objects of sight, but suggested to the imagination by the colour and figure, which are properly perceived by that sense. In short, those things alone are actually and strictly perceived by any sense, which would have been perceived, in case that same sense had then been first conferred on us. As for other things, it is plain they are only suggested to the mind by experience grounded on former perceptions.[14]

This subtly mixes shrewd truth with serious error. I shall try to separate them.

A minor point: I may be 'said to hear the coach' even if appropriate tactual and visual correlates are not 'suggested to my mind', for you may properly say 'He thinks he is hearing a thunderstorm, but really he is hearing a coach'. Still, it is true—and we can take this to be what Berkeley meant—that if *I* think that I 'hear a coach' then I must have not just my present auditory 'ideas' but also certain kinds of background knowledge as well.

Another preliminary point: Berkeley may think that what happens is that I put together my present auditory state and my memories of past experiences, and then, perhaps extremely quickly, *infer* that I 'hear a coach'; or he may think that my past experiences have 'programmed' me in such a way that my present auditory state *causes* me to believe that I 'hear a coach'. The former account would be wrong in most cases; the latter might, for all I know, always be right; but neither is what Berkeley needs. The vital point is that my belief that I 'hear a coach' is answerable to facts about what I shall or should experience under different conditions, and that it could be defended by 'reason and memory', i.e. by a disciplined appeal to the ways in which, in the past, certain visual and tactual 'ideas' have been associated with auditory states like my present one. That is what Berkeley needs for this part of his argument—an analytic thesis about the meaning of 'hears a coach', not a genetic one about how anyone comes to believe that he hears a coach.

Berkeley is right, then, in thinking that 'x perceives O at t', where O is not an 'idea', reports more than just what x's sensory state was at t. We may even concede that 'x perceives [non-idea] at t' is a conjunction of (a) something of the form 'x has [idea] at t' and (b) a statement about ideas had at times other than t and, perhaps, about what ideas would have been had at various times if certain conditions had obtained. Where Berkeley errs is in thinking that (a) is a genuine perception-statement while (b) is not. Once we allow that (a) is a paradigm of a perception-statement, we can hardly avoid saying that only ideas are perceived, and thence concluding that 'sensible things' are ideas or collections of ideas.

In at least four different ways Berkeley gives this error a specious plausibility, and so renders it easier to accept—or to make in the first place.

(1) There is a point of tactics. Berkeley begins by saying that what is only 'mediately' perceived is not genuinely perceived at all, and he illustrates this with an uncontroversial example: we all agree that God, truth and virtue are not perceived even when we see words which 'suggest' them. He conveniently overlooks the fact that in such a case no one would say that God etc. are 'mediately' perceived either. That is, the example does not, as it purports to, concern a use of 'perceive' *which we do have* but which on reflection we agree to be un-'strict' because the perception involved is only mediate. It turns out that Berkeley wants to construe 'mediate perception' so that it covers every use of 'reason and memory' to connect the ideas had at t with other actual and possible ideas; and that does imply that some of our ordinary perception-statements, such as 'x hears a coach', report only 'perceptions' of the allegedly suspect, 'mediate' variety. But that ought not to be allowed to gain plausibility from the 'God' example, for the latter draws the mediate/immediate line in a different place. This is shown by the fact that Berkeley's final position actually condemns his handling of the 'God' example.

He says that what we perceive immediately are not God, truth and virtue, but only words; but then it turns out that all we perceive immediately are our own visual ideas, and that the words—the ink-portions which could be seen at other times and by other people—are themselves perceived only mediately.

(2) The 'coach' passage itself has a false plausibility. One does not shrink from saying that 'I hear a coach' means 'I hear a sound made by a coach', and one might think that that is to grant Berkeley his main point. It isn't, though. Even if we concede that any statement about hearing an object ought, 'strictly', to be expressed as a statement about hearing a sound which is somehow associated with an object, this still does not give Berkeley what he wants. For he wants the immediate accusatives of the verb 'to hear' to be auditory 'ideas', and a sound is not an 'idea'. A sound is objective, physical, spatially located, interpersonally perceptible; while an auditory idea or sense-datum is none of these. Berkeley regularly confuses objective sounds with auditory sense-data, and this gives a specious plausibility to his thesis that strictly speaking one can hear nothing but a sound; where he must take 'sound' to mean 'auditory idea', but we are inclined to agree with what he says because we take 'sound' to mean *sound*. This equivocation with 'sound' apparently cannot be reproduced for the other senses, except perhaps for the sense of smell. The reasons for this seem to be complex and interesting, but a discussion of them would take me too far afield.

(3) Berkeley's uses of the cognates of 'strict' are probably a help to him: 'in truth and strictness, nothing can be heard but sound . . .', and '[only ideas] are actually and strictly perceived...'. These turns of phrase are dangerous because 'strict' is ambiguous. To use a word 'strictly' may be to use it narrowly, or to use it in an unusually careful and correct way; and one might be tempted in Berkeley's direction by a drift from one sense of 'strict' to the other.

(4) The expressions 'perceive by sense' and 'see with your eyes' are also relevant. It is not true that what I perceive at *t* is determined wholly by my sensory state at *t*; but the other relevant facts lie within the province of 'reason and memory', and we can understand Berkeley's thinking it safe to deny that these other facts have any bearing on what I perceive *by sense* at *t*. As for 'see with your eyes': of course there is no other way of seeing, but I

think that Berkeley uses this expression in an attempt to bolster his view that any account of what one sees must consist wholly of facts about one's *visual* intake ('*Seeing* is something you do with your *eyes*, not with your ears or your finger-tips')—whence it follows that one cannot see a tangible coach.

31. *The source of Berkeley's error*

Have I explained Berkeley's willingness to say that all we 'strictly' perceive are ideas and thus that objects are (collections of) ideas? Hardly. The points I have made might help us to understand Berkeley's fidelity to idealism even when some of its implausibilities begin to show through, but they do not explain what positive, substantial reasons he had for entertaining idealism in the first place.

This might explain it: seeing that Locke's position was untenable, Berkeley sought an account of perception which would show that we do perceive objects and would explain how we can know that we do; and the only account he could find was idealism, which says that we perceive objects because objects are ideas.

That explanation is moderately satisfying. If Berkeley saw idealism as the only alternative to the inaccessible world of Lockean 'real things', his splendidly clear view of the defects of Locke's position would of course lead him to opt for idealism and to maintain it in the face of almost any difficulty. But the explanation says that Berkeley could see no viable alternative to the veil-of-perception doctrine other than idealism—and one might ask for *that* to be explained. Specifically, given that phenomenalism is much more viable than idealism, why did Berkeley opt for the latter? This, which is the last 'Why?' in my current sequence, will be answered in the present section.

The answer cannot be that it did not ever occur to Berkeley to use typically phenomenalistic forms in elucidating statements about objects. Apart from his covertly phenomenalistic theory about (Berkeleian) 'real things', to be discussed in § 34 below, there are two isolated phenomenalistic passages. In one of them, he elucidates the statement 'The earth moves' by a phenomenalistic use of conditionals which, had he thought hard about it, he could scarcely have avoided carrying over into the analysis of

'There is a planet in such-and-such an orbit around the sun', and thence into the analysis of statements about the existence of objects generally:

The question, whether the earth moves or no, amounts in reality to no more than this, to wit, whether we have reason to conclude from what hath been observed by astronomers, that if we were placed in such and such circumstances, and such or such a position and distance, both from the earth and sun, we should perceive the former to move among the choir of the planets, and appearing in all respects like one of them.[15]

In his one other passage in this vein, Berkeley adumbrates a phenomenalistic analysis of a statement which is explicitly about the existence of an object:

The table I write on ... exists, that is, I see and feel it; and if I were out of my study I should say it existed, meaning thereby that if I was in my study I might perceive it, or that some other spirit actually does perceive it.[16]

So Berkeley was capable on occasion of taking a phenomenalist line. What has to be explained is his not building on such passages as these—his opting for a theory which, precisely because it excludes conditionals, spawns the host of difficulties which I shall examine in § 33. The explanation might be that Berkeley just didn't see in his occasional phenomenalist remarks the makings of a theoretical alternative to idealism; and this, though not interesting, could be correct and could also be all the explanation there is. If Berkeley's inattention to phenomenalism was a sheer oversight, it would be an honourable and understandable one, and we might be content to leave the matter there.

However, I shall take the matter further. For one thing, Berkeley's unpublished *Philosophical Commentaries* provide considerable evidence that at an early stage he not only envisaged phenomenalism as a theoretical option but was strongly inclined to accept it (see § 41 below). And in any case there are reasons for thinking that Berkeley was *pushed* away from phenomenalism by his views about meaning. The latter set up pressures within his system which yield the best explanation—whether as a rival to the 'oversight' explanation or as a deepening of it—of Berkeley's choosing idealism. It isn't important to know whether Berkeley ever considered espousing phenomenalism and then decided not

to because . . . etc. But the logical relationships within his philosophy are important: my main point is the non-biographical one
that Berkeley could not have embraced phenomenalism, and
thought its consequences through, without being forced to
revise radically certain assumptions of his about meaning. I now
proceed to defend this.

Let us grant that 'x perceives O at t' can be spelled out into
statements purely about the having of ideas, and that when thus
spelled out it reports only one actual *happening-at-t*, namely x's
having a certain idea at t. If 'x perceives O at t' has any further
content it must concern ideas had at times other than t or ideas
which would be had, at t or other times, if certain conditions
obtained. Berkeley takes this to imply that the only clear, clean
philosophically defensible sense we can give to 'x perceives O
at t' is the sense expressed by 'x has [idea] at t', i.e. the sense which
picks out the one relevant happening-at-t.

Suppose we deny this. Suppose we insist that there is nothing
wrong, shallow, or misleading about so construing 'x perceives O
at t' that it is equivalent to a set of statements which include not
only 'x has [idea] at t' but also ones of the form 'If C were the
case at t^* then [idea] would be had at t^*'. (Indicative statements
about ideas had at times other than t will be discussed in § 33, and
are here ignored.) Berkeley, I think, would object to this along
the following lines:—

'If all facts about sensible things can be expressed in the
language of ideas, you ought to be able to complete the equation
"O is . . ." in the language of ideas. But your claim, that "x perceives O at t" says things about what ideas would be had if certain
conditions obtained, prevents you from thus completing the
equation. Obviously, it rules out "O is the idea which x has at t";
and what alternatives are you left with? All you can say is that O
consists of the idea which x has at t together with other possible
ideas, ideas which would be had if certain conditions obtained.
But that is preposterous. It seems quite wrong, and is certainly
not helpful, to say that what x perceives at t is a class of possible
ideas of which one, and perhaps only one, is actual.'

We might complete the equation by saying 'O is a logical construction out of ideas'. This really evades Berkeley's challenge
though, and it would be better to say: although all the facts about
objects can be expressed in the language of ideas, the equation

'O is . . .' cannot be completed in that language. To analyse objectivity-concepts in the language of ideas, we must forgo such forms as '"table" means . . .' or 'A table is . . .', and adopt such forms as 'To say that there is a table is to say . . .' and 'To say that one perceives a table is to say . . .'. These forms make room for the conditionals which—let us admit it—*cannot* be captured by the form which Berkeley would insist upon using.

This is not to admit that our objectivity-concepts are peculiar or unsatisfactory; but Berkeley would think that it is, because he is incompletely liberated from Locke's theory of meaning. He seems to have shared with Locke and with other philosophers a view about meaning which, though not essential to the 'synchronous mental activity' analysis of meaning, is a natural accompaniment of it. This is the view that the unit of meaning is the individual word: not just that one understands a sentence by understanding its constituent words, but the much stronger, false view that the whole story about what a word means can be told without implying anything about how it can be put together with other words to yield meaningful sentences. According to this view, discrete word-meanings are judiciously assembled to yield sentence-meanings—just as words can be juxtaposed to yield sentences or bricks to yield buildings. Anyone who accepts this picture of how word-meaning relates to sentence-meaning is bound to think of a clarification or analysis as typically having a single word on one side and a phrase on the other. A theory of meaning which connects the meaning of a word with the roles it can play in sentences, on the other hand, removes the blinkers and enables us to see that an analysis may have to have a whole sentence on one side and one or more sentences on the other. As I mentioned in § 8 above, Berkeley himself sometimes countenances analyses of this kind; but he regards them as a special case— namely the special case where an expression has to be explained in this manner because it does not stand for anything in the world. There is clearly no encouragement *there* for Berkeley to adopt this pattern of analysis for objectivity-concepts generally.

(Against the Lockean view about how word-meaning relates to sentence-meaning we could bring the slogan 'The meaning of a *word* is determined by its use in *sentences*'; and against his general 'mental correlate' analysis of meaning we could bring the slogan 'The *meaning* of a word (or other part of language) is its *use*'.

Each slogan expresses a position owing much to Wittgenstein, though the former owes more to Frege;[17] each denies something accepted by Locke; it is hard to reject either without rejecting the other; and it is natural to express both, once their distinguishing emphases have been removed, by the single sentence 'The meaning of a word is its use in the language'. Having been plagued by my own tendency to go wrong about this, I think it may be worthwhile to say: we have here two positions, not one; answers to two quite different questions, not one.)

Our question, it will be recalled, was 'Why did Berkeley not exploit his conditionalizing passages and develop something like phenomenalism?' The 'sheer oversight' answer, even if true as intellectual biography, is unhelpful because it tells us nothing about the logical structure of Berkeley's philosophy. But we do learn something about this structure if the 'oversight' explanation is replaced or supplemented by an explanation drawing on the points I have been expounding:—Even if Berkeley considered giving theoretical significance to 'I should say it existed, meaning thereby that if I was in my study I might perceive it', he would be deterred by his inability to get the force of this conditional into an equation of the form 'The table in my study is . . .' with a completion expressed in the language of ideas. He might well be attracted by a phenomenalistic account of 'The table in my study exists' or 'There is a table in my study'; but he would have to regard any elucidation of such sentences as just an upshot of the more fundamental elucidation which is required, namely that of the word 'table'; and it is this which he could not give without deserting his use of conditionals.

The pattern is this: a wrong view in the theory of meaning engenders a narrowed view of what shape an analysis or meaning-elucidation may have to have; and this in turn engenders faulty analyses. In Chapter XIII we shall see this same pattern in Hume's treatment of the same problem. It is worth noting that Kant was much freer than either Berkeley or Hume from Lockean assumptions about meaning, and that he came much nearer than they did to formulating phenomenalism as a theoretical position. These two facts, I submit, are connected.[18]

---

[17] G. Frege, *The Foundations of Arithmetic* (New York, 1953), p. x. See also Zabeeh, *Hume*, pp. 83–4.

[18] See J. Bennett, *Kant's Analytic* (Cambridge, 1966), § 42.

32. *An anti-phenomenalist skirmish*

This section is an aside. In it I shall discuss the following re-markable but seldom remarked passage:

HYLAS: Yes, Philonous, I grant the existence of a sensible thing consists in being perceivable, but not in being actually perceived. PHILONOUS: And what is perceivable but an idea? And can an idea exist without being actually perceived?[19]

This fragment is, so far as I know, Berkeley's only explicit, pub-lished consideration of phenomenalism as a theoretical alternative to idealism. We can suppose that Hylas recalls the passing remark about the table in the study, and is inviting Philonous to build it into his theory by replacing 'The table exists only if it is per-ceived' by the more generous principle 'The table exists only if it is perceived or perceivable—i.e. would be perceived if certain con-ditions were satisfied'. Philonous replies not that Hylas' principle is wrong but that it is not really more generous. He says, in effect, that although phenomenalism looks more liberal it turns out to be equivalent to idealism after all.

As Berkeley states it, Philonous' reply presupposes that only ideas are perceivable; and that begs our question. But the argu-ment does not depend upon this—we can banish 'perceive' from it and still have something left. Hylas' proposal, with 'perceive' removed, is that for a sensible thing to exist is for certain ideas to be had *or havable*. Philonous' reply, I suggest, can be amplified into the following. 'The addition of ". . . or havable" makes no difference. A statement ending with ". . . kicked" might have its truth-conditions changed if we added ". . . or kickable"; but that is because kickable things can exist without being kicked, e.g. unsold footballs; whereas the only items which are "havable" in the relevant sense are ideas, and an idea can exist only if it is actually had. There are no havable ideas which are not actually had by someone, and so in replacing "had" by "had or havable" you have left things exactly where they were.'

Philonous is in error. He rightly thinks that '. . . had or havable' can differ in force from 'had' only if 'havable but not had' makes sense; and he rightly thinks that every actual idea is had; but he wrongly infers from this that every havable idea is

[19] *Third Dialogue*, p. 234.

had. If every actual idea is had, then every F idea is had, where 'F' stands for a predicate which picks out a sub-class of ideas of some kind; but 'havable' is not a predicate of this kind.

Here is another way of putting the same point. Hylas suggests that 'O exists' might be entailed by a statement about what ideas are havable, i.e. by something of the form:

(1) If P, then an idea of kind K is had.

Philonous equates (1) with

(2) There is an idea I of kind K such that: if P, then I is had.

The rest is plain sailing: if there is such an idea, then that idea is actually had; so the antecedent of the conditional 'If P, then I is had' is idle; and the whole of (2) is not weaker than

(3) An idea of kind K is actually had,

which is the sort of statement which Berkeley's idealism says must be used to express the content of 'O exists.' The mistake here, of course, is the equation of (1) with (2), which is on a par with equating 'If I drink this I shall have a headache' with 'There is a headache which I shall have if I drink this'.

These two glosses impose a heavy load on a pair of rhetorical questions totalling a mere sixteen words; but I submit that they do lay bare the structure of Berkeley's thought in the quoted passage. They don't do him much credit, but then I don't offer this line of thought as solidly explaining Berkeley's steady avoidance of phenomenalism. The deepest reason for that avoidance, expounded a few pages back, would bear on Hylas' proposal as follows. Hylas is suggesting that 'O exists' may be entailed by sets of statements of the form

If C_1 obtained, I_1 would be had

If C_2 obtained, I_2 would be had . . . etc.

Faced with this, Berkeley is under pressure to reply: 'But then what *is* the object O? Presumably it is the set of ideas $I_1, I_2, \ldots$; but if these are actual ideas then they are actually had, and your conditionals are idle. If on the other hand they are merely possible ideas, then how can a set of them *be* an actual object? In short, your conditional analysis of "O exists" won't let you say what the object O is—won't let you honestly complete the equation "O is . . ." in the language of ideas.' True, but the conditional analysis is none the worse for that. In thinking otherwise, Berkeley, would be making a mistake, but not one that could properly be viewed with condescension.

For those with an interest in intellectual biography, I offer the following unimportant conjecture: Berkeley eventually noticed that his two phenomenalistic remarks—about the earth's movement and the table in the study—might be thought to point to a theoretical alternative to idealism, and he tried to do something about this. I base this conjecture on two sets of facts.

Firstly, the two remarks in question occur in the *Principles*. I cannot find that Berkeley lapses into phenomenalistic conditionals, even briefly, anywhere in the *Dialogues*; except that his theory about 'real things' (see § 34 below) is a vehicle of a kind of phenomenalism which runs, presumably entirely unrecognized, all through both works.

Secondly, Berkeley's only explicit consideration of the phenomenalistic alternative is in the fleeting 'perceived/perceivable' argument which I have quoted from the *Dialogues*. His efforts to isolate a notion of '*immediate* perception' (see § 30 above), and to distinguish what is 'perceived' from what is merely 'suggested', were first undertaken, for a rather limited purpose, in the *New Theory of Vision*; there is very little like them in the *Principles*; but then they occur in a strenuous and extended form in the *Dialogues*, where they look very much like a conscious endeavour to show that the phenomenalist approach is wrong.

33. *Some consequences of Berkeley's error*

If objects are ideas, there cannot be unperceived objects. Idealism has other unwelcome consequences too, of which I shall present three here and a fourth in § 34. In every case we shall find Berkeley meeting the challenge, if at all, in the same way: by admitting idealism's apparent conflict with some of our ordinary ways of talking about objects, and then trying to explain the common locutions in question—not to discredit them but to show that they consist of a Berkeleian core plus an apparently non-Berkeleian periphery. The relationship of the periphery to the core is supposed to show that such locutions do not really conflict with idealism, or not in a way which tells against idealism.

This tactic, I shall argue, does not work. In a legitimate statement about a sensible thing, the main content is not a purely Berkeleian statement about an idea: what Berkeley relegates to the periphery is never as superficial or as *simple*, and is therefore not as peripheral, as he thinks it is. To see this is to see something about why phenomenalism is an advance on idealism.

Firstly, then: I cannot 'perceive' at t a collection of ideas some of which do not exist at t; so what I perceive at t must be a collection of t-dated ideas—no member of *that* collection can exist at another time; so I cannot perceive one object on separate occasions; so objects cannot have histories.

How would Berkeley have treated this point if it had occurred to him as a difficulty?[20] He might have said (i) that objects do have histories and that strictly speaking all I can perceive at t is a temporal part of an object, a few members of the idea-collection which constitutes the enduring object. But he would be more likely to say (ii) that 'in truth and strictness' I cannot perceive the same object twice, and that our uses of 'the same thing again' are inaccurate though excusable *façons de parler*.

Either way, he ought to state the criteria for two non-contemporaneous ideas' counting—whether in strict Berkeleian theory or in unstrict ordinary speech—as perceptions of a single thing. Berkeley would probably try: 'I_1 and I_2 are ideas of the same thing if and only if they are sufficiently alike'; but that is doubly inadequate. After seeing that apple yesterday, I ate it, so that my present visual field—though just like yesterday's—is not a seeing of the same apple. On the other hand, that clown has just changed his clothes, make-up and posture: my present visual field, though enormously unlike the one I had ten minutes ago, is a seeing of the same man. If Berkeley is to do justice to our ordinary notion of 'the same thing again', he must be prepared to grapple with complexities. This is important, for the following reason.

(i) Suppose that Berkeley admits into his theory the notion of 'perceiving the same thing twice'. Since this would be an attempt to avoid a conflict with ordinary language, achieved only by creating a different conflict ('Strictly speaking all one perceives

[20] See *Principles* § 95.

at t is a temporal part of an object'), it would be pointless unless it provided for the notion of 'perceiving the same thing twice' which we do in fact have—not merely some notion which could be thus expressed. Furthermore, Berkeley would be obliged not just to give us general permission to carry on speaking as we have been accustomed to doing, but to state explicit criteria for ideas' belonging to a single collection or pertaining to a single object. But explicit criteria for our ordinary notion of 'perceiving the same thing twice' would have to make it clear that the truth of 'I_1 and I_2 belong to the same collection (pertain to the same object)' may depend not just upon how I_1 and I_2 relate to one another and to other actual ideas, but also upon what ideas would have occurred if. . . . As soon as Berkeley allows that kind of thing *into his theory* he is well on the way to dropping idealism in favour of phenomenalism: he can no longer take seriously and strictly his thesis that objects are 'collections' of ideas.

(ii) Suppose then that Berkeley takes the other line: strictly speaking an object is a collection of contemporaneous ideas, and vulgar uses of 'the same man again' etc. can be explained by idealism but are not really sanctioned by it. It is not very plausible to say: '"Objects have histories" and "I saw it twice" are just *façons de parler*. They are all right in their way—one sees what people mean by them—but they aren't strictly true as they stand.' But the implausibility of this position matters less than how Berkeley would have to defend it. He would have to say that 'I see the man I saw an hour ago' mainly reports what my visual fields were like now and an hour ago, and peripherally adds some extra detail which in the careless vernacular is summed up in the claim that I saw 'the same man' on both occasions. The content which Berkeley would thus relegate to the periphery, however, could hardly be sketched in less than fifteen pages, and that is too much to treat as a mere scatter of limbs and outward flourishes around the Berkeleian core. In short, the approach which I have guessed Berkeley would take to this problem—and which he does take to related ones—vastly underestimates the weight and complexity, and thus the centrality, of those aspects of ordinary speech and thought which prima facie conflict with idealism.

The second difficulty is this: I cannot 'perceive' an idea which someone else 'perceives'; so either I never perceive a whole object but only 'my share of it', i.e. those members of it which occur in my mind, or objects are not interpersonally perceivable. Either way, idealism conflicts with ordinary speech and thought.[21]

Berkeley does grapple with this one. When Hylas asks 'Does it not follow from your principles that no two can see the same thing?', Philonous replies:

If the term *same* be taken in the vulgar acceptation, it is certain (and not at all repugnant to the principles I maintain) that different persons may perceive the same thing; or the same thing or idea exist in different minds. . . . But if the term *same* be used in the acceptation of philosophers, who pretend to an abstracted notion of identity, then, according to their sundry definitions of this notion (for it is not yet agreed wherein that philosophic identity consists), it may or may not be possible for divers people to perceive the same thing. But whether philosophers shall think fit to call a thing the *same* or no, is, I conceive, of small importance.[22]

Philonous adds, in effect, that we may say 'You and I see the same thing' meaning 'Our visual fields are alike', or we may say 'You and I cannot see the same thing' meaning 'You and I, since we are distinct from one another, cannot share a visual field'. This, he thinks, is the end of the matter:

Who sees not that all the dispute is about a word? to wit, whether what is perceived by different persons, may yet have the term *same* applied to it? . . . Suppose a house, whose walls . . . remaining unaltered, the chambers are all pulled down, and new ones built in their place; and that you should call this the *same*, and I should say it was not the *same* house . . . Would not all the difference consist in a sound?[23]

I suppose that 'philosophers who pretend to an abstracted notion of identity' are ones who would say: '*x* would ordinarily be said to be the same as *y*, but is *x* really the same as *y*?'; or 'Never mind how "same" is normally used—I want to know the true meaning of "same"' or '. . . I want to know what sameness really is'. The word 'abstracted' gratuitously drags Locke into this unattractive camp, but Berkeley's point itself is a sound one.

He draws from it, though, the moral that once the facts are agreed on there remains only a negligible verbal quibble, a dispute about 'a sound'. That does not follow, for the residual

---

[21] See D. Braybrooke, 'Berkeley on the Numerical Identity of Ideas', *Philosophical Review*, vol. 64 (1955).

[22] *Third Dialogue*, p. 247.   [23] *Third Dialogue*, p. 248.

'verbal' dispute, far from being trivial, may be a serious conceptual disagreement with philosophical consequences depending on it. Otherwise we could deflate Berkeley's attack on the veil-of-perception doctrine by saying: 'The doctrine lacks empirical content; so the dispute cannot concern the facts, and must therefore be merely verbal.' In fact, Berkeley rightly takes some 'verbal' questions seriously:

HYLAS: I own indeed, the inferences you draw me into, sound something oddly; but common language, you know, is framed by, and for the use of the vulgar: we must not therefore wonder, if expressions adapted to exact philosophic notions, seem uncouth and out of the way. PHILONOUS: Is it come to that? I assure you, I imagine myself to have gained no small point, since you make so light of departing from common phrases and opinions; it being a main part of our inquiry, to examine whose notions are widest of the common road, and most repugnant to the general sense of the world.[24]

Berkeley could defend his off-hand dismissal of the dispute about 'same' by maintaining that although some disputes about words are not trivial this particular one is. In support of this he may—and I think he would—say that it is perfectly clear (*a*) what it means to say that you and I perceive the same object, (*b*) what it means to say that we cannot, and (*c*) that it is entirely legitimate to use 'same' in either way; and similarly with 'the same house'. This brings us to the heart of Berkeley's error in the passage in question. He wants to say that strictly speaking two people cannot perceive the same thing, and to regard 'You and I see the same thing' as, though all right in its way, a 'vulgar' or non-theoretical use of 'same'; but he is prepared to countenance the vulgar usage because he thinks he can *easily* explain its meaning in strict or non-vulgar terms. That is why he is impatient with this debate—as one might be impatient with an argument over whether two people can have 'the same nasty experience'.

Well, Berkeley may think it easy, but he gets it wrong. His reference to 'the uniformness of what [is] perceived' implies an equation of 'You and I see the same thing' with 'Your present visual field is uniform with, or similar to, mine'. The latter is neither necessary nor sufficient for the truth of the 'vulgar' statement 'You and I see the same thing', and its analogues for the other senses are equally wide of the mark. To replace them by

[24] *First Dialogue*, pp. 182–3.

something viable, Berkeley would have to cope with complexities which would forbid him to dismiss this matter with a wave of the hand.

In short, Berkeley assumes that certain ordinary locutions which seem to conflict with his theory can be easily explained in terms of it; but this is because he has grossly underestimated the complexity of the vulgar concept of 'perceived by two people', and of the facts which that concept is designed to handle, which in its turn implies an underestimate of the concept's importance to us in our intellectual handling of our data. One symptom of this underestimate is the fact that Berkeley, while trying to stand back from the notion of 'perceived by two people', unwittingly helps himself to it when he scoffs at the dispute about 'whether *what is perceived by different persons,* may yet have the term *same* applied to it'.

In the strict Berkeleian theory, then, a 'collection' of ideas which constitutes a single object must be restricted to ideas which (1) all occur at the same time, and (2) all occur in the same mind. We now shrink the 'collection' still further.

The third difficulty is as follows. If what I see must be a visual idea, and what I touch a tactual idea, then what I see cannot be what I touch. Generalizing the point: two ideas belonging to different senses cannot be members of a single object-constituting collection, even if they occur in one mind at one time. This finally reduces Berkeley's sensible things to 'collections of ideas' which are so poverty-stricken that they can hardly contain more than one member each.

Here again Berkeley has two options. He could say (i) that what I *see* is not the whole of an object but only its visual part, i.e. the visual members of the collection; or he might (ii) stand by his thesis that we do not 'immediately perceive by sight any-thing but light and colours and figures' etc., and treat 'I saw it and heard it' as a vulgar locution which can be explained in terms of strict Berkeleian theory but has no place in it. As we have already seen, Berkeley takes option (ii): since 'in truth and strictness, nothing can be heard but sound', it follows that if I (as we should vulgarly say) 'hear a coach' which I neither touch nor see, 'the coach is not then properly perceived by sense, but suggested from experience'.[25]

[25] *First Dialogue,* p. 204.

Berkeley does not say that the coach we hear is distinct from any coach we might touch or see, but rather says that we do not hear the coach. He is assuming, not unnaturally, that if the phrase 'the coach' is to be connected with only some of the senses which would commonly be thought relevant, sight and touch have a stronger claim than hearing. In short, Berkeley takes 'the coach' to be the visible and tangible coach.

Visible *and* tangible? He is not entitled to that. He ought also to draw a line between sight and touch, saying that when I (as we should vulgarly say) 'see a coach' without touching it, 'the coach is not then properly perceived by sense—is not then actually seen—but is only suggested from experience'. Or, even less attractively, he might equate 'the coach' with what is seen, and deny that strictly it can be touched—but I doubt if he would take that option.[26]

Berkeley makes things too easy for himself in the coach passage, by stressing the hearing/sight-and-touch line to the neglect of the sight/touch line. He splits 'what is heard' off from the object itself, and makes this look reasonable: both because, as noted in § 30 above, he exploits the fact that a 'sound' may be either an objective sound or an auditory sense-datum; and also—this being my present point—because he keeps us comfortable about the object itself, i.e. the coach I do not strictly hear, by representing it as a rather fully-fledged coach which can at any rate be seen and touched. In the whole passage, Berkeley's commitment to driving a wedge between sight and touch is acknowledged only once: 'When we are said to see a red-hot bar of iron, the solidity and heat of the iron are not the objects of sight.' The point about heat, like the one about sound, can be granted without much discomfort; but 'solidity' is something else again, and Berkeley avoids a crisis of confidence over this point only by whisking it past the reader's eyes so quickly that it is hardly noticed. Also, as well as being too skimpy, the remark is misleading: granted that the solidity is not an object of sight, is the tangible bar of iron an object of sight? If it is, how can it also be an object of touch? If it is not, let Berkeley say so—not just in the safer context of the *New Theory of Vision*, where the point is indeed stressed, but also here in the context of an attempt to argue for outright idealism.

[26] See *New Theory of Vision*, § 46.

Here as before, though, the main point is not the implausibility of Berkeley's claim that 'I saw it and touched it' belongs to the not-strictly-true fringe of our language, but rather the inadequacy of his account of how the periphery relates to the centre. Option (i) would have required him to state criteria for the strict truth of 'I saw it and touched it', and option (ii) confronts him with essentially the same task: he must explain in 'strict' idealist terms what such vulgar locutions mean, or else lose his complacency over their apparent conflict with his theory.

Just to keep the pressure up, it is worth noticing that Berkeley himself *uses* these vulgar locutions, and indeed uses them to recommend his theory:

Is it not a sufficient evidence to me of the existence of this *glove*, that I see it, and feel it, and wear it?[27]

The table I write on, I say, exists, that is, I see and feel it.[28]

If at table all who were present should see, and smell, and taste, and drink wine, and find the effects of it, with me there could be no doubt of its reality.[29]

It is essential that Berkeley elucidate these remarks, but how can he do so?

In the 'coach' passage he says only that ideas of two senses are ordinarily said to be of a single thing because of a 'frequently perceived connexion' between ideas of the two kinds. 'From the experience I have had that such a sound is connected with [the tactual ideas which are central to our ordinary notion of] a coach, I am said to hear the coach.'[30] This view is expressed again later:

A *cherry* . . . is nothing but a congeries of sensible impressions, or ideas perceived by various senses: which ideas are united into one thing (or have one name given them) by the mind; because they are observed to attend each other. Thus when the palate is affected with such a particular taste, the sight is affected with a red colour, the touch with roundness, softness, &c. Hence, when I see, and feel, and taste, in sundry certain manners, I am sure the *cherry* exists, or is real.[31]

This is dismally inadequate. It rules out 'I tasted one cherry while seeing another and touching a third'; and there are hosts of other

[27] *Second Dialogue*, p. 224.
[28] *Principles* § 3.
[29] *Principles* § 84.
[30] *First Dialogue*, p. 204.
[31] *Third Dialogue*, p. 249.

'vulgar' locutions which, though entirely satisfactory in their own way, are belied or at least not covered by Berkeley's formula about ideas which are 'observed to attend each other'.

So, here as in the earlier cases, Berkeley assumes that a certain kind of vulgar locution can easily be expressed in terms of his theory; but he is wholly wrong about this; and so he is not entitled to claim that his theory expresses the clean, hard core of our language about the things we perceive.

34. *Appearance and reality*

We distinguish what is really the case in one's own immediate environment from what appears to be the case going by what one sees, feels, hears etc.; we allow that one may err about what an object is like on the basis of one's 'ideas' of it. This distinction seems to have no place in Berkeley's theory, for *there* a perceived object turns out to be a single idea, and Berkeley does not think one can err about the ideas one actually has. Here is his attempt to deal with this problem:

HYLAS: Since, according to you, men judge of the reality of things by their senses, how can a man be mistaken in thinking . . . an oar, with one end in the water, crooked? PHILONOUS: He is not mistaken with regard to the ideas he actually perceives; but in the inferences he makes from his present perceptions. . . . What he immediately perceives by sight is certainly crooked; and so far he is in the right. But if he thence conclude, that upon taking the oar out of the water he shall perceive the same crookedness; or that it would affect his touch, as crooked things are wont to do: in that he is mistaken. . . . But his mistake lies not in what he perceives immediately and at present (it being a manifest contradiction to suppose he should err in respect of that) but in the wrong judgment he makes concerning the ideas he apprehends to be connected with those immediately perceived: or concerning the ideas that, from what he perceives at present, he imagines would be perceived in other circumstances.[32]

This, apart from its claim that the man does perceive something crooked (see § 5 above), is unexceptionable. It raises a problem for Berkeley, though. His sketch of the ordinary distinction between 'the oar's real shape' and 'the oar's apparent shape' is acceptable because, and only because, it explains 'The oar is

[32] *Third Dialogue*, p. 238.

crooked' as a false statement about what ideas would be had if certain conditions obtained; but if conditionals enter into the analysis of 'The oar is crooked' when this is false, they must also enter into its analysis when it is true. So Berkeley here commits himself to a phenomenalistic account of the whole vulgar distinction between 'apparently F' and 'really F'.

Now, Berkeley has a decision to make about this distinction, or about the locutions which embody it. Are they to be (i) part of his theory, or (ii) relegated to the periphery—treated as permissible but unstrict idioms which a careful speaker might prefer to avoid? If Berkeley takes option (ii), then 'seen twice' and 'seen by both of us' and 'seen and touched' are joined on the periphery by '(not) really crooked'. But this last is on a continuum with '(not) really an oar': if the conditional element in 'The oar looks bent but isn't really' makes this statement a mere *façon de parler*, then the same goes for 'There appears to be an oar here but really there isn't' and for 'Not only does there appear to be an oar here, but there really is one'. This would commit Berkeley to saying not that Locke's theory mis-handles the distinction between appearance and reality, but rather that there is no such distinction, or at least none that is central to our thought and language. This is too much. Berkeley claims that his philosophy does justice to all our central beliefs about objects, e.g. that the 'sensible things' of his theory are the tables and mountains of daily life. Furthermore, as we shall see in Chapter VII, idealism's supposed ability to handle the appearance/reality distinction is reckoned by Berkeley as one of its chief merits. It would be intolerable if his 'sensible things' turned out after all to be of such a kind that any having of an idea was the perceiving of a sensible thing. On the other hand, if Berkeley takes option (i), and allows into his theory of 'sensible things' the implications of the quoted analysis of 'not really crooked', then that analysis is a Trojan horse which will smuggle phenomenalism into the city.

When Berkeley says 'The more a man knows of the connexion of ideas, the more he is said to know of the nature of things',[33] we have his dilemma in a nutshell. If (i) he takes what 'is said' into his own theory, then his account of sensible things becomes thoroughly phenomenalistic. If (ii) what 'is said' is excluded from his theory, then the latter omits *all* the core of our talk about 'the

[33] *Third Dialogue*, p. 245.

nature of things', right down to our talk about what things there really are.

This time, Berkeley chooses (i) inconsistency rather than (ii) bankruptcy. Although his official account of 'sensible things' is thoroughly idealist, he moves towards phenomenalism when discussing 'real things'. He does not think there are two sorts of things—sensible and real—but he uses 'real' when discussing the difference between genuine perception on the one hand and dreams, hallucinations, etc., on the other. In the rest of this section, I shall examine Berkeley's theory of 'real things'.

It starts from the fact, of which Locke also made much, that some of our ideas are forced upon us whether we like it or not:

I find I can excite ideas in my mind at pleasure, and vary and shift the scene as oft as I think fit. . . . But whatever power I may have over my own thoughts, I find the ideas actually perceived by sense have not a like dependence on my will. When in broad day-light I open my eyes, it is not in my power to choose whether I shall see or no, or to determine what particular objects shall present themselves to my view; and so likewise as to the hearing and other senses, the ideas imprinted on them are not creatures of my will. There is therefore some other will or spirit that produces them.[34]

The last sentence introduces an argument for God's existence which I shall discuss in Chapter VII. My present concern is with Berkeley's use of passivity to explain what 'real things' are. It would be absurdly implausible to say that every idea which comes to one unbidden is a (perception of) a real thing, for many dreams and hallucinations are clear cases to the contrary. Nor does Berkeley say that. Rather, he equates 'real things' with a sub-class of involuntary ideas:

The ideas imprinted on the senses by the Author of Nature are called *real things* . . . The ideas of sense are allowed to have more reality in them [than the ideas of imagination], that is, to be more strong, orderly, and coherent than the creatures of the mind . . . They are also less dependent on the spirit, or thinking substance which perceives them, in that they are excited by the will of another and more powerful spirit.[35]

A preliminary difficulty: Berkeley does not define 'idea of sense', and no definition could entirely legitimize his use of the phrase.

---

[34] *Principles* §§ 28–9.   [35] *Principles* § 33.

The point is not vital, and the reasons are complex, so I shall merely say dogmatically that we had better construe Berkeley not as using 'idea of sense' to explain '(idea of) a real thing', but rather as introducing both expressions together: 'There is a class of ideas which are strong, orderly and involuntary. These are called "ideas of sense". They are also, perhaps more interestingly, called "real things".'

Now we can approach the main problem raised by the passage. Berkeley here purports to be *adding* something to a theory according to which all we perceive 'in truth and strictness' are ideas. This theory denies that we strictly see anything we touch; it puritanically banishes from the mainland of our language of perception anything involving 'reason and memory'; and so on through all the other features of the theory which commit it to equating sensible things with single ideas rather than with collections of them. In the quoted passage Berkeley does not retract any of that. Rather, he claims to be describing a sub-class of ideas, each member of which is (the idea of) a real thing; as though the upshot were just the original sensible-things theory with a certain refinement added to mark off real sensible things from hallucinations and the like.

But consider what the 'refinement' is! Wanting to know whether a certain idea is (of) a real thing, I ask Berkeley for help. He tells me to discover whether the idea came to me unbidden, and whether it is 'strong' (he also says 'vivid', 'distinct', lively'); and I report that it passes both these tests. Berkeley rightly thinks that that is not enough: ideas count as (ideas of) real things, he says, only if they are also 'orderly and coherent', 'regular', 'constant', 'steady', 'not excited at random', 'connected'.[36] But *these expressions cannot intelligibly be applied to a single idea*. To bring them to bear on a present visual idea of mine, I must consider whether that idea—together with other past (and future? and possible?) ideas, of visual (and other?) kinds, had by myself (and other people?)—forms a pattern or sequence or set of ideas which is orderly, regular and so on. Whatever Berkeley does about the issues raised in those parentheses, he must concede that 'I now perceive a real thing' partly concerns my present idea's relations with ideas which I am not now having. So after all he has to agree that a certain kind of perception-

[36] All from *Principles* §§ 30, 33, and *Third Dialogue*, p. 235.

statement, which he does not relegate to the 'vulgar' periphery, involves considerations of 'reason and memory', of what is 'suggested to the mind' rather than sensorily present to it.[37] He has been forced into phenomenalism by the sheer pressure of his need to cope with the distinction between appearance and reality.

The clash between Berkeley's analysis of 'real thing' and the rest of his theory can be brought out by considering his thesis that no object can exist while unperceived. The only reasons Berkeley has for denying that an object can exist while not perceived are ones which depend upon 'An object is a collection of ideas, and so can exist only so long as its constituent members exist, i.e. are had or perceived'. But this is no longer available to him. It implies that, in a case where I perceive an object at t, an account of *what* I perceive can be given without going outside my sensory state at t; and that has been thrown overboard by the analysis of 'real thing'.

[37] See R. H. Popkin, 'The New Realism of Bishop Berkeley', Pepper pp. 14–16.

VII

BERKELEY ON GOD AND SCEPTICISM

35. *The passivity argument*

WE have briefly met an argument of Berkeley's for the existence of God, which I shall call the passivity argument. It goes like this:

(*a*) My ideas of sense come into my mind without being caused to do so by any act of my will;

(*b*) The occurrence of any idea must be caused by an act of the will of some being in whose mind the idea occurs;

therefore

(*c*) My ideas of sense occur in the mind of, and are caused by acts of the will of, some being other than myself.

This argument uses the dubious notion of an 'act of the will', and presupposes that only wills can be causes; but I defer discussion of these points until Chapter VIII. Also, the argument's conclusion falls short of theism, let alone Christian monotheism; but that is a matter of routine apologetics which I shall not discuss at all.[1]

The present chapter will be entirely exegetical. To understand Berkeley's writings one must disentangle certain strands in his thought which are not properly separated in any commentary I have seen. The passivity argument is involved in all this in several ways. Most immediately, it raises a small question which can serve as one end of a thread which will lead us through the tangle.

The question is this: why does Berkeley assume that every change of sensory state must have some cause, disregarding the possibility that an 'idea of sense' might just happen without any cause? Perhaps Berkeley is one of those who find it self-evident that every 'Why?'-question has an answer, that whatever happens is caused to happen. Warnock sees him like this:

---

[1] See Thomson, 'G. J. Warnock's *Berkeley*', p. 429 n.; R. H. Hurlbutt, 'Berkeley's Theology', Pepper; *Principles* §§ 57, 72, 151.

The true foundation of his view is, I believe, the conviction that to hold that events merely *occur*, without any purpose and volition behind them or anything analogous with purpose and volition, is to say something which is really quite *unintelligible*.[2]

This is mildly confirmed by a passage where, from the premiss that certain ideas 'are not creatures of my will', Berkeley moves *straight* to the conclusion that 'There is therefore some other will or spirit that produces them'.[3]

Later, though, Berkeley makes that same move through a lemma:

Those things which are called the works of Nature, that is, the far greater part of the ideas or sensations perceived by us, are not produced by, or dependent on the wills of men. There is therefore some other spirit that causes them, since it is repugnant that they should subsist by themselves.[4]

The last clause of this offers a reason why every idea must be caused by a spirit, namely that ideas cannot 'subsist by themselves'. In Berkeley's normal usage this would mean that ideas cannot exist without being had by someone: that is a point about the ownership, not the causation, of ideas, and it does not imply that every idea must be caused. Still, Berkeley does here offer an argument, albeit an invalid one.

Yet Warnock may well be right, for Berkeley could be gratuitously offering argumentative support for something which he does not seriously regard as needing it. Whether or not Berkeley attached weight to it, however, the argument is structurally interesting. I have accused Berkeley of treating 'Ideas cannot subsist by themselves'—by which he usually means 'Ideas must be owned'—as though it entailed 'Ideas must be caused'; but how could he have made so gross a mistake? If the only answer is: 'Philosophers do make mistakes, and this was one of Berkeley's', then this non-sequitur is about twice as bad, twice as crude and abrupt and unstructured, as anything else in the *Principles*. Fortunately, there is another answer. Without validating the argument, it renders Berkeley's acceptance of it intelligible.

Consider the following hypothesis: Berkeley frequently uses 'depend' and its cognates to express relations between ideas and

[2] Warnock, *Berkeley*, p. 123.   [3] *Principles* § 29.
[4] *Principles* § 146.

minds or spirits; in some of these uses '*I* depends on *S*' means '*I* is had by *S*', in others it means '*I* is caused by *S*'; and Berkeley is never aware of this ambiguity.[5]

If this is true, then we can explain Berkeley's non-sequitur. The clue is his saying that some ideas 'are not produced by, or dependent on' the wills of men. The word 'will' points to causation; but it does not entirely insulate 'dependent' from an interpretation in terms of ownership rather than causation, because for Berkeley 'wills' and 'spirits' are not two sorts of item—both words refer to thinking substances, the former stressing their capacity to act and the latter their capacity to perceive. If my hypothesis about Berkeley's use of 'depend' etc. is right, then we can diagnose his non-sequitur as follows. From a premiss which he does have:

Some ideas are not dependent upon (= caused by) any human mind,

together with another premiss which he does have:

Every idea is dependent upon (= had by) some mind,

he slides to the conclusion he wants:

Some ideas are dependent upon (= caused by) some non-human mind.

It does not matter whether this diagnosis is correct. It does matter whether the underlying hypothesis is true, and I now proceed to prove that it is.

36. *Berkeley's uses of 'depend'*

I have to show that Berkeley uses 'depend on' etc. ambiguously as between 'owned by' and 'caused by', and that he is unaware of this ambiguity. Some generous collaborators in Cambridge have possessed me of every occurrence of 'depend' and its cognates throughout the *Principles* and *Dialogues*. The facts are as follows.

There is an unclassifiable use of 'dependent' in Berkeley's account of number.[6] In half a dozen places 'depend' is used logically: one theory depends upon another, a difficulty depends upon a prejudice, and so on. In a dozen others the items whose

[5] The ambiguity has been noted by Day, 'George Berkeley', p. 448; and by D. Grey, 'The Solipsism of Bishop Berkeley', *Philosophy*, vol. 2 (1952), p. 344.

[6] *Principles* § 12.

'dependence' is spoken of are not ideas: God is independent of everything, we are dependent on God, and so on. And in three places Berkeley unclearly uses 'depend' etc. when putting words in Locke's mouth rather than expressing his own views.[7] None of these occurrences is relevant to my hypothesis. Of the remainder, all but four fall squarely—and with alarming symmetry—into one or other of two classes.

THE OWNERSHIP USES. On eight occasions Berkeley uses 'independent', 'dependent' (once) and 'independency' (once) to say something about the ownership of ideas.[8] In these passages, an idea's independence of a mind is its not occurring in that mind, and the question of what causes it is simply not raised.

THE CAUSATION USES. On eight other occasions Berkeley uses 'depend' etc. in discussing what causes ideas to be had by minds.[9] In these passages, an idea's 'independence' of a given mind is its not being caused, or willed into existence, by that mind. The ownership sense is positively excluded in most of these cases, where an idea is said *not* to depend upon a mind in which it *does* occur.

So the ambiguity is there. Is Berkeley aware of it? Is his silence about it due merely to his having no reason to remark upon the ambiguity because nothing in his works in any way involves it? No, for something in his works does involve it (the italics are mine):

Men knowing they perceived several ideas, whereof they themselves were not the authors, as not being excited from within, nor *depending on* the operation of their wills, this made them maintain, those ideas or objects of perception had an existence *independent of*, and without the mind, without ever dreaming that a contradiction was involved in those words.[10]

This alleges that a contradiction has been inferred from a true premiss, by an argument which must therefore be deemed invalid. The flaw in the argument, as stated, is that in the premiss 'not depending on' means 'not caused by', while in the conclusion 'independent of' means 'not owned or "perceived" by'. But

---

[7] *Principles* § 10; *Dialogues*, pp. 205, 216.
[8] *Principles* §§ 6, 89, 91; *Dialogues*, pp. 195, 200 (twice), 213, 261.
[9] *Principles* §§ 26, 29, 33, 106; *Dialogues*, pp. 196 (twice), 214, 235.
[10] *Principles* § 56.

Berkeley, fond as he is of diagnosing his opponents' errors, does not remark on this ambiguity. His failure to point it out, even when actively engaged in criticizing a fallacy which it may have helped to engender, irresistibly suggests that Berkeley is totally unaware of the ambiguity as a potential source of danger.

My hypothesis that Berkeley was unaware of the ambiguity is also supported by my use of it in § 35 above. The hypothesis lets us explain something which is otherwise inexplicable, namely Berkeley's gross move from 'cannot subsist by themselves' to 'must be caused'; and this fact is evidence for the hypothesis. There is no circularity in this.

I mentioned four relevant occurrences of 'depend' etc. which I excluded from my two-part classification; and we should keep track of these. One is the occurrence of 'dependent on' in the version of the passivity argument discussed in § 35, and a second is the occurrence of 'depending on' and 'independent of' in the passage last quoted. These stand outside my classification because they *involve* the ambiguity. The third unclassified occurrence is in a widely misunderstood passage which I shall discuss in § 39; and the fourth is in another of Berkeley's arguments for God's existence, to which I now turn.

37. *The continuity argument*

The famous limericks about 'the sycamore tree in the quad', like most commentaries, imply that Berkeley also argued for God's existence like this:

(*a*) No collection of ideas can exist when not perceived by some spirit;

(*b*) Objects are collections of ideas;

(*c*) Objects sometimes exist when not perceived by any human spirit;

therefore

(*d*) There is a non-human spirit which sometimes perceives objects.

The continuity argument, as I shall call it, proves nothing, if only because its idealist premiss (*b*) is false. Also, its conclusion is very weak. If (*c*) were replaced by a stronger premiss expressing the

whole content of the plain man's assumptions about the continuity of objects, a stronger conclusion would follow; but it
would still not be Christian monotheism. These points, however,
are not my main concern.

Why does Berkeley think he is entitled to premiss (c)? The
idealism expressed in (b) implies that nobody could have empirical
evidence for the existence of an object at a time when no human
perceives it, and this implication seems too obvious to be overlooked.[11] It has been suggested to me that an idealist might
accept (c) on grounds of simplicity, i.e. on the grounds that our
account of what things there are and how they behave runs more
smoothly if we postulate that objects can and usually do exist
during the gaps in our perceptions of them. But I can find no
evidence of Berkeley's favouring this line of thought, and it
would have been out of character if he had. I suggest, indeed,
that he would have been bound to regard the 'simplicity' defence
of (c) as a mere confusion between truth and convenience.[12] To
see that it could be more than that, one needs a deeper theory of
meaning than Berkeley ever had. So the puzzle remains.

A solution to it is found when we see how Berkeley words the
continuity argument:

HYLAS: Supposing you were annihilated, cannot you conceive it
possible, that things perceivable by sense may still exist? PHILONOUS: I
can; but then it must be in another mind. When I deny sensible things
an existence out of the mind, I do not mean my mind in particular,
but all minds. Now it is plain they have an existence exterior to my
mind, since I find them by experience to be independent of it. There is
therefore some other mind wherein they exist, during the intervals
between the times of my perceiving them: as likewise they did before
my birth, and would do after my supposed annihilation.[13]

The last two sentences of this, I suggest, exploit the ambiguity
of 'independent'. Berkeley takes the premiss that some ideas are
independent of (not caused by) my mind, muddles himself into
treating it as the premiss that some ideas are independent of (not
owned by) my mind, and so infers that some mind has ideas when

---

[11] See W. R. Dennes, 'Berkeley's Dilemma', Pepper p. 184; G. D. Hicks, *Berkeley*
(London, 1932), pp. 130–1.

[12] See A. Myerscough, 'Berkeley and the Proofs for the Existence of God',
Studies in Philosophy and the History of Philosophy, vol. 1 (1961), pp. 69–70.

[13] *Third Dialogue*, pp. 230–1.

I do not. How else could we explain his saying that 'I find by experience' that some ideas are 'exterior' to my mind in a sense which implies their existing 'during the intervals between the times of my perceiving them'. The mistake is a bad one anyway; but my diagnosis shows how it could represent not childish incompetence but rather Berkeley's falling into a trap laid by his own terminology.

When this is combined with the diagnosis of the passivity argument in § 35 above, a pleasing pattern emerges. Berkeley's basic tenets allow that (1) every idea is owned by some mind, and that (2) some ideas are not caused by my mind. The ambiguity of 'depend' etc. lets him interchange 'owned' and 'caused' without noticing that he is doing so. By putting 'caused' for 'owned' in (1), he steals the premiss he needs for the passivity argument; and by putting 'owned' for 'caused' in (2), he steals the premiss he needs for the continuity argument.

Explanations like these could not account fully for Berkeley's holding, as a matter of settled belief, any views to which he is not entitled; and I do not claim that they do. In most versions of the passivity argument Berkeley assumes without argument that what is not caused by my mind must have some other cause. Warnock is probably right in his conjecture that Berkeley held the principle 'Every happening is caused' as an unchallengeable axiom. This would create no conflict with his basic position, and would align him with the majority of philosophers up to his time.

What of the continuity argument? Idealism is consistent with the thesis that objects exist when no human perceives them, but it clamours for the latter to be justified. My point about 'depend' explains Berkeley's attempt to justify the thesis in one short passage, but it cannot explain his adopting it as a permanent intellectual possession. What *can* explain this?

Nothing; for there is no such fact to be explained. Berkeley does not regularly assume that objects exist when no human perceives them; he is not much interested in whether they do; and the continuity argument, which assumes that they do, is absent from the *Principles* and occurs in the *Dialogues* only in the two-sentence passage which I have quoted. That passage is right out of line with everything else Berkeley says about the continuity of objects, and should be dismissed as a momentary aberration.

These are unorthodox claims. Compare them, for example, with Warnock's view of the matter:

Berkeley . . . knows that any plain man would insist that the furniture in an unoccupied room actually does exist, not merely that it would exist if the room were occupied; and he himself thinks that it would be merely absurd to question this.[14]

This is the standard view. Let us test it against what Berkeley actually wrote.

38. *Berkeley's indifference to continuity*

Berkeley's first published reference to the 'continuity' issue, by which I mean the question of whether objects can exist when no human perceives them, is in his declaration:

that . . . all those bodies which compose the mighty frame of the world, have not any subsistence without a mind, that their being is to be perceived or known; that consequently so long as they are not actually perceived by me, or do not exist in my mind or that of any other created spirit, they must either have no existence at all, or else subsist in the mind of some eternal spirit.[15]

These are not the words of one who would add: 'Objects do exist when not perceived by creatures, so there must indeed be an eternal spirit which perceives them.' The natural continuation is rather: 'Unless we can show independently that there is an eternal spirit, we do not know that objects exist when not perceived by creatures.'[16]

The main textual evidence, however, must be presented in the light of Berkeley's theory of 'real things' and of 'reality'. Against a certain charge of scepticism Berkeley defends himself strenuously and often, saying that his system does not detract from the 'reality' of things, and explaining 'reality' in terms of strength, order and involuntariness (see § 34 above). Just as a reminder:

---

[14] Warnock, *Berkeley*, p. 115. See also ibid. p. 125; T. E. Jessop in *The Works of George Berkeley*, vol. 2, p. 81 n.; I. Hedenius, *Sensationalism and Theology in Berkeley's Philosophy* (Oxford, 1936), pp. 122-3; A. A. Luce, 'Berkeley's Existence in the Mind', Martin pp. 291-2; K. Marc-Wogau, 'Berkeley's Sensationalism and the *Esse est Percipi* Principle', Martin p. 325 (also in Engle).

[15] *Principles* § 6.

[16] Cf. A. A. Luce, *The Dialectic of Immaterialism* (London, 1963), p. 184.

The ideas imprinted on the senses by the Author of Nature are called *real things*. . . . The ideas of sense are allowed to have more reality in them, that is, to be more strong, orderly, and coherent than the creatures of the mind. They are also less dependent on the spirit, or thinking substance which perceives them, in that they are excited by the will of another and more powerful spirit.[17]

This is wholly in the region of the passivity argument: it concerns ideas which exist although not caused by me, and has nothing to do with ideas which exist when not had by me.

Berkeley keeps to this. As we follow him through, we shall find that: (*a*) his text sustains a surprisingly sharp distinction between strength/order/involuntariness on the one hand and existence-when-not-perceived-by-humans on the other; (*b*) he is remarkably faithful to his official account of 'reality', always defining 'real' in terms of the strength etc. of ideas which one *does* have, and thus positively divorcing the reality question from the continuity question; (*c*) his reiterated claim that he can do justice to the 'reality' of things is stressed and valued, as his answer to a serious accusation and as his basis for an important argument for God's existence; and (*d*) whenever he remarks that his principles permit continuity, the temperature is always low— Berkeley does not attach weight to this point, either as philosophical defence or as theological attack.

Here is Berkeley taking seriously the charge of scepticism:

It will be objected that by the foregoing principles, all that is real and substantial in Nature is banished out of the world . . . All things that exist, exist only in the mind, that is, they are purely notional. What therefore . . . must we think of houses, rivers, mountains, trees, stones . . . ? Are all these but so many chimeras and illusions on the fancy? To all which . . . I answer, that by the principles premised, we are not deprived of any one thing in Nature. Whatever we see, feel, hear, or any wise conceive or understand, remains as secure as ever, and is as real as ever. There is a *rerum natura*, and the distinction between realities and chimeras retains its full force. This is evident from *Sect*. 29, 30 and 33, where we have shewn what is meant by *real things* in opposition to *chimeras*, or ideas of our own framing.[18]

The question of 'reality' is here referred back to earlier sections where the matter has been discussed solely in terms of strength, order and involuntariness. Throughout sections 30 to 44, indeed,

[17] *Principles* § 33.   [18] *Principles* § 34.

Berkeley discusses 'reality', 'chimeras' and scepticism not only without mentioning continuity but positively forcing it aside by discussing only the strength etc. of ideas which humans do have.

Berkeley's next four sections (45–8) do concern continuity. He introduces this as a new issue: 'Fourthly, it will be objected that from the foregoing principles it follows, things are every moment annihilated and created anew' (45); and later (48) he refers back to 'the objection proposed in *Sect*. 45' not to 'the objection discussed throughout the past fifteen or more sections.' Now let us see what happens in the sections on continuity.

Berkeley is accused of implying that 'things are every moment annihilated and created anew . . . Upon shutting my eyes all the furniture in the room is reduced to nothing, and barely upon opening them it is again created.' Rather then replying 'Of course that would be absurd, but I am not committed to it', Berkeley counter-attacks:

If [my accuser] can conceive it possible either for his ideas or their archetypes to exist without being perceived, then I give up the cause: but if he cannot, he will acknowledge it is unreasonable for him to stand up in defence of he knows not what, and pretend to charge on me as an absurdity, the not assenting to those propositions which at bottom have no meaning in them.[19]

Only after arguing through two over-ingenious sections that 'the materialists themselves' are committed to the intermittency of objects does Berkeley remark that he is not thus committed:

For though we hold indeed the objects of sense to be nothing else but ideas which cannot exist unperceived; yet we may not hence conclude they have no existence except only while they are perceived by us, since there may be some other spirit that perceives them, though we do not. Wherever bodies are said to have no existence without the mind, I would not be understood to mean this or that particular mind, but all minds whatsoever. It does not therefore follow from the foregoing principles, that bodies are annihilated and created every moment, or exist not at all during the intervals between our perception of them.[20]

The crucial expressions are 'we may not hence *conclude*', 'there *may* be some other spirit', 'it does not therefore *follow*'. There is no hint of Berkeley's thinking that his accusers are right, or that

---

[19] *Principles* § 45.   [20] *Principles* § 48.

it is important to him to show that he can consistently agree with them, about the continuity of objects.

He does not even say anything like this: 'My accusers have no grounds for their correct belief that objects are continuous. My principles show that the belief can be justified only on theological grounds; in a way, it is itself a covertly theological belief. I wonder how my materialistic opponents like that!' That would be one version of the continuity argument; it cries out to be used by any idealist who thinks that objects are continuous or even respects the common belief that they are; and this is the place for it. But apart from the brief lapse which I discussed in § 37 above, Berkeley nowhere shows the slightest inclination to argue in such a way.

There remains a problem about Berkeley's sections 45–48. He starts by implying that the common view about continuity is one of 'those propositions which at bottom have no meaning in them', and ends by saying that the view is consistent with his principles—which implies that it has meaning in it after all. I shall explain this in § 40 below; but isn't it clear already that no explanation is likely to help the standard account?

Among those who attribute to Berkeley a care for the continuity of objects, a few have at least noticed that these sections of the *Principles* need some explaining.[21] Others have been less cautious, including one who writes: 'It would, [Berkeley] says, be absurd to suggest that "things are every moment annihilated and created anew".'[22] The quoted clause comes from the section in which, as we have seen, Berkeley elaborately refrains from calling the suggestion absurd and flings the charge of absurdity back into the faces of his accusers.

Moving on now, we find Berkeley later denying that he has so emptied the universe as to be in conflict with holy writ, and argues entirely from 'this business of *real* and *imaginary* [which] hath been already so plainly and fully explained'.[23] These sections,

---

[21] G. D. Hicks, *Berkeley* (London, 1932), p. 136; A. A. Luce, 'Berkeley's Existence in the Mind', Martin p. 290 n.; A. A. Luce, *Berkeley's Immaterialism* (London, 1945), pp. 120–2.

[22] Warnock, *Berkeley*, p. 115. See also F. Bender, *George Berkeley's Philosophy Reexamined* (Amsterdam, 1946), p. 69; A. C. Fraser, *Berkeley* (Edinburgh, 1909), p. 87; E. A. Sillem, *George Berkeley and the Proofs for the Existence of God* (London, 1957), p. 132.

[23] *Principles* § 84.

and the earlier ones to which they explicitly refer back, all concern involuntariness, order, etc., with not a word about objects' existing when not perceived by created spirits.

The only other reference to continuity in the *Principles* occurs in Berkeley's account of the meaning of 'external':

The things perceived by sense may be termed *external*, with regard to their origin, in that they are not generated from within, by the mind it self, but imprinted by a spirit distinct from that which perceives them. Sensible objects may likewise be said to be without the mind, in another sense, namely when they exist in some other mind. Thus when I shut my eyes, the things I saw may still exist, but it must be in another mind.[24]

'External', we might say in short-hand, may mean either 'real' or 'continuous'; but the line between the two is not smudged, for the latter is explicitly called *another* sense of 'external' (or 'without the mind'). The passage gives no support to the standard account of Berkeley's handling of continuity. He does not insist that objects are 'external' in the second sense; still less does he argue from this to any theological conclusion. Quite uncombatively, he contents himself with remarking that the things I saw *may* still exist but if they do it must be in another mind.

In short, the continuity issue—by which I always mean the issue about objects existing when not perceived by any human— receives scant attention in the *Principles*. This fact tells against the standard account, and the content of the few remarks Berkeley *does* make about continuity tells even more strongly.

What of continuity in the *Three Dialogues*? Apart from passages already mentioned, and one to be discussed in § 39 below, there is only the following difficulty which Hylas raises: 'Is it not . . . according to you plainly impossible, the Creation of any inanimate creatures should precede that of man? And is not this directly contrary to the Mosaic account?'[25] Philonous' reply is surprising: the Mosaic account is consistent with idealism because 'created beings might begin to exist in the mind of other created intelligences, beside men'. Perhaps trying to free himself from entire dependence on angels, he also toys with an essentially pheno- menalist line of thought: 'Things, with regard to us, may properly be said to begin their existence, or be created, when God decreed

---

[24] *Principles* § 90.   [25] *Third Dialogue*, p. 252.

they should become perceptible to intelligent creatures . . . You may call this a *relative*, or *hypothetical existence* if you please.'[26] The implications of this, if followed through, would clearly conflict with other parts of Berkeley's philosophy. (They would also deprive him of any chance of using the continuity argument. If O's existing can consist in the fact that if a human did such-and-such he would perceive O, then O's existing when no human perceives it does not entail that some non-human perceives it.) But that is not my present point.

What does concern me is that Philonous tries to deal with the first five days of creation in terms of angels, and of phenomenalism, but he does *not* suggest that the creation of the inanimate world might have consisted in things' coming to be perceived by God, or in ideas' coming into the mind of God. Why not? We cannot answer: 'Because that would reduce God's creation of the inanimate world to a mere conjuring up of ideas in his own mind'; for Berkeley demonstrably does allow the latter activity as a kind of creation.[27] The right answer is that Berkeley is here cramped by a specifically theological belief. The following sentences, though some appear in the text as rhetorical questions, clearly all express Berkeley's own convictions: 'God knew all things from eternity . . . Consequently they always had a being in the Divine Intellect . . . Therefore, nothing is new, or begins to be, in respect of the mind of God.'[28] Because there are no changes in God's mind, the notion of a datable creation must be construed as something other than 'coming into the mind of God' or 'coming to be perceived or imagined by God'. Hence Berkeley's struggles to find another construction.

Let us take seriously this reason for not construing the creation of the inanimate world as an act of the divine imagination, and see what it implies for the standard account. If the idea-content of God's mind is the same at any time as at any other, then God's present perceptions cannot secure the present existence of the book-case on which I have just turned my back; or, rather, God's present perceptions can secure this only if they also secure the present existence of the book-case which I destroyed three years ago, and of the one which will someday be made for my grandson out of planks cut from a tree which has not yet been planted.

[26] *Third Dialogue*, p. 253.
[27] *Philosophical Commentaries*, entry 830.   [28] *Third Dialogue*, p. 253.

We have seen that Berkeley does sometimes remark that the continuity of objects can be maintained only with help from an appropriate theology; and my concern has been only to deny the rest of the standard account—namely that Berkeley cares about object-continuity and that he accepts it as a premiss in a considered argument for God's existence. But now we see that his theology forbids him even the relaxed and unargumentative remarks which he clearly does make. If the idea-content of God's mind never changes, then no fact about God's present perceptions can imply the present existence of a given object—unless all objects are sempiternal. (There is a formally adequate escape-hatch, namely postulating that God's ideas have built-in dates, so to speak, so that we can credit God with always having the idea of my-bookcase-at-t_1, always having the idea of my-bookcase-at-t_2, and so on. But this would be totally un-Berkeleian. For one thing, it would trivialize Berkeley's picture of the continuity of an object as being secured by God's perceiving the object *while* I do not perceive it. Also, it would divorce the term 'idea' from all Berkeley's main explanations and explanatory paradigms.) What is more, just a page or two earlier Berkeley has said as much himself:

All objects are eternally known by God, or which is the same thing, have an eternal existence in his mind: but when things before imperceptible to creatures, are by a decree of God, made perceptible to them; then are they said to begin a relative existence, with respect to created minds.[29]

There is no room here for the continuity argument based on anything like a common-sense continuity premiss—i.e. a premiss which says that my suitcases do exist now although no creature perceives them, but which does not say, and indeed positively denies, that my suitcases have an eternal existence.

The main importance of this is as follows. I have asked 'How could Berkeley think he was entitled to the premiss that objects exist when not perceived by any human?', implying that he couldn't. Someone might object: 'You take too narrow a view of Berkeley's thought. He had a theology as well as a philosophy, and really did accept certain Biblical doctrines without argument, among them the Mosaic account of the creation. You may think

[29] *Third Dialogue*, p. 252.

this intellectually disreputable; but it is a fact, and if Berkeley's thought is to be understood the fact must be taken seriously.' Now, I doubt if revealed theology did penetrate Berkeley's philosophy to the extent that this implies. But if it did—if we are to give weight to Berkeley's unargued acceptance of certain theological tenets—then among the things we must give weight to is the doctrine that no changes occur in the idea-content of God's mind.

The latter doctrine is, as I have pointed out, inconsistent with remarks Berkeley does make about continuity. But if those remarks were strengthened so as to confirm the standard account, then, as has been noted by Armstrong but by no other commentator that I can find,[30] the inconsistency would be even grosser and more conspicuous; and this is another obstacle in the way of the standard account.

The Mosaic account of creation is discussed in the *Dialogues* only in the passage treated above, and in the *Principles* not at all. In the *Philosophical Commentaries* there are just four entries on the topic: one proposing a solution in terms of 'homogeneous particles', which I do not understand; another proposing to combine a 'homogeneous particles' solution with an essentially phenomenalist one; a third which merely says that the problem can be solved, but does not say how; and this: 'I may say earth, plants etc were created before Man there being other intelligences to perceive them before Man was created.'[31] The plural 'intelligences' makes it fairly clear that Berkeley is thinking of non-human, created intelligences. It looks as though, when he is in a frame of mind to take existence-when-not-perceived-by-humans *seriously*, namely a Biblical frame of mind, Berkeley is also reluctant to allow 'ideas in the mind of God' as even a possible solution.

I mentioned in passing that phenomenalism undermines the continuity argument, because it destroys the premiss that objects can exist only when perceived by some spirit. It may be worth remarking that even on a phenomenalistic basis Berkeley could have found *some* work for God to do in connexion with continuity, only it would not be the perceptual work which is

---

[30] D. M. Armstrong (ed.), *Berkeley's Philosophical Writings* (New York, 1965), p. 22.
[31] *Philosophical Commentaries*, entry 723. The other three entries are 60, 293, 339.

stressed by the standard account. According to the phenomena-list or conditionalizing analysis, the continuous existence of objects consists in the continuing truth of suitable conditionals; their truth rests on the continuation of lawlikeness or regularity in the occurrence of our ideas; and that regularity—according to Berkeley—is the work of the cause of our ideas, namely God. So the continuity of objects, on the phenomenalist account of what it involves, is secured not by God's continuing perceptions but by his dependable maintenance of order. I do not know whether this fact helps to explain anything in Berkeley's texts.

One other point about phenomenalism and God should be mentioned. If someone accepted a conditionalizing analysis of statements about the existence of objects, and also equated 'If it were the case that P, then a K idea would be had' with 'There is a K idea which would be had if it were the case that P', then *he* might think that the continuity of objects required a continual perceiver. For if that equation held, the existence of O now would require not merely the truth of a certain conditional to the effect that if it were the case that P then *I* would be had, but also the existence of *I* now; and so O could exist now only if *I* were now being had, which is to say only if O were being perceived now. And so, starting from a phenomenalist account of continuity, we reach God as a guarantor of continuity through continual per-ceptions. But of course we reach this through an equation which is quite wrong, as I argued when we first met it in § 32 above. One expositor of Berkeley credits him with a conditionalizing account of the existence of objects, *and* a firm conviction that God's continuing perceptions are needed to secure object-continuity; and he seems to think these two are consistent. The key remark is that, according to Berkeley, 'God is the home of the perceivable when it is unperceived by man',[32] which, if it expresses anything, surely expresses the mistake about conditionals which I have expounded above. I have no evidence that this mistake played any part in Berkeley's own thinking about continuity.

39. 'A false imaginary glare'

There is a passage in the Second Dialogue which is often adduced as evidence for the standard account, and indeed cited

[32] A. A. Luce, *Berkeley's Immaterialism* (London, 1945), p. 75. See also J. Collins, *The British Empiricists* (Milwaukee, 1967), p. 78.

as an occurrence of the continuity argument—i.e. the argument from the continuity of objects to the existence of a spirit who perceives objects while humans do not. I shall contest this reading of the passage in question.

Philonous asks rhetorically: 'How should those principles be entertained, that lead us to think all the visible beauty of the creation a false imaginary glare?'—he is dramatizing the charge that *his* principles imply this conclusion, not railing against Locke.[33] Hylas, by now converted to idealism as he understands it, replies stoically: 'My comfort is, you are as much a *sceptic* as I am.' Philonous denies that he is committed to scepticism, and offers a restatement of his position in the course of which he says:

To me it is evident, for the reasons you allow of, that sensible things cannot exist otherwise than in a mind or spirit. Whence I conclude, not that they have no real existence, but that seeing they depend not on my thought, and have an existence distinct from being perceived by me, *there must be some other mind wherein they exist*.[34]

Of these two sentences, the first certainly concerns the ownership of ideas. If the second does too, then the whole passage is a version of the continuity argument: objects cannot exist out of all minds, but do sometimes exist out of my mind, and must therefore sometimes exist in another mind. Even if this interpretation were right, so that the continuity argument had to be awarded four sentences in Berkeley's writings rather than two, my thesis of §§ 37–8 would be only marginally embarrassed; but in fact the interpretation is wrong.

Consider what leads up to the quoted sentences. Philonous says that his principles would oblige him to 'deny sensible things any real existence' *if* Hylas were right in taking 'the reality of sensible things' to consist in 'an *absolute existence* out of the minds of spirits'. He then continues:

But I neither said nor thought the reality of sensible things was to be defined after that manner. To me it is evident, for the reasons you allow of, that sensible things cannot exist otherwise than in a mind or spirit. Whence I conclude . . . etc.[35]

The argument is not: objects cannot exist out of all minds, yet do sometimes exist out of human minds, and must therefore sometimes exist in a non-human mind. Rather, it is that objects cannot

---

[33] *Second Dialogue*, p. 211.   [34] *Second Dialogue*, p. 212.   [35] Ibid.

exist out of all minds, but are undoubtedly real, and therefore
'real' must not be defined as 'capable of existing out of all minds'.
The ownership of ideas is relevant only because of Hylas' wrong
definition of 'real'.

I am maintaining that Philonous says 'they depend not on my
thought' as a quick way of saying 'they are real, in the correct
sense of "real" which I have explained'. (This is the last of the
four relevant occurrences of 'depend' etc. which I left unclassified
in § 36 above. I take it to be a causation use, but I did not classify
it then because the point is controversial.) Berkeley's concept of
reality, however, involves more than involuntariness, and I have
to explain why he lets Philonous omit any mention of strength
and order.

Well, this whole stretch of the Dialogue is an attempt to show
that there is something behind the veil of perception, something
whose existence does not merely consist in a set of facts about
ideas. Berkeley infers the existence of such a something, namely
God, from the existence of real things; but the existence of *some*
spiritual substance other than myself is, in Berkeley's view, entailed by the occurrence of *any* involuntary ideas, however weak
or disorderly. Details regarding wisdom, beneficence, divinity
etc. might require premisses about the (strength and) order of
some of our involuntary ideas, but the mere fact that some of our
ideas come to us unbidden is enough, for Berkeley, to show that
there is a spiritual substance other than ourselves. So the passage
as a whole can achieve its purpose by stressing involuntariness
alone, i.e. by Philonous' saying 'they depend not on my thought'
and meaning 'depend' in its causal sense.

Philonous finishes with '. . . there must be some other mind
wherein they exist'—is not this clearly a pointer towards the area
of the continuity argument? I think not. If it is, then it must be
read as meaning '. . . wherein they exist at times when they are
not in my mind', which really isn't very plausible. If we must
introduce an expansion, we can as well use '. . . wherein they
exist and which causes them'. On that reading, Berkeley's point
is that when I involuntarily have an idea I must be sharing it with
whatever spirit has caused it. This is an ownership point occurring
as a detail within an essentially causation line of thought, and
Berkeley puts it in just that way of a couple of pages further on,
when he says that since some of my ideas are involuntary 'They

must therefore exist in some other mind, whose will it is they should be exhibited to me'.[36] The first clause in that sentence is about ownership, but *not* about the perceptions of ideas by God at times when they are not perceived by me.

The other thing I have to explain in the two-sentence passage I am mainly discussing is Philonous' saying: '. . . seeing they depend not on my thought, *and have an existence distinct from being perceived by me* . . .' The difficulty here is that the second clause looks like a reference to ownership, rather than a rewording of the first which concerns involuntariness. I have to guess that the second clause drifted in through carelessness on Berkeley's part: on my interpretation the clause, though it may help to explain what immediately follows it ('. . . there must be some other mind wherein they exist'), is idle.

That is a point against my interpretation, but consider what its rival—the standard account—has to cope with! It must put ownership right at the centre; rest weight on 'have an existence distinct from being perceived by me'; represent Berkeley as introducing God, in a considered way, by means of the continuity argument; and do all this in a way which gives the two sentences in question an intelligible relation to what immediately precedes them. This last requirement, I submit, dooms the whole endeavour.

Nor could the rival exegesis make sense of what comes next. Immediately after '. . . there must be some other mind wherein they exist', Philonous says: 'As sure therefore as the sensible world really exists, so sure is there an infinite omnipresent spirit who contains and supports it.'[37] Here, the word 'really' points to my interpretation. Those who do not find the pointing unequivocal must be treating Berkeley's uses of 'real' and its cognates as vague gestures in the direction of strength/order/involuntariness/*continuity*; but the inclusion of the last term smudges a line which Berkeley draws sharply and adheres to rigidly.

Next, Hylas remarks that Philonous' position amounts only to what 'I and all Christians hold', namely that God 'knows and comprehends all things'. Philonous replies:

Ay, but here lies the difference. Men commonly believe that all things are known or perceived by God, because they believe the being of a

[36] *Second Dialogue*, 214–15.   [37] *Second Dialogue*, p. 212.

God, whereas I on the other side, immediately and necessarily conclude the being of a God, because all sensible things must be perceived
by him.[38]

He does not say *when* objects must be perceived by God, or relate
the argument to the common belief that objects exist when no
human perceives them. And when he repeats the argument a few
lines later—still discussing whether objects 'really' exist—he is
still silent on these points.

A little further on still the ownership issue is raised again,
but only, as before, in connexion with an improper account of
what 'real' means. Philonous challenges the 'abettors of impiety'
to show 'how any thing at all, either sensible or imaginable, can
exist independent of a mind'—and here 'independent' certainly
has the ownership sense.[39] But he does not say: 'You think that
objects exist when no human perceives them, but to justify this
you must postulate a non-human spirit.' His challenge is a perfectly general one: 'Make sense, if you can, of any position other
than idealism.' Berkeley clearly thinks this is relevant to God's
existence—but how? By way of the continuity argument or the
passivity argument? To answer that we must consult the whole
passage in which this episode is embedded, and then, I have
argued, we find not the continuity argument but—over and over
again—the passivity argument.

Finally, Hylas drags the discussion off-course by comparing
Philonous' position with 'a notion entertained by some eminent
moderns, of *seeing all things in God*'. Philonous laboriously tries to
part company from Malebranche, who is the 'eminent modern' in
question, then tires of comparisons and seeks once more to make
clear *his* view:

Take here in brief my meaning. It is evident that the things I perceive
are my own ideas, and that no idea can exist unless it be in a mind. Nor
is it less plain that these ideas or things by me perceived, either themselves or their archetypes, exist independently of my mind, since I
know myself not to be their author, it being out of my power to
determine at pleasure, what particular ideas I shall be affected with upon
opening my eyes or ears. They must therefore exist in some other mind,
whose will it is they should be exhibited to me.[40]

[38] *Second Dialogue*, p. 212.
[39] *Second Dialogue*, pp. 212-13. See also *Third Dialogue*, p. 235.
[40] *Second Dialogue*, pp. 214-15.

This is Philonous' final attempt to clarify what he has been saying all along. It is the clearest possible presentation of the passivity argument.

40. *Berkeley and 'the Mob'*

The standard account must also cope with other obstacles. In presenting them, and meeting certain objections to my own view, I am tempted to say with Berkeley: 'Let my adversaries answer any one of mine I'll yield—If I don't answer every one of theirs I'll yield.'[41]

Why, according to 'my adversaries', does the continuity argument not occur in the *Principles*? Because Berkeley chose to omit it? Why should he? And if he did think of it, why does it not occur even in his private notebooks, the *Philosophical Commentaries*? Did he then fail to think of it? He was aware of all the needed logical connexions and avowedly wrote the *Principles* against atheism—so how could he be guilty of such an oversight?

If the continuity argument is used consideredly, deliberately, in the *Dialogues*, why does it occur there only once, or—if the standard account can capture the 'false imaginary glare' passage—only twice, occupying at most four sentences embedded in discussions of quite different topics? And why is it wholly absent from *Alciphron*, which is Berkeley's most extended work of apologetics?

The passivity argument is celebrated as 'this great truth',[42] and is saluted by Hylas: 'The proof you give of a Deity seems no less evident, than it is surprising.'[43] The continuity argument, in both its occurrence and its pseudo-occurrence, slides by without the slightest fanfare. Why?

If Berkeley did assume that objects sometimes exist when not perceived by humans, this must be because he wanted to 'side in all things with the Mob';[44] and so he must have assumed, with the 'vulgar' or 'the Mob', that the closing of eyes etc. will *never* annihilate an ordinary object—which is what the standard account always takes him to assume. So the continuity argument concludes that God perceives objects when we do not, while the passivity

---

[41] *Philosophical Commentaries*, entry 349.
[42] *Principles* § 149.   [43] *Second Dialogue*, p. 215.
[44] *Philosophical Commentaries*, entry 405.

argument concludes that he perceives them when we do. The two are exactly complementary: without overlapping, they enable God's perceptions to cover the whole territory. Thus, Berkeley is supposed to have a perfectly economical two-part 'proof' of God's omniscience, or at least of his perceptual omnipresence; and the two parts of it correspond to the two functions which Berkeley allows to any spirit, namely perception (continuity) and will (passivity). Yet he is silent on this beautiful pattern in natural theology credited to him by the standard account. Why?

A prima facie possible answer is this: 'Berkeley did not see the two arguments as complementary because he did not clearly see them as distinct.' We have seen how sharply Berkeley distinguished continuity from reality. He discussed the intimate relations between perception and will, e.g. considering whether a spirit could have one without the other; but he did not fail to make, and was indeed almost obsessed by, the distinction between them.[45] So a relevant failure-to-distinguish on Berkeley's part could not concern the raw materials for the two arguments. It would therefore have to concern the arguments themselves, i.e. the raw materials as assembled in those particular ways. Furthermore, an asymmetry would have to be granted; for whenever Berkeley deploys the passivity argument it is quite clear that he knows exactly what he is doing and hasn't any tendency to muddle this argument with the continuity one. So all that can be left of the 'failure to distinguish' thesis is this: where Berkeley actually writes down a version of the continuity argument, he is not clear in his mind about the difference between what he is writing down and the passivity argument. I think that this is false as it stands; but if it were true, it would support my position and completely refute the standard account; for it is just one way of saying that Berkeley doesn't really *have* the continuity argument.

Since Berkeley claims to 'side in all things with the Mob', there is justice in the remark: 'It is *prima facie* hardly likely that Berkeley should be concerned about the reality of sensible things, but indifferent to their continuity.'[46] The unlikely, of course, is sometimes true. Also, although Berkeley was a self-appointed plain man, he was not a slave to the mob: he defended views which he knew the common man would dismiss out of hand—such as

[45] *Philosophical Commentaries*, entries 645, 659, 672a, 674, 708, 841.
[46] E. J. Furlong, 'Berkeley and the Tree in the Quad', Martin p. 402 (also in Engle).

that only a spirit can be a cause, not to mention the view that we eat and drink ideas—and he said that 'received opinions ... are not always the truest'.[47] But I don't want to say 'It is unlikely but true', or 'It isn't *very* unlikely'. For the fact is that it would be utterly astonishing if Berkeley, once his final idealist position was developed, had *not* been indifferent to the mob's pressure on the continuity question. The textual facts which doom the standard account, so far from being surprising, are just what should be expected by anyone who understands idealism. All one needs is the assumption that Berkeley honestly *meant what he said*: when in his non-phenomenalistic vein, he really did think that objects are collections of ideas; and so he really did think that the plain untheological man who asks about the continuity of objects will, if he clears his mind, see that there is nothing intelligible that *he* means by his question. Someone who has understood and accepted idealism can give sense to the question, namely the sense of 'Can objects exist in non-human minds when no human perceives them?' But Berkeley's writings were not aimed at a 'plain man' who had got as far as that.

This explains Berkeley's handling of the objection that 'from the foregoing principles it follows, things are every moment annihilated and created anew'.[48] He first implies that the objection has 'no meaning', and then later he gives it a meaning and argues that when thus construed it does not hold against idealism. There is no honest way for Berkeley to make capital out of this point. The two dishonest ways in which he might do so are the two central myths of the standard account. (1) He might say: 'Your objection was prima facie damaging; it would be a serious defect in my system if it ruled out continuity; but happily it does not do so.' But he does not think the objection is prima facie damaging. He thinks, and clearly says, that it is prima facie meaningless: the move which shows how it can mean something after all *is* the move which shows that it does not hold against idealism. (2) He might produce the continuity argument: 'Now, you see, you are committed to God's existence by one of your most deeply-rooted beliefs, namely that objects exist continuously.' But this would pretend that the plain man is entitled to use his assumptions about continuity as a premiss from which to infer God's existence; and on Berkeley's principles that would be mere cheating. He cannot

[47] *Principles* § 52.   [48] *Principles* §§ 45-8.

regard the belief in continuity as fully intelligible and as worthy
to be accepted except on the basis of an acceptance of idealism
and a belief in God's existence arrived at on other grounds.

It won't do to say: 'Berkeley could not attach sense to "object
existing when no spirit whatsoever perceives it", but he could
allow that this makes sense to a non-idealist.' Idealism would be a
curious doctrine indeed if its acceptance rendered unintelligible
something which previously made sense; and that is clearly not
how Berkeley sees it. He propounds it as a true theory about
what everybody means by 'object existing when . . .' and the
like; and he sees the difference between himself and a non-idealist
as the difference between one who can and one who cannot see
that 'object existing when no spirit whatsoever perceives it' is
senseless or self-contradictory. So he has an overwhelming reason
for showing no deference to—and not thinking it important to
accommodate his position to—the plain man's view that objects
exist when not perceived by humans. For most plain men will
hold this because they believe, more strongly, that objects do or
at least could exist when not perceived by any spirit whatsoever;
and those who don't hold this stronger view are already entirely
on Berkeley's side and he has nothing to say to them.

In short, it is because Berkeley is serious about idealism that he
brushes off the mob's protests about continuity, and has no considered use for the continuity argument. There is no problem
here; but there would be one if the standard account were correct.
The standard account misrepresents not only the textual details
but also the broad outlines of Berkeley's thought.

41. *Continuity in the 'Commentaries'*

When my thesis of this chapter was first published, it drew a
reply from E. J. Furlong,[49] who discerns three stages in Berkeley's
thoughts about continuity: (1) Early in the *Philosophical Commentaries*, the view that idealism is inconsistent with continuity; (2)
Late in the *Commentaries*, and in the *Principles*, the view that
idealism is compatible with continuity 'because God may perceive
things when we do not'; (3) In the *Dialogues*, the acceptance of the

[49] J. Bennett, 'Berkeley and God'; E. J. Furlong, 'Berkeley and the Tree in the
Quad'; both in Martin and in Engle.

continuity of objects as a premiss, and the argument from it to the existence of God.[50]

In support of (3), Furlong takes the 'false imaginary glare' passage to express the continuity argument. He explains its unclarity when thus construed, and also Berkeley's failure to highlight the continuity argument, by suggesting both that 'Berkeley saw the continuity and passivity arguments as two complementary portions of the one proof' *and* that 'Berkeley did not think of the continuity argument as clearly different from the passivity argument'.[51] These suggestions have, I think, been sufficiently discussed in § 40. In reply to the question 'How could Berkeley have thought himself entitled to the continuity premiss?', Furlong says that Berkeley could think this because he had an (invalid) argument for it. This refers to Berkeley's saying—in the one indisputable occurrence of the continuity argument, discussed in § 37 above—that 'It is plain they have an existence exterior to my mind, since I find them by experience to be independent of it'.[52] I submit that that little play on 'independent' is altogether too slight to bear such a load as the considered belief in continuity which is attributed to Berkeley by the standard account.

That stages (1) and (2) both occurred, I don't deny. But I can find no evidence that (2) shows up in the *Commentaries*—if we take (2) as involving the belief that idealism is compatible with continuity because *God might perceive things when we do not*. That is one matter on which I shall argue against Furlong.

There is also another. Furlong contends that all along Berkeley cared very much about continuity: he says, for example, that Berkeley moved from stage (1) to stage (2) with 'relief'.[53] His remark that Berkeley would be *likely* to care about it because the mob cares has already been discussed. He also suggests that Berkeley's apparently agnostic remarks about continuity—'the things I saw may still exist' etc.—are the understatements of a man who, although he cares very much, thinks his position is so strong he can afford to pull his punches. Such an explanation, though it might serve for an isolated passage, could hardly carry conviction if it had to be applied to *all* Berkeley's mentions of continuity. There would have to be some independent evidence of Berkeley's attaching real importance to the continuity issue—

[50] Furlong, op. cit. Martin p. 405.   [51] Ibid. pp. 408, 407.
[52] *Third Dialogue*, p. 230.   [53] *Furlong*, op. cit. pp. 404, 407.

but is there? Well, Furlong thinks there is some in the *Commentaries*, and that is the other point of his which I shall contest.

Even if the *Commentaries* showed Berkeley's overwhelming concern with continuity—despair in thinking that idealism rules it out, joy at the discovery that it does not—this would not refute my account of what goes on in the *Principles* and *Dialogues*. It would inform us of Berkeley's state of mind, and make us wonder why it was so imperfectly realized in his published works. But that problem, if we had it, might be solved by supposing that Berkeley changed his mind—that he came to see that he ought not to have agonized over continuity. The problem would not be helpfully solved by insisting that Berkeley did not change his mind and that the published works must, despite all appearances to the contrary, mean what the standard account says they mean.

So I don't have to argue on that point; and the other one, regarding *when* Berkeley first thought of God as a possible guarantor of continuity, matters even less to my exegesis and is less important in itself. (The two are connected to this extent: if the *Commentaries* do not show Berkeley moving from (1) to (2) at all, then *a fortiori* they do not show him doing so 'with relief'.) It is embarrassing to wrangle over inessentials, especially against a courteous and considerate opponent; but I shall proceed, because my real target is much larger than the two points I have mentioned. It is an over-all pattern of misinterpretation of the *Commentaries'* treatment of continuity—a set of misinterpretations which are accepted by Furlong and by many others and which are, in a special way, privileged. Students of Berkeley owe to the Rev. A. A. Luce—among much else—the first satisfactory text of the *Commentaries*, namely the wonderful diplomatic edition of the work, and also the only good text of it which is still generally available.[54] Luce has accompanied these texts with editorial notes—in the diplomatic edition very extensive ones—many of which are helpful in the highest degree, but some of which rather confidently give disputable interpretations. The latter include an exegesis, which I think I can disprove, of Berkeley's treatment of the continuity issue.

That faulty exegesis of the *Commentaries* would tend, causally,

---

[54] George Berkeley, *Philosophical Commentaries*, diplomatic edition by A. A. Luce (Edinburgh, 1944); also, along with other material, in *The Works of George Berkeley*, vol. 1, edited by A. A. Luce (London, 1948).

to induce acceptance of the standard account of continuity in the *Principles* and *Dialogues*; but that is not my only reason for discussing it. By taking issue with Furlong and Luce over the *Commentaries*, I get a chance to include in my book one sample of the sort of challenge which that fascinating work offers to anyone wanting to get to grips with Berkeley's mind.

I shall mention by number, in the text or the notes, every entry which bears directly on the existence of objects when not perceived, or when not perceived by humans. I shall ignore entries concerning 'reality' rather than continuity, and ones which, although implying that Berkeley might have a problem about continuity, show nothing about his attitude to it or even whether he was aware of it.

Entry 60, noted towards the end of § 38 above, proposes to solve the 'creation' form of the continuity problem by invoking 'homogeneous particles' (see also entry 293). I cannot connect that with the present debate. Nor shall I say more about entry 723, which I showed near the end of § 38 to be the worst possible springboard for the standard account. With those entries out of the way, we can take the rest in roughly their order of occurrence in the *Commentaries*.

Firstly, a group of more or less phenomenalistic entries, which all occur in the first half of the work.[55] This is fairly typical: 'The Trees are in the Park, that is, whether I will or no whether I imagine any thing about them or no, let me but go thither & open my Eyes by day & I shall not avoid seeing them.'[56] According to this, an object's existing now may consist in the fact that if I acted thus and so I should have such and such perceptions; which implies, of course, that an object can exist now even if no spirit whatsoever perceives it. Essentially the same view is sometimes expressed like this: 'Bodies etc do exist whether we think of 'em or no, they being taken in a twofold sense. Collections of thoughts & collections of powers to cause those thoughts. . . .'[57] This is the conditionalizing approach in a different guise. To say that a body is a collection of 'powers to cause thoughts' is to imply that a body's existing now may consist in the truth of certain conditionals about what people would perceive if they

---

[55] *Philosophical Commentaries*, entries 52, 98, 185, 185a, 282, 293, 293a.
[56] Entry 98.   [57] Entry 282.

did certain things. (The language of 'powers' also occurs else-where.[58])

In two of these phenomenalist passages, Berkeley weakens the position a little: 'Mem: to allow existence to colours in the dark, persons not thinking &c but not an absolute actual existence.'[59] Though against that entry Berkeley later recorded an apparent change of mind, a decision to retract the weakening rider: 'Colours in ye dark do exist really *i.e.* were there light or as soon as light comes we shall see them provided we open our eyes. & that whether we will or no.'[60] In entry 293 Berkeley seems to imply that bodies taken as 'combinations of powers to raise thoughts' may exist when not perceived; and this time caution is introduced in the afterthought entry 293a, where he says (confirming, incidentally, that 'powers' and conditionals are all of a piece): 'Bodies taken for Powers do exist w^n not perceiv'd but this existence is not actual. w^n I say a power exists no more is meant than that if in ye light I open my eyes & look that way I shall see it i.e ye body &c.' Fortunately, we need not linger on the unpromising distinction between 'existence' and 'actual existence'. Each of these conditionalizing passages, strong or weak, says something of the form: 'Even if no one now perceives O, the fact that if someone did A he would perceive O is sufficient to guarantee . . .' To guarantee what? If it guarantees that 'O exists now', with this construed strongly enough to answer the question throw n up by the continuity issue, then we have here a downright phenomenalist solution to the continuity problem; and such a solution, as I have pointed out, removes all need to invoke the perceptions of non-humans to guarantee the continuity of objects. If on the other hand what is guaranteed by the conditional is something less than an answer to the typical continuity-question, then what is being said is simply irrelevant to the continuity of objects.

Curiously placed in the middle of these conditionalizing passages there occurs entry 194:

On account of my doctrine the identity of finite substances must consist in something else than continued existence, or relation to determin'd time and place of beginning to exist. the existence of our thoughts (wch being combin'd make all substances) being frequently interrupted, & they having divers beginnings, & endings.

---

58 Entries 41, 80, 84.   59 Entry 185.   60 Entry 185a.

We might, with a little stretching, construe the '. . . but not an actual existence' passages as also saying that idealism is incompatible with continuity, i.e. with the continuity of objects' 'actual existence'. That would give us a total of three such passages; but the fact remains that entry 194 is the only direct evidence of Berkeley's having asked 'Given that objects are ideas, can an object exist when none of us perceive it?' and answered flatly 'No'. Does the passage manifest anxiety, regret or intellectual distress about this answer? On the contrary: the entry notes that Berkeley has a technical problem to solve, namely that of finding acceptable criteria for the re-identification of objects;[61] and the relevant point about continuity occurs merely as one half of a subordinate clause.

Next we meet a couple of entries which imply that 194 is wrong and that continuity can be allowed after all. One of them abruptly lists, but does not explain, '4 Principles whereby to answer objections', of which the first is 'Bodies do really exist tho not perceiv'd by us'.[62] What are we to make of this? Do the words 'by us' suggest that bodies exist when not perceived by God? That interpretation, besides being wilful in the extreme, would not yield what the standard account wants. For the entry says not that bodies *may* but that they *do* really exist when not perceived by us; so that on the suggested interpretation it represents the position Berkeley is claimed to hold in the *Dialogues*, not the position he is agreed to hold in the *Principles*. In terms of Furlong's account, it represents Berkeley as at stage (3) before he has reached stage (2).

Ignoring the mysterious and unhelpful entry 339, the next one that contradicts 194 is this:

I must be very particular in explaining w^t is meant by things existing in Houses, chambers, fields, caves etc w^n not perceiv'd as well as w^n perceiv'd. & shew how the Vulgar notion agrees with mine when we narrowly inspect into the meaning & definition of the word Existence wch is no simple idea distinct from perceiving & being perceiv'd.[63]

Whatever solution of the continuity problem Berkeley has in mind here, it cannot be the one he eventually settles for in the *Principles*. If it were, we should have to accept that in his *first* extended entry based on the distinction between 'not perceived'

---

[61] See also entry 192.   [62] Entry 312.   [63] Entry 408.

and 'not perceived by humans' he wrote the former phrase and meant the latter! I do not claim to know what line(s) of thought Berkeley did have in mind in the two entries last quoted, where he apparently claims to have solved the continuity problem without saying how.

The next relevant entry is 472:

You ask me whether the books are in the study now w^n no one is there to see them. I answer yes. you ask me are we not in the wrong for imagining things to exist w^n they are not actually perceiv'd by the senses. I answer no. the existence of our ideas consists in being perceiv'd, imagin'd thought on whenever they are imagin'd or thought on they do exist. Whenever they are mention'd or discours'd of they are imagin'd & thought on therefore you can at no time ask me whether they exist or no, but by reason of y^t very question they must necessarily exist.

One can hardly credit that Berkeley was satisfied with this argument, and yet apparently he was, for he published it twice.[64] In the *Commentaries*, however, he followed it by something which he understandably chose not to publish:

But say you then a Chimaera does exist. I answer it doth in one sense. i.e it is imagin'd. but it must be well noted that existence is vulgarly restrain'd to actuall perception. & that I use the word Existence in a larger sense than ordinary.[65]

That admission, when followed through, shows why the argument of 472 is so bad and so unavailable to Berkeley. It also enables us to show that the argument does not support the standard account of Berkeley's views on continuity, as follows. When I ask a typical continuity-question such as 'Do the works of my watch exist now, when I do not [actually] perceive them?', either I use 'exist' in Berkeley's 'larger sense' or I don't. If I don't then 472 does not answer my question. If I do use 'exist' in the larger sense, then 472 answers 'Yes, the works of your watch do exist now'; but it gives this answer because 'by reason of that very question they must necessarily exist', i.e. because of what I 'imagine' or 'think on' in asking the question, and not because of what any other spirit perceives.

[64] *Principles* § 23; *First Dialogue*, p. 200. See also *Philosophical Commentaries*, entry 518.

[65] Entry 473.

So it may well be that 472 purports to solve the continuity problem; but this 'solution' cannot be seen as a version of, or as a stage along the way to, the solution which invokes God's perceptions. If Berkeley's thoughts about continuity underwent a rectilinear development, the two entries last quoted do not stand anywhere on the line.[66]

There are just three more entries to be discussed.

In entry 477 Berkeley challenges the Cartesians about their belief in 'Bodies', and in the afterthought entry 477a—which is our present concern—he corrects this to a challenge about their belief in 'Matter', for 'bodies & their qualitys I do allow to exist independently of Our mind'. This is the earliest entry which Furlong explicitly claims to express the *Principles* position on continuity: 'Berkeley is, by implication, distinguishing between "Our mind" and—though he does not say so, but what else can it be?—God's mind.'[67] What else can it be? Well, it could be 'other intelligences'[68]—if indeed 'Our mind' is being used in a *distinguishing* way at all. Luce's note on this entry says: 'Note the capital "Our", distinguishing the human mind from the divine.' This strikes me as rashly dogmatic. The word 'Our', with a capital, appears twice in the *Commentaries*: this may, like some of Berkeley's other variations in the use of capitals, have no significance at all; or it may mean something special, but not of a distinguishing kind; or it may give 'Our' a distinguishing force, but not that of the human/divine distinction; or it may mean what Luce says it does. I cannot find a shred of evidence to support Luce's interpretation as against its three rivals; and there is one piece of evidence against it, namely that the other occurrence of 'Our', to which I shall come in a moment, cannot embody the human/divine distinction.

Also, if entry 477a is to be relevant to continuity *at all*, it must be using 'independently' in the ownership rather than the causation sense; and there is no evidence for that either.

Next we come to entry 801, of which Furlong makes much. After claiming that by the end of the *Commentaries* Berkeley 'had found a way, by distinguishing between our mind and some other

---

[66] For fuller discussions of them, see Prior, 'Berkeley in Logical Form'; and Thomson, 'G. J. Warnock's *Berkeley*'. Also K. Marc-Wogau, 'Berkeley's Sensationalism and the *Esse est Percipi* Principle', Martin 339.

[67] Furlong, op. cit. pp. 403-4.

[68] See entry 723.

mind, of . . ."siding with the Mob" and at the same time retaining
[idealism]', Furlong continues: 'And he states this achievement
as a point in his favour as compared with the Cartesians. This is
not the claim of one who was unconcerned about intermittency.'[69]
As evidence, he cites entry 801: 'I differ from the Cartesians in
that I make extension, Colour etc to exist really in Bodies &
independent of Our Mind. All y^s carefully & lucidly to be set
forth.' So this entry has to do double duty: it is to serve as
evidence that Berkeley has thought of the 'God's perceptions'
solution to the continuity problem, and as evidence that he cared
about continuity. As regards the latter point: we are presumably
invited to read the opening words as self-congratulatory, and as
revelatory of 'concern'; but I don't see why we should. Of course
it is virtually tautological that x prefers his view to y's different
one, and to that extent regards his having it as 'a point in his
favour'; but it doesn't follow that the view must be about a
matter which is of great concern to x, or that it is a view x arrived
at 'with relief'.

But never mind that. The main point is that entry 801 cannot
be about continuity at all. To suppose that it is requires (*a*) the
wholly unwarranted supposition that it is using 'independent' in
the ownership sense, and (*b*) that *Berkeley thought that Cartesians
did not allow that bodies can exist when no human perceives them.* That
was not a Cartesian view, and Berkeley cannot have thought that
it was. In face of this insuperable difficulty, the *a priori* assertion
that the entry must concern continuity, because 'Our' must be
meant to distinguish human minds from God's, hardly carries
conviction.

An acceptable reading must make the entry draw a contrast—
one which Berkeley could sanely have thought to be genuine—
between Berkeley and the Cartesians. Such a reading is available:
the entry could be saying that Berkeley allows to 'colour' the
same sort of mind-independence that he allows to 'extension'.
This genuinely contrasts his position with that of the Cartesians,
who held Locke's kind of view about the distinction between
primary and secondary qualities. It makes sense of the entry's
referring not to 'Bodies existing independent of Our Mind' but
to 'extension, Colour etc' existing 'really in Bodies & independent
of Our Mind'. And it fits with the fact that Berkeley has marked

[69] Furlong, op. cit. p. 404.

entry 801 with a marginal 'P', which means, according to his own explanation, that *its topic is 'Primary & Secondary Qualities'*!

There is just one entry to go, namely 802. This has a marginal 'P', but also an 'M'—this means 'matter', and occurs against many entries concerning the existence of bodies, reality, continuity and so on. So entry 802 has at least a chance of falling within the continuity area. Here it is: 'Not to mention the Combinations of Powers but to say the things the effects themselves to really exist even w^n not actually perceiv'd but still with relation to perception.' Luce says that the 'powers' theory 'is virtually discarded in 802 in favour of the position taken up in *Princ.* 45–8, where intermittency and the companion doctrines are stated *not* to follow from [Berkeley's] principles'.[70] This implies a reading, which Furlong also accepts, of entry 802 as rejecting any appeal to conditionals or 'combinations of powers', and as claiming that nevertheless objects can exist when humans do not perceive them—this claim being based on the possibility that God may perceive objects when humans do not.

This reading of 802 implies that Berkeley has failed, in four distinct ways in one sentence, to say what he meant. (1) It takes Berkeley to have written 'not to *mention* . . .' when he meant something much stronger. Yet when he says 'I must not mention . . .' in entry 441 he means just that. (2) It construes Berkeley's 'when not . . . perceived' to mean 'when not . . . perceived by humans', although the difference between 'perceived' and 'perceived by humans' is supposed to be the whole point of the entry. (3) It makes Berkeley's use of 'actually' idle, unless he is supposed to assume that human perceptions are actual while divine ones are not. (4) It takes Berkeley to have said 'but still with relation to perception' when he meant 'but still perceived by Someone', which is no wordier and is much clearer and more direct.

These difficulties would entitle one to reject the Luce–Furlong reading of entry 802, even if we had no alternative interpretation of it. But there is at least one quite plausible alternative, namely the following. Entry 802, like entry 441 with its 'I must not mention . . .', shows Berkeley in his role as a writer who is planning a book and thinking about problems of exposition. He intends to give a phenomenalistic or conditionalizing account of the existence of bodies when they are not perceived, saying that

[70] A. A. Luce, note on entry 52 in both editions. See also note on entry 802.

they can exist when 'not actually perceived' if they have the 'relation to perception' expressed in phenomenalistic conditionals; and in 802 he is primarily reminding himself 'not to mention the combinations of powers', i.e. not to use the technical term 'combinations of powers' even though it is one vehicle of the phenomenalist approach which he is contemplating.[71]

This interpretation assumes that Berkeley was capable of dealing with continuity through conditionals as late as this; but we know that he was.[72] It assumes that he had difficulties with the expression 'combinations of powers' which were not just difficulties with the underlying phenomenalism; but we know that he had.[73] It assumes that Berkeley knew that his use of 'combinations of powers' was equivalent to a phenomenalist use of conditionals; but we know that he did know this.[74]

The interpretation I have suggested, then, has Berkeley saying something which he could very well have been saying: and it relates reasonably to the text of 802 itself, encountering none of the four obstacles to the Luce interpretation. Even if my suggested reading is wrong, it is surely better than one which takes Berkeley to have written 'when not actually perceived but still with relation to perception' when he meant 'when not perceived by humans but still perceived by God'.

The position can be summed up as follows. Luce says that by a certain stage in the writing of the *Commentaries* '[Berkeley] has come to realize that immaterialism is strengthened, not weakened, by the admission of sensible bodies, perceived by God when not perceived by man.'[75] The first bit of this resembles Furlong's claim that Berkeley moved 'with relief' to the *Principles* position on continuity; and I can find no evidence whatsoever for it. Suppose we delete it, and take Luce to have said only that while writing the *Commentaries* Berkeley *became aware of the possibility* that bodies might exist when not perceived by men because they are perceived by God. This claim, which is weakened to the point where it does not conflict at all with my central thesis in the present chapter, still goes too far: it is not supported by any single one of the nearly nine hundred entries in the *Philosophical Commentaries*.

[71] See Grave, 'The Mind and its Ideas', p. 303; J. D. Mabbott, 'The Place of God in Berkeley's Philosophy', Martin p. 374.   [72] *Principles* § 3.
[73] *Philosophical Commentaries*, entries 84 and 282 (end).   [74] Entry 293a.
[75] A. A. Luce, note on entry 52, in the diplomatic edition (1944) only.

VIII

ACTIVITY AND CAUSALITY

42. *Berkeley on causation*

THE passivity argument requires the premiss that nothing can be a cause except (the will of) a spirit. This implies that fires do not make kettles boil; and one wonders why Berkeley should accept anything so implausible.

One explanation is that he found the following argument compelling: objects are collections of ideas; and ideas 'are visibly inactive, there is nothing of power or agency included in them';[1] so objects are inactive, are powerless, are not causes. This argument is unattractive. Its first premiss is false, and its second is tremendously unclear.

Berkeley's view, however, has another source which does not involve idealism. Whenever the vulgar say that something caused or made or produced something else, all they have to go by—all they are really entitled to report—is a sequence of events which instantiates a familiar pattern. Roughly and briefly: the vulgar report 'causes' although they have observed only regularities. Berkeley takes this to imply that the vulgar say more than they should:

> The connexion of ideas does not imply the relation of *cause* and *effect*, but only of a mark or *sign* with the thing *signified*. The fire which I see is not the cause of the pain I suffer upon my approaching it, but the mark that forewarns me of it.[2]

Berkeley thinks that visual ideas are God's future-tense language about the tangible world, and so he means 'the mark that forewarns me' literally. My sight of the fire is God's warning to me that if I step forward I shall be burned. The passage is clouded by Berkeley's having to identify 'the fire which I see' with my sight of the fire, but still the main point is clear enough: the relationship between a 'mark' and 'the thing signified' is taken to be just a God-ordained concomitance and *therefore* not to be causal.

---

[1] *Principles* § 25.   [2] *Principles* § 65.

In one place Berkeley distinguishes causes from regular accompaniments by crediting the word 'occasion' with two senses: it 'signifies, either the agent which produces any effect, or else something that is observed to accompany, or go before it, in the ordinary course of things'.[3] His description of science ('natural philosophy') makes the same point:

The difference there is betwixt natural philosophers and other men, with regard to their knowledge of the phenomena . . ., consists, not in an exacter knowledge of the efficient cause that produces them, for that can be no other than the *will of a spirit*, but only in a greater largeness of comprehension, whereby . . . agreements are discovered in the works of Nature, and the particular effects explained, that is, reduced to general rules.[4]

The denials in these passages go against the mob's assumptions about what can be a cause. Berkeley knows this, but:

In such things we ought to *think with the learned, and speak with the vulgar*. [Copernicans] say the sun rises, the sun sets, . . . and if they affected a contrary style in common talk, it would without doubt appear very ridiculous. A little reflexion on what is here said will make it manifest, that the common use of language would receive no manner of alteration or disturbance from the admission of our tenets.[5]

Still, in speaking with the vulgar we shall be saying what is not literally true:

In the ordinary affairs of life, any phrases may be retained, so long as they excite in us proper sentiments, or dispositions to act in such a manner as is necessary for our well-being, how false soever they may be, if taken in a strict and speculative sense. Nay this is unavoidable, since propriety being regulated by custom, language is suited to the received opinions, which are not always the truest.[6]

The point about Copernicans is this: when the vulgar say 'The sun rises', this is all right because it unambiguously marks out a particular kind of phenomenon; but astronomical discoveries have been made which show that the sun does not, strictly, *rise*. To preserve the analogy, the point about 'cause' will have to be this: the vulgar have a serviceable use of 'The fire caused the kettle to boil' and the like, but discoveries have been made which show that fires do not, strictly, *cause* anything to happen. What

[3] *Principles* § 69.   [4] *Principles* § 105.
[5] *Principles* § 51.   [6] *Principles* § 52.

discoveries can these be? Despite occasional phrases suggesting the contrary, Berkeley does not think he has made an empirical discovery about what causes there are: the basis of his position is in fact a view about the meaning of 'cause'—namely that nothing could strictly qualify as a 'cause' except the will of a spirit. This partly spoils the analogy with the Copernicans. It also sits uneasily with Berkeley's professed respect for ordinary language; he seems to be saying that the common meaning of 'cause' is not its correct meaning; and one is tempted to ask, nastily, whether he is imposing on us a 'philosophic' and 'abstracted notion of cause'.[7]

He might reply: 'I am not a slave to common parlance, from which I have already departed by denying that one can, strictly, see a tangible thing.' Now, Berkeley had reasons for saying that from premisses which everyone would accept it follows that a tangible thing cannot be seen; so that the vulgar, in claiming to 'see and touch the coach', are being unfaithful to their own basic perception-concepts; from which it does perhaps follow (I here slide over a controversial area) that such vulgar locutions are 'false if taken in a strict and speculative sense'. But can Berkeley take a similar line about 'cause'? He certainly needs to. If his position is not to remain a mystery, he must maintain that certain aspects of what we all mean by 'cause', or certain common assumptions about what causes must be like, do imply that objects cannot be causes—even if most people do not see the implication or do not honour it in their ordinary talk.

I think Berkeley would maintain something like this. Specifically, I think he would claim that the vulgar would agree that regularity is not enough. When he insists that 'The fire made the kettle boil' reports only that this kettle did—and that kettles ordinarily do—boil shortly after being placed on the fire, he seems to expect us to say: 'If that is all there is to it, then certainly the fire did not make the kettle boil.' This presupposes that we all expect a 'cause' to have some feature which is lacked by mere regularities but possessed by the wills of spirits—the voluntary or deliberate or purposive doings of persons. What could Berkeley have supposed this feature to be?

Well, he stresses the contingency of the observed regularities, and notes that we can easily suppose that any particular one of them might fail to obtain in a given case. Having said that the 'set

7 Cf. *Third Dialogue*, pp. 247–8.

rules' whereby God 'excites in us the ideas of sense' are called 'laws
of nature', Berkeley thinks it worthwhile to add: 'These we learn
by experience, which teaches us that such and such ideas are
attended with such and such other ideas, in the ordinary course of
things.'[8] In the next section, contingency and necessity are
explicitly contrasted: 'That to obtain such or such ends, such or
such means are conducive, all this we know, not by discovering
any necessary connexion between our ideas, but only by the
observation of the settled laws of Nature.'[9] Of the law of gravity
Berkeley says: 'There is nothing necessary or essential in the case,
but it depends entirely on the will of the *governing spirit*.' And in
the next section:

By a diligent observation of the phenomena within our view, we may
discover the general laws of Nature, and from them deduce [= infer
in some way] the other phenomena, I do not say *demonstrate* [= infer
deductively]; for all deductions of that kind depend on a supposition
that the Author of Nature always operates uniformly, and in a constant
observance of those rules we take for principles: which we cannot
evidently know.[10]

Does Berkeley think, then, that a genuine causal connexion must
be knowable *a priori*? Is this why he thinks that the vulgar would
agree, if they cleared their minds, that objects cannot be causes?
I think not; for this would also debar spirits from being causes,
on Berkeley's own account of the activities of spirits.

Berkeley stresses the contingency of the regularities which the
vulgar call 'causes', I suggest, so as to highlight the *inductive*
nature of our knowledge about them. He wants to stress that all
we know about fires in relation to kettles is that a certain pattern
has been observed in the past, to which we can add only a hope or
'a supposition' that the pattern will continue to hold in the future.
This inductiveness or backward-lookingness is arguably absent
in cases of 'the will of a spirit'. If I know that I am about to
scratch my elbow, having just decided to do so, it is plausible to
say that my knowledge—though not *a priori*, not knowledge of a
logically necessary consequence of my decision—is not inductively
based either. Because this is plausible we find contemporary
writers saying: 'There are two possible kinds of certainty about
one's own future actions—inductive certainty, and certainty

[8] *Principles* § 30.   [9] *Principles* § 31.   [10] *Principles* § 107.

based upon reasons, which is decision.'[11] My conjecture, then, is that Berkeley thinks that a genuinely causal connexion must enable us to predict *non-inductively* a state of affairs from an earlier state of affairs, and that the only such connexion we know of is that between a decision ('volition') and the subsequent action of a 'spirit'.

That would explain Berkeley's thinking that objects cannot be causes, and that spirits can. Would it explain his thinking that *only* spirits can be causes, i.e. that 'We cannot possibly conceive any active power but the Will'?[12] Yes, it would explain this too, given the idealist premiss that *ideas* (some of which are objects) and *spirits* are the only kinds of item there can be.

There is, however, a feature of Berkeley's use of language which might help to explain the position he takes, or at least the confidence with which he takes it. This partial explanation has nothing directly to do with idealism or with the supposed contrast between causes and regularities.

One of Berkeley's standard ways of saying that something is (not) a genuine cause is to say that it is (not) an 'agent'. This is natural enough, for there are etymological and semantic links between 'agent' and 'active' and 'act', and the last of these, especially in expressions like 'act upon', is closely connected with 'cause'. In English today, however, the word 'agent' tends in most contexts to suggest personal agency—not just something active but someone who acts. I have caught myself in lectures crediting Berkeley with the view that 'only agents can be causes', meaning that only spirits can be causes; and I think that it is natural thus to assume that 'agent' excludes everything of an inanimate kind. I suspect that this was also natural for a speaker of English in Berkeley's days; and, if that is right, Berkeley's use of 'agent' also as a synonym for 'cause' could at least tend to confirm him in his view that only spirits or persons can be causes.

Berkeley sometimes expects even Lockeans to agree that matter is 'inactive', despite the fact that the concession would rob them of a conclusion they want:

PHILONOUS: Doth not *matter*, in the common current acceptation of the word, signify an extended, solid, moveable, unthinking, inactive substance? HYLAS: It doth. PHILONOUS: And hath it not been made evident,

[11] S. Hampshire and H. L. A. Hart, 'Decision, Intention and Certainty', *Mind*, vol. 67 (1958), p. 4.   [12] *Philosophical Commentaries*, entry 155.

that no such substance can possibly exist? And though it should be allowed to exist, yet how can that which is *inactive* be a *cause*; or that which is *unthinking* be a *cause of thought*?[13]

I suggest that Hylas is supposed calmly to allow 'inactive' because this follows from 'unthinking', i.e. that Berkeley is at this point connecting 'active' with 'agent' and taking the latter to mean 'sentient being which acts with reasons' or the like; and that, having extracted Hylas' concession, Berkeley then falls back on the other way of using 'active', in order to argue that since matter is inactive it cannot be a cause.

An alternative explanation, suggested to me by Richard Sorabji, is that the supposed passiveness of matter might have been a residue from certain doctrines of Aristotle's; and that seems to me likely. But I think that the peculiarity of 'agent' also plays a part, especially when Berkeley says: 'When we talk of unthinking agents, . . . we only amuse our selves with words.'[14]

Another strand in Berkeley's thinking about causes ought to be teased out. I have quoted a rhetorical question of Berkeley's which implies that an unthinking thing could not cause thought— and this is not offered as a mere corollary of the stronger view that an unthinking being could not cause anything. Does Berkeley find it obvious that a thing which is not F cannot cause anything else to be F? Well, he says this: 'It is . . . extravagant to say, a thing which is inert, operates on the mind, and which is unperceiving, is the cause of our perceptions, without any regard either to consistency, or the old known axiom: *Nothing can give to another that which it hath not itself.*'[15] The clause 'without any regard . . . itself' was omitted in the third edition. Still, the thought it expresses may have other symptoms in Berkeley's writings: we cannot realistically assume that he would omit everything which he was in fact led to under the influence of the 'old known axiom'—and anyway the 'axiom' is interesting in itself.

There is, of course, absolutely no warrant for the 'old known axiom'; and it is part of a line of thought which can, though it probably does not in Berkeley, lead to grave trouble. One error to which it can lead—and, I conjecture, has led—is undue insistence upon certain sorts of 'conservation' law. Why were so many philosophers and scientists reluctant to accept gravitation

---

[13] *Second Dialogue*, p. 216.   [14] *Principles* § 28.
[15] *Third Dialogue*, p. 236.

as a fundamental type of physical phenomenon? Partly, of course, because it involves action at a distance; but also because it involves one body's acting upon another in a way which cannot be described as one's losing what the other gains. Thus Faraday: 'That a body without force should raise up force in a body at a distance from it, is too hard to imagine; but it is harder still, if that can be possible, to accept the idea when we consider that it includes the *creation of force*.'[16] Mary Hesse's *Forces and Fields*, from which that quotation comes, provides further evidence of the power which the 'old known axiom' has had over some men's thinking.

The 'axiom' that a thing which is not F cannot cause anything to be F has an even more damaging first-cousin, namely the view that it stands to reason that a thing which is F will cause other things to be F. The latter view implies that the facts about heat-transfer, say, hardly have the status of contingent facts: 'Of course the water, in cooling the iron, itself becomes hotter: in this case the iron is only passing on to the water the heat it already has.' Locke, for example, says that our observation of objects gives us no idea of 'a power in the one to move the other' save 'by a borrowed motion',[17] and implies that this idea is not the rock-bottom idea of power—presumably because it is only the idea of motion-*transfer* and thus of something which stands to reason or goes without saying. He puts the point more fully here:

Active power ... is the more proper signification of the word power ... Bodies, by our senses, do not afford us so clear and distinct an idea of active power, as we have from reflection on the operations of our minds ... For, when the ball obeys the motion of a billiard-stick, it is not any action of the ball, but bare passion. Also when by impulse it sets another ball in motion that lay in its way, it only communicates the motion it had received from another, and loses in itself so much as the other received ... The idea of the *beginning* of motion we have only from reflection on what passes in ourselves.[18]

The implications of 'it *only* communicates' are too multifarious to be followed out in detail here. But is it not apparent that Locke holds, *a priori*, the view that motion-origination needs to be

[16] Quoted in Mary B. Hesse, *Forces and Fields* (London, 1961), p. 223. See also pp. 157–63 and 222 –5.
[17] *Essay* II. xxiii. 28.
[18] *Essay* II. xxi. 4.

explained as motion-transfer does not? Hume understood all this perfectly.[19]

43. *Berkeley and Hume on volitions*

A certain theory about voluntary action, i.e. that activity of spirits which Berkeley thinks is the only genuinely causal activity, is implied here: 'I find I can excite ideas in my mind . . . It is no more than willing, and straightway this or that idea arises . . . Thus much is certain, and grounded on experience.'[20] That is the only published passage I can quote, but its general tenor is confirmed by several entries in the *Commentaries*:

Wn I ask whether A can move B. if A be an intelligent thing. I mean no more than whether the volition of A that B move be attended with the motion of B, if A be senseless whether the impulse of A against B be follow'd by ye motion of B.[21]

What means Cause as distinguish'd from Occasion? nothing but a Being wch wills wn the Effect follows the volition.[22]

There is a difference betwixt Power & Volition. There may be volition without Power. But there can be no Power without Volition. Power implyeth volition & at the same time a Connotation of the Effects following the Volition.[23]

Strange impotence of men. Man without God. Wretcheder than a stone or tree, he having onely the power to be miserable by his unperformed wills, these having no power at all.[24]

All these point to the same account of how a spirit acts: it performs a volition, and an upshot ensues—perhaps a little later or perhaps, as the words 'straightway' and 'attended' suggest, at the very same time as the volition. However the details are filled in, it seems clear that the volition and the upshot are supposed to be two distinct events related in some way which Berkeley does not explain. It looks as though the relation is one which can be known to hold only inductively: I find 'by experience' that certain volitions are attended or followed by certain upshots, and I trust (in God) that this correlation will continue to hold in future. On that view of the matter, though, Berkeley's whole account of causation

---

[19] *Treatise*, pp. 111–12. See also Leibniz, *Monadology* § 7; J. Laird, *Hume's Philosophy of Human Nature* (London, 1932), pp. 98–101.   [20] *Principles* § 28.
[21] *Philosophical Commentaries*, entry 461.   [22] Entry 499.
[23] Entry 699.   [24] Entry 107.

is hopelessly compromised, for all it has done is to relocate the inductive regularity.

My main purpose in this section, though, is to examine the volition-and-upshot account of deliberate (intentional, voluntary) action, not in relation to other theories of Berkeley's but just on its own merits.

The claim that any voluntary or deliberate action involves a volition and an upshot might be offered as (1) an analysis, an account of what it means to say that a doing was deliberate, voluntary, intentional or the like; or as (2) a contingent thesis about the mechanics of deliberate doings, a thesis which represents 'I get my head scratched by first performing a volition' as logically on a par with 'I get the light on by raising the switch'. Offered as (2) contingent, the volition-and-upshot theory is merely tiresome: there is no evidence for it, and no philosophical reason for caring whether it is true or not. So I shall confine myself to the theory considered as (1) an analysis of the general notion of intentionalness—which I suspect, and shall assume without proof, to be the version of the theory which attracted Berkeley.

The theory does not work. Purporting to explain 'x did A for a reason, or intentionally, or deliberately', all it offers us is 'A occurred because x performed a volition'. But if 'performing a volition' or 'performing an act of the will' is to be intelligible to us as referring to a *doing,* then it in its turn re-raises the question about intentionalness. Did he perform the volition *so that* his fingers would move in such a way as to relieve the itch in his scalp? If he did, then the notion of intention—which is tied to 'so that'—has not been analysed or explained, but merely relocated. On the other hand, if such notions as intention don't apply to volitions, does not that concede that volitions are not performed after all, but merely happen? And in that case the analysis implies that no one ever really *does* anything: what we call actions are really just the upshots of happenings.[25]

Berkeley may have thought of 'volitions' as episodic wants or desires ('the volition of A that B move' sounds like 'the desire of A that B move'). On that model, it might indeed be right to say that the question of the intentionalness or voluntariness of volitions does not arise; for we cannot sensibly ask why, or with what

[25] G. Ryle, *The Concept of Mind* (London, 1949), p. 67.

intention, someone underwent a spasm of desire. But then on that model the whole analysis collapses: it is obviously false that what happens in intentional action is that (a) one wants certain events to happen, and (b) in consequence of that want events do happen. By mere wanting I can no more get my fingers crossed than I can move mountains. Only bad philosophical theory could lead anyone to deny this very obvious truth.

Hume's treatment of the volition theory has points of interest which might be mentioned here. He thinks that knowledge of the future can only have an inductive basis, and so he sees the volition theory as the locus of a possible threat. Specifically, he sees it as a possible basis for the view that our deliberate doings give us direct experience of a kind of 'power' or 'necessity' binding one event to another, i.e. binding the volition to the upshot. (He was slow to notice the threat. A brief discussion of it is squeezed into the Appendix of the *Treatise*,[26] whereas in the first *Enquiry* it occupies nearly half the section 'On the Idea of Necessary Connexion'.)

Some of the time, Hume seems to agree that any 'activity of a spirit', to use Berkeley's phrase, involves a volition and an upshot, and to dispute only the claim that these two putative events are non-inductively connected. He hints at an acceptance of the volitions theory in the *Treatise*, and in the *Enquiry* he goes much further:

The influence of volition over the organs of the body ... is a fact, which, like all other natural events, can be known only by experience, and can never be foreseen from any apparent energy or power in the cause, which connects it with the effect, and renders the one an infallible consequence of the other. The motion of our body follows upon the command of our will. Of this we are every moment conscious. But the means, by which this is effected ... must for ever escape our most diligent enquiry.[27]

Somewhat later, after arguing that external events yield only brute-fact sequences, so that our predictions in that realm must rest on our faith that regularities discovered in the past will continue to hold in the future, Hume continues:

The same difficulty occurs in contemplating the operations of mind on body—where we observe the motion of the latter to follow upon the volition of the former, but are not able to observe or conceive the tie which binds together the motion and volition, or the energy by which the mind produces this effect.[28]

Even those who agree with Hume about the inductive basis of all predictions are likely to be discontented with his account of deliberate action. It is easy to see why. They agree with (i) Hume's denial that a deliberate doing involves a volition which is non-inductively related to an upshot, but dissent from (ii) his implied affirmation that a deliberate doing does involve a volition and an upshot. All he needs, to defend his theory of causation, is the denial (i); and the implausibility of certain parts of his discussion stems wholly from his affirmation (ii). The latter, incidentally, occurs mainly at the beginning and end of the discussion; throughout most of the middle stretch Hume confines himself to the denial.

44. *Activity and passivity*

Berkeley confidently applies the active/passive dichotomy to human spirits, in ways which raise problems.

His usual paradigm of activity is the voluntary conjuring up of ideas: 'I find I can excite ideas in my mind at pleasure, and vary and shift the scene as oft as I think fit.'[29] The capacity for this kind of imagining—let us call it 'imaging'—is not essential to the human condition, and some people lack it entirely. Berkeley can take imaging as a paradigm of activity only because he virtually equates it with thinking. His Lockean approach to meaning and understanding encourages a Lockean view of thinking as the mental manipulation of ideas or images; and so Berkeley has to think that active imaging is a vital part of the life of any whole man.

Sometimes, indeed, he writes as though he thinks that the active/passive line coincides exactly with the thinking/perceiving line: 'But whatever power I may have over my own thoughts, I find the ideas actually perceived by sense have not a like dependence on my will.'[30] And there is also this curious passage:

Thoughts do most properly signify or are mostly taken for the interior operations of the mind, wherein the mind is active, those y^t obey not the acts of Volition, & in wch the mind is passive are more properly call'd sensations or perceptions, But y^t is all a case.[31]

The phrase 'all a case' means 'all one' or 'all the same'. The passage as a whole, I think, means this:

The word 'thoughts' is properly or usually taken to signify the interior operations of the mind, wherein the mind is active. Mental operations that obey not the acts of volition, and in which the mind is passive, are more properly called 'sensations' or 'perceptions'. But the content of what goes on is just the same in both cases.

This reflects Berkeley's general tendency to assimilate the intellectual to the sensory: thoughts and perceptions are both transactions with ideas of a single kind, and the two labels merely mark the difference between the active and the passive commerce with ideas.

For a contrast, consider Kant's position. He did not regard the distinction between thoughts and perceptions as a superficial one, and so *a fortiori* he did not *define* it as the distinction between active and passive engagement with ideas. But although he enforced a fundamental distinction between thoughts and perceptions—between 'concepts' and 'intuitions'—Kant thought that humans are in *fact* active in their thinking and passive in their intake of 'intuitions' or raw data. This led him into difficulties which I cannot follow out here: for example, into unprofitable speculations about whether some non-human beings might have 'active intuitions', i.e. might be active in respect of their intake of data as we are in respect of our intellectual operations *upon* data.

My present concern is with what Kant and Berkeley have in common. For Berkeley it is a merely verbal matter, an upshot of the standard meanings of 'thought' and 'perception'; while for Kant it is a deep truth about the human mind; but they do at any rate agree that we are active in respect of our thoughts and passive in respect of our perceptions.

The thesis that we are active in all our thoughts might be denied on the grounds that thoughts sometimes just come, and sometimes 'run away with' the thinker; but I shall not pursue that point. What of the converse thesis? Berkeley does not quite say that the only thing we actively do is to think; but his illustration

[31] *Philosophical Commentaries*, entry 286. See also entry 821.

of the active/passive dichotomy is always thinking/sensing and never swimming/sensing—which makes one wonder. Physical activity, indeed, is never prominent in Berkeley's picture of the human condition, and it drops almost completely out of sight when the active/passive distinction is at work.

That fact gives grounds for suspicions, and these increase when we turn to the 'passive' side of the antithesis. Berkeley says that we are passive in respect of all our 'sensations' or 'actual perceptions'; and this commits him, as does his theory of 'real things', to the conclusion that passivity is a *sine qua non* of any perception of a 'real thing' or objective state of affairs. This conclusion is false, however, and looks true only if one thinks about the non-interfering onlooker and forgets the active, physically involved observer. Like Kant, Berkeley neglects the fact that humans have bodies.

Even in passive or non-interfering observations there may be a relevant kind of physical activity. Berkeley does pay some attention to this, for example by distinguishing my activity in drawing air in through my nose from my passivity in respect of the olfactory sensation which I then have.[32] The interplay between activity and passivity, however, goes much further than this.

When I see a real arm going up, my visual intake is the perception of a 'real thing', and Berkeley's theory implies that I am passive in respect of it. But if the arm is mine, and goes up because I voluntarily raise it, then I am not passive in respect of its going up; and so, one would have thought, I am not passive in respect of the change of my visual state as I see it going up. Berkeley may say that here I am involved both actively and passively, but as soon as he adds any details to this he is in trouble.[33]

Suppose he says that I (*a*) actively raise my arm but (*b*) passively undergo the corresponding change of visual state. That will be no use unless (*b*) passivity is taken to cover not only the visual but also the tactual and other sensory states which would count as perceptions of my arm's upward movement—e.g. what I feel when my hand touches the ceiling. But then this way of distinguishing the area of my activity from that of my passivity implies a distinction between (*a*) my arm's going up and (*b*) *any* 'ideas' which would ordinarily count as perceptions of my arm's

[32] *First Dialogue*, p. 196.
[33] See D. M. Datta, 'Berkeley's Objective Idealism', Steinkraus pp. 114–18.

going up. I think it is clear that this flatly contradicts Berkeley's idealism and takes him a giant stride towards the veil-of-perception account of what it is for something really to be the case in the objective realm, e.g. for an arm really to go up.

Berkeley's only alternative is to say that I am active in respect of my volition and passive in respect of the upward movement of my arm. That he would take this way out of the difficulty is suggested by his remark that 'man without God' would be wretched because of his 'unperformed wills'. Taking this latter phrase to mean 'volitions not followed by the willed upshot', this implies that what does actually happen ('with God') is that I actively will and that the upshot is wholly in God's hands and thus wholly outside the scope of my genuine activity. An even more striking instance of this line of thought will be discussed in my next section.

I have already noted that this version of the volition theory commits Berkeley to giving causal statements an inductive basis after all; but there is more wrong with it than that. The theory was supposed to explain what it is for a movement to constitute my actively doing something, or to be a case of the activity of a spirit; but now we find that no bodily movement ever is a case of a spirit's actually doing something. All I ever do is to *will*, and what happens to my body is not really up to me, so that Berkeley is not even entitled to his modest asseveration that 'We move our Legs our selves'.[34] In this version of it, the volition theory is self-defeating, for it implies the non-existence of the very class of phenomena it was designed to explain.

Berkeley's difficulties over the active/passive dichotomy result from the intersection of *his* premises with a conceptual tangle which presents a problem to every philosopher. There is a theory-neutral question about how the active/passive distinction should be brought to bear upon cases of physical activity, and I do not pretend to know how to answer it.

45. *Spirits*

Berkeley has a special problem about the physical actions of other people. It is natural to construe the passivity argument of § 35 above as saying 'Any change in my sensory state which is

[34] *Philosophical Commentaries*, entry 548.

not my doing is God's doing', which implies that your ideas when you perceive my raising my arm are caused solely by God. Berkeley, however, construes it otherwise:

Though there be some things which convince us, human agents are concerned in producing them; yet it is evident to every one, that . . . the far greater part of the ideas or sensations perceived by us, are not produced by, or dependent on the wills of men. There is therefore some other spirit that causes them.[35]

The crux of the argument, it seems, is what is (not) caused by *men* rather than what is (not) caused by *me*. In chapter VII I deliberately suppressed this issue by using both formulations interchangeably, but now it is time to prise them apart.

This requires us to examine Berkeley's use of 'spirit other than myself', which requires us first to look into 'spirit'.

After much wavering in the *Commentaries*, Berkeley settles in the published works for a view of spirits as mental substances, which he takes to be substrata:

Thing or *being* is the most general name of all, it comprehends under it two kinds entirely distinct and heterogeneous, and which have nothing common but the name, to wit, *spirits* and *ideas*. The former are *active, indivisible substances*: the latter are *inert, fleeting, dependent beings*, which subsist not by themselves, but are supported by, or exist in minds or spiritual substances.[36]

The word 'supported', like the phrase 'substance or support' further on,[37] ominously echoes the Lockean substratum analysis of the concept of substance. But there is more here than just a verbal echo. Berkeley's treatment of spiritual substance has a deep structural feature which brings it under the same axe as the Lockean substratum theory, namely its dividing the mental world into two *kinds* of item—ideas and spirits, mental-properties and mental-property-bearers.[38] The objection I brought against the substratum analysis in § 11 above is perfectly general: it condemns anyone who says 'Property-bearers are items of a kind', and condemns him no less if he also says, as Berkeley does, 'There are no properties except mental ones'.

Berkeley is clearly in a difficulty here; and, since he himself

[35] *Principles* § 146.
[36] *Principles* § 89.   [37] *Principles* § 135.
[38] For a different view, see Tipton, 'Berkeley's View of Spirit'.

has attacked the substratum analysis in Locke's version of it, he has a problem about consistency. I shall try to show, partly using materials in Chapter III above, how we can resolve this well-known tension in Berkeley's thought in a manner which leaves him if not triumphant at least intelligible.

Berkeley himself sees that 'spirit' needs special defence, primarily because he regards 'spirit' as an intelligible term although one could not have an idea of spirit. In the following passage the prima facie problem is stated badly because of underlying bad theory, and Berkeley's handling of it is also unsatisfactory for a reason I shall explain later:

> Surely it ought not to be looked on as a defect in a human understanding, that it does not perceive the idea of *spirit*, if it is manifestly impossible there should be any such *idea*. And this, if I mistake not, has been demonstrated in *Sect.* 27: to which I shall here add that a spirit has been shown to be the only substance or support, wherein the unthinking beings or ideas can exist: but that this *substance* which supports or perceives ideas should it self be an *idea* or like an *idea*, is evidently absurd.[39]

Berkeley here argues: spirits are not ideas, so spirits cannot resemble ideas, so there cannot be an idea of spirit. The premiss is true, and perhaps it entails the lemma; but the lemma does not entail the conclusion, for it is just not true that an idea of x must resemble x. Whatever the impediment is to there being any ideas of spirit, it cannot be that. Notice also the curiously blustering nature of the passage: Berkeley says imperiously that *of course* there can be no idea of spirit, as though he were up against someone who thinks that there can be such an idea or, even more absurdly, someone who thinks it is 'a defect in a human understanding' that it cannot form such an idea. But these opponents are straw men. What has to be dealt with is the adversary who says that if there cannot be an idea of spirit then the word 'spirit' is illegitimate or at the very least that we cannot know that there are spirits. Berkeley has an answer for that adversary too, but in the quoted passage he bypasses the answer by misrepresenting the challenge.

Before trying to improve on that account of what the problem is, let us look at Berkeley's main way of solving it. His core statement on the subject is this: 'How often must I repeat, that I

[39] *Principles* § 135.

know or am conscious of my own being; and that I my self am not my ideas, but somewhat else, a thinking active principle that perceives, knows, wills, and operates about ideas.'[40] In brief: I know what 'spirit' means, because I am a spirit myself, and I know what 'I' and 'myself' mean.

In this connexion Berkeley introduces the word 'notion'— casually in the Third Dialogue,[41] more deliberately in the second edition of the *Principles*. Still taking himself or his mind as his paradigm of a spirit, he says that even if he has no idea of spirit at least he has a 'notion' of it, and that this suffices to render the term 'spirit' a legitimate one.

That way of expressing his position is not quite right, though. Berkeley is not saying 'I have a notion of myself and *therefore* understand the word "myself" and know truths about myself'. If he were, we might join some writers in regretting Berkeley's not having told us just what 'notions' are,[42] or we might join others in speculating about what deep insight into meaning is being concealed behind Berkeley's reticence about 'notions';[43] but both responses are misguided. Berkeley's real position can be expressed thus: 'I have a notion of myself, *which is to say* that I can understand the word "myself" and can know truths about myself', with or without the rider '. . . even though I have no idea of myself'. That is, Berkeley does not have an unexplained premiss about 'notions' from which he infers that he can under- stand 'myself' or 'my mind' without having corresponding ideas. Rather, he has the premiss that he does understand 'my mind', yet has no corresponding ideas; and he expresses these facts, or at least the former of them, by saying that he has a 'notion' of his mind. This is well confirmed by the text:

We have some notion of soul, spirit [etc.]—in as much as we know or understand the meaning of those words.[44]

In a large sense indeed, we may be said to have an idea, or rather a notion of *spirit*, that is, we understand the meaning of the word, other- wise we could not affirm or deny any thing of it.[45]

[40] *Third Dialogue*, p. 233.   [41] *Third Dialogue*, pp. 231–2.
[42] R. Grossman, 'Digby and Berkeley on Notions', *Theoria*, vol. 26 (1960); J. W. Davis, 'Berkeley's Doctrine of the Notion', *Review of Metaphysics*, vol. 12 (1959). For further examples, see references by Davis.
[43] I. T. Ramsey, 'Berkeley and the Possibility of an Empirical Metaphysics', Steinkraus pp. 17–19; A.-L. Leroy, 'Was Berkeley an Idealist?', Steinkraus p. 136.
[44] *Principles* § 27.   [45] *Principles* § 140.

I have some knowledge or notion of my mind, and its acts about ideas, inasmuch as I know or understand what is meant by those words. What I know, that I have some notion of.[46]

So it is not really right to say: 'According to Berkeley, some understanding is based on ideas, some on notions.' It is better to say: 'Berkeley uses the word "notion" to express his claim that not all understanding is based on ideas.'

Berkeley's basic problem about 'spirit', expressed in as un-Lockean a way as possible, is as follows: it seems plausible to say that if I am to have any disciplined theoretical use for a given classificatory term, I must know what it would be like to encounter something to which the term applies: my understanding of 'house', for example, involves my knowing how to distinguish houses from non-houses amongst the items with which I am sensorily confronted. But this sets a standard which cannot be met by the term 'spirit' in Berkeley's sense of it, for nothing could count as a sensory encounter with a spirit.

The difficulty could be put to Berkeley in the form of a challenge: 'What right have you to think that there is anything to which "spirit" applies?' Berkeley's answer, I think, amounts to this: 'I have ideas; and, by definition of "spirit", whatever has ideas is a spirit; so I am a spirit. You cannot expect me to take seriously the suggestion that perhaps I do not exist or do not have ideas.' If the challenger said: 'So you think you do have ideas of spirit, from your encounters with yourself?' Berkeley's reply would be: 'No—all my confrontations are ones in which *I* confront *something else*. I am, so to speak, the receptacle which holds all of my data, and it does not make sense to try to include myself, or that to which "I" refers, among these data. Don't ask where you can *find* a spirit—you *are* one.'

That exercise in sympathetic misinterpretation does seem to fit the broad outlines of Berkeley's treatment of 'spirit'. It credits him with having a prima facie problem which could, though unhappily, be expressed in the words 'There can be no idea of spirit'. It credits him with thinking that a defender of 'spirit' must take himself as the paradigm spirit. And it credits him with the view that a full explanation of *why there cannot* be an idea of spirit carries with it an explanation of *why it does not matter that there cannot* be an idea of spirit—that is, why it is legitimate to use

[46] *Principles* § 142.

'spirit', or at least 'I', even if one has no corresponding idea. These three features of my interpretation correspond to three of the most conspicuous features of Berkeley's own discussions of 'spirit'.

On this account of the problem and of Berkeley's solution of it, neither the problem nor the solution has anything to do with substrata. Perhaps it does involve the notion of a mind as a spiritual substance—an item upon which ideas are adjectival and which is not itself adjectival upon anything—but it does not involve Berkeley in wrongly analysing the concept of substance in terms of naked substrata. It is true that Berkeley does use substratum language in talking about spirits, and this gives him a (bad) reason for saying that we cannot have ideas of spirits. But, whether or not he realized it, he also has a much better reason for thinking that the concept of spirit, or of himself as a mental or spiritual substance, is a special case which needs special explanation; and his treatment of the problem is coherent only when seen in the light of that better account of what the problem is. If we continue to see the problem as 'How can we make sense of "kind of item which supports mental properties"?', the answer is that we cannot make sense of this, and Berkeley's appeals to 'I know or am conscious of my own being' are of no avail. If on the other hand the problem is 'How can I make sense of "myself" or of "I", if these terms do not refer to an item which I can sensorily encounter?', then some of Berkeley's remarks contain the makings of an answer.

Now, what about the consistency problem? Berkeley does, as I have mentioned, use the language of the substratum analysis in talking about spirits, apparently assuming that if there are substances there are substrata—items of a *kind* that cannot have any defining properties. Can he square this with his peremptory rejection of the substrata canvassed by Locke? The point is forcefully made by Hylas:

You admit . . . that there is spiritual substance, although you have no idea of it; while you deny there can be such a thing as material substance, because you have no notion or idea of it. Is this fair dealing? To act consistently, you must either admit matter or reject spirit.[47]

Philonous replies:

[47] *Third Dialogue*, p. 232.

I do not deny the existence of material substance, merely because I have no notion of it, but because the notion of it is inconsistent, or in other words, because it is repugnant that there should be a notion of it ... In the very notion or definition of material substance, there is included a manifest repugnance and inconsistency. But this cannot be said of the notion of spirit. That ideas should exist in what doth not perceive, or be produced by what doth not act, is repugnant. But it is no repugnancy to say, that a perceiving thing should be the subject of ideas, or an active thing the cause of them.[48]

The move from 'I have no notion of it' to 'the notion of it is inconsistent', though problematical in several ways, is clearly a shift from the attack on substrata to the attack on material substances—these being understood as radically mind-independent items, not necessarily as involving the substratum analysis. In short, Berkeley is now retroactively changing the whole structure and strategy of his attack on 'material substance', asking the reader to ignore the attack on substrata as such and to take him as having addressed himself solely to the veil-of-perception doctrine. In effect, Berkeley is now claiming to have followed the strategy which I described in § 17 above.

Berkeley's treatment of the 'consistency problem' confirms my thesis in Chapter III above, that the substratum and 'real thing' issues are different and that Berkeley tended to conflate them. For we have now found Berkeley retracting his criticisms of the substratum analysis as such, and asking that his attack on 'material substance' be viewed wholly as a criticism of the veil-of-perception doctrine. It would be pleasant to contend that he has in fact accepted the substratum analysis all through, but I do not think that can be maintained: Berkeley's discussions of Locke do contain those few cogent remarks which are genuinely addressed to the substratum analysis and not a confused mixture of it with other doctrines. But they are few, and are peripheral to Berkeley's main anti-Lockean concerns; and those facts render his subsequent acceptance of the substratum analysis less surprising than it might otherwise have been.

Now, at last, we can return to the question of 'other spirits'. It is not clear that Berkeley has entitled himself to the notion of 'spirit other than myself'. His claim to be able to make sense of 'spirit' rests on the argument: I am myself, so I know myself, so

I have a notion of myself, so I have a notion of spirit. If he is to apply 'spirit' to anything else, he ought to provide further explanations—which he does not. I shall not press that point, however; for my main concern is with what Berkeley says *about* other spirits, i.e. his treatment of 'the problem of other minds', of which he was arguably the discoverer. He says:

We cannot know the existence of other spirits, otherwise than by their operations, or the ideas by them excited in us. I perceive several motions, changes, and combinations of ideas, that inform me there are certain particular agents like my self, which accompany them, and concur in their production. Hence the knowledge I have of other spirits is not immediate, as is the knowledge of my ideas; but depending on the intervention of ideas, by me referred to agents or spirits distinct from myself, as effects or concomitant signs.[49]

Berkeley goes on to say that sometimes the agent cannot be a human one. Let that pass: we shall give him God, and merely ask what right Berkeley has to say that the agent ever *is* a human one.

He concedes that 'we have neither an immediate evidence nor a demonstrative knowledge of the existence of other finite spirits' but claims that 'there is a probability' that such spirits exist because 'we see signs and effects indicating distinct finite agents like our selves'.[50] The claim is, then, that 'There are finite spirits other than myself' is for me an explanatory hypothesis, a conjecture which explains my data better than any other: I have visual ideas which would ordinarily count as my seeing you raise your arm, and I speculate that there is another human spirit whose activity helps to explain the visual ideas in question.

This approach to the 'other minds' problem is notoriously full of difficulties, and for Berkeley they are peculiarly acute. The visual ideas I seek to explain by the hypothesis that there is another human spirit are perceptions of reality, and Berkeley is firmly committed to saying that they are caused by God. If another human spirit is to be involved, it must be less directly: the spirit causes x to occur, and God is somehow spurred by x's occurrence to cause a change in my visual state.

Berkeley himself says as much in a passage where he approaches the other minds problem by contraposition, as it were: by stressing

[49] *Principles* § 145.   [50] *Third Dialogue*, p. 233.

the indirectness of one's experience of other human spirits he seeks to argue that one perceives God in at least as straightforward a way as one perceives other humans. Then he overplays his hand, arguing that we are *more* in touch with God than with one another, partly because his 'effects' are 'infinitely more numerous and considerable, than those ascribed to human agents', and also—this being what gives the game away—because it is God who 'maintains that intercourse between [human] spirits, whereby they are able to perceive the existence of each other'.[51] This could be taken in either of two ways, corresponding to the two possible values of x at the end of my preceding paragraph. (1) You cause your body to move, and God causes me to perceive its movement or to perceive it as it moves; or (2) you perform a volition to move your body, and God causes your body to move and therefore causes me to perceive its movement. Either way—and neither of them sits happily with Berkeley's basic principles— God is the immediate cause of any change in my sensory state of which I am not the cause.

But if God is the immediate cause, then what is explained by the hypothesis that there is another human spirit involved in the situation? Berkeley will surely not say that your volition or your arm-movement causes God to cause the change in me; so presumably he must say that your action, whatever it is, serves as a non-causal trigger which somehow spurs or prompts God to cause a change in me. What God can do on a hint, though, he can do on his own initiative; so your role in the situation is dispensable; so there is no warrant for my conjecture that you have a role in the situation or, therefore, that you exist at all.

At this point, Berkeley's difficulties are astonishingly like Locke's over the veil-of-perception doctrine. There is a passage in the Second Dialogue where Hylas tries to contend that although God causes our changes of sensory state, 'matter' has a role either as his 'instrument' in causing these changes or as the 'occasion' of his doing so.[52] The 'occasion' proposal amounts to saying that God, in deciding whether to cause a given idea in me at a certain time, allows himself to be guided by the facts about what sorts

---

[51] *Principles* § 147. See also *Alciphron* IV, §§ 4–5.

[52] *Second Dialogue*, pp. 218–220. See also G. D. Hicks, *Berkeley* (London, 1932), p. 148; and R. Jackson, 'Locke's Version of the Doctrine of Representative Perception', Martin p. 139 n.

of 'matter' I am in fact in the presence of at that time. Philonous' crisply efficient exposure of the idleness of 'matter' in this theory (as distinct from his claims that it is impious to suppose God would attend to unthinking substance, and that 'matter' is meaningless anyway) can be modelled over into a proof that in Berkeley's own theory 'other human spirits' are idle to the same degree and for the same reasons.

Berkeley is in fact deeply committed to saying: 'I am alone in the universe with God. There are sensible things, but these are a sub-class of my mental states and God's; there are perhaps mental states which God has and I do not, and many of my mental states must be God's also; but there cannot be any reason for supposing that the universe contains any spirits, or mental substances, other than the two of us.' There may be an escape from this through an appeal to God's benevolence; but short of that, i.e. considering the existence of other human spirits simply as explanatory of the given data, Berkeley ought to say 'I do not need that hypothesis'.

IX

EMPIRICISM ABOUT MEANINGS

46. *Ideas and impressions*

HUME'S view of meaning is essentially Locke's: to understand a word is to associate it with a kind of 'idea', and 'ideas' are quasi-sensory states. For Hume, too, thinking consists in mentally manipulating these same 'ideas'; and so he shares with his predecessors a general picture in which no radical lines are drawn between thinking, imagining, meaning, understanding. The inclusion of 'imagining' in the list suggests that Hume will draw no sharp and absolute line between, for instance, what goes on when one thinks out a problem and what goes on when one sees a potato. This is indeed the case. Hume does have a special label—'impressions'—for the sense-data of normal perception, but he represents the difference between 'ideas' and 'impressions' as merely one of degree:

Those perceptions, which enter with most force and violence, we may name *impressions*; and under this name I comprehend all our sensations, passions and emotions, as they make their first appearance in the soul. By *ideas* I mean the faint images of these in thinking and reasoning.[1]

The generic word 'perception' echoes Berkeley's view that all we strictly perceive are what *he* calls 'ideas', and also Locke's use of 'perceive' to cover all mental activity (see § 4 above). As Hume says roundly: 'To hate, to love, to think, to feel, to see; all this is nothing but to perceive.'[2] His 'perceptions' are Locke's and Berkeley's 'ideas'; and his distinction between 'ideas' and 'impressions' marks the difference in the degree of 'force' or 'vivacity'—a difference which was equally recognized, though in different language, by Locke and Berkeley. In Hume, then, we again have the assimilation of the intellectual to the sensory.

I remarked in § 4 that this assimilation, or the double use of

---

[1] *Treatise*, p. 1. See also p. 319 and Kemp Smith, *The Philosophy of David Hume*, ch. 10.

[2] *Treatise*, p. 67.

'idea' which it generates, is relevant to Locke's empiricism about meanings, i.e. to his theory that to understand a classificatory word one must either (a) have been sensorily confronted by items to which it applies or (b) know how to define it by means of words which one understands. In particular, the double use of 'idea' makes meaning-empiricism look simpler, and perhaps more obviously true, than it really is. Meaning-empiricism, however, is also influenced by the sensory/intellectual assimilation in other and subtler ways, and in §§ 47–8 I shall discuss these as they figure in Hume's writings.

Hume, as is well known, took over all the main elements of Locke's meaning-empiricism, except for the part about abstract ideas which he thought Berkeley had refuted. I choose to focus my discussion of meaning-empiricism on Hume partly because it plays a more active role in his work than in Locke's—presumably because Hume saw more clearly its potential as a weapon of destructive criticism, or had a greater will to use it as such. Confronted by an expression which his theory implies to be meaningless, Locke's usual response is not to condemn the expression but to soft-pedal on the theory. Hume tries to do better than this, and never shrinks from following the argument wherever it honestly seems to him to lead. As that wavering account suggests, I am unsure whether the basic difference is one of insight or one of nerve.[3]

I centre the discussion on Hume also because his mind was tougher and more persistent than Locke's; the power of the intellectual/sensory assimilation to generate error is seen more clearly in Hume because he, far more than Locke or Berkeley, abides by it and does his hard thinking in terms of it. This is why, so far as the themes of this book are concerned, Hume is at once the most instructive and the oftenest wrong of the three philosophers.

The phrase 'tougher and more persistent' needs qualification. I shall explain why, through a small case-study which also adds needed details about the idea/impression dichotomy.

Since 'impressions' are by definition nothing but forceful perceptions, Hume can reasonably think that all our sensory intake in experience of the objective realm consists of 'impressions'; but he ought also to allow an 'impression' status to much of

[3] See Gibson, *Locke's Theory of Knowledge*, pp. 10–11, 28.

what occurs in vivid dreams, hallucinations, etc. Sometimes, however, he uses 'impression' as though it covered *only* the data of ordinary experience of the objective realm. This narrowing tendency, although Hume explicitly disavows it[4] and although it conflicts with his view that there are impressions of reflection as well as sensation, is strongly manifested in his preparedness to treat meaning-empiricism as a view about understanding in relation to *experience of the objective*, while always expressing it as a thesis about understanding in relation to *impressions*. I'll return to this in a moment.

Hume believes that thought is a transaction with ideas; but his definition of 'idea' as 'faint perception' ought to discourage him from saying conversely that every transaction with ideas is a case of thinking—unless of course he follows Descartes and Locke in using 'thought' etc. to sprawl over the whole range of the mental. Yet we have seen that he calls ideas 'the faint images of [impressions] in thinking and reasoning', which strongly suggests that any having of ideas is to count as 'thinking' in some fairly normal sense of that word.

The two preceding paragraphs yield this: Hume's official position is that (*a*) the impression/idea line is just the lively/faint line within perceptions; but he tends to slip into the assumptions, neither of which square with that, that (*b*) impressions occur only in experience of the objective realm, and that (*c*) ideas occur only in thinking and reasoning. Suppose that all these were present in Hume's mind while he was considering what to say about vivid hallucinations. He would be led by (*b*) to say that such hallucinations involve ideas, not impressions; (*c*) would let him infer from this that hallucinations are cases of thinking; and a memory of (*a*) might persuade him that they only just qualify—that they are close to the borderline between thinking and non-thinking. It is not a libel on Hume to suppose he could get into such a muddle:

Every one of himself will readily perceive the difference betwixt feeling [impressions] and thinking [ideas]. The common degrees of these are easily distinguished; tho' it is not impossible but in particular instances they may very nearly approach to each other. Thus in sleep, in a fever, in madness, or in any very violent emotions of soul, our ideas may approach to our impressions.[5]

[4] *Treatise*, p. 2 n. See also Zabeeh, *Hume*, pp. 39–41.
[5] *Treatise*, pp. 1–2.

Even if I have misunderstood that passage, Hume does tend to equate 'impressions' with 'perceptions of the objective realm'. That fact alone makes my point, which is this: if Hume combined that equation with his official account of the idea/impression distinction, he would be equating 'experience of the objective realm' with 'intense or violent sensory states'; and this, considered as an account of what it is to perceive something objective, would be simple to the point of idiocy.

Hume was capable of such optimistic simplifications; but this is because of a defect in his peripheral vision, so to speak, and not because he could not deal in complex depth with a problem when he had it in focus. I have accused him of one simplification about thinking and another about objectivity. Since he did not see that 'thinking and reasoning' presents a philosophical problem in its own right, Hume's stray remarks about it seldom rise above the level of the quoted passage. But he did address himself squarely to the analysis of objectivity-concepts, and his treatment of such concepts, although deeply flawed, is a peerless example of disciplined depth and complexity.

47. *Hume's meaning-empiricism*

'All our simple ideas . . . are deriv'd from simple impressions, which are correspondent to them, and which they exactly represent.'[6] Hume adopts Locke's distinction between 'complex' and 'simple' ideas, the former linked with definable words, the latter with words whose meanings—Hume thinks—must be learned through confrontation with examples. The simple/complex antithesis has worked much mischief in the theory of meaning generally, but I shall not harry it here.

Each time Hume defends his meaning-empiricism, he claims to have two arguments for it.[7] *Firstly*, everyone who has a given simple idea also has one or more impressions which are 'correspondent' to it, i.e. which resemble it in everything but strength. This cannot be coincidence: 'Such a constant conjunction, in such an infinite number of instances, can never arise from chance; but clearly proves a dependence of the impressions on the ideas, or of the ideas on the impressions.'[8] Furthermore, the impressions must

---

[6] *Treatise*, p. 4.   [7] *Treatise*, pp. 3–7; *Enquiry* §§ 14–17.
[8] *Treatise*, pp. 4–5.

cause the ideas, and not vice versa, since the ideas never come first. Our simple ideas, therefore, are copies of impressions—i.e. they are caused by impressions and resemble them. *Secondly*: 'If it happen, from a defect of the organ, that a man is not susceptible of any species of sensation, we always find that he is as little susceptible of the correspondent ideas. A blind man can form no notion of colours; a deaf man of sounds.' [9] It is clear that this will yield only a special case of the first argument.

If we take this at face value, as a theory about the preconditions for having unlively 'perceptions' or quasi-sensory states, what evidence can Hume have for it? He may claim to know about his own ideas by 'reflection', but what of the ideas of others? He speaks of the ideas of the blind and the deaf, asserts that the 'Laplander or Negro has no notion of the relish of wine', [10] and confidently uses 'we': 'That idea of red, which we form in the dark . . .', 'We find, that any impression . . . is constantly followed by an idea, which resembles it', 'When we analyze our thoughts or ideas . . . we always find that they resolve themselves into such simple ideas as . . .'[11] How could he know?

A related question: what would count as evidence against the theory when so construed? Of his thesis that every simple idea is preceded by a correspondent impression Hume says:

Every one may satisfy himself in this point by running over as many [ideas] as he pleases. But if any one should deny this universal resemblance, I know no way of convincing him, but by desiring him to shew . . . a simple idea, that has not a correspondent impression. If he does not answer this challenge, as 'tis certain he cannot, we may from his silence and our own observation establish our conclusion.[12]

The theory's truth is, indeed, to depend solely upon whether anyone can 'shew' or 'produce' a simple idea not preceded by a correspondent impression:

Those who would assert that this position is not universally true nor without exception, have only one, and that an easy method of refuting it; by producing that idea, which, in their opinion, is not derived from this source. It will then be incumbent on us, if we would maintain our doctrine, to produce the impression, or lively perception, which corresponds to it.[13]

---

[9] *Enquiry* § 15. See also Locke, *Essay* II. ii. 2.   [10] *Enquiry* § 15.
[11] *Treatise*, pp. 3, 5, and *Enquiry* § 14.   [12] *Treatise*, pp. 3–4.
[13] *Enquiry* § 14.

To be able to assess the theory, then, we must know how to go about 'producing' an idea.[14]

Clearly, Hume will not bow to any fool or knave who claims to have a counter-example, any congenitally blind man who says 'I have an idea of purple'. To 'produce' an idea one must not merely *say* but *show* that one has it; and Hume is confident that his challengers will fail in this larger task, e.g. that a congenitally blind man who says 'I have an idea of purple' won't be able to give us reasons for believing him.

But the blind man might well satisfy us that he is not lying, and then Hume's only resort would be to say that the blind man did not know what 'purple' means. This, I suggest, is the source of his confidence: he is sure that the congenitally blind man would not be able to 'produce' an idea of purple because he would not be able to satisfy us that he knew what 'purple' means. In short, no one is to count as having an idea of purple unless he knows the meaning of 'purple' or a synonym of it in some other language.

Now, what of the people whose ideas Hume counts as positive evidence for this theory? He has not asked them what ideas they have, and even if he did why should he believe their answers? He must say: 'Well, they clearly understand the word "purple", and that is good enough for me.' If he does not say this, then it is perfectly obscure how he can have any positive evidence for his theory as applied to anyone but himself. If he does say it, then anyone counts as having an idea of purple if he understands 'purple' or a synonym of it in some other language.

Combining the two results: someone counts as having an idea of purple if and only if he understands 'purple' or a synonym thereof. Hume's theory is not that *ideas* pre-require impressions, but that *understanding* pre-requires impressions.[15]

I could have *jumped* to this conclusion. 'When Hume speaks of "ideas" his real topic is meaning and understanding, for his analysis of these is basically Lockean.' The longer route, however, displays more of the logical structure. The salient points are that when Hume's theory is taken at face-value we cannot bring evidence to bear upon it; that the evidence which Hume would probably have allowed has the effect of turning the theory into

[14] See Zabeeh, *Hume*, pp. 75–6; A. H. Basson, *David Hume* (Pelican Books, 1958), pp. 35 ff.
[15] Thus D. G. C. MacNabb, *David Hume* (London, 1951), pp. 27–9.

one not about ideas but about understanding; and that this transformation solves the evidence-problem only because understanding consists not in having Humean ideas but in something for which there are public criteria.

So we should see Hume as having a theory about how impressions are pre-required for understanding—with 'understanding' properly understood. His official equation of 'understanding' with 'having ideas', since it dictates his wording of the theory and also affects details in his handling of it, cannot be neglected; but the theory ought not to be seen as primarily one about ideas.

It comes down to this. We may say, in short-hand, that Hume accepts (1) 'Ideas follow impressions', (2) 'Understanding is having ideas', (3) 'Understanding follows impressions'. If we see (3) as inferred from (1) and (2), then (1) stands on its own feet and so cannot be assessed, and the meaning of (3) is dictated by (2) so that (3) cannot be assessed either. So we shall do better to take (3) as accepted on its own merits, i.e. as a theory which really is about understanding. This credits Hume with knowing what understanding really is, and of course he does know this. His theoretical acceptance of (2)—which leads him to express (3) as (1)—is belied by his preparedness to identify cases of understanding on the basis of the criteria we ordinarily do employ—criteria which lie in the public domain and do not concern 'ideas'. There is nothing mysterious, or even unusual, about a philosopher's misdescribing a concept which he is well able to use properly.

Taking Hume's theory to have the form 'You cannot understand W unless you have first . . .', we still have problems regarding it. I now present three of them.

Understanding is having certain linguistic abilities; we can tell whether someone understands a given word; and we could discover a case of understanding which was not preceded by impressions of the sort demanded by Hume's theory. What someone understands now is not logically tied to what he underwent earlier: the account of 'newly born' adults in Shaw's *Back to Methusaleh* is a perfectly consistent fantasy. Hume himself sees his theory as refutable by counter-evidence, yet he will not retract it at the drop of a hat. After denying that he has ever had an impression of a necessary connexion in the outer world, he asks:

[Should I therefore] assert, that I am here possest of an idea, which is not preceded by any similar impression? This wou'd be too strong a proof of levity and inconstancy; since the contrary principle has been already so firmly establish'd, as to admit of no farther doubt; at least, till we have more fully examin'd the present difficulty.[16]

Elsewhere he is even stubborner, as when he argues that we cannot attach sense to 'time during which nothing happens':

That we really have no such idea, is certain. For whence shou'd it be deriv'd? Does it arise from an impression of sensation or of reflexion? ... If you cannot point out *any such impression*, you may be certain you are mistaken, when you imagine you have *any such idea*.[17]

Here and elsewhere Hume seems to treat meaning-empiricism as *a priori* true, as not after all vulnerable to counter-examples. A well-tested empirical theory has some power to discredit an occasional putative counter-example: 'Helpful as you have found him, I doubt if Schmidt is really a good psycho-analyst since he hasn't himself been analysed.' But Hume thinks his theory can fatally discredit whole classes of alleged counter-examples: he mainly uses it, indeed, to argue that *nobody* has an 'idea' of eventless time, necessary connexion, the self etc. Why can't his opponents say that these are precisely the classes of 'ideas' for which the theory is false?

There is another puzzle about Hume's position. If a congenitally blind man showed that he understood 'purple', Hume's theory would be refuted, and this would deprive him of his main argument for saying that certain expressions are meaningless. In such an eventuality he would be committed to conceding that perhaps those expressions are meaningful after all, and yet it seems clear that such a concession would really be misplaced: the linguistic abilities of a blind Patagonian are irrelevant to the intelligibility of 'eventless time' and the rest.

A third puzzle: Hume is concerned with whether certain expressions make sense, or whether we understand anything by them, and he thinks that these questions have some importance. But if it really does matter *now* whether a given expression makes sense, then its making sense or not ought to show *now*: we ought to be able to settle the question by attending to the present and the future. Yet Hume, in trying to answer the question through

[16] *Treatise*, p. 77.   [17] *Treatise*, p. 65.

his theory, implies that it is best answered by looking to the past—as though the best way of assessing a psycho-analyst were by considering how he was trained.

Summing up these three difficulties: Hume offers an empirical theory as though it were an *a priori* one; and the theory which he offers turns out to be largely irrelevant to the matters which he wants it to illuminate. I now proceed to explain why.

48. *The genetic nature of Hume's theory*

The crucial trouble is that Hume's theory is genetic rather than analytic: he expresses it as a theory about what must occur before there can be understanding, rather than about what understanding is, or about what it is for an expression to have a meaning.

He would have done better to say something like the following. An expression E in our public language has a meaning only if we can tell whether a given person understands it, and our evidence for that must consist in how he uses it. Suppose he uses it correctly in statements whose truth-value does not depend upon the state of his environment at the time of speaking—in verbal definitions, necessary truths, contingent generalizations etc. This will assure us of his understanding of E if, but only if, we know that he understands the other words used in those statements. Someone's saying 'Red things tend to irritate bulls' or 'Red things are always coloured' is not evidence of his understanding 'red' if his grasp of 'bulls' or 'coloured' is seriously in doubt. This looks like a vicious circle; and our only escape from it is through the fact that 'using E correctly' may involve relating E correctly not only to other expressions but also to bits of the objective world. The basis for our common understanding of a language is our ability to agree on statements of the form 'That is a . . .' where 'that' refers to something accessible to all of us; and E cannot be accounted as meaningful unless it is—or connects with expressions which are—usable in statements of that kind. The connexions may be lengthy and tenuous, and of course they need not consist in strings of verbal definitions; but if there is to be the possibility of evidence for or against the claim that somebody understands E, then there must be *some* coherent way of connecting E with the empirical world—the world given to us through our impressions.

That would preserve the empiricist spirit of Hume's theory, while turning it from a genetic into an analytic one. The first difficulty mentioned near the end of § 47 would not now arise. The theory would make claims about what it is for an expression to be understood or to have a meaning; and these could be refuted only by philosophical argument. An alleged counter-example would be a putatively meaningful expression which was denied to be connectable with the world in the required way; and an adherent of the theory would have to deal with such an expression by considering whether it does have a meaning and whether it lacks empirical connexions. If it turns out to have one and lack the other then the theory is false; and in that case it is obviously reasonable to demand a retrial for the other expressions which have been condemned on the strength of the theory—which removes the second difficulty. Furthermore, the scrutiny of a supposed counter-example would not be an exercise in personal biography: the decisive facts lie in the present and future, not in the past; which removes the third difficulty.

Much of what Hume says in deploying his meaning-empiricism can be modelled over into a theory which is not genetic and—harking back to the first theme of § 47—not about ideas. This can be done, indeed, too far for it to be a coincidence. I do not say that Hume 'really meant' to offer an analysis of meaning and understanding; but I do suggest that what he said about ideas as copied from impressions is explained, somewhat and somehow, by the fact that his remarks can be 'translated' into analytic truths about meaningfulness in relation to empirical cashability. Let us examine one striking example of how far such modelling or 'translating' can go.

To get a protracted sound from a tuning-fork you must rap it hard in the first place; and, analogously, Hume could think it obvious that the first in a series of similar 'perceptions' must be 'lively' or 'vivacious' if it is to linger on in the form of conjured-up perceptions on later occasions. He certainly does take 'vivacity' to be a quantum which is transmitted, with some loss, from an impression to the ideas which follow it:

When any impression has been present with the mind, it again makes its appearance there as an idea; and this it may do after two different ways: either when in its new appearance it retains a considerable degree of its first vivacity, and is somewhat intermediate betwixt an impression and an idea; or when it entirely loses that vivacity, and is a perfect idea.[18]

Now, this view of 'vivacity' which comes right from the heart of Hume's theory considered as a theory about the origins of ideas, implies a reason for saying that any simple idea must be preceded by a *lively* perception. But I have remarked that he tends to equate 'impression' with 'sensory intake from the objective world': he does not care whether a blind man could have a vivid hallucination of something purple. Let us translate 'lively' into 'pertaining to the objective realm', as well as turning Hume's theory into one about understanding rather than ideas, and construing it as analytic rather than genetic. Under this threefold 'translation', the statement 'Ideas must be preceded by *lively* perceptions' becomes 'What is understood must be connectable with experience of the *objective* realm'. The stress on 'lively', which was encouraged by the primitive face-value form of the theory, re-appears as a stress on 'objective'. The latter stress can be justified within the triply-transformed version of the theory: you cannot know that I understand E unless there is something we can both connect with E—that is, something interpersonal and thus objective.

(I do not offer these transformations as an act of fond indulgence towards Hume—an indulgence which I refused to extend to Berkeley when in § 10 above I pointed out how un-Wittgensteinian his views on meaning are. The point is simply that it is profitable to look at Hume in the light of these 'up-dating' transformations —they throw light on his text, and help to bring to the surface many instructive complexities. In contrast with this, the representation of Berkeley as Wittgensteinian about meaning flattens out complexities in the text, as well as abolishing the explanation which I gave in § 31 of Berkeley's opting for idealism rather than phenomenalism.)

I have not laboured to present a fully articulated theory about meaningfulness in relation to empirical cashability, for I do not think that Hume's sort of meaning-empiricism is much helped by a precise, general theory. Berkeley, for example, in his excellent criticisms of the veil-of-perception theory, needs no magisterial principles about the limits on intelligibility. He shows that Locke's doctrine fails to answer the set questions, to draw the

[18] *Treatise*, p. 8. See also pp. 98, 144.

needed distinctions, to explain the relevant facts, to connect helpfully with other philosophical problems, or to bear in any way upon possible experience. His case would not have been stronger or more interesting if he had adduced a general theory of meaning to justify the further conclusion '. . . and therefore Locke's doctrine is meaningless'.

Hume, too, often proceeds by detailed, down-to-earth argument rather than by blanket applications of his meaning-empiricism; and often enough he is not arguing for a conclusion about meaninglessness at all, but is trying to see *what* an expression means by seeing *how* it connects with the empirical world.

It is fortunate that Hume's work is not too deeply rooted in his theory; for whenever the latter is taken as sufficient in itself the results are calamitous. For example, his discussion of 'empty space' and 'empty [= eventless] time' is badly warped by his simple-minded search for 'impressions of', and by his trust in the spurious simple/complex dichotomy.[19] From the defensible premiss that nothing could count as an impression of empty space or of empty time, Hume infers that neither 'empty space' nor 'empty time' has a meaning. I think that there could be empty space and that there could be empty time;[20] but, whether I am right or wrong about that, these are certainly separate issues which require different arguments.

I am not sure that Hume's uses of the theory suffer major damage from its genetic nature. Many philosophers present analytic claims in a genetic guise without being thereby led into further errors. Still, geneticism can do harm. For example, phenomenalism is sometimes taken to be the thesis that we *advance* from sense-datum statements to ones about the objective realm; and then it is open to empirical as well as philosophical objections which have no force against phenomenalism construed as an atemporal thesis about the logical relations between objectivity-statements and statements about sense-data.

It is worth noting that the two principal defects in Hume's statement of meaning-empiricism are connected: in two distinct ways, the stress on 'ideas' is a positive encouragement into geneticism.

[19] *Treatise* I. ii. 3.
[20] Proved by S. Shoemaker, 'Time without Change', *Journal of Philosophy*, vol. 66 (1969).

First, superficially, it is tempting to think of ideas as copies of impressions, and therefore to think that impressions must come first. With 'ideas' replaced by 'capacities to use words correctly' or the like, this temptation disappears. The second way in which 'idea' encourages geneticism lies deeper. Hume wants to settle controversial questions of the form 'What, if anything, does E mean?' Because his answers are controversial he must argue for them; but if his arguments appealed explicitly to criteria having to do with the use of E—criteria on which, no doubt, he silently relies in uncontroversial cases—he would be forced to see and admit that his equation of meaning with ideas is hopelessly wrong. So he has to tackle these controversial questions in a way which draws our attention, and his own, away from E itself and towards issues about 'antecedent impressions' which are in fact irrelevant to the matter in hand. Taking them to be relevant is espousing a genetic rather than an analytic form of meaning-empiricism.

X

HUME'S PHILOSOPHICAL LOGIC

49. *The general picture*

HUME closes the *Enquiry* with a famous peroration about the destructive power of his 'principles';

When we run over libraries, persuaded of these principles, what havoc must we make? If we take in our hand any volume; of divinity or school metaphysics, for instance; let us ask, *Does it contain any abstract reasoning concerning quantity or number?* No. *Does it contain any experimental reasoning concerning matter of fact and existence?* No. Commit it then to the flames: for it can contain nothing but sophistry and illusion.[1]

As this implies, Hume works with a dichotomy: things which can be said or thought or asked concern either 'relations of ideas' or 'matters of fact'.[2] These phrases are commoner in the *Enquiry* than in the *Treatise,* but both works are permeated by the dichotomy and by Hume's conviction of its importance.

It is, in fact, a simplification of a trichotomy. Hume says that statements may be based upon 'knowledge' or 'proofs' or 'probabilities':

By knowledge, I mean the assurance arising from the comparison of ideas. By proofs, those arguments, which are deriv'd from the relation of cause and effect, and which are entirely free from doubt and uncertainty. By probability, that evidence, which is still attended with uncertainty.[3]

The better known dichotomy puts 'knowledge' on one side of the line and 'proofs and probabilities' on the other.

'Proofs' differ from 'probabilities' only superficially in Hume's scheme: the former are conclusive, the latter inconclusive, causal arguments. Hume thinks that even 'proofs' leave room for doubt or uncertainty, but only because there are limits in principle to the strength of the evidence which 'experience affords us'; and he prefers to reserve 'probability' for the kind of evidence which

---

[1] *Enquiry*, final paragraph.　　　　[2] *Enquiry* § 20; *Treatise*, p. 463.
[3] *Treatise*, p. 124.

would count as inconclusive even by ordinary untheoretical standards: 'One wou'd appear ridiculous, who wou'd say, that 'tis only probable the sun will rise to-morrow, or that all men must dye; tho' 'tis plain we have no further assurance of these facts, than what experience affords us.'[4] The scope of 'probability' is thus restricted in deference to the vernacular, and Hume admits that he sometimes forgets to defer and uses 'probability' to cover everything except what he calls 'knowledge'.

Notice that two people might accept a single statement, one because he has a 'proof' of it and the other because he finds it 'probable'; and that anything accepted as 'probable' could, in principle, eventually be given a 'proof'. I should add that the association of 'probabilities' with inconclusive causal arguments is belied by Hume's weak discussion of 'the probability of chances';[5] but it holds good in the areas of his thought which concern me here.

Although Hume agrees that by mundane standards there is no doubt that the sun will rise tomorrow, he does not think we have 'knowledge' that it will. This restricted use of 'knowledge' reflects the view that one cannot 'know' that P if there is any possibility at all that not-P: I know that P only if there is no possibility, however remote and theoretical, of my being wrong about it. Let us consider the sources of this popular mistake.

It is necessarily true that if 'x knows that P' is true then so is P. Someone might wrongly infer from this that if 'x knows that P' is true then P is necessarily true: this would restrict what could be known to what is necessarily true, and thus imply that we cannot know that the sun will rise tomorrow. This diagnosis has been offered for the narrowed use of 'know'; but, although the muddle is a possible one, it seems to me improbable and I can find no evidence that anyone has ever been guilty of it.

An intrinsically more plausible diagnosis, which seems to reflect what goes on when apprentice philosophers are induced to deny that they 'really *know*' things which in unreflective moments they would confidently claim to know, is the following. It is clearly wrong to say anything of the form 'I know that P but I might be wrong'; and this might seem to imply that knowledge is incompatible with possibility-of-error; whence it follows, since there is admittedly some possibility of error as to the sun's rising tomorrow, that we do not know that the sun will rise tomorrow.

What is wrong with that 'know'-narrowing argument? Here is a possible answer:

The argument takes 'might be wrong' and 'possibility of error' too generously. The inadmissibility of 'I know that P but I might be wrong' depends upon our taking 'might be wrong' as claiming some possibility-of-error which is considerable by everyday standards; but the conclusion of the argument takes it to include every sort of possibility-of-error.

This reply won't do; for it wrongly concedes that 'I know but I might be wrong' is admissible just so long as the possibility-of error in question is extremely remote. The suggested reply is also wrong in silently conceding that (1) 'It is wrong to say "I know that P but I might be wrong"' does entail (2) 'Knowledge is incompatible with possibility-of-error', just so long as 'might be wrong' is given the same degree of strength, so to speak, as 'possibility-of-error'. In fact, (1) does not entail (2) at all. Just as 'P but I do not believe that P' is improper, even though truth is compatible with disbelief-by-me; so also 'I know but I might be wrong' is improper, even though knowledge is compatible with possibility-of-error.

The impropriety of 'I know but I might be wrong' arises from this fact: to say 'I know that P' is to say that P and to say or imply that there are no possibilities of error worth mentioning in the present context—which explains why it is wrong to go straight on to mention possibilities of error.

That approach, I submit, shows what is really wrong with the 'know'-narrowing argument. It also explains the fact that, for a single P, it may be all right for me to say 'I know that P' to one person but wrong for me to say it to another. If their stakes in the matter are relevantly different, I may be entitled to give to one but not to the other the special kind of assurance implied by the claim to 'know'.

Philosophers often try, and always fail, to state necessary and sufficient conditions for something to count as a case of knowledge. I suggest that they fail because there are no 'cases of knowledge' in the sense required by such an endeavour. If someone says 'I know that P' when P is false, or he does not believe it, or he has virtually no evidence for it, then indeed we may say that his knowledge-claim is false, that he does not know that P, that this is not a case of knowledge. But that kind of rebuttal of a knowledge-claim is so marginal as to be almost a joke: imagine actually saying to someone 'You didn't know that P' on the grounds that P was false, or that he did not believe that P. Most real-life assessments of first-person claims to knowledge concern whether the speaker ought to have said that P in the form 'I know that P'—whether he was entitled to give that kind of assurance to that hearer on that evidence. Such assessments depend upon factors—many of them non-epistemic—which could not be captured in a statement of necessary and sufficient conditions for knowledge.

Whatever the philosophical mistakes which explain it, we can afford to take Hume's use of 'knowledge' as a mere oddity, and attend only to what he brings under this label: 'By knowledge, I mean the assurance arising from the comparison of ideas.' The word 'comparison' reflects Locke's theory that all relations stem from comparisons (see § 2 above). We can take it that Humean 'knowledge' is, as he sometimes explicitly says, what we get by discovering *relations* amongst ideas. Furthermore, since 'ideas' here are meanings, Humean 'knowledge' that P involves establishing P's truth purely on the basis of the meanings of the words in which it is expressed; so that analytic or logically necessary truths are the only ones that can be 'known'.

So Hume's dichotomy splits the bases on which statements may be accepted into (1) analysis, and (2) the adducing of causal evidence. Now we must get down to details.

50. *Intuition and demonstration*

When Hume spares from the flames any 'abstract reasoning concerning quantity or number', he implies that 'quantity or number' is the only object of 'knowledge', the only topic about which we can discover truths by 'comparing ideas'. His considered view is indeed close to this, and one wonders why the province of knowledge, or of necessary truths, should be thus limited. I shall try to explain.

Hume inherited from Descartes, through Locke, a distinction between intuition and demonstration. Here is Locke's account of it:

The mind perceives that *white* is not *black*, that a *circle* is not a *triangle*, that *three* are more than *two* . . . Such kinds of truths the mind perceives at the first sight of the ideas together, by bare intuition; without the intervention of any other idea: and this kind of knowledge is the clearest and most certain that human frailty is capable of . . . [But sometimes] those ideas, concerning whose agreement or disagreement the inquiry is made, cannot by the mind be so put together as to show it. In this case then, when the mind cannot so bring its ideas together as by their immediate comparison . . . to perceive their agreement or disagreement, it is fain, *by the intervention of other ideas* (one or more, as it happens) to discover the agreement or disagreement which it searches . . . Where the agreement and disagreement is by this means plainly and clearly perceived, it is called *demonstration*.[6]

This distinguishes self-evident analytic truths from ones which need proof. Here is an example, in language as Lockean as I can make it (for 'number' throughout read 'number > 2'). A dull schoolboy cannot see that no prime number can be the successor of a prime number: he does not 'perceive the disagreement' between the ideas of *prime number* and *successor of a prime number*. His teacher invites him to place next to his idea of *prime number* the idea of *number not divisible by 2*, and to juxtapose that with the idea of *odd number*, and that in its turn with the idea of *successor of an even number*. The schoolboy sees that each of these leads to the next, and that the last of them 'disagrees' with the idea of *successor of a prime number*; and thus he achieves by demonstration the knowledge which intuition would not give him.

This example masks a flaw in Locke's theory. Remembering that Locke assumes that any two ideas either 'agree' or 'disagree', consider what he can mean by these terms.

(1) His examples of disagreeing pairs of ideas are white/black and circle/triangle, which suggest that an idea-disagreement corresponds to a predicate-inconsistency. But then an idea-agreement corresponds to a predicate-consistency: the idea of white 'agrees with' that of square, for instance. This leaves Locke with no way of expressing the notion of entailment. The schoolboy sees that each idea 'leads to' the next, but Locke cannot say what this 'leading to' consists in. It cannot be mere 'agreement', if agreement is consistency; for, from the fact that each idea is consistent with the one before and 'successor of a prime' is

<hr />

[6] *Essay* IV. ii. 1–3.

inconsistent with the last, it does not follow that 'successor of a prime' is inconsistent with the first.

(2) The word 'comparison', and the reporting of idea-disagreements in the form 'x is not y', suggest that x agrees with y only if x is identical with (or, perhaps, entails) y. Then the idea of white 'disagrees with' that of square, because the former 'is not' the latter; but the idea of red does perhaps 'agree with' that of colour. On this interpretation an idea-agreement corresponds to a predicate-identity or -entailment, and a disagreement is the absence of such an entailment relation. This would enable Locke to say, in the schoolboy example, that each idea's 'leading to' the next is its 'agreeing with' the next; but now he cannot say how the idea of 'successor of an even number' relates to that of 'successor of a prime'. To say merely that they 'disagree' is, on the present interpretation, to say that neither entails the other—and that does not yield the desired conclusion.

The inferential procedures which Locke calls 'demonstration' require two relations—entailment and ruling-out—but Locke allows himself only the single relation of 'agreement'. It is true that 'P entails Q' is equivalent to 'P rules out not-Q'—but could Locke use that fact to repair his position? Could he, for example, take option (1) which correlates idea-disagreement with predicate-inconsistency, and express 'Red entails coloured' as 'Red disagrees with not-coloured'? No, because he is not entitled to 'not-coloured'. What idea could he claim to correspond to that expression? He sometimes implies, in other contexts, that what corresponds to 'not-coloured' is the absence from my mind of any idea of colour; but that is obviously hopeless. To take just one of its defects: how can I have an idea of red in my mind and also have— for purposes of *comparison*!—an absence from my mind of any idea of colour?

We shall see in Chapter XI that some of Hume's difficulties connect with that one, but my present concern is with other aspects of the intuition/demonstration distinction.

Hume uses the word 'intuition' sparingly, but he does sometimes draw the line in Locke's terms: 'Three of these relations are discoverable at first sight, and fall more properly under the province of intuition than demonstration.'[7] The distinction itself, however worded, runs all through his work. To take an example

[7] *Treatise*, p. 70.

which links with the opening of this section, when Hume says that 'the sciences of quantity and number . . . may safely . . . be pronounced the only proper objects of knowledge and demonstration',[8] he is not denying that there are necessary truths, known solely by 'comparison of ideas', outside the realm of mathematics. His view is rather that only 'quantity and number' admit of long, analytically valid arguments to conclusions which, because they are not obviously necessary, can count as 'knowledge' of an interesting and untrivial sort. In brief: necessary truths about 'quantity and number' may be known by demonstration, whereas all other necessary truths are known by single intuitions.

It is not true that only 'quantity and number' admit of protracted chains of logically valid reasoning. But Hume's attempts to explain this alleged fact throw light on the dangers of construing problems about meaning and necessity in terms of 'ideas'.

He changes his mind about what he has to explain. In the *Treatise* he treats geometry as wholly empirical:[9] this is because he equates meanings with ideas, takes ideas to be faded sense-data, and reifies sense-data—an accumulation of errors which lets him argue that we have no idea of infinitely divisible space because we have no infinitely divisible spatial ideas! In the *Enquiry* he distinguishes pure from applied geometry, and allows that there can be demonstrative proofs in the former; I needn't go into details on this, as the matter has been fully treated by Flew.[10] I shall discuss the view of the *Enquiry*, that the province of 'demonstration' is co-extensive with that of arithmetic, algebra and pure geometry, though what I shall say could easily be adapted to fit the *Treatise* position which excludes geometry altogether.

Here is one of Hume's explanations of the alleged fact (emphases mine):

As the component parts of quantity and number are entirely *similar*, their relations become intricate and involved; and nothing can be more curious . . . than to trace, by a variety of mediums, *their equality or inequality*, through their different appearances. But as all other ideas are clearly *distinct and different* from each other, we can never advance farther, by our utmost scrutiny, than to observe this *diversity*, and, by an obvious reflection, pronounce *one thing not to be another*.[11]

---

[8] *Enquiry* § 131.   [9] *Treatise*, pp. 70–2.
[10] *Enquiry* §§ 20, 27; Flew, *Hume's Philosophy of Belief*, pp. 61–3.
[11] *Enquiry* § 131.

The phrase 'by an obvious reflection' needs comment. Although 'reflection' is Hume's usual word for introspection, or looking into oneself, an 'obvious reflection' here means an obvious or easy intuition. For Hume this is not an ambiguity in the word 'reflection', because he thinks that it *is* by introspection, by looking inward, that one establishes trivial necessities. I shall discuss this further in § 52 below.

In the quoted passage the italicized expressions show the influence of the notion of *comparing* ideas. Outside mathematics, once we have established such a truth as that 'Black is not white' there is nothing more we can do with it: we cannot link it with others to form a 'demonstration'. In mathematics the case is different. It is true that a square is not a triangle; but that is not the end of the matter, for it is also true that, for instance, a square is composed of two triangles with certain special features and inter-relations. It is true that six is not four; but it is also true that six is composed of four and another number whose square is four, and so on. Facts like these enable us to string 'intuitions' together to form 'demonstrations' of untrivial necessary truths. Such demonstrations are wholly based on comparisons (we 'trace the equality or inequality' of our mathematical ideas); but they do not stop dead with 'x is not y', because even where x and y are distinct they may have parts in common ('the component parts of quantity and number are entirely similar'). That explains why, in mathematics, we can generate a network of assertions and denials of identity, starting with just one pair of ideas *and their parts*.

The notion of an idea's 'parts' is connected, by Hume as by Locke, with an idea's being 'complex'.[12] If ideas are meanings, their complexity is of a logical kind: the idea of man is complex because it has as parts the ideas of animal and of rationality. But ideas are also images or sense-data, and this gives 'part' a different role to play: my idea of a man has as parts my idea of a head, my idea of a torso, my ideas of legs etc. This is quite different from the logical interpretation of 'complex' and 'part', and has no place in any coherent theory of necessary truth. Yet Hume relies on it in the quoted passage. That is why, in glossing a treatment of the ideas (= meanings) involved in mathematics, I let myself say that a square is composed of two triangles. That ought to have been blatantly irrelevant; but Hume would have equated it with 'An

---

[12] See Gibson, *Locke's Theory of Knowledge*, pp. 51–2.

idea (= image) of a square is composed of two ideas of triangles', which in turn he would have construed as a statement about the logical complexity of the concept of squareness or the meaning of 'square'.

There is worse to come. For all its confusions, we can grasp the broad shape of Hume's explanation: there can be demonstrations in mathematics because those ideas are inter-related in 'intricate and involved' ways, whereas non-mathematical ideas are so simply related that they can enter only into disconnected trivialities—they admit only of separate 'intuitions' which don't interlock to yield demonstrations. But Hume also has another account of why demonstration is confined to mathematics: in non-mathematical studies ('moral sciences') we soon reach the end of what can safely be said about the inter-relations of the ideas involved, because the further our arguments proceed the more vulnerable they are to ambiguity, unclarity and the like:

The great advantage of the mathematical sciences above the moral consists in this, that the ideas of the former, being sensible, are always clear and determinate, the smallest distinction between them is immediately perceptible, and the same terms are still expressive of the same ideas, without ambiguity or variation. An oval is never mistaken for a circle, nor an hyperbola for an ellipsis . . . But the finer sentiments of the mind, the operations of the understanding, the various agitations of the passions, though really in themselves distinct, easily escape us, when surveyed by reflection . . . Ambiguity, by this means, is gradually introduced into our reasonings: Similar objects are readily taken to be the same: And the conclusion becomes at last very wide of the premises.[13]

This says that there can be demonstrations (only) in mathematics because (only) *mathematical ideas are 'clear and distinct'*; we cannot reason long with other ideas without risking substantial error. Yet in his other explanation Hume says that with non-mathematical ideas there is no lengthy reasoning to be done, risky or otherwise, precisely because *non-mathematical ideas are 'clearly distinct and different from each other'*. The two explanations conflict violently; and it is hardly surprising that Hume's one attempt to deploy both at once is a disaster.[14]

The passage last quoted has other sinister features, including the

---

[13] *Enquiry* § 48.   [14] Ibid., second paragraph.

implication that the only non-mathematical topics are psychological ones, and the extraordinary view of 'ambiguity' which seems to be presupposed. These, however, would take me too far afield.

51. *Matters of fact*

The other half of Hume's dichotomy contains 'proofs and probabilities', which he says provide our only basis for statements about 'matters of fact'. That phrase occurs mainly in the *Enquiry*, but it raises problems common to both works.

The terms 'proof' and 'probability', as I have remarked, distinguish two kinds of basis for a statement: that I shall sleep well tonight is a matter of probability for me, but of proof for the man who has just slipped me a dose of chloral. But the line separating proofs-and-probabilities from 'knowledge' is a line between two classes of statement—those which cannot, and those which can, be established just by 'comparing ideas'. Hume's label 'matter of fact', which he takes to correspond to his category of proofs-and-probabilities, is very clearly meant to mark off a class of statements.

Hume says that all our beliefs about matters of fact involve causal considerations. Let us consider what he might mean by this.

(1) Perhaps he means that any argument for a conclusion about a 'matter of fact' must involve an appeal to causal laws: 'When it is asked, *What is the nature of all our reasonings concerning matter of fact?* the proper answer seems to be, that they are founded on the relation of cause and effect.'[15] That, as it stands, is false; for one can have a demonstrative argument to a 'matter-of-fact' conclusion, just so long as it has 'matter-of-fact' premises. I think Hume would grant this, and that the above passage mis-expresses his view. Let us try again.

(2) Hume's view may be that the total grounds for any belief about a 'matter of fact', even if they include demonstrative elements, must also involve causal considerations: 'All belief of matter of fact or real existence is derived merely from some object, present to the memory or senses, and a customary conjunction between that and some other object.'[16] That is, if I reasonably hold a belief about a 'matter of fact', a full account of why I hold it will mention my acceptance of at least one statement

---

[15] *Enquiry* § 28. See also § 22.   [16] *Enquiry* § 38.

about a causal connexion or 'customary conjunction'. This also seems false, as Hume himself implies:

If I ask why you believe any particular matter of fact, which you relate, you must tell me some reason; and this reason will be some other fact, connected with it. But as you cannot proceed after this manner, *in infinitum*, you must at last terminate in some fact, which is present to your memory or senses; or must allow that your belief is entirely without foundation.[17]

So the giving of reasons may 'terminate in some fact, which is present to your . . . senses'; but if the original question had been why you believe *that* to be a fact, then you could have answered: 'Because I see [feel, hear] it', without appealing to causal considerations.

(3) I think that Hume's thesis about the causal basis for 'matter-of-fact' beliefs is meant to apply only to beliefs which are not warranted by the believer's present perceptions and memory. Hume sometimes expresses it in that form:

All reasonings concerning matter of fact seem to be founded on the relation of *Cause and Effect*. By means of that relation alone we can go beyond the evidence of our memory and senses. If you were to ask a man, why he believes any matter of fact, which is absent . . . etc.[18]

In similar vein, of a supposed person who lacked 'the idea of cause and effect': 'Such a person, without more experience, could never employ his conjecture or reasoning concerning any matter of fact, or be assured of anything beyond what was immediately present to his memory and senses.'[19] These passages show that Hume is mainly interested in 'absent' matters of fact, i.e. ones which go beyond present perceptions and memory; and I agree with him that all beliefs about *those* must be based on causal considerations. But there remains the problem of why, if Hume wanted to say something only about 'absent' matters of fact, he so often drops the qualification 'absent' or any equivalent of it.

The explanation, I suggest, is that Hume tends to identify 'matters of fact' with 'absent matters of fact'. He certainly does not do this outright. If he did, his phrase 'any matter of fact which is absent' would be pleonastic. But much of his text would be explained by the hypothesis that Hume tends unconsciously to make this identification, tends to be satisfied of a statement's

[17] *Enquiry* § 37. [18] *Enquiry* § 22. [19] *Enquiry* § 35.

'factuality' only in proportion as it is not wholly warranted by present perceptions and memory.

If that seems unbelievable, remember that the phrase 'wholly warranted by present perceptions' arguably does not cover any belief about the objective realm, even one about the present state of a contiguous bit of it—such as my belief that I now see trees through my study-window. This is because of the fact, on which phenomenalism is built and which Berkeley also used in his account of 'reality', that my belief that those are trees out there involves beliefs about what I should experience if . . ., what I shall experience when . . ., and perhaps also what I did experience when . . . So my belief that there are trees out there could be said to concern 'a matter of fact which is absent', in Hume's sense, and could also plausibly be said to have a causal basis. Hume often handles objectivity-beliefs uncritically; and his most strenuous attempt to analyse them is not very phenomenalistic (see Chapter XIII below); but there is also a causal-phenomenalist strand in his thinking about them. In so far as he construes them phenomenalistically, he has grounds for thinking of them as concerning 'absent' matters of fact and for saying that their acceptance always depends in part on causal considerations.

What of statements or beliefs about one's own present inner state? I can think of no reason why Hume should classify these too as involving something 'absent', and no reason why he should think that they are causally supported. My conjecture that he tends to identify 'matters of fact' with 'matters of "absent" fact', then, commits me to the following: Hume would tend to deny, or would want to deny, that statements about one's own present inner state report 'matters of fact' at all. Implausible as this is, I stand by it.

It does not matter that 'I have a headache now' states what would ordinarily be called 'a matter of fact'; if the propriety of the label 'matter of fact' were in question, then I ought to have protested earlier that it is in the ordinary sense 'a matter of (mathematical) fact' that 29 is a prime number. The implausibility of the position I am taking has to do with what Hume puts on each side of his dichotomy, not with the labels he uses. If 'I have a headache now' does not fall on the side labelled 'matter of fact', then it must fall on the other side of Hume's dichotomy. Hume's explanations and examples make it clear that this other side—the one comprising statements which can be established by 'comparing ideas'—includes all necessary or analytic truths; and I am suggesting that Hume also includes in it present-tense statements about sensory states, images, bodily sensations and the like. Is it even remotely credible that, in what Hume thinks to be a theoretically basic and powerful classification, one class should contain such a heterogeneous mixture as this? Yes it is, as I now proceed to show.

52. *Two kinds of safety*

Someone who thinks that we establish analytic truths by examining our 'ideas' is likely to see this as an introspective activity: to know that red things infuriate bulls I must attend to the outer world, but to know that red things are coloured I need only look inwards at my ideas of red and of colour. Thus we find Hume saying that 'reflection'—meaning 'introspection'—can establish simple logical truths.

The trouble could go even deeper. It is arguable that in reporting my present inner state I am *safe*. It is plausible to say that in making such a report, since I claim nothing about the past or future or about the objective other-than-me, I run no risk of honest error. It is also plausible to say that logical or analytic truths are safe; that red things infuriate bulls could come to be false, but the proposition that red things are coloured—the proposition which we do now express by the sentence 'Red things are coloured'—must be true for all eternity.

Let us uncritically accept these two theses about safety, in the somewhat naive form they have in much of the philosophical literature. My first point is that they obviously involve two different kinds of safety. That I now have a headache is not a proposition which has to be true, or which could not turn out to be false. The safety which is commonly thought to attach to it consists only in the fact that if I think I now have a headache then I have one—the proposition could have been false, but I cannot honestly be in error about it. The proposition that red things are coloured, on the other hand, is not the locus of any special epistemological privileges. One could honestly be in error about it (or at any rate about less trivial logical truths), through sheer conceptual ineptitude.

The difference between these two sorts of safety—sometimes called 'incorrigibility'—deserves more attention than it has been given. Descartes began to attend to it in the *Meditations*: trying to isolate propositions which he could safely assert, he considered such necessary truths as that $2+2 = 4$, and found no basic safety in them because he saw that he could raise the question 'Might I be wrong in thinking that it *is* a necessary truth that $2+2 = 4$?' All this, however, leads into deep waters in which I am not qualified to swim. It will be generally granted, I think, that the two sorts of safety are indeed two.[20]

But this might be denied by someone who gave an introspective account of logical discovery. Such a person might think that in establishing a necessary or analytic truth I attend only to my own 'ideas', i.e. to certain of my own inner states; and he might infer from this that I am safe in saying that all red things are coloured for the same reason, and in the same way, that I am safe in saying that I now have a headache.

There is a hint of this mistake in an early work of Descartes: 'Each of us can see by intuition that he exists, that he thinks, that the triangle is bounded by three lines only . . . and the like.'[21] It is true that Descartes had a peculiar view about the logical status of 'I think' and 'I exist', but he did not arrive at it until after the above passage was written. The passage, I submit, does show Descartes jumbling introspective psychology with logic. He is putting 'I think' on a level with 'Triangles have three sides', on the grounds that each is known by 'intuition', i.e. by inspection of one's 'ideas'.

Locke introduces the intuition/demonstration distinction purely in terms of logical truths, and then raises a question about objectivity-statements:

There can be nothing more certain than that the idea we receive from an external object is in our minds: this is intuitive knowledge. But whether there be anything more than barely that idea in our minds; whether we can thence certainly infer the existence of anything without us, which corresponds to that idea, is that whereof some men think there may be a question made.[22]

[20] See A. J. Ayer, 'Basic Propositions', in *Philosophical Essays* (London, 1954), pp. 105–7.
[21] Descartes, *Regulae* III.
[22] *Essay* IV. ii. 14. See also ix. 3.

Locke sees no ambiguity in describing as 'intuitive' my knowledge of elementary analytic truths and my knowledge of my present inner states. And the notion of safety is involved: I can play safe by staying with meanings and asserting nothing synthetic, or by staying with my inner states and asserting nothing about the objective realm.

Now, Hume uses 'idea' less generously than Descartes and Locke: some of their 'ideas' are his 'impressions'. But this is no safeguard against the mistake I am considering. Since impressions are supposed to differ from ideas only in vivacity, Hume cannot say that they differ in the degree of 'evidence' with which they can be known. Nor does he try to: 'Since all actions and sensations of the mind are known to us by consciousness, they must necessarily appear in every particular what they are, and be what they appear.'[23] So Hume says that I am safe in reporting any of my present inner states, whether impressions or ideas; and he may think that this has something to do with the certainty of necessary truths, since these concern ideas. The way is open for him to join Descartes and Locke.

He does join them. Of the four kinds of relational statements which can be known by intuition or demonstration, Hume says that three—those involving resemblance, contrariety and degrees in quality—are matters of intuition rather than demonstration. His defence of this drifts gradually away from the area of necessary truths, which is the home ground of the intuition/demonstration distinction, towards that of truths about sensory states:

Three of these relations are discoverable at first sight, and fall more properly under the province of intuition than demonstration. When any objects *resemble* each other, the resemblance will at first strike the eye, or rather the mind; and seldom requires a second examination. The case is the same with *contrariety*, and with the *degrees* of any *quality*. [With regard to the latter,] tho' it be impossible to judge exactly of the degrees of any quality, such as colour, taste, heat, cold, when the difference betwixt them is very small; yet 'tis easy to decide, that any of them is superior or inferior to another, when their difference is considerable. And this decision we always pronounce at first sight, without any enquiry or reasoning.[24]

[23] *Treatise*, p. 190.
[24] *Treatise*, p. 70. Discussed in Zabeeh, *Hume*, pp. 91–2.

The phrase, 'the eye, or rather the mind', which shows Hume's suspicion that his intended discussion of necessary truths is getting out of hand, is particularly enjoyable.

To see how wildly he lets the subject change, consider the 'degrees of any quality'. Suppose that *x* looks pure maroon: Hume implies that *x looks redder than y* is easier to establish if *y* looks purple than if *y* looks bluish-maroon. This, though true, has nothing to do with the difference between obvious and unobvious necessary truths. The necessity of *A maroon thing is redder than a purple thing* is no more obvious than that of *A maroon thing is redder than a bluish-maroon thing*. On the other hand, even if my handkerchief is maroon and my tie purple, it is not necessary at all that *My handkerchief is redder than my tie*. If this statement were necessary, it would not be because of the (apparent) colours of my handkerchief and my tie, but because of the meanings of 'my handkerchief' and 'my tie'. Hume would use the phrase 'the idea of my tie' to mean both 'a faded visual appearance of my tie' and 'the meaning of "my tie" ', and in that fact lies his big mistake.

Reverting briefly to the topic of § 51: I suggested that when Hume distinguishes (*a*) what can be known by comparing ideas from (*b*) matters of fact, he intends (*a*) to cover analytic truths and first-person subjective statements, and (*b*) to cover objective synthetic statements. This makes (*a*) a very mixed bag, but we now see that Hume tolerates just such a mixture. And that account of the dichotomy, though I do not insist that it is correct, would at least explain why Hume says that everything in class (*b*) has a causal basis.

53. *A muddle about relations*

Hume's conflation of logical with psychological truth yields a rich harvest of error in a paragraph which merits analysis, both for its own sake, and as an object-lesson.[25]

The phrase 'philosophical relation' which occurs in it needs to be explained. Hume says that 'relation' has two senses.[26] Firstly, a technical sense, for which Hume uses 'philosophical relation': any true statement of the form *xRy*—for example that *x* is unlike *y*—asserts the holding of a philosophical relation between *x* and *y*.

Secondly, a vernacular sense, for which Hume uses 'natural relation': there is a natural relation between x and y only if the plain man would describe them as 'related' or 'connected'; and Hume thinks that relations which qualify as 'natural' by this criterion are also the ones which have a certain role in his theory about the 'association of ideas' (see § 63 below). So philosophical relations are just *relations* in the broadest sense, and natural relations form a sub-class of these: in the phrase 'philosophical relation' the adjective does not have a narrowing function.[27] Since natural relations have no role in the paragraph I want to discuss, I can safely use the unqualified 'relation' to mean what Hume means by 'philosophical relation'.

Our paragraph treats of a distinction between (a) relations which 'depend entirely on the ideas, which we compare together', and (b) relations which 'may be chang'd without any change in the ideas'. An (a)-relation holds between two ideas purely by virtue of what each separately is like, and so it can cease to relate them only if one of them changes in itself. A (b)-relation's holding between two ideas is not simply an upshot of the nature of each idea separately: it could hold, and then later not hold, between two ideas without either's altering in itself.

If 'ideas' are meanings, Hume could be distinguishing (a) analytic from (b) synthetic statements, as follows. (a) The statement that *Every brother is male* expresses a relation between the ideas of brotherhood and of maleness—one which must hold just so long as these two ideas remain as they are. To deny this would be to say that 'Every brother is male' could become false without any change in the meaning of 'brother' or 'male'. (b) The statement that *Every brother is intelligent* could be true, and then later false, even though neither 'brother' nor 'intelligent' had changed its meaning; so the relation it expresses between the ideas of brotherhood and of intelligence does not 'depend entirely' on the natures of those two ideas. That is why the statement could change truth-value without any relevant semantic change.

This is all slightly unsatisfactory; for if 'Every brother is male' did become false through a change in the meaning of 'brother', we shouldn't want to say that the idea of brotherhood had

---

[27] Thus J. A. Robinson, 'Hume's Two Definitions of Cause', Chappell p. 138. Contrast B. H. Laing, *David Hume* (London, 1932), pp. 96-8; A. H. Basson, *David Hume* (Pelican Books, 1958), pp. 54-5.

changed—implying that there is one item, the idea of brotherhood or the meaning of 'brother', which has retained its identity and merely undergone an alteration. It would be more natural to say that there had been a change in *which* idea counted as 'the idea of brotherhood'. But the former, poorer formulation is the one I have had to adopt in fidelity to Hume's text; so I admit that the interpretation of the (*a*)/(*b*) distinction as the analytic/synthetic distinction can be maintained only with some strain. I do not retract the interpretation, however, for it is clear that Hume does want the (*a*)/(*b*) distinction to distinguish (*a*) relations between ideas which do yield analytic truths from (*b*) ones which do not.[28] This is shown by his describing (*a*) as the class of relations 'which depending solely upon ideas, can be the objects of knowledge and certainty';[29] and it is also shown in other ways to which I shall come shortly.

Now, Hume argues that (*a*) contains only four species of relations, whence it follows that every necessary truth—everything in the province of 'knowledge'—involves a relation belonging to one of those four species. Hume himself draws this conclusion, when he says that these four are 'the only infallible relations'.[30] This would be an extremely important and powerful result, if it were true; but in fact it is false. If 'Every brother is male' expresses a relationship between the ideas of brotherhood and maleness, it is the relation embodied in 'Every . . . is . . .'; but that relation is asserted to hold between the ideas of brotherhood and intelligence by the statement 'Every brother is intelligent'. There are no grounds for saying that 'Every . . . is . . .' is ambiguous as between these two statements. To contrast them in respect of the 'relations of ideas' they involve, we must attend not to what each statement asserts but to the *grounds* of its truth: the analytic one is true because the idea of brotherhood includes that of maleness, whereas neither of the two ideas involved in the synthetic statement includes the other. But now Hume is in trouble in a different way; for *non-inclusion* between a pair of ideas is—just as much as *inclusion*—a relation which can cease to obtain only if one of the related ideas changes; so that both these relations fit Hume's formula for (*a*)-relations. Also, Hume thinks that the (*a*)/(*b*) line divides relations generally; but our latest attempt has

[28] Thus Zabeeh, *Hume*, p. 85.   [29] *Treatise*, p. 70.
[30] *Treatise*, p. 79. See also pp. 463–4.

given us only a line with *inclusion* on one side and *non-inclusion* on the other—with nothing said about any other relations whatsoever. So we must conclude that Hume's line between (*a*) analytic and (*b*) synthetic truths does not correspond in the intended way to any line between two classes of relations-between-ideas.

In our paragraph Hume does also use the (*a*)/(*b*) distinction to draw a line between two classes of relations. But that is only because he uses it for two distinct purposes whose distinctness he does not see. In this second version of it, the line between (*a*) and (*b*) has nothing to do with that between (*a*) analytic and (*b*) synthetic, or between (*a*) 'knowledge' and (*b*) proof-and-probability. It is in fact the line between (*a*) *reducible* and (*b*) *irreducible* relations, in senses of these terms which I now proceed to explain.

'James is in debt to John' is a relational statement, and indebtedness-to-John is thus a relational property of James. What about 'James is a debtor'? This lacks the verbal form typical of overtly relational statements; but a debtor must be in debt *to someone*, and this makes it reasonable to count 'James is a debtor' as a relational statement and indebtedness as a relational property. The following rule looks right:

> F is a relational property = There is a relation R such that, for any x, $Fx \rightarrow$ (*There is a y such that $y \neq x$ and xRy*).

Thus, indebtedness is a relational property while impecuniousness is not; jealousy is, but depression is not; fatherhood is, but maleness is not.

Given the notion of a *relational property*, I can now define 'reducible' and 'irreducible' as these apply to *relations*:

> R is reducible = For all x and y, there are non-relational properties F and G such that $(Fx \ \& \ Gy) \rightarrow xRy$.
> R is irreducible = R is not reducible.

Thus, 'is warmer than' expresses a reducible relation, because x *is warmer than y* is entailed by x *is at 42°C. and y is at 17°C*. Other examples would be 'has the same shape as' and 'has more legs than'. By way of contrast, 'is married to' expresses an irreducible relation: no conjunction of statements attributing non-relational properties to John and to Mary can entail that John is married to Mary. (When Locke says that relations are 'not contained in the real existence of things' but are 'something extraneous and super-induced', he may mean that all relations are reducible.[31] Similar remarks by Leibniz certainly have that meaning—a point which is argued by Rescher from whom I have borrowed the terms 'reducible' and 'irreducible' and, with a slight modification, the distinction they embody.[32])

Now, Hume's distinction between (a) relations which 'depend entirely on the ideas, which we compare together' and (b) relations which 'may be chang'd without any change in the ideas' is intended partly as the distinction between (a) reducible and (b) irreducible relations. This is suggested by the words in which Hume introduces the distinction. It is confirmed by what he says about where the distinguishing line falls. He says that (a) contains just four (species of) relations, namely resemblance, contrariety, degrees in quality, and proportions in quantity and number. Instances of these would be, respectively, 'has the same colour as', 'has a different colour from', 'is warmer than' and 'has more legs than'; and all of these are reducible relations. As for the three (species of) relations which Hume says exhaust (b): one of them, identity, is so obscurely handled that I must set it aside; but the other two—causation, and relations of time and place—are irreducible relations.

Furthermore, some of Hume's explanations and examples of the (a)/(b) distinction make sense only as applied to the distinction between (a) reducible and (b) irreducible relations. For example, he puts spatial relations in (b) because 'the relations of *contiguity* and *distance* betwixt two objects may be chang'd merely by an alteration of their place, without any change on the objects themselves or on their ideas';[33] and this can only be read as the assertion that spatial relations are irreducible, i.e. that no conjunction of non-relational descriptions of x and y can entail, say, that x is a mile from y. (This interpretation assumes that a thing's having such and such a 'place' is a relational property of it, and so indeed it is.)

The reducible/irreducible line does divide relations, but now we

---

[31] *Essay* II. xxv. 8.
[32] N. Rescher, *The Philosophy of Leibniz* (Englewood Cliffs, N. J., 1967), pp. 71–5.
[33] *Treatise*, p. 69.

have deserted relations between *ideas*. Hume nearly admits this by referring to 'the relations of contiguity and distance betwixt two *objects*'. And when he says that a (*b*)-relation can cease to hold even if there is no change in 'the objects or their ideas', there are signs of strain: he needs to say 'objects' but has committed himself to saying 'ideas'. He often uses 'idea of' to mean something like 'appearance of', and he tends to blur the line between the appearances of an object and the object itself. These two facts make it easier for him to slide back and forth between 'object' and 'idea of object', but they do not falsify my account of what it is in our paragraph that forces him into this slide.

So Hume is doing two things at once, and is led by his double use of 'idea' to miscount them. Within the class of statements he distinguishes (*a*) analytic from (*b*) synthetic, and within the class of relations he distinguishes (*a*) reducible from (*b*) irreducible; and he does not realize that these are two distinctions and not just one. Immediately after drawing what he thinks to be his one distinction, Hume says:

'Tis from the idea of a triangle, that we discover the relation of equality, which its three angles bear to two right ones; and this relation is invariable, as long as our idea remains the same. On the contrary, the relations of *contiguity* and *distance* betwixt two objects may be chang'd merely by an alteration of their place, without any change on the objects themselves or on their ideas . . .

'On the contrary' here means 'On the other hand': Hume wants to present an antithesis, something from each side of a single distinction. But all he is saying is: 'It is *analytic* that the internal angles of a triangle = 180°, but on the other hand spatial relations are *irreducible*.' This is not very creditable, but my interpretation does at least make it intelligible: since Hume conflates the analytic/synthetic and reducible/irreducible distinctions, he naturally thinks that analytic/irreducible expresses a proper contrast.

This interpretation is reinforced when Hume, having said in effect that spatial relations are irreducible, adds that an object's 'place depends on a hundred different accidents, which cannot be foreseen by the mind'. Of course the foreseeability of an object's 'place' is irrelevant to the irreducibility of spatial relations. Hume's point, I think, must be that truths about where things are 'cannot be foreseen by the mind' and are therefore never analytic or necessary!

That Hume's two distinctions are entirely independent is shown by the existence of the four cases:

analytic/reducible: *A maroon thing is redder than a purple thing.*

analytic/irreducible: *A subterranean thing is some distance away from a stratospheric thing.*

synthetic/reducible: *My handkerchief is redder than my tie.*

synthetic/irreducible: *My cellar is at least a mile away from Telstar.*

As I remarked earlier, it would be very interesting to learn that only four kinds of relations can figure in necessary truths—if it were true. In fact, any relation can enter into analytic statements, including the causal relation: 'Any earthquake which causes every house to fall down causes every small house to fall down' is an analytic truth whose main verb is 'causes'. It is not an interesting truth, but its existence shows that if Hume is to prove that causal laws are not logically necessary he will need something subtler than the block-busting claim that every statement involving the causal relation is synthetic. We must suppose that Hume agrees with this; for he does adduce other, much subtler, arguments. These will be the theme of my next chapter.

XI

HUME ON CAUSATION: NEGATIVE

54. *Introduction*

HUME attacked certain wrong analyses of the concept of cause, and propounded one of his own.[1] Before discussing his positive analysis in my next chapter, I shall devote the present one to his negative work on the topic and to certain issues arising therefrom.

Hume's targets are all accounts of causation in terms of the notion of a 'necessary connexion' between the objects or happenings which are said to be causally related. He does eventually allow a kind of sense to the phrase 'necessary connexion', but not a sense such that 'x is necessarily connected with y' is a plain statement of fact about a relation which holds between x and y. Throughout this chapter I shall use 'necessary connexion' to mean 'necessary connexion considered as objectively holding between the objects or events which are said to be causally related'. Hume argues that when the phrase 'necessary connexion' is taken in that way it is condemned, by his meaning-empiricism and certain other true premisses, as meaningless. The argument, cleansed of its geneticism and of its references to 'ideas', goes like this: since it cannot be verbally defined, the phrase 'necessary connexion' does not have a complex meaning; and since we do not experience instances of 'necessary connexion', that phrase does not have a simple meaning; so it has no meaning at all.

That application of Hume's meaning-empiricism, though better than his own versions, is still crippled by its dependence on the simple/complex dichotomy, which reflects a naive view of the ways in which an expression can be meaningful. Consider, for example, the claim that 'necessary connexion' cannot be verbally defined. Hume says little in defence of this except: 'The terms of *efficacy, agency, power, force, energy, necessity, connexion*, and *productive quality*, are all nearly synonimous; and therefore 'tis an absurdity to employ any of them in defining the rest.'[2] But one *wants* the two sides of a definition to be synonymous! Hume's point must be that his list contains *single* words each of which is 'nearly

---

[1] *Treatise* I. iii. 1-9, 14; *Enquiry* §§ 48-61.   [2] *Treatise*, p. 157. See also p. 77.

synonymous' with each of the others, so that the list does not provide the materials for a definition which usefully spells out the definiendum's 'complex' meaning in 'simpler' terms. The list, though, is a cheat: instead of the words 'necessity' and 'connexion' it should contain the phrase 'necessary connexion', for it is only the latter which can plausibly be described as 'nearly synonymous' with 'power', 'efficacy' etc. Now the phrase 'necessary connexion', which Hume does often take as central, might give his opponents room to manoeuvre:

'Connexion' makes sense in 'I have severed my connexion with the Communist Party', as does 'necessary' in 'Mathemetical truths are necessary'; and so the disputed phrase has a complex meaning which is caught by the definition of 'x is a necessary connexion' as 'x is necessary and x is a connexion'.

This would be absurd, of course, but it is not clear that Hume is in a position to say so. I have remarked that he condemns 'necessary connexion' only when the phrase is supposed to refer to a relation objectively holding between pairs of objects or events; and he might complain that the absurd definition proposed above does not give the phrase a meaning of *that* sort. This complaint, though just in itself, is not available to Hume. For the complaint presupposes that the issue about 'necessary connexion' concerns whether the phrase can legitimately be used to do certain sorts of work, and that description of the problem lies right outside the ambit of Hume's official theory about simple and complex ideas.

The moral of all this is that Hume's problem about 'necessary connexion' is less simply structured than his form of meaning-empiricism, with its cramping use of the simple/complex dichotomy, implies it to be. The disputed phrase might be meaningful because it has an empirical cash-value of a complex sort, even if it could not be verbally defined by means of words which are ostensively definable.

Fortunately, Hume's practice belies his theory. He produces agile and free-ranging arguments to show that 'necessary connexion' cannot do the work demanded of it by those who embody it in wrong analyses of the concept of cause. To grasp the value of those arguments, however, one must see that Hume's achievement in this area does not fit the narrow programme dictated by his theory of meaning.

I need to explain 'the work demanded of "necessary connexion" by those embody it in wrong analyses of the concept of cause'. This work requires that 'necessary connexion' refer to a relation holding objectively between events and happenings; but to say that is not enough, for Hume is not interested in denying that '*x* is necessarily connected with *y*' could be taken to mean, say, that *x* is a mile away from *y*. The other vital aspect of the criticized use is this: it has been thought that one could be entitled to say, on a non-inductive basis, things of the form 'There is or has been an F; Fs are necessarily connected with Gs; so there will be a G.' An 'inductive basis' for a prediction is one involving something in the nature of an unprovable assumption—an act of faith or hope—that some regularity or pattern which has so far obtained will continue to obtain. A non-inductive basis, such as some philosophers have hoped to secure by the discovery of 'necessary connexions', is one which supports a prediction without involving any mere assumption about a matter of brute, future fact. Hume's negative discussion of cause, then, could be described as a set of arguments for the conclusion that no prediction can have a stronger-than-inductive basis, that the element of guesswork about the future is ineliminable. Observe that in stating Hume's conclusion we have to desert the terms supplied by his theory of meaning.

The thesis that there are relevant 'impressions of necessary connexions' is the only part of our topic which can be expressed in purely Humean terms; and I shall dispatch it in § 55. In § 56 I shall present criticisms—including Hume's—of the view that we are entitled to hypothesize or conjecture that some objects or happenings are 'necessarily connected' so as to yield a better-than-inductive basis for predictions. These alleged 'necessary connexions' will be assumed to be offered as something less than logical necessitations; but for the rest we shall not insist upon knowing exactly what 'necessary connexion' is supposed to mean here. Mercifully, Hume waives such demands, and adopts the kind of tactic described in § 27 above, arguing that on his opponents' own partial explanation of 'necessary connexion' nothing could qualify for that label. This will bring us finally to the view that predictions can have a non-inductive basis which gives them the highest possible degree of security, because there are *logically* 'necessary connexions' between objects or events. Unlike some writers, I do not think that this position was so decisively refuted by Hume as to need no further discussion.

55. *Impressions of necessary connexion*

Do we have any 'impressions of necessary connexion' between events? The only plausible basis for an affirmative answer goes like this: when I act voluntarily, I am conscious within myself of a necessary or more-than-inductive connexion between the act of my will and the willed upshot. Hume denies this (see § 43 above), and he is right to do so; but the falsity of the position is the least of its troubles.

Let us go back to Locke.[3] He tries to explain the empirical basis for our concept of making or producing or causing, which he calls our 'idea of power':

Power also is another of those simple ideas which we receive from sensation and reflection. For, observing in ourselves that we do and can think, and that we can at pleasure move several parts of our bodies which were at rest; the effects, also, that natural bodies are able to produce in one another, occurring every moment to our senses,—we both these ways get the idea of power.[4]

One source of the idea of power, then, is our observation of our own doings. When Locke re-states his view somewhat later, he refers instead to our observation of our own changes of inner state, including changes which we passively undergo and by implication excluding our physical activities. In this respect the earlier formulation is better, and truer to the main lines of Locke's thought. The later one, however, does better on the second alleged source of the idea of power. Here is what it says:

The mind being every day informed, by the senses, of the alteration of those simple ideas [= qualities] it observes in things without . . .; reflecting also on what passes within itself, and observing a constant change of its ideas, sometimes by the impression of outward objects on the senses, and sometimes by the determination of its own choice; and concluding from what it has so constantly observed to have been, that the like changes will for the future be made in the same things, by like agents, and by the like ways,—considers in one thing the possibility of [being] changed, and in another the possibility of making that change; and so comes by that idea which we call *power*.[5]

---

[3] Following Gibson, *Locke's Theory of Knowledge*, ch. 5, §§ 12–14.
[4] *Essay* II. vii. 8.   [5] *Essay* II. xxi. 1.

The earlier version says that we observe 'the effects that natural bodies *produce* in one another', whereas the latter allows us actually to observe in 'things without' only their 'alterations'. The more circumspect version is the better. We do not observe producings as such, but only happenings; and if we classify some of the latter as producings, saying that *x* happened 'because' *y* happened, the question of why and by what criteria we do this is precisely what has to be explained by someone trying to lay bare the empirical basis for 'the idea of power'.

Assembling the better parts of Locke's two versions, then, we get the following. My idea of power arises in the first instance from my 'observing a constant change of [my] ideas, . . . by the determination of [my] own choice', since what I observe in these cases is more than mere change; and I then apply it to 'things without', although all I observe in them are mere changes, by some kind of transfer. Hume's résumé will serve: 'Some have asserted, that we feel an energy, or power, in our own mind; and that having in this manner acquir'd the idea of power, we transfer that quality to matter, where we are not able immediately to discover it.' [6] But the supposed transfer is unintelligible. Locke could not say: 'The statement that *the fire made the water boil* is exactly analogous to the statement that *I made my arm go up* (by deliberately raising it)'; for that would imply that the fire knowingly and deliberately boiled the water. He must say, then, that 'The fire made the water boil' is *partly* analogous to 'I made my arm go up': in the former statement, 'made' has a sense which involves more than mere alteration, which is directly cashable only in respect of one's own deliberate doings, but which can also be applied in the absence of deliberateness and even of sentience. Compare that with: 'Trees may have pains, in a sense of "pain" which does not involve the having of conscious states though it can be grasped only by those who have pains and are conscious of them.' If one is better than the other, Locke does not show how.

Hume challenges the transfer, but not because it moves from the personal to the impersonal. Even if we had the desiderated 'idea of power' and could intelligibly apply it to 'things without', Locke would still have to show that powers, thus understood, *do* in fact operate in the objective realm. (Perhaps Locke is grappling with this point when he speaks of our 'concluding' from our patterned past that we shall have a patterned future; but he offers no argument entitling us to 'conclude' this, nor does he explain how the conclusion could entitle us to apply the idea of power to outer things. He may have in mind something like this: 'We do infer a patterned future from a patterned past; this inference is invalid unless there are powers which secured the past patterns and which guarantee future ones; so there are such powers.' One hesitates to credit Locke with so crude a non-sequitur, but the text offers no clear alternative.) Hume scrutinizes some arguments purporting to fill this gap, and shows them to be faulty. He argues further that nothing *could* count as 'powers' or 'necessary connexions' which provide a stronger-than-inductive though weaker-than-logical basis for predictions;[7] and that line of argument goes through independently of what experiential basis is claimed for the alleged idea of power. This is one reason, though by no means the only one, for rejecting out of hand the naive view that experimental work such as Michotte's has somehow provided evidence against Hume's position on causation.[8]

'Do we experience within ourselves any exercise of "power", any kind of non-inductive basis for saying how we shall act?' An affirmative answer to this, I have maintained, is not sufficient for a non-Humean account of causation: because a self-based concept of power cannot be applied to inanimate things; and also because no concept of power, however based, could provide a non-inductive basis for prediction about the objective realm. It remains only to add that an affirmative answer to the question is not straightforwardly necessary, either, for a non-Humean account of causation. As Hume implicitly concedes, someone might make a case for saying 'Objective regularities are explained by the operation of powers' without giving any independent account of what 'power' means. It is at least prima facie possible that the word's meaning might be adequately embodied not in verbal definitions or in ostensions but rather in its use in various theories —e.g. in a theory, if there were one, giving us grounds for hypothesizing that there are powers. If Hume's theory of meaning were correct, it would be vitally important to search for 'impressions of necessary connexion' or '. . . of power', and this would require

---

[7] See D. F. Pears, 'Hume's Empiricism', Pears, pp. 13–15.
[8] A. E. Michotte, *The Perception of Causality* (London, 1963).

us to assess certain views about what is experienced in deliberate action. Since the theory is not correct, the impression-hunt can be called off and the serious philosophy can begin.

56. *The conjecture theory*

'Observed regularities in the behaviour of objects make it reasonable to suppose that empirical happenings are connected by some kind of power or necessary connexion. The surface fact that F events are regularly succeeded by G events is explained by the conjecture that F events produce or necessitate G events.' This view, whether or not amplified by the claim that we can experience our own exercises of 'power', has defects which Hume efficiently exposes. I shall present his two main objections, and a third which is not his, to this 'conjecture theory'.

(1) The conjecture that empirical order is the observable upshot of underlying powers or necessary connexions has the form of: 'Every major scholarship since 1960 has gone to an Etonian—the examiners must be prejudiced.' The 'prejudice' guess could be a reasonable one, for it might be the only alternative to a highly improbable level of Etonian excellence; but we cannot analogously defend the 'necessary connexion' hypothesis as being the only alternative to something we know to be highly improbable. That connects with another vital contrast between the two cases: the conjecture that the examiners are prejudiced has content because we could discover that they are indeed prejudiced (they admit it), or that after all they are not (we see for ourselves the excellence of the Etonian scripts); but nothing could count as independently confirming or refuting the conjecture that observed order reflects underlying necessities.

There are many variations on this theme. 'Observed order, if not due to an underlying necessity, must be sheer coincidence; and no sane man would accept a coincidence of such astronomical proportions.' A coincidence is the occurrence of one or more items which are both F and G, where there is no causal relation between their being F and their being G although one might have expected there to be one—e.g. a set of horses which win, and are backed by me, although my bets are based only on my liking for the horses' names. The above argument has the form: 'If something's being F does not necessitate its being G, then the

F-G association is just a coincidence'; but this assumes that if Fness does not necessitate Gness then it does not cause it—which is just the point at issue.

Those criticisms of the conjecture theory are, I think, essentially Humean: for example they reflect the spirit of the middle part of *Treatise* I.iii.6. The relevant parts of Hume's text, however, are a little difficult to handle because they contain a trap, a source of exegetical and philosophical error, which I want to deal with right away. The trouble is that Hume runs two questions in the same harness. He wants to know: 'First, For what reason we pronounce it *necessary*, that every thing whose existence has a beginning, shou'd also have a cause? Secondly, Why we conclude, that such particular causes must *necessarily* have such particular effects . . . ?' [9] After devoting several pages to the former question, he says: 'I find it will be more convenient to sink this question in the [latter one]. 'Twill, perhaps, be found in the end, that the same answer will serve for both questions.' [10] Let us proceed with caution.

The two questions are quite different: one concerns the status of a claim about the scope of causal laws, while the other concerns the analysis of the concept of a causal law. Either question could arise without the other's doing so. Someone might think that every event must have a cause, while rejecting a necessitarian analysis of the concept of cause and seeking nothing stronger than an inductive basis for predictions. Conversely, someone might—perhaps in the interests of miracles or of freedom—deny that whatever happens is caused to happen, while believing that when something *is* caused to happen this involves its being 'necessitated' in some strong sense. Why, then, does Hume take the two questions together?

He does so partly for the reason he gives, namely that 'the same answer will serve for both'. We shall see in § 63 that Hume's positive theory of causation would, if it were true, explain both the belief that determinism is not merely true but somehow necessary, and the belief that causation involves 'necessity' in some strong sense. But this is only to say that Hume's two questions are connected through a false theory: it does not reveal any real link between them.

There is in fact a real link, a human one, between the two

---

[9] *Treatise*, p. 78.   [10] *Treatise*, p. 82.

questions, though it is not the one implied by Hume's positive theory. Many people, whom we may loosely label 'rationalists', find it intolerable to say of anything that it just is the case: they cannot tolerate absolutely brute facts, and assume that any question of the form 'Why is it so?', asked about a logically contingent state of affairs, must have an answer. For a rationalist, the thesis that whatever happens is caused to happen conveniently embodies his assumption that 'Why did it happen?' can always be answered, namely by something of the form 'Because it was caused to happen by . . .' That form of answer, though, will not satisfy the rationalist if part of what it means is: 'F events just are, as a matter of fact, always followed by G events'; for on that analysis the answer actually increases the dose of sheer unexplained brute fact which has to be swallowed. The rationalist cast of mind, in short, generates the assumptions both that determinism must be true and that causal explanations and causally based predictions cannot have an inductive basis.

Hume may have been dimly aware of this connexion between his two questions. Consider this passage:

The . . most popular explication of this matter, is to say, that finding from experience, that there are several new productions in matter, such as the motions and variations of body, and concluding that there must somewhere be a power capable of producing them, we arrive at last by this reasoning at the idea of power and efficacy. But . . . reason, as distinguish'd from experience, can never make us conclude, that a cause or productive quality is absolutely requisite to every beginning of existence.[11]

This denies our right to 'conclude' on *a priori* grounds—*what*? There is no clear answer, because Hume could be using 'cause' either (*a*) as a vehicle of the necessitarianism which he is opposing or (*b*) as a theory-neutral term whose analysis is at issue. On interpretation (*a*), the passage says only that we cannot prove that observed order reflects underlying necessities; on (*b*) it says that much ('productive quality'), and also says ('cause') that we cannot prove that every happening has a cause. On one reading, the passage is not an argument but a mere counter-claim, while on the other it adds to the counter-claim an irrelevancy. It is just possible, though, that the passage involves an unconscious mixture of (*a*) and (*b*)—a stumbling attempt to link necessitarianism with

[11] *Treatise*, p. 157.

dogmatic determinism through the rationalist cast of mind which is often their common source.

(2) Hume's second attack on the conjecture theory is aimed at a version of it which he expresses thus:

After experience of the constant conjunction of certain objects, we reason in the following manner. Such an object is always found to produce another. 'Tis impossible it cou'd have this effect, if it was not endow'd with a power of production. The power necessarily implies the effect; and therefore there is a just foundation for drawing a conclusion from the existence of one object to that of its usual attendant. The past production implies a power: The power implies a new production: And the new production is what we infer from the power and the past production.[12]

Waiving the demand for a clear account of what 'power' means, and the demand for a proof that the past production implies a power, Hume offers a further criticism:

It having been already prov'd, that the power lies not in the sensible qualities of the cause; and there being nothing but the sensible qualities present to us; I ask, why in other instances you presume that the same power still exists, merely upon the appearance of these qualities?[13]

The conjecture theory, Hume is contending, ought to run like this: 'We observe F events to be followed by G events, and thence conclude that all those F events have had, as well as the sensible qualities which define Fness, an insensible quality which might be called a G-power: any event which has a G-power necessitates the occurrence of a G event. When we observe a new F event, we can predict a G event on the non-inductive ground that since this F event has a G-power it *must* be followed by a G event.' But even if we grant that all those past F events have had a G-power, Hume asks, why say that this new one has a G-power also? All we observe in it are those sensible qualities which make it an F event. In assuming that it also has a G-power we are assuming that the past association of Fness with G-power has continued through into the present case; and that is precisely the kind of past-to-future act of faith which the 'power' theory was supposed to free us from. It would be more economical, and no less satisfactory, to jettison 'G-power' and merely assume that the past association of Fness with Gness will continue through

[12] *Treatise*, p. 90.   [13] *Treatise*, p. 91.

into the present case. In my judgement, this argument of Hume's is flawless.

(3) The conjecture theory could be open to a further attack. Hume does not use it, probably because it concerns a form of the theory which he did not envisage anyone's actually adopting. I want to expound it, in preparation for matters to be discussed in my next section.

Never mind what 'necessary connexion' or 'power' mean; grant that the past production implies a power; and grant too that we can know that this new F event has a G-power; *still* there remains a difficulty. Or at any rate there is a difficulty if we can say this much about the meaning of 'power': '*x* has a G-power' provides a stronger-than-inductive ground for '*x* is followed by a G event', but not a logically compelling ground. (The stronger version, in which '*x* has a G-power' *entails* that *x* is followed by a G event, will be discussed later.) On this reading of 'power', it always makes sense to ask: 'Granted that *x* occurs and has a G-power, will a G event actually ensue?' This is to ask whether the G-power will be operative on this occasion, and the answer must be inductively based: G-powers have so far operated unfailingly, and we guess or hope or trust that they will continue to do so. This, however, re-establishes the inductive basis for the prediction.

In Peirce's defence of the thesis that 'general principles are operative in nature', which he apparently construes as an anti-Humean view which frees predictions from an inductive basis, the game is beautifully given away by the clause which I italicize:

With overwhelming uniformity, in our past experience, ... stones left free to fall have fallen. Thereupon two hypotheses only are open to us. Either (1) the uniformity with which those stones have fallen has been due to mere chance and affords no ground whatever ... for any expectation that the next stone that shall be let go will fall; or (2) the uniformity with which stones have fallen has been due to some active general principle, in which case *it would be a strange coincidence that it should cease to act at the moment my prediction was based upon it*. That position, gentlemen, will sustain criticism. It is irrefragable.[14]

This replaces a Humean hope that stones will continue to fall by a Peircean hope that 'active general principles' will continue to 'act'.

[14] C. S. Peirce, *Collected Papers* (Cambridge, Mass., 1934), vol. 5, § 100.

57. *The shift to logical necessity*

The conjecture theory aims to give predictions a stronger-than-inductive basis; but it can offer no defence of (1) 'Past F events have had a G-power', and only inductive defences of (2) 'This new F event has a G-power' and (3) 'This event's G-power will be operative'. These difficulties are cumulative: neither the second nor the third can be cleanly raised until its predecessor has been resolved. Still, let us momentarily forget the first two problems, and attend to (3).

This difficulty would not arise if 'power' were so construed that 'x has a G-power' entails or leads by logic to 'x is followed by a G event'. For then the question 'Will x's G-power be operative?' or 'Given that something occurs which has a G-power, will a G event ensue?', would be of the form: 'Given that ϕx, and that ϕx entails ψx, is it the case that ψx?' The question may be called improper, or self-answering, or answerable by logic; but certainly it is not one to be answered on an inductive basis. So let us take the theory to be thus modified: we now construe 'x has a G-power' as *entailing* that x is followed by a G event.

But now the theory purports to explain the fact that every past F event *has been followed by a G event* by saying that every past F event has had a G-power, meaning that it *has had some property its possession of which entails its having been followed by a G event*. But this is no explanation at all, since it is logically equivalent to what is supposed to be explained.

I base this claim on the general logical point that

All ϕs are ψ

is logically equivalent to

For some f: all ϕs are f, and being-f entails being-ψ.

That the second entails the first is obvious. That the first entails the second is no less certain; for if the first is true then we have a guaranteed candidate for the required 'some f' in the second—namely ψ itself. Since this equivalence holds as a matter of elementary logic, one could never explain the fact that all ϕs are ψ by saying that all ϕs have some property their possession of which entails their being ψ.

To put the point yet more generally: whatever proposition P may be, one could never explain the fact that P by saying that something is the case which entails that P. If P is true then *of course* there is a true proposition which entails P—namely P. And if you want P to be entailed by some *other* true proposition, the latter can still be routinely constructed by conjoining P with any truth you like.

Applying this back to our original topic: if every F event has been followed by a G event, then it follows trivially that every F event has had a property which entails its having been followed by a G event—namely the property of being-followed-by-a-G-event. Or, if you want to invoke some *other* property, take 'being H and followed by a G event' where H is any property you like which the event happens to have.

If we want to explain why it is the case that P, offering a genuine explanation in which the notion of logical necessity has a working role, then the necessity must not be left lurking in the background: we shall have to be prepared to say that P is itself a logically necessary proposition. So if the necessitarian theory is to escape vacuity it must come right out and say boldly that it is logically necessary that *All F events have been followed by G events*. The necessity must inhere in that proposition as it stands: we cannot say that the proposition, though itself contingent, is true because of a logical necessity. From now on, let us construe the theory in this bold form—since nothing less will do.

In this form of it, the theory no longer postulates a 'G-power' which is contingently associated with Fness and which somehow necessitates the ensuing of a G event. In its earlier form, the statement (1) 'Past F events have had a G-power' was one which our necessitarian could not defend—indeed he could not even say what might count as cogent reasons for it. But in the present form of the theory (1) means 'It is logically necessary that past F events have been followed by G events'; we know how to go about establishing truths of the form 'It is logically necessary that . . .'; and so the necessitarian, whether or not he can establish the ones he wants to, at least is not doomed from the outset. To that extent his problem over (1) is solved.

So is his problem over (2) 'This new F event also has a G-power'. In the theory's new form, there is no question of (2)'s being defended on inductive grounds: there is no act of faith that 'the past association between Fness and G-power' will continue, for the theory does not now postulate any such 'association'.

If it is logically necessary that all past F events were followed by G events, then it is logically necessary that all F events, including this new one, are followed by G events; and that is all there is to say about it. (Notice that I can deal with (2), now, only by absorbing (3) into it. I remarked at the end of § 56 that the distinction between (2) and (3) depends upon a non-logical-necessity interpretation of 'G-power'. Having dropped that interpretation, we lose this distinction.) The strategic position is this. The conjecture theory was faced with three insoluble problems: nothing could count as evidence for (1), and only inductive evidence could support (2) and (3). By the single operation of transforming it into a logical-necessity theory—according to which 'An F event occurs' supports 'A G event will occur' because it is logically necessary that F events are followed by G events—we have removed all three difficulties. For (1) has now become a statement of a kind which there are ways of establishing, and (1) now entails both (2) and (3). So someone who seeks a non-inductive basis for predictions is, whether or not he realizes it, under tremendous conceptual pressure to adopt a logical-necessity account of causation.

Hume seems to be half-aware that his opponents are under this pressure. Without explicitly saying that nothing less than logical necessity will serve, he frequently slides into assuming that his only really serious target is the thesis that predictions can be licensed by logically necessary truths. To apply the 'idea of power' in a particular case, he says,

We must distinctly and particularly conceive the connexion betwixt the cause and effect, and be able to pronounce, from a simple view of the one, that it must be follow'd or preceded by the other. This is the true manner of conceiving a particular power in a particular body . . . Now nothing is more evident, than that the human mind cannot form such an idea of two objects, as to conceive any connexion betwixt them, or comprehend distinctly that power or efficacy, by which they are united. Such a connexion wou'd amount to a demonstration, and wou'd imply the absolute impossibility for the one object not to follow, or to be conceiv'd not to follow upon the other.[15]

The references to what we can 'conceive' or 'comprehend distinctly' point to a logical-necessity interpretation of 'power'; and the highly explicit last sentence points even more clearly in that

[15] *Treatise*, pp. 161–2.

direction. I suggest that when Hume speaks of 'the true manner of conceiving a . . . power' he is claiming that although 'powers' are not always construed in this logical-necessity way they ought to be—since otherwise the 'power' theory falls at the first hurdle.

In discussing 'the will, considered as a cause', Hume says:

The will being here consider'd as a cause, has no more a discoverable connexion with its effects, than any material cause has with its proper effect. So far from perceiving the connexion betwixt an act of volition, and a motion of the body; 'tis allow'd that no effect is more inexplicable from the powers and essence of thought and matter. Nor is the empire of the will over our mind more intelligible.[16]

The words 'essence' and 'intelligible' here point to the logical-necessity position. When Hume says that the relation between volition and upshot is not 'intelligible', he means not that we cannot understand it but that we cannot see it as necessary.

Of many other examples which could be given, I select one in which 'conceive' and 'unintelligible' and 'comprehend' play roles like those just discussed:

The generality of mankind [when confronted by] the more common and familiar operations of nature . . . suppose that, in all these cases, they perceive the very force or energy of the cause, by which it is connected with its effect, and is for ever infallible in its operation. They . . . hardly conceive it possible that any other event could result from it . . . But philosophers, who carry their scrutiny a little farther, immediately perceive that, even in the most familiar events, the energy of the cause is as unintelligible as in the most unusual, and that we only learn by experience the frequent *Conjunction* of objects, without being ever able to comprehend anything like *Connexion* between them.[17]

In that passage Hume sets out to deny that we observe anything but regularities, but slides into denying that we discover logically necessary connexions between causes and their effects.

An important by-product of the shift to logical necessity is that from now on we shall be discussing the relations between certain pairs of propositions, namely the antecedents and consequents of prediction-licensing conditionals. No relation of this kind can qualify as itself being the causal relation, for the latter holds not between propositions, or facts reported in propositions, but between events.[18] Still, the discussion will be indirectly relevant

---

[16] *Treatise*, p. 632.   [17] *Enquiry* § 54.
[18] See D. Davidson, 'Causal Relations', *Journal of Philosophy*, vol. 64 (1967).

to the concept of cause, in ways which will emerge in my next chapter. The slight shift away from the announced topic of the present chapter is forced upon us by the need to stay with Hume, and so I make no apology for it.

58. *Causal laws as logically necessary*

We now approach Hume's principal target, namely the view that 'An F event occurs' can support 'A G event will occur' because it is logically impossible that an F event should fail to be followed by a G event—or, in more Humean language, because causes lead to their effects by a 'demonstrative' or 'absolute' necessity. Hume rejects this view, but it is not perfectly clear why.

His best-known argument runs as follows. Given any pair of event-types F and G which are thought to be causally linked, it is possible to 'conceive' an F's occurring not followed by a G; and if this is conceivable it is logically possible; so that no prediction can, in the way demanded by the theory, be licensed by a logically necessary proposition. In Hume's words:

There can be no *demonstrative* arguments to prove, *that those instances, of which we have had no experience, resemble those, of which we have had experience*. We can at least conceive a change in the course of nature; which sufficiently proves, that such a change is not absolutely impossible. To form a clear idea of any thing, is an undeniable argument for its possibility, and is alone a refutation of any pretended demonstration against it.[19]

This is unclear. If 'we can conceive' means 'it is logically possible for there to be', then the argument's conclusion appears, naked and unadorned, amongst its premisses. Hume probably intends 'we can conceive' psychologically; but then the conclusion does not follow, for logical impossibilities can be and sometimes are 'conceived', as when Wells conceived travel into the past and Hobbes conceived a squaring of the circle. Kneale has pointed out that if psychological conceivability implied logical possibility, certain mathematical problems could be solved out of hand. (1) No one knows whether Goldbach's conjecture is true—the question of its truth is an open one; so (2) mathematicians find it 'conceivable' that the conjecture is true; so (3) the conjecture is logically possible; but (4) Goldbach's conjecture is a mathematical statement which is impossible if false, and therefore true if possible; and so, from (3) and (4), we get (5) Goldbach's conjecture is true![20] And a similar argument will also yield the conclusion that Goldbach's conjecture is false. The absurdity of the argument lies in the move from (2) to (3), that is, it lies in Hume's principle that what is pyschologically conceivable is logically possible.

If we had to leave the matter there—saying that Hume's only argument depends upon the assumption that whatever is necessary or impossible is obviously so—then this part of Hume's work would be a downright bore. I shall eventually conclude that his attack on necessitarianism does indeed have little solid content, but this is not a conclusion to reach summarily. For one thing, in addition to the argument from 'conceivable' to 'possible' Hume has other things to say which I shall discuss in § 62 below. Also, I want to throw some light on the still-common belief that Hume demonstrated a substantive result about how causality relates to contingency, a belief implying that there is such a result (as indeed there is), that Hume affirmed or at least accepted it (which is dubious), and that he supplied good arguments for it (which is certainly false). There is, in short, a tangle of issues here.

The best route into it is through attempted salvage. Let us start by construing the conceivable/possible argument in such a way that it is neither grossly circular nor grossly invalid, as follows. One cannot imagine anything which is elementarily logically impossible—such as a four-sided triangle; and it is arguable that any logical impossibility, if spelled out in enough detail, involves simple impossibilities of this 'inconceivable' kind. This implies that Wells could 'conceive' of time-travel only because he did so schematically, leaving out dangerous details. I can imagine someone working at his desk, shouting 'I have found a fraction equal to $\sqrt{2}$!', receiving the plaudits of an admiring world, and so on; but I cannot imagine the fraction he has discovered together with the correct calculation which shows it to equal $\sqrt{2}$.

This view about detail—which seems to me right—would be better expressed in terms not of imagining or 'conceiving' but of *describing*. It comes to this: if S is a logically impossible story, then it entails obvious logical impossibilities—or it implies both the

[20] W. C. Kneale, *Probability and Induction* (Oxford, 1949), pp. 79–80.

answers 'Yes' and 'No' to certain questions. The impossibility may not be manifest in S as stated, but it can always be *displayed* by asking the right questions. Let S be 'Someone has found values of m and n such that m and n have no common factors and $m/n = \sqrt{2}$.' Then we can ask 'Is m an even number?' The answer must be 'Yes', because if m is odd then $(m/n)^2$ is odd, which 2 is not. But the answer must also be 'No', because if m is even (and n, sharing no factors with m, is odd), then $(m/n)^2$ is divisible by 4, which 2 is not. These rock-bottom contradictions correspond to the inconceivabilities on which Hume relies.

Hume would agree that any logical impossibility can be 'displayed': I am sure he thinks that any 'demonstrative' truth can be demonstrated, and a 'demonstration' is simply a judicious assemblage of 'intuitions' (see § 50 above). Furthermore, in the quoted argument he does say: 'To form a *clear* idea of any thing, is an undeniable argument for its possibility', and we might take 'clear' as invoking the notion of conceiving in detail. It is even more plausible so to construe the Cartesian phrase 'clear and distinct', when Hume says that 'whatever can be conceiv'd by a clear and distinct idea necessarily implies the possibility of existence'.[21] So we might conjecturally reconstruct his argument as follows:

Let S be a statement to the effect that an F event occurs and is not followed by a G event (choose any F and G you like). Probe S as you will, subject it to questions as searchingly hostile as you can devise, you will never display a simple contradiction in it; so there is no impossibility in it; so it is not logically necessary that F events are followed by G events.

In this version, Hume's argument bridges the gap between the psychological and logical notions of 'conceivability'; for now the crucial premiss says that the falsity of a causal law—or prediction-licensing statement—can always be 'conceived' in as much detail as one likes; and this does imply that it is logically possible.

Some anti-Humeans reject the premiss that any logical impossibility is displayable. Kneale says that causal laws express necessities of the same kind as are involved in logical truths, but that we cannot prove them *a priori*—which amounts to saying that their contradictories are not displayably impossible.[22] If he means that causal laws are true because of necessities in the world,

---

[21] *Treatise*, p. 43.   [22] Kneale, op. cit. pp. 71, 78–89.

without themselves being necessary, then he is open to the objections canvassed in §§ 56–7 above. But his view may be that causal laws are themselves necessarily true but not displayably so. I do not know how to argue for the view that every necessity or impossibility is displayable, except from a controversial premiss which I shall take up in my next section. In the meantime I must leave it at that; if some logical necessities are undisplayable, Hume's argument fails.

Also, conversely, if all logical necessities are displayable, Hume's argument goes through. From the premiss 'No impossibility can be displayed in the supposition that an F event occurs and is not followed by a G event' he can validly infer the conclusion 'The prediction that a G event will occur because an F event occurs cannot be licensed by a logically necessary proposition'. It is time, though, to ask what entitles Hume to this premiss. His latter-day supporters seem unaware that the premiss needs to be backed by arguments; and his opponents, with notable restraint, also omit to demand its credentials. This puzzling fact of contemporary intellectual history connects with some important philosophical points, and is worth explaining. I have been told: 'Nobody argues for that premiss because it is *obviously* true'—a remark which does not solve the problem but merely instantiates it.

59. 'Causal laws are synthetic': a bad argument

There is a view about logical necessity which appears in embryonic form in Hume[23] and flowers in the work of Wittgenstein, namely that logical necessity derives wholly from facts about meanings; or that to know whether P is necessary one needs only to know facts about the meanings of the words in which P is expressed; or, for short, that *all necessary truths are analytic*. This implies that all necessities are displayable, though it is not the only possible basis for that view. Anyway, my concern with 'All necessary truths are analytic' has to do not with its relation to the displayability thesis but rather with another role which it plays in our comedy.

It is commonly taken as obvious that if all necessary truths are analytic then no causal laws are necessary, and so the debate over

[23] But see W. A. Suchting, 'Hume on Necessary Truth', *Dialogue*, vol. 5 (1966–7).

the consequent has been ingested by the debate over the antecedent. Those who accept the analyticity thesis apparently think
that its implications for causal laws are too obvious to need
mentioning; while those who think that causal laws are necessary
launch their main attack against the analyticity thesis, as though
their position were obviously doomed unless *that* could be refuted.

Hume's supporters and his opponents, in short, agree that no
causal laws are analytic. I agree too; but the only argument for
this position which I can find in the literature is, though popular,
invalid. Before proceeding to expound and criticize it, I shall give
it a setting.

How can we show that a given (kind of) proposition is not
necessary? Perhaps by showing that it is false, but this move is
not available when the proposition in question is a causal law.
Another technique is this: we may show P's contingency by
describing a world in which P is false, with enough pertinent
detail to satisfy everyone that if there had been a lurking impossibility it would have been displayed in the given description. This
procedure is essentially indecisive: we may rightly be certain, but
we cannot directly prove, that the description does not harbour a
still-undisplayed impossibility. Also, the technique could be con-
vincingly applied to our present problem only by describing in
fine detail a whole possible world—Hume's snap 'conceptions'
are nowhere near adequate.

We might be able to devise a technique based on the following
kind of proof which is used in connexion with formal systems.
We can sometimes *prove* that a given formula F is not a theorem
in a given system S, by showing that F lacks a certain property ϕ
which is (*a*) possessed by each axiom of S, and (*b*) hereditary with
respect to the rules of S—which is to say that no rule of S can
lead from a formula having ϕ to a formula lacking ϕ. For example,
if S's axioms are all tautologies, and tautologicalness is hereditary
with respect to S's rules, then clearly the non-tautology (P & Q)
is not a theorem in S; that is, it cannot be reached from those
axioms by those rules. It does not matter in the least *what* property ϕ is, just so long as the axioms all have it and it is hereditary
with respect to the rules. For example, there might be a system
each of whose axioms had an even number of symbols, and whose
rules could not lead from an even- to an odd-numbered formula;
and those two facts about the system, once they were established,

would suffice to prove that the formula (P & P) was not a theorem of the system. In this case ϕ would be the peculiar property of having-an-even-number-of-symbols, but the proof would be none the worse for that.

To devise a structurally analogous proof that no propositions of kind K are necessary, we should need to find some property ϕ which verified both the general premiss:

> *Every necessary proposition follows from propositions which have ϕ, by moves with respect to which ϕ is hereditary,*

and the special premiss:

> *No K proposition has ϕ.*

Given both premisses, the desired conclusion would immediately follow.

The general premiss is verified by ϕ = logical necessity; but for that value of ϕ the special premiss is identical with the conclusion. So we must look for some other value of ϕ which verifies the general premiss.

Many philosophers think that the general premiss is true for the value ϕ = uninformativeness. If they are right, then it follows that no causal laws are necessary; for causal laws are not 'uninformative' in any reasonable sense—which is just to say that the special premiss is true for the values ϕ = uninformativeness and K = causal. This instance of the general premiss therefore demands our scrutiny.

To say that the general premiss is true where ϕ = uninformativeness is to say that all necessary truths are uninformative; and this is often said to follow from the lately-gained insight that all necessary truths are analytic. If all necessary truths are analytic then, arguably, every necessary truth follows by trivially valid moves from trivially necessary premisses; where a proposition is 'trivially necessary' if someone who questioned its truth would thereby show that he did not understand it, and a move is 'trivially valid' if the corresponding conditional is trivially necessary. Furthermore, we can allow that any trivially necessary proposition is uninformative, lacks content, tells us nothing about the world. So we may grant that every necessary truth follows from uninformative premisses by trivially valid moves. But this is not enough to verify the general premiss for the value ϕ =

uninformativeness; for we also need the second limb of the general premiss, namely that uninformativeness is hereditary with respect to trivially valid moves, i.e. that one cannot get by trivially valid moves from uninformative premisses to informative conclusions. This, however, is simply false. To discover that a proposition is necessary by proving it *is* to derive something informative from something uninformative by trivially valid moves.

Standard objection: 'You are using "informative" in a psychological sense, taking a proposition to be informative if it could come as news to an intelligent person, or could be found illuminating or surprising or interesting. But philosophers who say that because necessary propositions are analytic they are "uninformative" or "without content" are using these expressions in a logical rather than a psychological sense.' Well, what is it for a proposition to be, logically speaking, devoid of content? The usual answer is that a proposition is logically 'contentless' or 'uninformative' if it is 'consistent with every possible state of the world', or 'could not be refuted by any possible empirical discovery', or 'rules out none of the possibilities', or the like. But then the claim 'If P is necessary then P lacks content' is itself not just necessary but trivially so: it is an elementary consequence of what 'necessary' means that a necessary proposition must be 'contentless' or 'uninformative' in this sense. The claim was that 'If necessary then contentless' is to be accepted on the strength of 'If necessary then analytic, and if analytic then contentless', but now it turns out that 'If necessary then analytic' is simply irrelevant.

Credence is still given to the myth that 'Necessary truths are uninformative' expresses a truth which (*a*) stems from the premiss that necessary truths are analytic, (*b*) represents a recent and interesting discovery about necessary truths, (*c*) was taught to us by Wittgenstein, and (*d*) would have been denied by the 'rationalists' or 'deductive metaphysicians' of the past. I deny that 'Necessary truths are uninformative' expresses a truth of which *any* of (*a*) to (*d*) are true. As regards (*d*) in particular: no philosopher, whatever his views as to the nature of logical necessity, has thought that a necessary proposition could be inconsistent with some possibility, or could be refuted by some possible empirical discovery. There is an extraordinarily persistent desire to convict the rationalists, qua rationalists, of some general mistake about what can be learned by *a priori* means or what can be logically necessary; but there is no reason to think that the desire can be satisfied. There is only the illicit satisfaction of accusing the rationalists of errors of which they were not guilty, for example by saying that Descartes did not know, as we do, that the conclusion of a deductively valid argument is 'implicit in' its premisses.[24] Warnock says: 'This thesis of Hume's is sometimes reduced to the formula that empirical propositions cannot be logically necessary: and this—being a truism, though doubtless not a trivial one—has been very widely accepted. And rightly so.'[25] This is much better than most treatments, but why does Warnock allow that the truism is 'not a trivial one'?

Returning to our main theme: the general premiss is indeed true for the value ϕ = uninformativeness = logical necessity; but this is just a wordy version of our first false start, namely ϕ = logical necessity, and it too makes the special premiss identical with the conclusion. The question of whether causal laws are 'uninformative' in this sense—this unreasonable sense—is the question of whether causal laws are logically necessary. We had hoped to settle it by argument, not by dogma.

If Hume's conclusion is to be established, then, we shall have to find a fresh argument for it, such as the one in § 61 below.

60. *Hume and the bad argument*

Does Hume think that he has a substantive principle to the effect that 'No necessary truth has factual content'? Whether or not he thinks it follows from 'All necessary truths are analytic', or thinks it implies 'No causal laws are necessary', does he at any rate think that he has it? He sometimes seems to:

All the objects of human reason or enquiry may naturally be divided into two kinds, to wit, *Relations of Ideas,* and *Matters of Fact.* Of the first kind are the sciences of Geometry, Algebra, and Arithmetic; and in short, every affirmation which is either intuitively or demonstratively certain ... Propositions of this kind are discoverable by the mere operation of thought, without dependence on what is anywhere

---

[24] For this and other examples, see J. Bennett, 'A Myth about Logical Necessity', *Analysis*, vol. 21 (1960–1). For an impeccable handling of the point, see J. Hospers, *An Introduction to Philosophical Analysis* (Englewood Cliffs, 1953), pp. 131–2.

[25] G. J. Warnock, 'Hume on Causation', Pears p. 60.

existent in the universe . . . Matters of fact . . . are not ascertained in the same manner; nor is our evidence of their truth, however great, of a like nature with the foregoing. The contrary of every matter of fact is still possible; because it can never imply a contradiction . . .[26]

This looks like the twentieth-century myth, expressed as the claim that necessary truths never state 'matters of fact'. But the situation is not as simple as that.

The myth assumes that we have a pre-theoretic notion of 'fact' which supports a cogent argument for the conclusion that no necessary truth states a matter of fact or has factual content. Hume, on the other hand, explains 'matter of fact' only *through* his dichotomy between 'relations of ideas' and 'matters of fact'. He seems not to intend his choice of the latter label to embody a weighty claim to the effect that necessary truths never state 'matters of fact' in some independently clear sense. He may be hinting that anything which would ordinarily be deemed a 'matter of fact' will be found to lie on that side of the methodological divide, i.e. will be found to be incapable of proof by *a priori* means; but he shows no signs of wanting to use this hint combatively or argumentatively.

It is true that Hume connects 'matter of fact' with 'cause', in ways examined in § 51 above. But that connexion has the form 'If factual, then cause-involving'. It does not have the form 'If causal then factual, and if factual then contingent', which is the connexion alleged by myth.

It is also true that Hume uses the phrase 'matter of fact *and existence*', and maintains as a general thesis that no existential statement can be logically necessary: 'Whatever *is* may *not be*. No negation of a fact can involve a contradiction. The non-existence of any being, without exception, is as clear and distinct an idea as its existence.'[27] This, however, does not tar him with the brush of the current myth, for the latter has no patent on the thesis that all existential statements are contingent. Hume's reasons for the thesis, we may note in passing, are peculiarly murky. In the long passage quoted above, his use of 'what is anywhere existent in the universe' suggests that Hume tends to equate (1) what exists with (2) what exists in the universe, and this with (3) what exists in the objective realm, and this with (4) what is the case about the objective realm, and this with (5) what

[26] *Enquiry* §§ 20–1.   [27] *Enquiry* § 132. See also *Treatise*, p. 94.

is the case about anything beyond our own ideas and impressions, and this finally with (6) what is contingently the case. In this Humean route from existentialness to contingency, the crucial move is that from (4) through (5) to (6)—a move whose logic, and whose indebtedness to the double use of 'idea', I have discussed in § 52 above.

These, however, are matters of relative detail. To see how wrong it is to regard Hume as foreshadowing the twentieth-century view that necessary truths don't state facts, we must examine the use which he does make of his dichotomy between 'relations of ideas' and 'matters of fact'.

The fundamental point is that Hume sees the dichotomy as *exhaustive*. He wants to ask the hostile question 'Is what you are saying of *this* kind or of *that*?', in order to attack anyone whose only honest answer to the question is 'Neither'. He thinks that the 'school metaphysician', for instance, must answer 'Neither': he cannot claim that his results are reached by 'demonstration' (as Hume understands it) or by empirical methods; and so he is under a challenge, which Hume thinks he cannot meet, to explain the nature of his inquiry. Now, in this situation it is just irrelevant that Hume has the label 'matters of fact' for matters which are established by empirical means. He attacks 'school metaphysics' and 'divinity' through the methodological contents of the two sides of his dichotomy, not through the labels that he affixes to them.

To use his dichotomy in the manner of the twentieth-century myth, Hume would have to argue not from the joint exhaustiveness but from the mutual exclusiveness of the two sides of the dichotomy. He would have to attack someone who, when asked 'To which side does that statement belong?' answered not 'Neither' but 'Both'. But this answer is harmless if it means that the statement is based on a mixture of *a priori* and empirical considerations. The answer 'Both' could fall foul of Hume's dichotomy only if it meant that the basis for the statement is (*a*) wholly *a priori* and (*b*) partly empirical; but who would ever be so silly as to maintain that? For Hume to have any real target—any opponent whom he can attack as trying illegitimately to occupy both sides of the dichotomy at once—he will have to desert his view of the dichotomy as a methodological one. Instead of seeing it as a division between two ways of establishing truths, he will have to see it as a division between one *way of establishing truths* ('relations of ideas') and one *kind of truth* ('matter of fact'). If he did this, he could argue from the *label* 'matter of fact' in the manner of the current myth, saying to his opponent: 'You claim that your conclusion is provable *a priori* yet states a matter of fact; but you can't have it both ways.'

But Hume simply does not do this; and if he did, it would be wholly contrary to the spirit of the use which he does make of his dichotomy. Some proponents of the twentieth-century myth give Hume 'credit' for having begun what they have completed. I submit that this is unfair to him.

61. *'Causal laws are synthetic': another argument*

Any causal law or prediction-licensing statement must entail conditionals of the form 'If P then Q', where P is about the world only up to time *t* and Q is about the world at some time later than *t*—so that at *t* one could say 'P has come true, but whatever makes Q true or makes Q false has not yet happened'. This is an attempt to capture the vague notion of 'predicting the future on the basis of the past and present' which I take to be the focal point of Hume's inquiry into what he calls 'the idea of necessary connexion'.

The necessitarian thesis which Hume denies, then, is that the following is possible:

> P *is not about the future, Q is about the future, and P entails Q.*

If that formulation does not embody the point at issue, then the point eludes me entirely; but I think it will be agreed that the crux of the dispute lies somewhere in the region indicated. The formulation is so vague, and the region thus so wide, that we cannot make much progress until more precision is achieved. But that can wait a little.

Here is an argumentative move against the necessitarian. To say that P *is not about the future* is to report on P's content, or on what P says. The necessitarian thinks that a Q which is about the future may be entailed by a P which is not. Of such a P he must say that its *content does not*, but its logical *consequences do*, reach into the future; or that it *does not say* but *does entail* something about the future. This presupposes a certain kind of line between a proposition's content and its consequences. There cannot be a content/consequences line of the presupposed kind. So the necessiarian's view is wrong.

To explain what kind of content/consequences line the necessitarian needs but cannot have, I must invoke the thesis that all necessary truths are analytic or that all deductively valid truths are analytically valid. According to this thesis, one cannot trace out the logical consequences of a proposition unless it is expressed in a sentence. Furthermore, to trace them out is to assemble certain facts about the meaning of the relevant sentence in relation to the meanings of other sentences: knowing that (premiss)→ (first lemma) is knowing certain facts about the meanings of those two sentences; similarly for (first lemma)→(second lemma), and so on. The epistemological raw material for entailment-tracking, then, is the same as for determining the meaning of sentences or the content of propositions. This suggests that it may be hard to separate content from consequences in such a way that a proposition can entail something about the future without itself being about the future.

'But we do distinguish content from consequences.' Indeed we do. For example, if I am to report someone in oratio obliqua, I need not reproduce his sentences just so long as I produce sentences which mean what his did; but my report of 'what he said' must not include everything entailed by what he said. In short, I must reproduce the content but not the consequences of what he said. Another example: someone says 'Given that . . ., it does not follow that . . .', with the blanks filled by S_p and S_q which standardly mean that P and that Q respectively; and we know that P does entail Q. If we could not distinguish content from consequences we should have to say that this person uses S_p or S_q non-standardly—e.g. that he wrongly takes S_p to express not P but some other proposition which does not entail Q. But sometimes, rather than describing his error in that way, we are content to say that he wrongly thinks that P does not entail Q. That is, we credit him with meaning by S_p and S_q what we do, using them to express P and Q respectively, and accuse him of being in error not about content but about consequences.

Our content/consequences distinction, however, is one of degree, and it can be stopped from sliding only by somewhat arbitrary decisions. Someone who says 'Given that x is a triangle, it doesn't follow that x has three sides' is in trouble over content not consequences: if he is sincere, and understands 'follow' etc. properly, then he must be giving a non-standard meaning either to 'is a triangle' or to 'has three sides'. What about 'x is a triangle' in relation to 'x has three angles'? and 'x has as many sides as angles'? and 'x is half a quadrangle'? We want a line somewhere, but there is no one obviously right place to draw it. Similarly with the oratio obliqua example. If someone says 'Some men in Borneo are cannibals', I can fairly if stiltedly report: 'He said that some men in Borneo eat the bodies of members of their own species.' Can I also say: 'He said that some men in Borneo eat the bodies of other men'? and '. . . eat human flesh'? and '. . . eat flesh'? and '. . . are carnivorous'? Granted that the last two omit part of what he said, do they also add to it, going beyond the content into the consequences? When the question is thus raised in the abstract, there is no obviously right answer; and we may prefer one answer or another, depending on the special features of the situation. Usually, I suppose, 'He said that some men in Borneo are carnivorous' would be regarded as going beyond the mere reporting of content; but not always—e.g. not if on the reported occasion someone had said 'The men in Borneo are all vegetarians, you know', and the reported speaker had snapped back 'Some men in Borneo are *cannibals*!'

So our 'intuitions' about the content/consequences line vary with context, and the thesis that all necessary truths are analytic explains why. (Proposition-content is sentence-meaning; and the latter, according to the analyticity thesis, is on a continuum with proposition-consequence.) The prospects look bad for any attempt to develop an entirely general, context-independent, person-neutral distinction which will look reasonable in all its applications.

All that, however, merely provides a setting (not a premiss) for the following argument which shows that the necessitarian cannot have the kind of content/consequences distinction that *he* wants.

What sorts of P and Q will interest the necessitarian? Suppose we point out that (S_p) 'Smith has just taken a lethal dose of a fast-acting poison' can be so construed as to express a falsehood unless Smith dies soon, so that P entails (Q) that Smith will soon be dead. The necessitarian will dismiss that as uninteresting. 'It does not show what an entailment-based prediction is like. If P entails

Q in this case, that is only because P says something about the future, i.e. covertly says that Smith has done something as a result of which he will die soon.' Would the necessitarian be less disappointed by an S_p whose meaning-involvement with the future was less obvious? If he is the man I want to argue with, he will say: 'No. I want a prediction Q entailed by a P which *is* not about the future, not merely a P which *seems* not to be about the future.' Suppose then that we try to construct a case in which (1) P entails Q; (2) Q is explicitly about the future; (3) part or all of S_p's meaning is equally expressed by S_r, and S_r's by S_t, and S_t's by S_u, . . . and so through to S_q; and (4) in this sequence the earliest sentence which explicitly expresses something about the future is one which would not ordinarily count as just a way of expressing (part of) what S_p expresses—e.g. would not be acceptable in an oratio obliqua report on an uttering of S_p. This is a case in which everything which is explicitly 'about the future' will, by ordinary standards, qualify as a consequence of P rather than as part of its content. If the necessitarian accepts this as a fair sample of an entailment-licensed prediction, I have no argument with him.

But he is unlikely to accept it. If he sees that this case differs only in degree from one where S itself expresses something about the future, and remembers why he wanted a necessitarian theory in the first place, he will say: 'This still doesn't exemplify an entailment-licensed prediction Q from facts about the present and the past. You insist that the facts about the present and past be reported in a sentence: I'll go along with that, just so long as you don't muddy the waters by choosing a sentence which jumbles facts about the present and past with claims about the future. The sentence S_p must have a meaning which in no way reaches forward into the future; it must make an absolutely clean cut across the world at a particular time; for otherwise we cannot know that P *has* come true at a time when the events which verify or falsify Q still lie in the future.'

But if all necessary truths are analytic, the necessitarian cannot have what he wants. To satisfy him that P entails something about the future we shall, inevitably, have to convict S_p of having a meaning which is tainted by the future.

That completes my argument for saying that no necessary proposition can license a prediction. The conclusion is not trivial:

it rests on the relatively recent and partly Wittgensteinian insight that all necessary truths are analytic, and it denies something which has been believed by some able philosophers. (It has in fact all the properties which are wrongly attributed to the thesis that no necessary proposition can have content, be informative, state a fact about the world.) Philosophers such as Descartes and Locke really did think that a proposition might (*a*) be acceptable with a special kind of assurance because it concerns only the past and present, yet (*b*) lead by purely logical and demonstrative means to a conclusion about the future; and they might well have avoided this mistake if they had seen more clearly how meaning relates to necessity. To say this is not to libel them. It is not to be compared with accusing them of thinking that a necessary proposition can exclude a possibility or be refutable by a possible experience, or that premisses can entail a conclusion which is not 'implicit' in them.

I have no decision-procedure. Suppose the necessitarian adduces a plausible example—a Q which is about the future, and a P of which it is plausible to say that it entails Q and plausible to say that it is not in any way about the future. In such a case we may have no grounds for saying 'He is wrong because P does not entail Q' or for saying 'He is wrong because P is, in a way, about the future'. Usually, either diagnosis will be quite reasonable—which is just to say that either interpretation of S_p will be reasonable—and it will seldom if ever matter which is offered. The force of my conclusion is not to pick out a class of prediction-licensing statements and say that Descartes and others were wrong in thinking that any of *those* could be necessary. Rather, it is to criticize the general belief that a proposition could both license predictions and be logically necessary.

(Analogously, the principle 'A purely descriptive proposition cannot entail an evaluative one' does not pick out and condemn particular arguments. If an argument has an evaluative conclusion and a semblance of validity, we can usually choose between calling the argument invalid and calling the premiss evaluative. All the principle does is to reject the general thesis that a conditional can both be logically necessary and have a non-evaluative antecedent and an evaluative consequent. Since no one has ever accepted that general thesis, the principle is a bore; but that is not my problem.)

One last point. Our language is theory-loaded, so that its sentences do not split neatly into those which do and those which don't express something 'about the future' or 'about times later than t'. That fact, which explains our having the choice referred to in the paragraph before last, was not recognized by Hume—as witness his assumptions about the atomistic way in which language relates to ideas, and thus to impressions, and thus to the world. Now, when a philosopher says that science will eventually 'demonstrate' or show *a priori* that gold always dissolves in aqua regia, this may express the necessitarian ideal I have joined Hume in criticizing, but it may instead reflect a real understanding of what the logic of theory-laden terms such as 'gold' and 'aqua regia' might be in a mature science. Probably both factors will be involved: the necessitarianism which Hume opposes does exist in the literature, but we ought to remember that it does not show up in the language as neatly and unequivocally as Hume seems to suppose. To isolate linguistically the notion of a temporal cut across the world is a laborious and clumsy task, for reasons of which Hume was less aware than many of his opponents.

62. *'Distinct ideas'*

The argument of the preceding section is not one that Hume explicitly adduces; but it reaches his conclusion from fairly Humean premises, and I think he would have welcomed it. Apart from the 'conceivability' argument, which is incomplete even on the kindest interpretation, Hume really has no arguments against causal necessitarianism. In §§ 59–61 I have implied a partial explanation of why others have thought that Hume decisively refuted necessitarianism. I now want to explain why Hume himself thought this.

The explanation can start here:

All ideas, which are different, are separable . . . It follows . . . that if the figure be different from the body, their ideas must be separable as well as distinguishable; if they be not different, their ideas can neither be separable nor distinguishable.[28]

Hume often affirms the biconditional 'different↔separable', though the work done here by 'different' is often done by 'distinct', 'other', and 'two'. Here is another example:

[28] *Treatise*, pp. 24–5.

Every thing, that is different, is distinguishable; and every thing, that is distinguishable, may be separated, according to the maxims above-explain'd. [And conversely] if . . . they be not different, they are not distinguishable; and if they be not distinguishable, they cannot be separated.[29]

If ideas are concepts or meanings, the notion of the 'difference' or 'distinctness' of ideas is a purely logical one: to say that the idea of squareness is 'distinct from' that of blackness is to say that as between 'x is square' and 'x is black' there is no entailment either way; or, perhaps, that it is not the case that there is an entailment both ways. (The difference between these two versions does not matter for my present purposes.) And to say that one idea is 'separable from' another is, apparently, to say that a state of affairs can be imagined to which one idea is applicable but not the other. Given these interpretations, the biconditional says that *It is logically possible that* $(Fx \ \& \sim Gx) \leftrightarrow$ *One can imagine an F which is not G.* Thus construed, it is uninteresting: it is just an expression of misplaced confidence in the 'conceivability' test for logical possibility.

Now consider this:

Whatever is distinct, is distinguishable; and whatever is distinguishable, is separable by the thought or imagination. All perceptions are distinct. They are, therefore, distinguishable, and separable, and may be conceiv'd as separately existent, and may exist separately, without any contradiction or absurdity.[30]

This purports to move from a premiss about distinctness, through a lemma about separability, to a conclusion about logical possibility. If 'distinct' has to be explained through 'logically possible', the premiss is identical with the conclusion and the passage covers no ground. Yet I do not see how else Hume could explain what 'distinct' means in this passage. Certainly, we shall not get a clue from the peculiar sentence 'All perceptions are distinct'! The passage is in fact one of several in which Hume 'moves' from distinctness through separability to possibility, in contexts where he could explain 'distinct' only in terms of 'possible'.[31] In similar vein, I have been told that no fact can entail 'another' fact; and Warnock remarks that 'nothing that happens in the world can be

---

[29] *Treatise*, p. 36. See also p. 18.   [30] *Treatise*, p. 634.
[31] *Treatise*, pp. 86–7; *Enquiry* § 27.

connected . . . necessarily with anything else that happens in the world';[32] but our only criteria for 'otherness', or for a happening's being something 'else', are such as to trivialize both these claims. Here is the 'move' again, but this time with a certain difference:

As all distinct ideas are separable from each other, and as the ideas of cause and effect are evidently distinct, 'twill be easy for us to conceive any object to be non-existent this moment, and existent the next, without conjoining to it the distinct idea of a cause or productive principle. The separation, therefore, of the idea of a cause from that of a beginning of existence, is plainly possible for the imagination; and consequently the actual separation of these objects is so far possible, that it implies no contradiction nor absurdity; and is therefore incapable of being refuted by any reasoning from mere ideas; without which 'tis impossible to demonstrate the necessity of a cause.[33]

If ideas are meanings and 'distinctness' is a logical relation, then 'The ideas of cause and effect are evidently distinct' is false: it is analytic that every cause has an effect, and vice versa. Perhaps Hume means to say that 'the ideas of cause and beginning of existence are distinct'. On that reading, the passage moves from the premiss that those two ideas are 'evidently distinct' to the conclusion that 'Something begins to exist without a cause' expresses a logical possibility. Once more, the old troublesome question arises. Can Hume so explain 'distinct' that his premiss is 'evidently' true yet still at a decent argumentative distance from his conclusion?

I don't think he can. But if we stand back from the quoted passage and try to say roughly and briefly what its central contention is, the following seems right: 'Hume is contending that, given any pair of events which are related as cause and effect, it is logically possible that either should have occurred without the other's occurring.' If that is right, then it isn't clear that the phrase 'distinct *ideas*' belongs here at all. Hume's trouble in the first sentence may be due to the fact that he is trying to use the language of 'distinct ideas' when his real concern is with pairs of distinct *events*.

At any rate, Hume does sometimes apply the notion of 'distinctness' not to ideas but directly to events:

[32] Warnock, loc. cit. See also R. W. Church, *Hume's Theory of the Understanding* (London, 1935), p. 73.
[33] *Treatise*, pp. 79–80.

The mind can never possibly find the effect in the supposed cause, by the most accurate scrutiny and examination. For the effect is totally different from the cause, and consequently can never be discovered in it. Motion in the second Billiard-ball is a quite distinct event from motion in the first; nor is there anything in the one to suggest the smallest hint of the other.[34]

To spell out event-distinctness in terms of idea-distinctness would be a Herculean labour of misrepresentation. We ought to allow event-distinctness to stand on its own feet, as partly defined thus: if A occurs earlier than B, then A is a 'distinct event' from B. This explanation does not render Hume's premiss equivalent to his usual conclusion that A could occur without B's occurring. What we now have is not the triviality associated with idea-distinctness, but rather the substantive thesis that there cannot be an entailment-licensed prediction—or, rather, that is what the passage would contain if Hume had there clearly and forcefully drawn his usual conclusion.

Here is a passage where Hume does draw the standard conclusion from a premiss about the distinctness of events (which, here as elsewhere, he calls 'objects'):

Nothing is more evident, than that the human mind cannot form such an idea of two objects, as to conceive any connexion betwixt them, or comprehend distinctly that power or efficacy, by which they are united. Such a connexion wou'd amount to a demonstration, and wou'd imply the absolute impossibility for the one object not to follow, or to be conceiv'd not to follow upon the other: Which kind of connexion has already been rejected in all cases.[35]

This occurs in the thick of Hume's attack on necessitarianism. I think he is assuming that if A causes B then A and B are obviously distinct, are obviously 'two' events, because they occur at slightly different times. (For present purposes the adverb 'distinctly' is a red herring.) From their distinctness in that sense, Hume infers their logical independence, i.e. infers that either could occur without the other. The inference is not trivial. Rather than complaining that the corresponding conditional says nothing, we must complain that it says more than Hume can justify.

We are back at square one: Hume wrongly thinks he has shown

[34] *Enquiry* § 25.   [35] *Treatise*, pp. 161–2.

that there cannot be an entailment-licensed prediction. But now we can at least partly explain his thinking this. I suggest that he has mixed up (a) the trivial truth that if concept C_1 is 'distinct' from C_2 because logically independent of it, then they are logically independent, with (b) the substantive thesis that if event A is 'distinct' from B because non-synchronous with it then they are logically independent. This helps to explain why Hume lets himself down so lightly: he has an indisputably true thesis, and a substantive thesis, and he cannot distinguish between them; so he naturally thinks he has a single thesis which is both substantive and indisputably true. This account is consistent with Hume's known intellectual character; and I think it helps to illuminate nearly all his uses of 'distinct', 'other' etc. in this area, though the task of expounding them all in orderly fashion has defeated me.

This mix-up is helped by the fact that for Hume an 'idea' may be (a) a concept or meaning, or (b) a datable mental event which does not differ importantly from an impression. When he speaks of 'perceptions' as 'distinct', he is poised to set off in either of two directions. (a) Thinking of the sub-class of 'perceptions' which are 'ideas', and thinking of these not as datable occurrences but as meanings or concepts, he could be led to the notion of concept-distinctness or logical independence. (b) Thinking of 'perceptions' as mental happenings, he could be led to the notion of event-distinctness or non-simultaneity.[36] Furthermore, Hume can see (b) as unrestricted in scope: all we know about events is known through our impressions, and so—Hume can think— any result about 'distinct' impressions will imply a result about 'distinct' events of any kind whatever.

Still, although Hume's basic handling of 'idea' may thus have encouraged the assimilation of (a) to (b), it did not make it inevitable. Even the most credulous acceptance of the view that ideas are both meanings and mental occurrences still leaves room for the needed distinction between meaning-distinctness and event-distinctness. Hume, even with his basic premises, could have seen that one event (temporal criterion) might consist in the having of two ideas (logical criterion), as when someone has ideas of blackness and squareness at t; and that two events (temporal criterion) might consist in the having of a single idea (logical criterion), as when someone has ideas of squareness at t_1 and again

<hr>

[36] See *Treatise*, pp. 10, 27, 66.

at t_2. Had he seen that much, Hume would not have conflated the two sorts of distinctness, and so would not have jumbled (*a*) with (*b*). But, despite one flickering suggestion to the contrary,[37] I do not think that he did see that much.

[37] *Treatise*, p. 106, near top.

XII

HUME ON CAUSATION: POSITIVE

63. *Why we predict*

HUME thinks that predictions can have only an inductive basis. Our basis for predicting a G event, given that an F event has occurred, may be the fact that in the past F events have always been followed by G events. Or it may be more complex: the recent F event may be the only F event we know of; but we might still predict 'A G event will occur' because this is entailed by 'An F event has occurred' together with some set of general statements which *have* been often instantiated, and never counter-instantiated, in the past. And perhaps the basis for a prediction may be more complex still. The basic logic of the situation, how-ever, is captured by the simplest version: F events have always been followed by G ones, and so when a new F event occurs we predict a G one. On the maxim 'Don't scratch where it doesn't itch', I shall not strive for a realistic account of our predicting behaviour. The cruces of Hume's theory can be handled wholly in terms of the above over-simplification.

Hume offers to explain the fact that, when we have found F events to be followed by G events, we expect a new F event to be followed by a G one. The explanation utilizes two of his theories.

The first is his theory about 'the association of ideas'.[1] Offered as embodying a set of empirical facts which 'I pretend not to explain', this theory states the conditions under which statements of the following form are true: 'If *x* has an F perception at *t*, then he tends to have a G perception then or shortly thereafter.' Such a statement will be true if F perceptions have been associated with G perceptions in *x*'s past experience—using 'associated' as a stand-in for any member of a certain set of relations listed in the theory. The member of this set which matters to us now is that of being-followed-closely-by: the theory implies that if F per-ceptions have been followed closely by G perceptions in *x*'s past

---

[1] *Treatise* I. i. 4. See also p. 283.

experience, and *x* has an F perception now, then *x* probably has or soon will have a G idea. In initially expounding the theory, Hume omits to say that an F *impression* tends to induce a livelier G idea than would be induced, other things being equal, by an F *idea*. He implies this later: 'When any impression becomes present to us, it not only transports the mind to such ideas as are related to it, but likewise communicates to them a share of its force and vivacity.'[2] Hume seems also to think that the frequency of the past F-G association will determine not just the probability of a G idea's occurring next time but also its liveliness if it does occur.[3] This is backed by a speculative cerebral physiology which can safely be ignored.[4]

The second contributor to Hume's explanation of why we predict is his analysis of the concept of belief. A belief is just a lively idea: the difference between believing that London is on fire and entertaining the thought of its being on fire is just that between a more and a less lively idea of London ablaze:

As belief does nothing but vary the manner, in which we conceive any object, it can only bestow on our ideas an additional force and vivacity. An opinion, therefore, or belief may be most accurately defin'd, A LIVELY IDEA RELATED TO OR ASSOCIATED WITH A PRESENT IMPRESSION.[5]

The first clause records Hume's insight that one can believe, disbelieve, entertain etc. the same proposition. He thinks that the common propositional content which a belief, disbelief etc. can share is an idea, which implies that believing does not differ from disbelieving or wondering, say, in the ideas that are involved. In inferring from this that the difference can only consist in 'the manner in which' the ideas are had, Hume is assuming that someone's having a certain belief is just a fact about what ideas he has and how he has them. This assumption is unwarranted, and the resultant analysis of belief is beyond redemption. It implies, for example, that there is no difference between believing that the Sahara is warm and entertaining the thought that it is extremely hot! (Hume links his analysis of belief with some sound remarks about 'the idea of existence'.[6] The supposed connexion

---

[2] *Treatise*, p. 98.   [3] *Treatise* I. iii. 11, last sentence.
[4] *Treatise*, pp. 60–1.
[5] *Treatise*, p. 96. See also p. 86, and Flew, *Hume's Philosophy of Belief*, pp. 100–3.
[6] *Treatise*, pp. 94–5. See also pp. 66–7.

between these two topics is a bad mistake which has been set right by Geach.[7])

When Hume stipulates that an idea which is to count as a belief must be 'related to a present impression', he is presumably focusing on the special case of a belief for which one has present sensory evidence. He is also paving the way for his account of why we predict.

Put the analysis of belief together with the 'association of ideas' theory, and the desired explanation of why we predict rolls smoothly out.[8] If my F perceptions have always been closely followed by G perceptions, and I now have an F impression, then it follows by the association theory that I am virtually certain to have a lively G idea, and this, according to the analysis of belief, is the same as having a belief.

What am I believing when I have a suitably lively G idea? Hume must answer: 'You are believing that an event will soon occur which, if you observe it, will induce a G impression in you.' This shows optimism about how the classifying of sensory states relates to the classifying of objective events; but I reserve that topic for my last chapter. It also shows optimism about tenses: at most, Hume is entitled to 'You are believing that an event did/does/will occur . . .' Given that his sole aim is to explain why we *predict* as we do, this is no small defect.

The explanation is bound to fail, because Hume's analysis of the concept of belief is so bad. His 'association of ideas' theory is an empirical one which may contain some truth, though really it is too vague to be evaluated. Even if it is wholly true, it is simply irrelevant to our predictions—our beliefs about the future—because Hume is wrong about what a belief is. In rejecting his analysis of belief we cut the pipeline through which the explanation of why we predict is supposed to draw factual nourishment from the theory about the association of ideas; and so the explanation withers away.

64. *'Necessary connexion'*

Hume bases his analysis of the concept of cause on his theory about why we predict. Fortunately, the analysis partly survives the rejection of its supposed basis.

[7] P. T. Geach, 'Assertion', *Philosophical Review*, vol. 74 (1965), pp. 458–9. See also Passmore, *Hume's Intentions*, pp. 97–9.   [8] *Treatise*, pp. 92–3.

According to Hume, the concept of cause has three ingredients. One of them, spatial contiguity, was once controversial but would now be generally agreed not to be part of the concept of cause: 'action at a distance', whether or not it actually occurs, is at least possible.[9] The second alleged ingredient in the concept of cause is temporal priority. Hume sought to defend this, arguing that 'if any cause [were] co-temporary with its effect' the upshot would be 'the utter annihilation of time'.[10] His argument is invalid, though. At best, it shows that *some* causes are not 'co-temporary' with their effects: it offers no serious obstacle, and I doubt if any can be offered, to the supposition that some causes are synchronous with their effects. Of more interest is the suggestion that a cause might occur *later* than its effect: this suggestion was made—I think for the first time in serious philosophical literature—in a quite recent paper by Dummett. This provoked an energetic response, which still continues.[11]

The complex issues raised by that literature can, fortunately, be ignored without prejudice to the third ingredient which Hume finds in the concept of cause:

An object may be contiguous and prior to another, without being consider'd as its cause. There is a NECESSARY CONNEXION to be taken into consideration; and that relation is of much greater importance, than any of the other two above-mention'd.[12]

However, necessary 'connexions' of the sort Hume allows cannot give predictions a stronger-than-inductive basis, nor are they relations which hold objectively between the 'objects' or events which we take to be causally related. We move from 'post hoc' to 'propter hoc' if and only if the events in question instantiate some pattern which has been regularly adhered to in the past, but:

There is . . . nothing new either discover'd or produc'd in any objects by their constant conjunction, and by the uninterrupted resemblance

---

[9] See M. B. Hesse, *Forces and Fields* (London, 1961), *passim*; Flew, *Hume's Philosophy of Belief*, pp. 125–6.

[10] *Treatise*, p. 76.

[11] M. Dummett, 'Can an Effect Precede its Cause?', *Proceedings of the Aristotelian Society*, suppl. vol. 28 (1954). See also Flew, *Hume's Philosophy of Belief*, pp. 126–30. There is a fairly full bibliography in J. L. Mackie, 'The Direction of Causation', *Philosophical Review*, vol. 75 (1966), p. 442 n.

[12] *Treatise*, p. 77.

of their relations of succession and contiguity. But 'tis from this resemblance, that the ideas of necessity, of power, and of efficacy, are deriv'd. These ideas, therefore, represent not any thing, that does or can belong to the objects, which are constantly conjoin'd.[13]

So the third ingredient—'necessary connexion'—must concern what happens in the mind of the person who, observing an F event, predicts a G event.

To explain how, I must mention a fact which I have not so far stressed, namely that Hume's 'association of ideas' theory is a causal one: if F and G perceptions have often enough been associated in my past experience, and I now have an F impression, I can't help having a G idea. If the F-G association is less well entrenched, I may not be entirely at its mercy; and the most Hume will say of the over-all 'uniting principle among ideas' is that it is 'a gentle force, which commonly prevails'.[14] But in the paradigm prediction-situation, he thinks, the predicter is in the grip of something: he is forced to have his lively idea, i.e. to make his prediction. Now, someone who is being bundled along in this way may not understand what is happening to him; but he will feel it happen. There is a characteristic 'impression of reflexion' which goes with being causally compelled or 'determined' to expect something to occur, and this impression is the basis for the idea of necessary connexion. Thus:

After a frequent repetition, I find, that upon the appearance of one of the objects, the mind is *determin'd* by custom to consider its usual attendant, and to consider it in a stronger light upon account of its relation to the first object. 'Tis this impression, then, or *determination*, which affords me the idea of necessity.[15]

And again:

The repetition neither discovers nor causes any thing in the objects, but has an influence only on the mind, by that customary transition it produces: ... this customary transition is, therefore, the same with the power and necessity; which are consequently qualities of perceptions, not of objects, and are internally felt by the soul, and not perceiv'd externally in bodies.[16]

This is Hume's account of the 'idea of necessary connexion' which combines with the ideas of contiguity and priority to make up the idea of cause.

[13] *Treatise*, p. 164.   [14] *Treatise*, p. 10.
[15] *Treatise*, p. 156.   [16] *Treatise*, p. 166.

Hume expects resistance. Granted that any causal judgement implies something about contiguity and priority, and implies something else as well, it seems implausible to say that the 'something else' concerns the effect on the speaker's own mind of a certain event or of others like it. It seems to us clear that what we add to the contiguity-priority claim is something about a further relation between the two events themselves—and could we be wrong about that? Hume thinks we could:

> This contrary biass is easily accounted for. 'Tis a common observation, that the mind has a great propensity to spread itself on external objects, and to conjoin with them any internal impressions, which they occasion, and which always make their appearance at the same time that these objects discover themselves to the senses.[17]

This seems to imply that when we speak of 'causes' we merely project onto the world our compulsive expectations, as though a rational man would always replace 'It must happen' by 'I must expect it to happen'. Yet Hume tries to avoid dismissing causal statements as disguised autobiography or as manifestations of a universal neurosis; and if my exposition so far makes this surprising, that is because I have omitted part of the story. Here is Hume's final, official, considered analysis of the concept of cause:

> We may define a CAUSE to be [1] 'An object precedent and contiguous to another, and where all the objects resembling the former are plac'd in like relations of precedency and contiguity to those objects, that resemble the latter.' If this definition be esteem'd defective, because drawn from objects foreign to the cause, we may substitute this other definition in its place, viz. 'A CAUSE is [2] an object precedent and contiguous to another, and so united with it, that the idea of the one determines the mind to form the idea of the other, and the impression of the one to form a more lively idea of the other.'[18]

(He associates these with causation's roles as (1) a philosophical and (2) a natural relation. One sees what he means, but the suggestion is better ignored.) Definition (1) can be seen as Hume's answer to the charge that he reduces all causal talk to statements about contiguity and priority plus misleadingly worded statements about the speaker's state of mind. But the defence is not really good enough.

---

[17] *Treatise*, p. 167.

[18] *Treatise*, p. 170. See also *Enquiry* § 60, and the good discussion in A. H. Basson, *David Hume* (Pelican Books, 1958), pp. 72–8.

Hume himself knows that (1) will be objected to, as implying that the truth of '*x* causes *y*' depends upon events which occurred years before *x* and *y*. He knows also that (2) will be disliked because it excludes the past only by introducing another 'foreign' element, namely the speaker's state of mind. Hume challenges 'the persons, who express this delicacy' to 'substitute a juster definition'. Such a definition would have to capture 'necessary connexion' in a net no wider than the connected events themselves, i.e. one which did not reach out into the past or into the speaker's mind; and Hume's negative work makes him sure that this cannot be done.

Granting him that, there is still a difficulty about Hume's two definitions. If his explanation of why we predict is correct, then any case which is known to satisfy (1) will also satisfy (2), and perhaps Hume can safely assume the converse; but the two definitions are not equivalent—they cannot both be correct accounts of what we mean by 'cause'.[19] Furthermore, Hume has provided no basis for saying that (1) describes what we mean by 'cause': when we object that our causal statements are not misleadingly worded reports on our own states of mind, Hume cannot reply 'Well, then, forget about (2), and take me as propounding (1) as my analysis of your talk about causes'. Granting for purposes of argument that (1) is true when and only when (2) is true, Hume must say that what we *mean* by 'cause' is given by (2), so that our causal statements are revealed as disguised intellectual autobiography after all; unless he takes the even less attractive option of saying that our uses of 'cause' are mere mouthing which we are forced into by the causal factors alluded to in (1) and (2). So he is not yet out of the wood. What ought to be an analysis of the concept of cause still has the appearance of an exposé.

65. *Predicters as victims*

Part of the trouble is that Hume offers a *causal* theory. I do not allege circularity; if it is wrong in principle to elucidate causal language through a theory about what causes us to use it, that is not because such a procedure is circular.[20] The complaint is

[19] See *Treatise*, p. 400; and the exchange between J. A. Robinson and T. J. Richards on 'Hume's Two Definitions of "Cause"', in Chappell.

[20] See D. G. C. MacNabb, *David Hume* (London, 1951), pp. 112-15; Flew, *Hume's Philosophy of Belief*, pp. 121-3.

rather that causes tend to shoulder aside *reasons*. Hume does not, simply by assigning causes for our causal beliefs, imply that there are no reasons for them; but by treating only of their causes—by his silence about reasons for them—he does suggest that these beliefs cannot be supported by reasons, and even that they are unreasonable.

This is not merely a matter of suggestion. A causal theory is a genetic one, and Hume's genetic emphasis leads him to denigrate causal beliefs in quite specific ways. In considering any belief's intellectual standing, all Hume will do is demand its birth-certificate; and so, confronted by a belief for which there are reasons, he asks only whether it is arrived at through a consideration of reasons. He often finds that it is not. More clearly than many philosophers, Hume saw how few of our beliefs are reached through any ratiocinative endeavours. But then he offers an alternative account of our route to most of our beliefs, and allows this to dominate his intellectual assessment of them:

A person, who stops short in his journey upon meeting a river in his way, foresees the consequences of his proceeding forward; and his knowledge of these consequences is convey'd to him by past experience . . . But can we think, that on this occasion he reflects on any past experience . . . ? No surely; this is not the method in which he proceeds in his reasoning. The idea of sinking is so closely connected with that of water, and the idea of suffocating with that of sinking, that the mind makes the transition without the assistance of the memory. The custom operates before we have time for reflexion . . . Experience may produce a belief and a judgment of causes and effects by a secret operation, and without being once thought of.[21]

That passage refers to 'reasoning', but only in the very large sense in which Hume can also say that 'all reasonings are nothing but the effects of custom'.[22] 'Reasoning' in this sense may consist simply in a rapid and uncontrollable transition from an impression to a belief:

Because such a particular idea is commonly annex'd to such a particular word, nothing is requir'd but the hearing of that word to produce the correspondent idea; and 'twill scarce be possible for the mind, by its utmost efforts, to prevent that transition.[23]

More strongly still:

[21] *Treatise*, pp. 103–4.   [22] *Treatise*, p. 149.
[23] *Treatise*, p. 93.

Our judgments concerning cause and effect are deriv'd from habit and experience; and when we have been accustom'd to see one object united to another, our imagination passes from the first to the second, by a natural transition, which precedes reflection, and which cannot be prevented by it.[24]

Furthermore, Hume thinks that in causally explaining a belief in this way he is filling a gap created by the absence of any reasons for it:

We have already taken notice of certain relations, which make us pass from one object to another, even tho' there be no reason to determine us to that transition; and this we may establish for a general rule, that wherever the mind constantly and uniformly makes a transition without any reason, it is influenc'd by these relations.[25]

This is quite wrong. If a belief is reached without the weighing of reasons, we may inquire into its causes or we may prefer to offer no account of its genesis. Either way, the question of whether *there are* reasons for it remains completely open.

There are two replies that Hume might make to this.

(1) The first is that if I could not help acquiring a given belief— if I was just being hustled along by ungentle forces—then it doesn't matter whether there were reasons for it. 'I could have reached it through deliberation if I hadn't been forced to it in another way'—this, he might say, is cheap comfort.

That uses too broad a brush. The existence of reasons for a belief may be relevant to my acquisition of it even if I did not consider and approve those reasons. In acquiring the belief I may have been unreflectively applying an intellectual policy which I sometimes subject to reflective scrutiny. Or it may be that if the circumstances had been different, I should have deliberated, weighed reasons, and concluded against the belief in question. In at least those two ways, if indeed they are two, reasons can be relevant to what happens even when they are not actually entertained and assessed. The acquiring of a belief can occur under the governance of reason even if it does not result from episodic reasonings.

Indeed, this often happens. We often form an expectation 'immediately, without allowing any time for reflection',[26] without

[24] *Treatise*, p. 147.   [25] *Treatise*, p. 92.
[26] *Treatise*, p. 133.

being completely the victims of our pasts. In implying the contrary, Hume represents our predictions as vastly more involuntary, unreflective and instinctive than they often are; and ignores all the cases where we do, and the others where we could but don't, pause and consider.

Hume's over-insistence on our intellectual passivity also ignores the causal judgements which look interrogatively rather than confidently towards the future. We often adopt hypotheses with little support from past experience, in order to test them against future experience: '[We] approach nature in order to be taught by it, [not] in the character of a pupil who listens to everything that the teacher chooses to say, but of an appointed judge who compels the witnesses to answer questions which he has himself formulated.'[27] Hume, in fact, does not address himself to predictions in general, but only to *beliefs* about the future; and his theory does not cover non-credulous, tentative, interrogative predictions. He clearly thinks that beliefs are the whole story: 'We have no other notion of cause and effect, but that of certain objects, which have been *always conjoin'd* together, and which in all past instances have been found inseparable.'[28] It may be noted that in general, and not just in his theory of causal beliefs, Hume exaggerates our intellectual passivity. The one basic aspect of our conceptual scheme which he credits to our initiative is one he regards as a mistake (see §§ 75–7 below).

(2) The other reply Hume might make to the charge that he wrongly denies us reasons for our predictions is that our so-called 'reasons' are not really reasons. We sometimes do and often could engage in what we *call* 'assessing and approving reasons for a prediction', but that description—he might say—is wrong. For any such 'reasons' must concern the past, and could bear on a prediction only through some general principle to the effect that the past can be a reliable guide to the future. Since we cannot give reasons for any such principle, none of our more specific 'reasons' for specific predictions are really reasons at all.

The answers which have been given to this constitute the literature on 'the problem of induction'; for example, the answer —sufficiently exploded by Urmson—that what we mean by 'reason for a prediction' is defined by the kinds of considerations

---

[27] Kant, *Critique of Pure Reason* B xiii.
[28] *Treatise*, p. 93. See also *Enquiry* § 32.

which we do in fact adduce as reasons for a prediction.[29] There is one answer which is correct as far as it goes, and it goes far enough for my present purposes. Hume writes as though someone might be aware of a stream of impressions while making no predictions about what lies ahead; and it is against this background that he can represent us as having to make predictions, as though refraining from them were an intelligible alternative which we are psychologically powerless to adopt. But Kant has shown that someone who has impressions and knows what they are like must construe some of them as perceptions of an objective, and thus largely causally ordered, realm. This is a claim not about psychological compulsion but about the logical requirements for self-consciousness. It implies that a self-conscious creature must, qua self-conscious, use concepts which commit him to treating the past as a guide to the future; but it is quite different from Hume's thesis that we self-conscious creatures are psychologically unable to refrain from treating the past as a guide to the future. Neither thesis entails the other, but the two may be combined. (Kant's thesis, indeed, gives support to Hume's; for it is implausible to suggest that anyone could choose to relinquish the beliefs which are logically required for self-consciousness.) When they are combined, the resultant picture differs significantly from that presented by Hume's thesis on its own. For now the refusal to link past with future, while still something we are not capable of, is also something which would constitute an abdication from any knowledge of our own sensory histories. In the Kantian picture, even with Hume's claim added, our willingness to predict the future on the basis of the past no longer appears as incurable shut-mindedness, for the contrasted 'open-mindedness' is not a state that we can intelligibly suppose that we might be in.

Sometimes Hume himself expresses the Kantian insight, or something like it. For example, he says: 'Principles which are permanent, irresistable, and universal, such as the customary transition from causes to effects . . ., are the foundation of all our thoughts and actions, so that upon their removal human nature must immediately perish and go to ruin.'[30] But he is not fully

[29] J. O. Urmson, 'Some Questions Concerning Validity', in A. Flew (ed.), *Essays in Conceptual Analysis* (London, 1956).
[30] *Treatise*, p. 225, slightly repunctuated.

consistent about this—compare 'permanent, irresistable, and universal' with 'a gentle force, which commonly prevails'.[31] Also, the 'ruin' of 'human nature' to which Hume refers, rather than being a Kantian loss of the logical pre-requisites for self-consciousness or the like, may be merely the loss of dispositions which are needed for biological survival in our sort of world. Hume's words do not point unequivocally in either direction, and that fact shows how far he was from having the Kantian insight as a consciously-held item of theory. It is also relevant that Hume does not argue from a principle's being 'irresistable' or the like to its being in any way justified. For further discussion of this whole matter, the reader is referred to Passmore and to an important paper by Wolff.[32]

66. *An analytic salvage*

The difficulties we have been making for Hume might have been avoided if he had not had a genetic theory in the first place. Let us see what happens to his analysis of 'cause' if we systematically remove all its implications about what causes or otherwise leads us to make predictions.

A good start would be to deprive him of the words 'habit' and 'custom'. Compare:

(1) It is my habit, when faced by an F, to expect a G.
(2) It is my custom, when faced by an F, to expect a G.
(3) Whenever I am faced by an F, I expect a G.

Among these three, I suggest, entailments run downwards but not upwards. Specifically, (1) adds to the content of (3) a strong implication that my practice of expecting a G when faced by an F has arisen in some way of which I have not been the conscious master, which also suggests that I cannot now relinquish the practice at will. (2) differs from (3) in the same way but in lesser degree. For some absorbing semantic details, see the entry on 'Habit' in the *New English Dictionary*.

The proposal to strip Hume's theory of its geneticism involves replacing (1) and (2) by (3)—by statements which report what

---

[31] *Treatise*, p. 10.
[32] Passmore, *Hume's Intentions*, pp. 40–1, 54–6; Wolff, 'Hume's Theory of Mental Activity'.

people do without implying anything about what leads them to do it. Recent philosophy has provided a usefully clinical and non-genetic term which fits (3) while having the grammar of 'habit' and 'custom', namely the word 'disposition'. We can express (3) in the form 'It is my disposition, when faced by an F, to expect a G'. This is to be understood in Ryle's way: to credit someone with a disposition is to speak not of what he feels like doing but only of what in general he does do or would do if . . . Hume's 'habits', then, are dispositions plus an implication about what causes them. If we replace 'habit' by 'disposition', the resultant statements are neutral about causes and indeed about origins generally. My disposition to expect a G when faced by an F might be a habit or a deliberately adopted policy or something else again.

With this replacement made, Hume no longer has any theory about what leads us to predict, and so *a fortiori* he does not have the theory that we are caused or compelled to predict. This loss is sheer gain, but it raises a question. Hume's account of the 'idea of necessary connexion' depends upon the abolished theory: the 'idea' is a copy of that impression of being compelled or 'deter-mined' which, according to the theory, we have whenever we make an inductively based prediction. If the theory is dropped, what is left of Hume's 'idea of necessary connexion'?

Nothing. And a good thing too.[33]

Hume can say that we are disposed to make inductively-based predictions, and can say that these dispositions are, so to speak, the human reality underlying our uses of the notion of cause. He can further say that any particular causal statement, whether or not the speaker is caused to make it by patterns in his past experience, is about—or is answerable to—regularities in past and future experience; so that '*x* caused *y*' is a statement of a universal kind. More fully, to say that *x* caused *y* is to say—let us concede—that *x* is contiguous and prior to *y*, and is also to bring this pair of events *under a rule*.

(This is a natural outgrowth of our original impoverishment of Hume's theory, i.e. of the replacement of 'habit' by 'disposition'. If I am disposed to expect a G when faced by an F; and if I am not utterly the prisoner of this disposition, but have it partly as a matter of intellectual policy which I can reflect on and

[33] See Wolff, op. cit. pp. 111-14.

criticize; then this amounts to saying that I adopt a rule to the effect that when Fs are found Gs are to be expected. A case where I apply this rule is just one where I act according to the corresponding disposition.)

On this account of it, the concept of cause is a rule. That is all right, for every other concept is a rule too. For Hume, a concept is paradigmatically a quasi-sensory occurrence, an 'idea'. Looking for a third ingredient in the concept of cause, and assuming that it would have to be such an occurrence, he could find only the supposed feeling of being compelled to predict. This, as he realized, makes the concept of cause out to be highly peculiar: causal statements turn out to involve an element of self-reporting of an unsuspected kind. But the only alternative would be to represent 'x causes y' as a statement about x and y and indefinitely many other events. This would also introduce something 'foreign' to x and y, and would provide no corresponding quasi-sensory occurrence—no picture, no 'idea'. To keep his analysis of cause in touch with his theory of meaning, Hume had to continue to look inwards, and thus to insist that there is a felt compulsion to predict. He rightly expected his account to be shocking, and not just by disappointed necessitarians; but the shock is removed as soon as we drop Hume's theory of meaning and are thus freed to look outwards instead of inwards.

Summing all this up: Hume says that I have the idea of cause only if I have certain habits. Remove the genetic element, and we have: I have the concept of cause only if I have certain intellectual dispositions. If an 'idea' is a quasi-sensory episode, there seems to be no way of connecting it with a disposition except by connecting it with (how it feels to be gripped by) a habit; but if we replace 'idea' by 'concept' and understand the latter term correctly, we are on safe ground again. Indeed, we can go a step further: to have the concept of cause *is* to have certain intellectual dispositions; and to apply the concept in a given case is, deliberately or at least controllably, to realize the disposition in that case; which is the same as applying a rule to the case.[34] Once we are liberated from Hume's type of meaning-theory we can see that all this is normal, and that it has the same basic structure as a correct account of what it is to have and apply the concept of redness or of stupidity. All our concepts involve an element of

[34] See D. F. Pears, 'Hume's Empiricism', Pears pp. 28–9.

generality; overlooking this, Hume adopted the 'idea' theory; then, finding in the concept of cause an element of generality which is too obvious to be overlooked, he had to protect his 'idea' theory from it by the fruitless manoeuvres which have been my topic in the present chapter.

67. 'The Humean view'

What we have salvaged from Hume is very close to 'the Humean view of causation' as it is now generally understood. The 'Humean view' has the following form:

The difference between 'e_1 caused e_2' and 'e_1 preceded e_2' is that the former entails that there is a law which . . .

A 'law', as I am using the word, is a true, contingent, universally-quantified conditional statement which satisfies certain further conditions—to rule out vacuousness, triviality, eccentricity etc.—which nobody has yet successfully formulated.[35] The problem, of course, is to state the conditions without using any such term as 'causal' and without appealing to counterfactual conditionals. I believe that the problem can be solved, although Goodman's work has shown that a solution must be much more radical than most adherents of 'the Humean view' had previously thought.[36] I shall have nothing more to say about it.

The above formula is incomplete in a different way which I do now want to discuss, namely, its not saying how the relevant law relates to e_1 and e_2. Here is one possible position: any true singular causal statement must have the form 'The F event caused the G event' where F and G stand for suitably law-connected properties—so that from the singular causal statement we can automatically read off the law by virtue of which it is true. At the other extreme is the thesis of pure extensionality: the statement that e_1 caused e_2 is true—no matter how it refers to e_1 and e_2— just so long as those two events do in fact have properties which are law-connected in the appropriate way. Between the two extremes there are many possible intermediate positions, each

---

[35] See W. Kneale, 'Natural Laws and Contrary-to-Fact Conditionals', *Analysis*, vol. 10 (1950); reprinted in M. Macdonald (ed.), *Philosophy and Analysis* (Oxford, 1954).

[36] N. Goodman, *Fact, Fiction and Forecast* (Cambridge, Mass., 1955).

laying down more or less weak conditions on how the relevant law must relate to the language used in the singular causal statement; but I doubt if any of these has much to recommend it. The thesis of pure extensionality, which has been persuasively defended by Davidson, seems to me to be right;[37] and it is certainly plausible enough to motivate an inquiry into its relationship to Hume.

When he is defining 'cause' in ways which come nearest to the now-favoured 'Humean view', emphasizing 'constant conjunction' etc. rather than 'the determination of the mind' etc., Hume says:

. . . and where all the objects resembling the former are plac'd in like relations . . . to those objects, that resemble the latter;[38]

. . . and where all the objects similar to the first are followed by objects similar to the second.[39]

To these we might also add:

. . . and in inlarging my view to consider several instances, I find only, that like objects are constantly plac'd in like relations of succession and contiguity.[40]

These formulations suggest pure extensionality, just so long as we construe 'resembling' and 'like' and 'similar to' to mean 'resembling [etc.] *in some respect*' with no limitation on what the respect is. If Hume has some limitation in mind, he does not specify it and I cannot see what it could be. It can hardly be 'in respect of properties referred to in the original singular causal statement', for Hume does not think of his theory as concerning causal *statements* in the first place.

As against this, he sometimes seems to think of the move from the singular causal judgement to the corresponding law as being entirely automatic. Indeed, he writes as though the law had to do only with the very same pair of events ('objects') which are the subject of the singular judgement:

When any object is presented to us, it immediately conveys to the mind a lively idea of that object, which is usually found to attend it.[41]

[37] D. Davidson, 'Causal Relations', *Journal of Philosophy*, vol. 64 (1967).
[38] *Treatise*, p. 170.   [39] *Enquiry* § 60.
[40] *Treatise*, p. 170.
[41] *Treatise*, p. 169.

There must be a constant union betwixt the cause and effect.[42]

... an object followed by another, and whose appearance always conveys the thought to that other.[43]

No doubt this is careless writing rather than bad theory. Still, these turns of phrase discourage the view that Hume had clearly understood and firmly accepted the extensional thesis, or any position implying that a given singular causal judgement might be backed by any one of a range of laws.

In Hume's own work, of course, the 'Humean view' is embedded in a psychological theory, and one might wonder whether the latter made it hard for him to accept the extensional thesis. I do not see how it can have done so. If I think that e_1 caused e_2, I must, according to Hume's psychological theory, feel e_1's effect on my mind, whereby it determines me to form a vivid idea of e_2; but I need not know why e_1 has this effect on me. No doubt I must know that it has this effect by virtue of some property that it has; and perhaps I must also know that this property has, in my past experience, been law-connected with some property that e_2 has; but since I need not know what either property is, I need not be in a position to formulate the relevant law. So the psychological half of Hume's positive theory of causation also leaves it open to him to say that a singular causal statement *entails that there is a relevant law* but does not *entail the relevant law*.

In just one place that I know of, Hume fairly explicitly avails himself of this option:

The difference in the effects of two resembling objects must proceed from that particular, in which they differ. For as like causes always produce like effects, when in any instance we find our expectation to be disappointed, we must conclude that this irregularity proceeds from some difference in the causes.[44]

By allowing us to 'conclude' that there is 'some difference', Hume clearly implies that we may be in a position to assert a singular causal judgement but not to assert the relevant law. It may be significant, though, that Hume is here expounding a point of relative detail, not stating his central position. And it is surely

---

[42] *Treatise*, p. 173.   [43] *Enquiry* § 60.
[44] *Treatise*, p. 174.

significant that the immediately preceding paragraph goes in exactly the opposite way:

Where several different objects produce the same effect, it must be by means of some quality, which we discover to be common amongst them. For as like effects imply like causes, we must always ascribe the causation to the circumstance, wherein we discover the resemblance.[45]

The repeated use of 'we discover' strongly suggests that we cannot make the singular causal judgement until we know what the relevant law is.

In short: one of Hume's paragraphs commits him to the extensional thesis; most of his turns of phrase suggest that he is far from accepting that thesis; yet there is no obstacle to his accepting it, either in his explicit statements of the 'Humean view' or in the associated psychological theory. I conclude that Hume did not consciously face up to the issue over extensionality—or the more general issue over just how the singular causal judgement must relate to the relevant law—and so there is no straight answer to the question I have raised.

How does the 'Humean view' relate to Hume's negative work? After attacking a range of opponents, Hume is now propounding a theory which includes the two elements constituting the 'Humean view': that a singular causal judgement can be true only if a corresponding generalization is true, and that that generalization is contingent. Is this double-thesis arrived at *through* the negative work discussed earlier? It is usual and natural to think of Hume's positive theory as a rival to the views he has earlier rejected, all of them being answers to a single question or at least to closely related questions. But is this really so?

A partial affirmative answer can be given straight away. According to the Humean view, 'e_1 caused e_2' implies something about events other than—or 'foreign to'—e_1 and e_2 themselves, and Hume's defence of this rests on his earlier rejection of 'impressions of necessary connexion' (see § 55 above). Given that rejection, he can argue that if causation is not just contiguity and priority it must involve *some* foreign element; and that conclusion, though not as extraordinary as Hume thinks, is nevertheless a substantive part of the 'Humean view'. So one part of Hume's

[45] *Treatise*, p. 174.

negative work, namely his denial that there are impressions of necessary connexion in the outer world, does render a definite though minor service to his positive theory.

Is that all? One would hope to be able to represent Hume's attack on necessitarianism also as helping to clear the way for his positive theory of causation.

There is, however, an obstacle to relating the anti-necessitarian polemic to (the 'Humean view' contained within) the positive theory. It is the fact, noted at the end of § 57 above, that according to the 'Humean view' the causal relation holds between *events,* whereas the rejected necessitarianism makes sense only as a thesis about relations between the members of certain pairs of propositions—specifically, between the antecedent and consequent of any prediction-licensing conditional. Hume did not clearly see the need to construe necessitarianism in this way, but that fact is no help. I want to know what connexions there are, not merely what connexions Hume might have thought that there are, between anti-necessitarianism and the 'Humean view'.

So it is no help to be told, for example, that Hume might have sought to relate the two as follows: the attack on necessitarianism shows that causation is not a necessary or analytic relation, and the positive theory takes over from there, giving details about what sort of contingent or synthetic relation it is. This, though Hume might have said it, is unacceptable. Relations cannot be divided into necessary and contingent, and Hume's attempt so to divide them is, as I have shown in § 53 above, a hopeless muddle.

Let us try again: Hume's negative thesis implies that causal statements are contingent, and his positive theory adds details about what sort of contingent statements they are. But this is no use if it means that all causal statements are contingent, for the 'Humean view' rightly does not deny that many causal statements are logically necessary. It does say that *some* are contingent, but can we really see Hume's anti-necessitarian polemic as a defence of *that*? Are we to suppose that he envisages a necessitarian opponent who denies that there are any logically contingent causal propositions? This is surely wrong. Just as a Humean can admit that any cause-effect pair does instantiate some logically necessary conditionals, so a necessitarian can admit that such a pair instantiates contingent conditional truths.

Yet those of us who think of ourselves as broadly 'Humean'

about the concept of cause are apt to think that we accept some non-trivial thesis about causality and contingency—we think that in our total system of causal propositions it is the contingent ones that count, that are the source of life, or the like. How can this metaphor be unpacked? The only suggestion I can make is this: in our total system of causal propositions it is the contingent ones that have *predictive value*.

Our causality-contingency thesis, on this account of it, is just a special case of the more general thesis which I salvaged from Hume's anti-necessitarianism, namely the general thesis that there cannot be entailment-licensed predictions. So if I have handled both matters correctly we do have the sought-after link between the negative and positive positions. In one way the link is perhaps a tenuous one, for it connects the negative position not with the concept of cause as such but only with a certain use to which causal propositions may be put—namely licensing predictions. Still, it seems reasonable to regard this as a very central and important use of causal propositions. There is significant support for this in a recent paper of Dummett's, where he continues to explore the question of whether it makes sense to suppose that one might cause something to have happened.[46] One result which emerges from his probing inquiry is that even temporally reversed causation, if it makes sense at all, does so only on condition that it is governed by laws which have predictive value. Anyway, I do not insist that Hume's negative thesis is closely and intimately linked with the 'Humean view' about causation—all I have wanted to do is to show what link there is. If the result is that Hume's total work on causation is more broken-backed than one had thought, so be it.

[46] M. Dummett, 'Bringing about the Past', *Philosophical Review*, vol. 73 (1964).

XIII

HUME ON OBJECTIVITY

68. *The problem stated*

HUME'S section entitled 'Of Scepticism with regard to the Senses' is his principal discussion of objectivity-concepts.[1] It is extremely difficult, full of mistakes, and—taken as a whole—a total failure; yet its depth and scope and disciplined complexity make it one of the most instructive arguments in modern philosophy.[2] One philosopher might be judged superior to another because he achieved something of which the other was altogether intellectually incapable. By that criterion Hume surpasses Locke and Berkeley—because, and only because, of this one section.

The section is the subject of a book by H. H. Price.[3] I admire and owe much to Price's penetrating analysis; but if I am to link this part of Hume's work with the rest of my account of the central Empiricist themes, I need to tackle it in my own way. This last chapter, therefore, will be a discussion of 'Of Scepticism with regard to the Senses'.

Hume aims to discover 'what causes induce us to believe in the existence of body', but fortunately his aim is poor. Most of the section can be seen as addressed to the question, which is not causal and not even genetic, 'What reasons are there for our belief in the existence of body?' I shall pretend that that is the question Hume is asking. Turns in his argument which belie this will be noted as they arise.

To believe in 'the existence of body' is to believe that there are items which are 'continuous' and 'distinct'. The question about continuity is just the question 'why we attribute a continu'd existence to objects, even when they are not present to the senses'. The meaning of 'distinct' is more complex: 'Under this last head I comprehend [objects'] situation as well as relations, their *external* position as well as the *independence* of their existence and operation.'[4]

---

[1] *Treatise* I. iv. 2. See also *Enquiry* §§ 117–23.
[2] Thus H. H. Price, 'The Permanent Significance of Hume's Philosophy', p. 11.
[3] H. H. Price, *Hume's Theory of the External World*. All further references to Price in this chapter refer to this book.   [4] *Treatise*, p. 188.

Let us get 'external' out of the way. The word is meant spatially:
an object is 'external' to me if it and I are in different places.
Since 'All bodies are spatially located' is analytic, an analysis of
'body' might have to explore the concept of spatial location. But
Hume's real topic is not the belief that there are, specifically,
bodies. Rather, it is the more general belief that there are *objects*—
objective particulars which admit of the distinction between
appearance and reality, can exist unperceived, and so on. He is not
assuming that we know what it is for an item to be objective, and
asking: 'What is it for an objective item to be a body?' Rather, he
is asking: 'What is it for an item to be objective?'[5] Perhaps the
latter question also involves spatial location, since arguably any
objective realm must be spatially organized; but Hume does not
argue for this view, and seems not to hold it. Or one might ask
both questions: 'What is it for an item to be objective?' and then:
'What is it for an objective item to be a body?'; but Hume here
shows no interest in the second of these. I conclude that spatial
externality does not lie at the centre of his inquiry.

Hume concedes as much. In one passage which I do not understand he seems to be giving a wrong reason for saying that externality need not be discussed.[6] Later, though, he does better. He
implies that, just because his prime concern is with objectivity
generally, spatial externality does not merit a central place in it:

When we talk of real distinct existences, we have commonly more in
our eye their independency than external situation in place, and think
an object has a sufficient reality, when its Being is uninterrupted, and
independent of the incessant revolutions, which we are conscious of in
ourselves.[7]

That, incidentally, is Hume's last mention of spatial externality
in this section. From there on he uses 'external' only to mean
'objective', and not with any specifically spatial connotations.[8]

So our concern is with continuity and independence. The few
early episodes where spatial externality has a role will be noted
as they occur.

It remains only to explain 'independent'. This refers to independence 'from the perception' of the observer: it seems that

---

[5] Thus Price, p. 19.   [6] *Treatise*, p. 188.
[7] *Treatise*, p. 191.
[8] *Treatise*, pp. 195 three occurrences), 199, 205 (three), 216–18 (four).

'*x* exists independently of my perception of it' means 'That *x* exists is not due solely to the fact that I perceive it', which presumably means '*x* could exist when I was not perceiving it'. To have an independent existence, it seems, is just to be capable of having a continuous existence.

It follows that continuity entails independence, but I am not prepared to add, as Hume does: 'and *vice versa*, if [objects'] existence be independent of the perception and distinct from it, they must continue to exist, even tho' they be not perceiv'd.' [9] The word 'must' makes this too strong to be accepted without argument. Still, something like it can be defended. It is arguable that one's only hope of showing that there are no continuous objects would be by showing that there cannot be any—i.e. that the notion of a continuous object is logically defective. But independent objects are, precisely, ones which can be continuous; and so—the argument would run—if there are independent objects then there isn't the remotest chance of anyone's showing that there are no continuous objects. This might justify Hume in saying that continuity and independence stand or fall together. Later, we shall see, he forgets this view of his: in the central mistake in the whole section, he apparently tries to keep independence upright while allowing continuity to collapse.

69. *A rejected answer: the senses*

Through some four pages Hume argues that 'the senses . . . are incapable of giving rise to' the belief in independent and continuous objects—'The Belief', for short. The general idea seems to be as follows.

Why do people believe that there are pains? It is both natural and Humean to think that 'Because they have pains' is a complete answer: the existence of pains is a raw, primitive datum of experience, not something reached by inference—valid or invalid—from our primitive data. Pains are just given; or, in the unhappy genetic mode, the belief that there are pains is 'produced by the senses'. Hume, I think, is trying to rebut an analogous account of The Belief. Expressed non-genetically, our question is: 'What facts about our experience enable us to apply objectivity-concepts?', and Hume seeks to show that the answer cannot be: 'The fact

[9] *Treatise*, p. 188.

that the existence of objective items is just given, or is a raw datum of experience.' Let us look at the details.

Hume first argues that the continuity of objects cannot be a raw datum of sense-experience,[10] for that would require 'that the senses continue to operate, even after they have ceas'd all manner of operation'. From this he rightly infers that if the senses unaided are to yield any part of The Belief it can only be that part which consists in the belief that there are (external and) independent objects.

The senses might be thought to 'suggest [the] idea of distinct existences' in either of two ways, of which the former evokes Locke and the latter is probably supposed to evoke Berkeley. Hume devotes one paragraph to expounding and refuting the Lockean one. The 'Berkeleian' alternative is expounded in the succeeding paragraph and then rebutted in the two after that.

Could the senses, unaided, produce the belief that there are external and independent items 'beyond' our impressions? Hume rightly says that they could not: 'A single perception can never produce the idea of a double existence.' I shall not linger on this.

There remains, then, only the prima facie possibility that the senses confront us with impressions in such a way as to make us believe that they—the impressions themselves—are external and independent.[11] Hume contends that if our senses did this they would be subjecting us to 'a kind of fallacy and illusion' about our impressions—'not concerning their nature, but concerning their relations and situation'—and he argues that such an illusion could not occur. His first argument concerns 'ideas of self and person', and is quite unsatisfactory. The second is this:

[It is not] conceivable that our senses shou'd be more capable of deceiving us in the situation and relations, than in the nature of our impressions. For since all actions and sensations of the mind are known to us by consciousness, they must necessarily appear in every particular what they are, and be what they appear.

One is suspicious of this confident claim that we are inerrant not only about the internal characteristics of our inner states but also about their situation (spatial externality) and relations (independence); but perhaps it does not matter, since this target of Hume's is not an attractive one anyway.

[10] *Treatise*, pp. 188–9 ('To begin with the senses . . . and external existences.').
[11] *Treatise*, pp. 189–90 ('If our senses . . . might be mistaken.').

Rather than arguing further that the senses *cannot* delude us into believing in distinct items, Hume says, he will merely argue that they *do not* do so. This misrepresents what follows, namely: a three-pronged attack on one specific argument purporting to show that the senses produce the belief in external items;[12] and a repetition, which I shall not discuss, of his earlier reasons for saying that the senses cannot produce the belief in independent items.

The argument about externality to which Hume addresses himself is this:

Our own body evidently belongs to us; and as several impressions appear exterior to the body, we suppose them also exterior to ourselves . . . In casting my eye towards the window, I perceive a great extent of fields and buildings beyond my chamber . . . No other faculty is requir'd, beside the senses, to convince us of the external existence of body.

The suggestion is that the elsewhereness of bodies is sometimes a raw visual datum: we simply see things to be at a distance, and that's that. This argument, uniquely in the whole section, concerns spatial externality and nothing else; and just for that reason it is peripheral to Hume's main theme. Still, two of his three replies to it are interesting.

The first reply is this:

Properly speaking, 'tis not our body we perceive, when we regard our limbs and members, but certain impressions, which enter by the senses; so that the ascribing a real and corporeal existence to these impressions, or to their objects, is an act of the mind as difficult to explain, as that which we examine at present.

This, though ill-expressed, has a valid core. An inquiry into our whole system of objectivity-concepts is not entitled to take 'I have a body', which itself expresses a view about the objective realm, as both true and not in need of explanation. Hume implies that I know about my body only by observing it, which ignores the fact that I also *move* my body; but this leaves his central point standing.

Hume's opponent might fairly complain that words have been crammed into his mouth: he has been made to construe 'external' as meaning (*a*) 'somewhere other than where my body is' rather

<hr />

[12] *Treatise*, pp. 190–1 ('To begin with . . . rational philosophers.').

than (*b*) 'somewhere other than where I am'. These are different, for the notion of 'where I am' does not require me to have a space-filling, objective body, since it can be adequately based on my perceptual slant on the world, i.e. on the fact that at any given time I perceive the objective realm from a particular point of view. So a thing's spatial 'externality' might be understood as its being at a distance from my spatially located but unextended point of view; and if (*a*) is thus replaced by (*b*), Hume's first counter-attack fails.

There is another point. In § 68 I argued that Hume ought not to set spatial externality at the centre of his investigation, and that point holds good on either reading—(*a*) or (*b*)—of 'external'. But if Hume insists upon (*a*) then there is a further reason for deposing externality. For according to (*a*) the *question* 'Are there any external items?' presupposes that *there is* at least one item, namely the questioner's body, to which the whole range of objectivity-concepts can be applied.

Hume's second reply alludes to 'sounds, and tastes, and smells'. It is extremely unclear, and is best seen as adumbrating an un-impressive argument which he deploys a little later and which I shall deal with now.[13] We can divide our perceptions into (1) those pertaining to primary qualities, (2) those pertaining to secondary qualities, and (3) 'pains and pleasures' and, one presumes, 'passions' generally. Of these three classes Hume says:

Both philosophers and the vulgar suppose the first of these to have a distinct continu'd existence. The vulgar only regard the second as on the same footing. Both philosophers and the vulgar, again, esteem the third to be merely perceptions; and consequently interrupted and dependent beings.

Despite Hume's obscuring failure to distinguish the qualities of things from our impressions of things, an argument of a kind can be discerned in these two paragraphs. Hume proceeds to say that secondary qualities, 'as far as appears to the senses', are just as objective as primary ones, as is shown by the failure of the vulgar to drive a wedge between (1) and (2). But then (2) secondary qualities are also on a par with (3) pains and the rest:

For as they are confest to be, both of them, nothing but perceptions arising from the particular configurations and motions of the parts of body, wherein possibly can their difference consist? Upon the whole,

---

[13] *Treatise*, pp. 192-3 ('To confirm . . . their existence.').

then, we may conclude, that as far as the senses are judges, all perceptions are the same in the manner of their existence.

This argument is useless, because it assumes that secondary qualities are 'nothing but perceptions', which is simply false (see § 23 above). Hume does in fact regularly credit 'the modern philosophy' with discovering that secondary qualities are not in objects because they are in the mind. For example, his argument that primary qualities alone are not sufficient for a working concept of body (see § 18 above) is the interesting part of a larger, shoddier argument along these lines: bodies do not really have secondary qualities, so at most they have primary qualities; but there cannot be bodies with only primary qualities; so there cannot be bodies. Since the first premiss is wholly indefensible, there is no value in any argument depending upon it.

Hume's third reply goes to the heart of the matter: 'Even our sight informs us not of distance or outness (so to speak) immediately and without a certain reasoning and experience, as is acknowledg'd by the most rational philosophers.'[14] This relies on Berkeley's thesis that our spatial concepts are primarily tactual and kinaesthetic, and only secondarily visual, so that things' 'outness' is not primitively given through the visual sense.[15] 'We sometimes see things to be at a distance from ourselves'—this is true, but it is logically not a bit like 'We sometimes feel pains to be acute'. That my present visual field does count as the seeing of something at a distance is a fact which involves a great deal more than my present sensory state.

As I have already mentioned, Hume then repeats his claim that the senses cannot produce the belief in independent objects. This is where he confesses that spatial externality is not very central to his concerns, and drops it for good. The paragraph after that is just a résumé of what has gone before.

70. *Also rejected: reason*

In one pregnant paragraph, Hume argues that The Belief cannot be produced by reason:

Whatever convincing arguments philosophers may fancy they can produce to establish the belief of objects independent of the mind, 'tis

[14] *Treatise*, p. 191.   [15] Berkeley, *New Theory of Vision* § 46.

obvious ... that 'tis not by them, that children, peasants, and the greatest part of mankind are induc'd to attribute objects to some impressions, and deny them to others.[16]

This argument depends on the genetic formulation: the vulgar are not led to The Belief by reasoning, because they are not given to 'weighing [their] opinions by any philosophical principles'. Against the analytic thesis that The Belief—however arrived at—is defensible on the basis of reason, Hume's argument is powerless.

I do not pretend to know what 'on the basis of reason' means. The best salvage I can offer for Hume's serial discussion of 'the senses', 'reason' and 'imagination' as bases for The Belief is as follows.[17] 'The senses are the basis' means that the existence of continuous and independent objects is a primitive *datum of* sense-experience. 'Reason is the basis' means that the existence of such objects can be validly defended by *arguments from* sense-experience. Having rejected these two, Hume concludes that The Belief 'must be entirely owing to the imagination', which I take to imply, among other things, that it is *illegitimately* derived from or based upon the deliverances of the senses. That is, Hume will explain The Belief in a manner which, he thinks, will condemn it.

If I have the strategy right, then we must protest that 'reason' has not had its day in court. As well as its dependence on the genetic formulation, Hume's argument has another flaw. He often takes 'reasoning' to cover causal reasoning. His remark that 'our sight informs us not of distance ... without a certain reasoning' presupposes this generous use of the word, and also concedes, as Hume must, that children and peasants do 'reason' in this sense. In our present paragraph, Hume uses 'reasoning' narrowly, to cover only the sophisticated 'weighing [of] philosophical principles'; but in that case are the possibilities exhausted by 'the senses', 'reason' and 'imagination'?

Hume restricts 'reason' at this stage, no doubt, so as to postpone his discussion of whether The Belief is based on everyday causal thinking; but he also has another motive for concentrating on what he calls 'philosophical principles'. He wants to contend that such principles don't just fail to justify The Belief but positively contradict it:

For philosophy informs us, that every thing, which appears to the mind, is nothing but a perception, and is interrupted, and dependent

---

[16] *Treatise*, p. 193.   [17] Cf. Berkeley, *Principles* § 18.

on the mind; whereas the vulgar confound perceptions and objects, and attribute a distinct continu'd existence to the very things they feel or see. This sentiment, then, as it is entirely unreasonable, must proceed from some other faculty than the understanding.

This needs consideration on its own merits.

The vulgar do indeed attribute continuity etc. to 'the very things they feel or see', but this does not imply that they attribute continuity to their perceptions. Hume thinks that it does, because 'every thing which appears to the mind is nothing but a perception', by which he means that 'the very things [we] feel or see' are themselves perceptions. The 'philosophy' which 'informs us' that only perceptions 'appear to the mind' has a choice. (*a*) If 'appearing to the mind' is simply being perceived, then what is said is just false. (*b*) If 'appearing to the mind' is what Berkeley would call being immediately perceived, then this philosophy 'informs us' correctly, but what 'appears to the mind' is—despite Berkeley's contrary view—different from what is felt or seen. Either way, Hume is wrong. I shall return to this matter in § 78.

Hume's view, then, is that 'as long as we take our perceptions and objects to be the same' we cannot justify The Belief by an appeal to reason: on the ground just given, and also because if they are 'the same' then 'we can never infer the existence of the one from that of the other'! He then proceeds to compound the error:

Even after we distinguish our perceptions from our objects, 'twill appear presently, that we are still incapable of reasoning from the existence of one to that of the other: So that upon the whole our reason neither does, nor is it possible it ever shou'd, upon any supposition, give us an assurance of the continu'd and distinct existence of body.

How will Hume defend so large a claim? The answer is that, as we shall see in § 78, he equates 'distinguishing our objects from our perceptions' with 'putting our objects beyond the veil of perception'. If we are not to identify 'our objects' with our perceptions, he thinks, we must relate them in the manner of Locke's theory of reality; and, since he is satisfied by Berkeley's arguments against Locke, he confidently asserts that reason cannot justify The Belief in 'objects' construed in *that* way.

In a nutshell: there are Berkeleian 'objects', but they are not

independent and continuous; Lockean 'objects' would be independent and continuous, but there cannot be grounds for
saying that there are any; so The Belief cannot be justified in
either its vulgar or Berkeleian form or its non-vulgar or Lockean
form. Apart from the identification of the vulgar position with
Berkeley's, all this is absolutely right. But *tertium datur*.

71. *A partly accepted answer*

Since we attribute continuity etc. to some but not all of our
impressions, Hume says, there should be some common feature
marking off those to which we accord this dignity. He still wants
to describe, though not now to justify, our deployment of
objectivity-concepts. So he hunts for the common feature. After
pointing out that the involuntariness and 'superior force and
violence' of some of our impressions are not the whole story,
Hume continues: 'These vulgar opinions, then, being rejected,
we must search for some other hypothesis, by which we may discover those peculiar qualities in our impressions, which make us
attribute to them a distinct and continu'd existence.'[18] With that
he embarks on three paragraphs which I shall discuss throughout
the present section.[19] They deal with continuity only, independence being silently dropped.

All those objects, to which we attribute a continu'd existence, have a
peculiar *constancy*, which distinguishes them from the impressions,
whose existence depends upon our perception . . . [That is too strong,
for] bodies often change their position and qualities, and after a little
absence or interruption may become hardly knowable. But . . . even
in these changes they preserve a *coherence*, and have a regular dependence on each other.[20]

Constancy and coherence, then, are what the imagination fastens
on when it selects certain impressions as being 'of' something
objective.
    Something has gone wrong already. The question was: 'What
features of our impressions induce the imagination to objectify
some of them?', but Hume's answer speaks of the constancy and

[18] *Treatise*, p. 194.
[19] *Treatise*, pp. 194–7 ('After a little . . . present to my perception.').
[20] *Treatise*, pp. 194, 195.

coherence not of impressions but of objects. The above passage treads down the needed distinction, as does this:

My bed and table, my books and papers, present themselves in the same uniform manner, and change not upon account of any interruption in my seeing or perceiving them. This is the case with all the impressions, whose objects are suppos'd to have an external existence; and is the case with no other impressions.

An analyst of objectivity-concepts, one would think, should be more sensitive to when he is using such concepts himself. But the impurity of Hume's use of 'constant' and 'coherent' is not fatal; for we can—taking clues from Price—reconstruct constancy and coherence as features of sets of impressions, as follows.[21] Coherence is just orderliness: a 'coherent' set of impressions is one conforming to some generalization to which many other sets also conform. Constancy is a special case of coherence: a 'constant' set of impressions is one conforming to the generalization 'Each member of the set is exactly like the preceding member'. This account allows, as Hume intends, that a set of impressions may be 'constant' even if there is a gap between my having some of its members and my having the rest.

Hume now asks why the impressions that we associate with objects should be just the members of constant and coherent sets. As he unhappily puts it, how do those two features 'give rise to so extraordinary an opinion' as The Belief? He answers through a complex example from which I select two episodes: (1) I hear a creaking noise and believe that a door is opening behind me, and (2) I read a letter 'from a friend, who says he is two hundred leagues distant', and I 'spread out in my mind the whole sea and continent between us'.

(Notice that (2) concerns a continent when I do not perceive it at all, while (1) concerns a door when I at least hear it. Hume speaks of the door's being 'open'd without my perceiving it', as though hearing it creak did not count as perceiving it. (1) is not irrelevant, for it raises the question of a visible item's existing when I do not see it; but all the same Hume has overlooked a significant difference between the two examples.)

These examples are to illustrate the force of constancy and coherence. Here is what Hume says about the door:

[21] Price, pp. 32–6, 65.

I never have observ'd, that this noise cou'd proceed from any thing but the motion of a door; and therefore conclude, that the present phaenomenon is a contradiction to all past experience, unless the door, which I remember on t'other side the chamber, be still in being.[22]

I shall argue that this cannot exemplify the kind of thinking which 'produces' The Belief, because we cannot regard any phenomenon as 'a contradiction to all past experience' unless we have already accepted The Belief. A little later, Hume says it again:

I am accustom'd to hear such a sound, and see such an object in motion at the same time. I have not receiv'd in this particular instance both these perceptions. These observations are contrary, unless I suppose that the door still remains, and that it was open'd without my perceiving it: And this supposition, which was at first entirely arbitrary and hypothetical, acquires a force and evidence by its being the only one, upon which I can reconcile these contradictions.[23]

What contradictions? The notion of 'contradiction' has no place here unless I already accept a large body of theory: the proposition that I inhabit a world of objects, many hypotheses about their general behaviour, and some hypotheses of the form 'I have perceptions of kind K only when in the presence of objects of kind K*'. Given all this, and some particular perception, I may have to postulate the existence of an unperceived object—or of a visible but unseen one, or the like—on pain of contradiction. But Hume's examples are supposed to illustrate the kind of thinking which underlies The Belief as a whole, and down at that level a 'perception' cannot threaten to contradict anything—whether a theory or, through the theory, other perceptions. Wanting to explain how we answer the question 'Are there objects—*doors* for instance?' Hume has at best explained how we answer the question 'Am I now hearing a door?' or 'Is there a door behind me now?', as asked by someone who knows that there are objects, including doors, and who knows a good deal about them. This is the gravest case yet of Hume's failure properly to set the scene for an analysis of objectivity-concepts.

He says this about the letter:

'Tis evident I can never account for this phaenomenon, conformable to my experience in other instances, without spreading out in my mind the whole sea and continent between us, and supposing the effects

---

[22] *Treatise*, p. 196.   [23] *Treatise*, pp. 196–7.

and continu'd existence of posts and ferries, according to my memory and observation.[24]

Hume does sometimes mention 'contradictions' in discussing the 'letter' example, and we could force that reading onto the quoted sentence, taking 'account for, conformable to my experience in other instances' to mean 'render consistent with my other experience'. But we could instead take it to mean 'explain, without contradicting my other experience'. This would put Hume on firmer ground: spreading out the sea and the continent is no longer removing a contradiction but providing an explanation.

The following view now emerges:—I have a conceptual framework which lets me connect my various sensory episodes to form a coherent whole: I bring the brute, disconnected facts of my sensory history under a *theory* in terms of which I can adduce some of these facts as explaining others, can predict further ones, and so on. This theory does its work only because, through it, statements about past perceptions can imply statements about present and future ones. Also, the theory is—for reasons to be discussed in § 72—so structured that through it certain perception-statements can imply the existence of objects when I do not perceive them. In a given sensory situation I may have to choose between (*a*) accepting that there is such an object, (*b*) relinquishing the theory and thus my only chance of explaining my sensory present, and (*c*) retaining the theory while denying that there is an object which I don't perceive—thus committing myself to a falsehood about my sensory past. This is the case where I must choose (*a*) if I am to 'account for [my present perception] conformable to past experience': if I choose (*b*) I cannot 'account for' the perception, and if I choose (*c*) my explanation will not be 'conformable' to my past experience.

Hume could have taken the same line about the door: I want to 'normalize' my auditory experience by relating it to other experiences through a theory which includes The Belief. That would have improved on the question-begging reference to 'reconciling contradictions'.

That Hume is guilty of the worse of the two accounts is certain, but I have given only a slim textual basis for the better of them. Here is more:

[24] *Treatise*, p. 196.

There is scarce a moment of my life, wherein there is not a similar instance presented to me, and I have not occasion to suppose the continu'd existence of objects, in order to connect their past and present appearances, and give them such an union with each other, as I have found by experience to be suitable to their particular natures and circumstances.[25]

The crucial words are 'connect' and 'union'. The same point is made earlier, when Hume says that although our 'passions' have some 'coherence or regularity in their appearances', we do not relate them to objects because:

On no occasion is it necessary to suppose, that they have existed and operated, when they were not perceiv'd, in order to preserve the same dependence and connexion, of which we have had experience. The case is not the same with [impressions which we bring into] relation to external objects. Those require a continu'd existence, or otherwise lose, in a great measure, the regularity of their operation.[26]

From now on, I shall hold Hume to this version, ignoring the 'contradiction-removing' account which sometimes intrudes into the text.

At best, Hume's scene-setting is imperfect. For example, he speaks of reading a letter, rather than of having certain visual and tactual impressions. This could be just short-hand, a way of getting on with the example; but when one remembers that throughout this passage Hume discusses only continuity, ignoring independence, one's suspicions grow. Perhaps, rather than setting aside the notion of an independent object, he is quietly helping himself to it. Perhaps he thinks his problem has the form: 'Given that I sometimes perceive (independent) objects, why do I think they exist when I don't perceive them?' One remark made in his 'explanation-providing' vein does seem to assume that perceived objects raise no problem: 'Objects have a certain coherence even as they appear to our senses; but this coherence is much greater and more uniform, if we suppose the objects to have a continu'd existence.'[27] Still, this does not prove that Hume is helping himself to the notion of a perceived object—meaning a perceived item which really is objective. Recall that he aims to consider The Belief in its vulgar form in which, he thinks, objects are identified with perceptions. If he keeps to this aim, the question 'Does he assume the existence of perceived objects as well as of perceptions?'

[25] *Treatise*, p. 197.   [26] *Treatise*, pp. 195–6.   [27] *Treatise*, p. 198.

cannot even be raised, since it implies a distinction between 'perceived objects' and 'perceptions'. Partly out of fidelity to the vulgar, but partly also out of sheer unthoroughness, Hume often fails to draw this distinction. See, for example, the quoted remarks about the passions.

But if this aspect of Hume's procedure dominates our discussion, we shall get nowhere. At certain points in the section he rests weight on his view that the vulgar are committed to thinking that impressions exist when no one has them, and these episodes should not be neglected. But the section as a whole has a logical structure—is better than a handful of contradictions floating in a sea of tautologies—only because Hume does *not* consistently identify objects with perceptions. In discussing continuity he sometimes assumes objectivity: he makes, and fails to analyse, many statements saying that we perceive objects. Independent objects? There is no way of saying; but the statements in question do assert that we perceive objects and not just that we have perceptions. Hume might well deny that they involve more than the having of perceptions, but he would be wrong.

So far, none of that matters much. The 'explanation-providing' account can be adapted to cover all our beliefs involving objectivity-concepts, including ones about objects—meaning *objects*—which exist when not perceived. Schematic as the account admittedly is, it seems to be on the right lines; and so we might think that Hume is within measurable distance of completing his task.

Not a bit of it! He will eventually conclude that the desire to find a rationale for The Belief is a disease for which 'carelessness and in-attention alone can afford us any remedy'. This dismal turn of events is explained by a passage, the pivot on which the whole section turns, which we must now examine.

72. *Why more is needed*

We have before us the move from coherence to continuity: what kind of move is it? The question is Hume's. He wants to know whether the move, as described by him, is a special case of some more general intellectual phenomenon, some broader and deeper 'principle' or mental disposition. Two candidacies are discussed.

First, there is the suggestion that 'this conclusion from the coherence of appearances' is 'of the same nature with our reasonings concerning causes and effects'. I think that this suggestion is correct, and sometimes Hume does too;[28] but now he rejects it on the grounds that causal reasoning is, while the move from coherence to continuity cannot be, a matter of habit.[29] In support of this, he represents the move to continuity in the following way. We have noticed 'a connexion betwixt two kinds of objects in their past appearance to the senses', but 'are not able to observe this connexion' on a particular occasion; whereupon we 'suppose . . . that these objects still continue their usual connexion, notwithstanding their apparent interruption.' In such a case, that is, we 'bestow on the objects a greater regularity than what is observ'd in our mere perceptions'; and it is this regularity-increasing aspect of our procedure which, Hume thinks, cannot be squared with the procedure's being an habitual one. His reason for this is that ''tis not only impossible, that any habit shou'd ever be acquir'd otherwise than by the regular succession of . . . perceptions, but also that any habit shou'd ever exceed that degree of regularity'. No habit can carry us from regularity in our perceptions to the supposition of 'a greater degree of regularity in some objects', because that would involve 'a contradiction, *viz*. a habit acquir'd by what was never present to the mind'.

This argument apparently trades on 'habit', and would not work if we substituted the origin-neutral term 'disposition'. But never mind that. How is the argument, as it stands, supposed to work? Granted that a habit must arise from sequences of perceptions ('acquir'd by what was present to the mind'), why can it not in some way reach out beyond the perceptions which constitute its basis ('exceed that degree of regularity')? I cannot see that Hume gives any answer to this. The argument is also defective in another way. Its description of the move from coherence to continuity, though extremely unclear, seems fairly clearly to desert the best parts—namely the 'explanation-providing' emphasis—in Hume's earlier treatment of the door, the letter, and so on. I shall return to this point shortly.

Having shown—he thinks—that the inference to continuity is

[28] *Treatise*, pp. 74, 108.
[29] *Treatise*, pp. 197–8 ('But tho' this conclusion . . . other principles.').

not causal in type, Hume explores one other suggestion. This is that the inference is an instance of a certain procedure of extrapolation which he says we often follow. He describes the procedure metaphorically, and illustrates it unclearly; but his sketch of the inference to continuity, when that is seen as an instance of the extrapolating procedure, is clear and literal:

Objects have a certain coherence even as they appear to our senses; but this coherence is much greater and more uniform, if we suppose the objects to have a continu'd existence; and as the mind is once in the train of observing an uniformity among objects, it naturally continues, till it renders the uniformity as compleat as possible. The simple supposition of their continu'd existence suffices for this purpose, and gives us a notion of a much greater regularity among objects, than what they have when we look no farther than our senses.[30]

Hume does not deny that the inference to continuity is in this way a special case of a general kind of extrapolating procedure. His view seems to be that it is a case of that procedure, but that this fact is not enough to explain our preparedness to make the inference from coherence to continuity. The 'principle' behind the extrapolating procedure, Hume says abruptly and dogmatically, is 'too weak to support alone so vast an edifice, as [the belief in] the existence of all external bodies'. And on the basis of this blatantly unargued assertion he sets off on a new tack—not exploring further the underlay of the move from coherence to continuity, but developing an entirely different account of the basis for The Belief.

Part of the explanation for this extraordinary behaviour, no doubt, is just that Hume does have an alternative account of how we come by The Belief, and he is determined to work it in somehow. This is all right in itself, for there is no reason why The Belief should not have two distinct bases. Hume ought not to pretend that he must find a second basis if he is 'to give a satisfactory account of' The Belief because the first basis rests on a principle which is 'too weak to support alone so vast an edifice' etc.; but this complaint is not a very serious one.

Still, something has gone wrong. Hume has seen a valuable part of the truth; and yet the section will end with his treating The Belief as entirely indefensible, because he thinks we must choose between the Lockean and Berkeleian forms of it and he

[30] *Treatise*, p. 198. See also pp. 47–9.

sees that neither will do (see § 78 below). How does he maintain this view of the situation in face of his manifest success, in the 'door' passage, in showing that The Belief does have a certain kind of legitimacy? The answer is not just that he is going to turn his back on that success, but that he has already misrepresented it as a failure.

Consider again his opaque account of how the move from coherence to continuity differs from causal reasoning. I suggest that underlying his point about 'habit' there is a non-genetic point that could be expressed as follows:

In causal inferences we argue from perceptions which we have to others which we have; whereas in moving from coherence to continuity we go from perceptions which we have to ones which we don't have, or to states of affairs which we don't perceive. It follows that these two sorts of intellectual transition—never mind what disposes us to make them—are thoroughly different from one another.[31]

This needs elucidation. The inference from coherence to continuity is said to involve a move 'beyond the perceptions' reported in the premisses. But then in causal inferences we go from the observed to the *not-yet*-observed, and in that sense go 'beyond the perceptions' we have at the time the prediction is made. Hume's contrast between these two movements of the mind requires him to represent the move to continuity as a move from the observed to the *never*-observed. He is asking, in effect, 'Given all the perceptions we ever have, why do we move to statements about perceptions which nobody ever has?'

If I am right in thinking that Hume sees his contrast between causal reasoning and the inference from coherence to continuity in this light, he must think it shows not merely that the two 'are at the bottom considerably different from each other', but that the latter cannot be justified at all. For if there is the difference indicated above, the belief in continuous objects has no bearing at all on any of the impressions we actually have, and so cannot facilitate the intellectual handling of our experience, and so is wholly idle.

This view of the belief in object-continuity is wrong. In showing how, I shall assume the correctness of my hypothesis that the view is one which Hume himself tends to adopt—but I do not want to insist upon this.

Hume, on my hypothesis about him, is caught up in a new form of an error which we have already met: by attending only to those fragments of an object's history when it is not being perceived, he implies that none of our other statements about objects, i.e. statements about objects when they are perceived, raises any problems for him or lies within the scope of his inquiry. He will say that since all those others concern perceived objects they are not problematic, because perceiving an object is just having a perception. But he will be wrong. That class of supposedly unproblematic statements includes many which, despite Hume's denial, do involve objectivity-concepts of the sort he is trying to investigate.

We can get a new angle on this error of Hume's by approaching it through a detail in his own treatment of coherence. He says, according to my hypothesis, that our belief in continuous objects has no experiential cash-value; but how does this square with his view that we postulate continuity in order to make something or other 'more uniform'? This must mean that the postulation makes 'more uniform' what we say about our experience; but this is just to admit that it does facilitate our intellectual handling of our experience, does have experiential cash-value; and so Hume is caught in an inconsistency.

But that is an objection *ad hominem*, which Hume can escape. Let us suppose that he does so in the obvious way—by retracting all he says about the 'door' and 'letter' examples, and declining to claim that anything at all is achieved by the belief that objects exist when unperceived. Then we can get to the real root—and the real instructiveness—of his error.

When I see a door, turn my head away, and then turn back and see it again, my two visual impressions are connected by the statement that each is the seeing of a door. For example, the judgement that the first is the seeing of a door supports the prediction that when I turn my head back I shall have the second visual impression. In ways like this I bring objectivity-concepts to bear upon impressions which I do have; and Hume should admit that such procedures are useful, and are broadly causal in nature. If he concedes both points, then he can hardly avoid acknowledging that to perceive an object is not just to have an impression, and thus admitting that he ought not simply to have helped himself to the notion of a perceived object. Even with all those concessions made, however, Hume might still say: 'But the fact remains that the utility of "perceived object" does not help me with my problem about the utility of "unperceived object". Even if it is helpful to be able to say "I now see a door" both at t_1 and t_3, I have shown that it cannot be helpful to say "There is now a door which I don't see" at t_2.'

But the benefits of 'perceived object' come through a theory of which 'unperceived object' is an *integral* part: we cannot lop off statements asserting the existence of objects while unperceived, while retaining the 'useful' objectivity-statements which classify some of our perceptions as perceptions of objects. For example, the 'sea and continent' are supposed to raise a problem for me only in respect of their existence when I don't perceive them; but the statement 'There is a sea between us *now*' is connected, through my general world-theory and thus through the conceptual framework which is its bone, with statements about perceptions which I do have at some time or other—what I shall observe if I take a certain journey, what I heard my friend say when asked 'What route will you take?' and so on. I have no way of linking these perceptions of mine which doesn't involve my agreeing that the sea is there right now.

Hume's procedure is analogous to this: 'It is obviously useful to have an arithmetical theory for numbers which we actually use, but why should our theory also make room for numbers which no one ever has used, does use, or will use? Our number-theory implies that there is the number 7,352,866,914,008,253— and even adds the baroque extravagance that this so-called number is divisible by three! The theory would be more defensible if we cleansed it of such excrescences.' This is obviously, as Hume's is less obviously, a proposal to trim the body by amputating not a limb but something more like the bones or the veins or the nerves.

Perhaps it is logically true that genuinely objective items must sometimes exist unperceived. But I rest my case on the weaker thesis that the only way I can helpfully bring objectivity-concepts to bear on *my* impressions—or you on yours, or Hume on his— is through a theoretic structure which, together with the given experiential data, implies that objects sometimes exist while unperceived. The only ground *we* have for claiming sometimes to

perceive objects are equally grounds for claiming that objects
sometimes exist when we do not perceive them.

It we equate perceived objects with perceived items which are
'independent', then the view I have been advocating echoes
Hume's own claim that independence and continuity stand or fall
together. As I remarked at the end of § 68, it is a pity that at this
crucial point in the section the claim is forgotten.

73. *Preliminary to a completion: identity*

In his second explanation of why we have The Belief, Hume
connects continuity with identity. He gets the connexion wrong,
but in an instructive way.

He also brings constancy into the limelight. Just because constancy is a special case of coherence, the logical structure of his
treatment of the 'door' and 'letter' examples is such that constancy
could have played a part in that discussion along with coherence.
Hume says in effect that constancy now enters the picture, but it
would be less misleading to say that coherence now drops out
of it.

Hume sketches the argument of his next ten pages as follows.[32]
Consider a limited case of constancy: I have a perception P_1,
followed by others unlike it, followed in turn by P_n which is
extremely like P_1; as when—to break into objectivity language—
I look at a door, turn away briefly, then look again. It is natural
for me to identify P_n with P_1, to think not merely that P_n resembles
but that it *is* P_1. To hide from myself the error of my ways, I try
to 'disguise' or even 'remove' the 'interruption' which has
occurred between P_1 and P_n, by 'supposing that these interrupted
perceptions are connected by a real existence' which I did not
perceive. To 'suppose' something is just to have an idea, but if
the idea acquires enough vivacity it becomes a belief. And this is
how I come to believe that there is something which existed
throughout a period when I did not perceive it.

Of the four parts in which this is to be expounded and defended,
the first is a general account of the concept of identity.[33] Hume
packs a great deal into these pages, and some relevant material

---

[32] *Treatise*, pp. 199–200 ('When we have . . . the propensity.').
[33] *Treatise*, pp. 200–1 ('First, As to . . . multiplicity or number.').

occurs elsewhere.[34] I shall devote the present section and three more to Hume's analysis of identity.

What honest work can the concept of identity do? Hume rightly sees a problem here; but he expresses it badly, centering it on the sentence 'An object is the same with itself'. The difficulty about this, he says, is that (a) if 'object' and 'itself' stand for the same thing then we have only the concept of unity rather than of identity, while (b) if they stand for different things the sentence expresses a falsehood.

These remarks do not isolate a problem. I think that Hume wants to present a problem about the form '...is the same with...' or '. . . is identical with . . .' generally. The problem is that (a) if the blanks are filled in the same way the result is an analytic truth, while (b) if they are filled in different ways the result is a falsehood; and so, apparently, there are no true contingent identity-statements. Hume has tried to generalize over everything of the form '. . . is the same with . . .' by taking the single sentence 'An object is the same with itself', but the generalization does not work. That sentence just is analytic; or, in Hume's version, it just does involve the concept of unity; and we cannot construe it, with linguistic propriety, in such a way that it expresses a falsehood. If we are to have something which easily admits of two sorts of handling, each open to a prima facie objection, we must replace the rigid analytic truth 'An object is the same with itself' by the adaptable sentence-*form* '. . . is the same with . . .', in respect of which we can choose how to fill the blanks.

My version of the problem differs from Hume's not only in its point of focus but also in regard to the complaint against alternative (a): where I say that (a) renders the statement analytic, Hume says that it introduces the concept of unity rather than of identity. But why should it not involve both these concepts? Why, indeed, assume that they are distinct concepts? If my account of the problem is right, we are looking for contingent identity-statements; these must not have the form 'x is identical with x'; and we *might* say that any such statement must in some way involve two items and not just one, or must be genuinely relational, or— as Hume horridly puts it—must 'contain a predicate and a subject'. These increasingly poor formulations are headed towards the claim that contingent identity statements must not be mere

[34] *Treatise*, pp. 253–8.

unity-statements. This, I think, must be what led Hume to mis-represent the search for contingency as the avoidance of unity.

I adopt the hypothesis that I have correctly described Hume's real problem, and shall expound him on that basis. If the hypo-thesis is wrong, I cannot expound him at all.

Hume's problem has been solved. If we put '. . . is identical with . . .' between a pair of expressions which (a) have different meanings yet (b) refer to the same thing, the result will be an identity-statement which avoids both (a) analyticity and (b) falsehood. In the terminology of Frege, who first made this matter really clear, we can formulate an identity-statement which is both true and contingent by finding a pair of terms with different *senses* but the same *reference*—as in 'The Progressive Party's candidate for mayor is the man who supervised the wiring of the Dreamland Theatre'.[35]

With this in mind, consider how Hume sets the problem up. He describes the (a) alternative—which I connect with analyticity —as that in which 'the idea expressed by [one term is] no ways distinguish'd from that meant by [the other]', suggesting that the two terms have *the same sense*. The (b) alternative—the one that leads to falsity—is not explicitly described; but Hume's rejection of it, on the grounds that 'a multiplicity of objects can never convey' the idea of identity, suggests that the two terms have *different references*.

Is Hume leading up to the Fregean solution? Is he poised to remark that (a) and (b) are not exhaustive because two terms might differ in meaning yet refer to one 'object'? He is not. The true Fregean logic of the situation may have influenced some level of his mind, inducing him to expound (a) mainly with 'idea' and (b) wholly with 'object'; but he does not see this choice of ter-minology as heralding a clear third alternative. This fact can be explained. From one end: Humean 'ideas' are meanings, but are also a species of 'perceptions'. From the other: Hume often uses 'object' to mean merely 'item that can be referred to', and thinks that perceptions are our only subject-matter, our only 'objects'. So 'idea' slides into 'perception' which is then equated with 'object'. We naturally pull 'idea' out towards 'sense', and pull 'object' the other way towards 'reference', leaving clear Fregean

[35] G. Frege, 'On Sense and Reference', in P. Geach and M. Black (eds), *Translations from the Philosophical Writings of Gottlob Frege* (Oxford, 1952).

space in between. But there are forces in Hume's thought which draw 'idea' and 'object' together, closing the gap.

Yet Hume does apparently think that the dilemma can be escaped:

We cannot, in any propriety of speech, say, that an object is the same with itself, unless we mean, that the object existent at one time is the same with itself existent at another. By this means we make a difference, betwixt the idea meant by the word *object*, and that meant by *itself*, without going the length of number, and at the same time without restraining ourselves to a strict and absolute unity.[36]

I take this to mean that 'x is identical with y' can steer a course between falsehood and analyticity ('number' and 'unity') only if x is an item existent at one time and y is an item existent at another. To understand and assess this, we must place it in a wider setting.

74. *Serial identity-statements*

From now on I shall be concerned only with contingent identity-statements. All subsequent uses of 'identity-statement' should be understood as tacitly qualified by 'contingent' or 'non-analytic'.

Any true identity-statement which does not use pronouns or proper names must contain two partial descriptions, neither entailing the other, of some one item. In a *synchronous* identity-statement, the descriptions relate as 'F at t' does to 'G at t'; for example, 'The man who has been standing in the corner is the one who has been bidding against you for all the best pieces'. In a *serial* identity-statement, they relate as 'F at t_1' does to 'F at t_n' or to 'G at t_n'; for example, 'The car I drove today is the one I drove yesterday' or '. . . is the one I washed yesterday'. In allowing serial identity-statements but not synchronous ones, Hume omits half the story. My guess as to why he does so is not worth space: our real concern is not with his suppression of synchronous identity-statements but with what he says about serial ones.

In saying that an identity-statement can be true only if it is a serial one, Hume strongly implies that some *are* true, but he does not quite say this outright. He may in fact think that no serial identity-statement is strictly true, which view he would share with others. Commenting on the answers to a problem set in *Analysis*, Prior writes:

The one wholly exasperating thing in the sixteen entries is the talk in one or two of them of a 'strict' sense of 'one and the same' in which no object existing at one time can be the same individual as an object existing at another time ... So far from being a peculiarly 'strict' sense of the phrase in question, this seems to me a hideous muddle ... To say that my successive instantaneous states are not one state but several is one thing, while to say that I in those states am not one but several individuals is to say quite another thing, and a thundering silly thing at that.[37]

Still, there is some excuse. A serial identity-statement does involve distinct things-at-a-time. In the language of Quine's classic discussion of identity, such a statement refers to distinct *thing-stages*.[38] (For Quine a thing is a time-taking process whose 'momentary parts' are thing-stages, but I prefer to allow a 'stage' to take time also—as much or as little as is needed for the analytic purpose in hand.) When I say 'The car I drove today is the car I washed yesterday' I do refer to two items, two car-stages, which are certainly distinct because their durations do not even overlap. So how can it be strictly correct to say that one of them *is* the other?

The answer to this is that 'The car I drove today is the one I washed yesterday' does not identify one thing-stage with another. Its first five words do not refer to a car-stage at all, nor do its last five. Rather, they refer—through a partial description of its state during part of its history—to an enduring car.[39] We *can* express 'The car I drove today is the car I washed yesterday' in terms of car-stages, but we must be careful to express it not in the form

The F car-stage is identical with the G car-stage

but rather in the form

The F car-stage has relation R to the G car-stage;

where R is the relation of being so linked as to constitute stages of a single car. In short, serial identity-statements are in a way

[37] A. N. Prior in *Analysis*, vol. 17 (1956–7), pp. 122–3.

[38] W. V. Quine, 'Identity, Ostension, and Hypostasis', in *From a Logical Point of View* (Cambridge, Mass., 1953), pp. 65–6.

[39] See Price, pp. 47–8.

about thing-stages, but they do not assert identities between thing-stages.

Hume does not say that serial identity-statements are never strictly true, but perhaps he ought to. In the preliminary sketch reported early in § 73 he says:

When we have . . . found, that the perception of the sun or ocean, for instance, returns upon us after an absence or annihilation with like parts and in a like order, as at its first appearance, we are not apt to regard these interrupted perceptions as different, (which they really are) but on the contrary consider them as individually the same, upon account of their resemblance. But as this interruption of their existence is contrary to their perfect identity, and makes us regard the first impression as annihilated, and the second as newly created, we find ourselves . . . involv'd in a kind of contradiction.[40]

Even if my perceptions P_1 and P_n are very similar, Hume here says, it is wrong for me to identify P_1 with P_n if they are dissimilar from the intervening perceptions $P_2, \ldots, P_{n-1}$. But it would be wrong to identify P_1 with P_n even if the intervening perceptions were exactly like them; my perception P_1 at t_1 is an episode in my sensory history, and my perception P_n at t_n is *another*: they are numerically distinct just because they are differently dated, whatever happened in the interval $t_2, \ldots, t_{n-1}$.

If my sensory state is qualitatively uniform from t_1 right through to t_n, we might wish to say that I have had a single perception lasting through that period. For example (moving for idiomatic convenience from perceptions to pains), one might say 'The headache that is distracting me now is the very same one that made me lose my temper an hour ago'. But that is to say that the two pain-episodes are parts of a single longer one—which is different from, and inconsistent with, the claim that the earlier one *is* the later one.

So someone who tries as Hume does to restrict himself to what can be said in terms of one's perceptions or inner states is almost bound to commit himself to denying that any serial identity-statement is strictly true. Hume is thus committed by the passage last quoted, and also by his initial account of the problem about how to avoid both 'unity' and falsehood—an account which leaves no room for a valid escape between the horns of the dilemma. Whether Hume accepts what he is thus committed to is

[40] *Treatise*, p. 199.

another matter; but I am inclined to agree with Price that Hume does think, although he does not ever explicitly say, that no serial identity-statement is strictly true.[41]

The principal evidence for this is Hume's account of the paradigm identity-statement, the kind which is true if any identity-statements are true. Even this, he says, involves a 'fiction of the imagination' which works as follows;

'Tis by means of it, that a single object, plac'd before us, and survey'd for any time without our discovering in it any interruption or variation, is able to give us a notion of identity. For when we consider any two points of this time, we may place them in different lights: We may either survey them at the very same instant; in which case they give us the idea of number, both by themselves and by the object; which must be multiply'd, in order to be conceiv'd at once, as existent in these two differents points of time: Or on the other hand, we may trace the succession of time by a like succession of ideas, and conceiving first one moment, along with the object then existent, imagine afterwards a change in the time without any *variation* or *interruption* in the object; in which case it gives us the idea of unity. Here then is an idea, which is a medium betwixt unity and number; or more properly speaking, is either of them, according to the view, in which we take it: And this idea we call that of identity.[42]

It is just after this that Hume says that we cannot 'in any propriety of speech' formulate identity-statements other than serial ones. (The quoted passage is introduced by two and a half sentences, including the word 'fiction', which refer back to an earlier discussion and which raise an extraordinary difficulty.[43] They do not help us with the bit I have quoted—but I spare the reader the pages of exegesis which are needed to justify this claim.)

The passage is most unclear. For one thing, in describing what gives us 'the idea of number' Hume assumes that 'a single object' *can* last throughout the relevant period of time—it is this one object which is 'multiplied' when we bring two moments in its history together in a single thought. But the question of whether one object can last through time is just what Hume ought to be answering or at least analysing. The existence of enduring items is not only necessary but also sufficient for there to be true serial identity-statements; so what can we make of a purported analysis

[41] Price, pp. 39–41.   [42] *Treatise*, p. 201.
[43] *Treatise*, p. 65. See also pp. 36–7.

of identity-statements which adopts, as true and not in need of analysis, the assumption that there are items which endure? Also, of course, there is the omnipresent difficulty: how much of an objectivity-load is Hume putting on 'object'? The answer ought to be 'None', because Hume is still trying to explain how we arrive at objectivity-concepts; but it is not clear that he fully realizes this.

For all the passage's opaqueness, though, one thing seems clear: it purports to describe a *mistake* inherent in all serial identity-statements. It locates an 'idea' which may be that of 'number' or of 'unity', Hume virtually says, according to which aspects of the situation we *overlook*. A little later Hume comes even closer to saying this outright.[44]

Admittedly, there is evidence the other way, as when Hume says that 'the interruption of our perceptions' is 'the only circumstance that is contrary to their identity', which implies that if there is no interruption a genuinely true identity-statement can be made. Still, Hume's considered view may be weaker than that: he may mean just that the 'interruption' is the 'only circumstance' that stops the case from being a paradigm case of identity, with the reservation that even paradigm identity-statements are not quite true. Similarly, when he implies that in some cases we can 'in propriety of speech' assert an identity-statement,[45] he may mean that those are the paradigm cases in which we *do* assert such statements, while still thinking that what we then assert is tainted with falsehood. I know of nothing in Hume's attitude to linguistic norms which rules out this interpretation.

Because of the impatience of Hume's writing and the weakness of its theoretical underlay, one cannot be sure whether he sees the paradigm serial identity-statement as strictly true or merely as the best we can do. It is not important to decide. But it is important, we shall find, to see how firmly Hume is committed to the 'merely the best we can do' position: it has a place in his thought, if not in his mind.

75. *Identity and objectivity*

What Hume needs, of course, is to distinguish 'my perception' from 'what I perceive', for it is only the former that always yields

---

[44] *Treatise*, the paragraph on pp. 203–4.   [45] *Treatise*, p. 201.

falsehood when used to fill the blanks in '. . . at t_1 is identical with . . .at t_n'. Had he worked with the form 'What I perceive at t_1 is identical with what I perceive at t_n', he would not have been committed to saying that every instance of his paradigm kind of identity-statement is false.

There would also have been other consequences. Hume says that each paradigm identity-statement concerns an item which is 'invariable' throughout the period spanned by the statement. He seems really to think that there is something suspect, some falling short of the paradigm, in any serial identity-statement which spans a period of time during which the item in question has altered, i.e. in any whose two descriptions relate as 'F at t_1' does to 'G at t_n' rather than as 'F at t_1' does to 'F at t_n'. Certainly, there is a limit to how much 'variation' a serial identity-statement can stand: it cannot be true that the postage-stamp I have just licked is the book I read last night. But it does not follow, and is not true, that an item's altering always makes the re-identification of it less secure or correct. Why does Hume think otherwise?

Part of the explanation lies in a minor mistake of his which I need not discuss;[46] but another part lies in his taking as his paradigm a statement identifying one perception with a later perception. That fact, which is what implies that even the paradigms are false, also explains why he regards any 'variation' as a further defect: any dissimilarity between the two perceptions makes it just that much more obvious that it is a mistake to identify them with one another. Replace 'perceptions' by 'items which are perceived', and this source of error—I mean the error Hume commits, not the one he describes—will evaporate.

But to distinguish 'my perception' from 'what I perceive' *is* to employ objectivity-concepts! Am I being unfair, then? Am I demanding that Hume, in the course of explaining the underlay of all our objectivity-concepts, use a distinction which itself involves such concepts? No. My claim is that, just because Hume ought at this stage to eschew objectivity-concepts, he is not entitled yet to introduce the concept of identity. Identity *is* an objectivity-concept. If Frege is right, we can formulate an identity-statement only if we assign two or more properties to some item, or can credit some item with a history. But the pursuit of objectivity-concepts largely consists in the endeavour to do precisely those

[46] *Treatise*, the paragraph on pp. 255–6.

two things: the inadequacy of Berkeley's account of objectivity emerged sharply in his inability to explain how one thing could be perceived in more than one way, or at more than one time.

(In saying that identity is an objectivity-concept I am agreeing with Kant about the concept of personal identity as applied to oneself. And I am snubbing such degenerate identity-statements as 'The headache that is now distracting me is the one I had an hour ago', which uses the language of identity but cannot be accounted a serious and central use of the concept of identity.)

In trying to analyse identity-statements while depriving himself of objectivity-concepts, therefore, Hume is bound to run into trouble. Let us credit him with thinking that no serial identity-statement is strictly true. We can then give him credit for seeing the crucial difficulty in which he has landed himself, but we must also add that he has turned it on its head. Hume depicts us as having the concept of identity, wanting but failing to give it a grip on our perceptions, and therefore being led—in ways yet to be fully explained—to postulate the existence of objective items as a way of getting identity to work. It is as though someone said: 'We took to *distinguishing* things so as to have a use for our technique of *counting*.'

Hume puts the cart before the horse. His inquiry embodies the fine insight that there is a deep and intimate connexion between identity and objectivity as such; but he does not see that the connexion is of such a kind that the worst possible route into objectivity is through identity.

76. *The answer completed*

Hume next proceeds to explain 'why the constancy of our perceptions makes us ascribe to them a perfect numerical identity, tho' there be very long intervals betwixt their appearance'. The explanation occupies three pages,[47] but its core can be stated briefly, as follows. According to Hume's 'association of ideas' theory there are various values of R such that: if two ideas are related by R, the mind moves naturally and easily from one of them to the other. Of these values of R—these 'natural relations' —the most potent is *similarity*. To this Hume now adds a further principle, namely that we tend to 'mistake one idea for another' if

[47] *Treatise*, pp. 201–4 ('I now proceed . . . for the other.').

they are so related that there is a smooth mental slide between them. It therefore follows that when one perception is extremely like another, we actually mistake one for another and so assert an identity between them. The tendency to do this is so powerful that even an 'interruption' between the two perceptions does not deter us:

An easy transition or passage of the imagination, along the ideas of these different and interrupted perceptions, is almost the same disposition of mind with that in which we consider one constant and uninterrupted perception. 'Tis therefore very natural for us to mistake the one for the other.[48]

As Hume remarks in an important footnote, there are two points here: we mistake the mind's movement across an 'interruption' for a movement where there is no interruption, and *therefore* we mistake a case of similarity for one of identity—or mistake one idea for another.

Hume handles all this very badly, as he is bound to do. His failure to look hard enough at the concept of identity shows strikingly in his way of asking what kinds of situation tempt us to assert false identity-statements:

Now what other objects, beside identical ones, are capable of placing the mind in the same disposition, when it considers them, and of causing the same uninterrupted passage . . . from one idea to another? . . . If we can find any such objects, we may certainly conclude, from the foregoing principle, that they are very naturally confounded with identical ones, and are taken for them in most of our reasonings.[49]

Whatever 'objects' may be, one hopes that Hume would not say that they are of two kinds—identical and non-identical! But to cleanse his text of the implication that this is a proper way to classify objects, he would have to work down to a deeper level, and subject to critical scrutiny the uneasy amalgam of phenomenal and objective terms with which he is trying to work. It won't do to say that I have wished 'identical object' onto Hume when all he needs is 'identical pair of objects', for the latter phrase is as silly as the former. In the standard phrase 'identity of indiscernibles' the final 's' is a logical solecism.

In this morass, let us consider just one detail: why, in Hume's view, does an 'interruption' bring (or add) falsity to a serial identity-statement? It is arguable that an objective item existing at t_1 and at t_n must exist throughout $t_2 \ldots t_{n-1}$, but a cogent argument for this would need a clearer picture than Hume's of what is involved in analysing objectivity-concepts—e.g. it could not blithely equate 'perceiving an object' with 'having a perception'. We cannot see Hume as entering into that debate. His reason for demanding continuity operates at an altogether more primitive level.

Hume's view about 'interruptions', as about 'variations', can be explained only by reference to the fact that even his paradigm identity-statements are not strictly true. If we see that on Hume's account every serial identity-statement wrongly identifies one perception with another, we can see the significance of interruptions: if the two identified perceptions are interrupted, this is an extra reminder of the fact that they are two and that identification of them is therefore wrong. Hume offers no explanation of why interruptions make so much difference; and perhaps he would have rejected this one, denying that there need be any falsity in a paradigm identity-statement. But I still maintain that the above does in some manner explain why Hume says what he does about continuity in relation to identity.

He sometimes tries to give significance to interruptions while presenting the paradigm cases as strictly true, by contrasting 'different and interrupted perceptions' with 'one constant and uninterrupted perception'. The latter phrase suggests that where there is no interruption the identity-statement really is true, because it concerns a single, long-lasting perception. To repeat a point made briefly in § 74: even if I have one long perception P lasting from t_1 through to t_n, the paradigm identity-statement, on Hume's own account of it, is still false; for it identifies the part of P occurring at t_1 with the part occurring at t_n, and these parts or sub-episodes are distinct. Among the passages which firmly commit Hume to agreeing about this is the one last quoted. He says there that in the paradigm case, as in the 'interrupted' one, there is an 'uninterrupted passage' of the mind 'from one idea to *another*'. This is not just a momentary lapse: without it, Hume has no account of why we mistake interrupted cases for paradigm ones, and thus—as we shall see in a moment—no explanation of why we postulate the existence of objects when they are not perceived.

The next part of Hume's exposition is plain sailing.[50] An 'interruption' between P_1 and P_n 'seems contrary to the identity'—the falsity of the statement identifying P_1 with P_n stares us in the face. Yet if they are sufficiently alike the inclination to identify them is nearly irresistible—we can 'never without reluctance yield up' the identity-statement. In order to avoid yielding it up we obliterate the reminder of its falsity in the only way we can, namely by 'feigning' or pretending that there was no interruption.

At this point, Hume explicitly insists upon his reading of the vulgar form of The Belief: we feign the existence of *perceptions* which would fill the gap—not by pretending that we had such perceptions, but by pretending that they existed at the relevant time even though nobody had them. Hume anticipates the objection that we could never 'assent to so palpable a contradiction' as that of supposing 'a perception to exist without being present to the mind'.[51] His surprising reply—namely that this is not a contradiction—will be discussed in my next section; but first let us rush through to the end of the story.

It remains only to show how our 'feigning' becomes downright belief.[52] The explanation is simple: the feigning consists in having ideas of unowned perceptions; and these ideas, being related both by causation and by resemblance to impressions which are actually had, will borrow vivacity or liveliness from the latter. Vivacity will also be increased by the sheer frequency with which the feigning is performed. But according to Hume's analysis of belief, to have a very lively idea of something's being the case *is* to believe that it is the case. That completes Hume's explanation of why we believe that there are items which exist when we do not perceive them.

This terminal episode in Hume's presentation of his 'system' requires no comment.

77. *Unowned perceptions*

Hume says that 'the unthinking and unphilosophical part of mankind, (that is, all of us, at one time or other)'[53] assent to the proposition that *some perceptions exist when nobody has them*, which

[50] *Treatise*, pp. 205–6 ('The persons . . . more fully afterwards.').
[51] *Treatise*, p. 206.
[52] *Treatise*, pp. 208–10 ('But as we here . . . by that circumstance.').
[53] *Treatise*, p. 205.

I shall call 'P'. I have argued in § 5 that P involves a logical or conceptual error comparable to 'There are instances of squareness which do not consist in something's being square', and sometimes Hume seems to agree. In the present context, however, he denies that P is logically defective.[54]

He thinks that he has to defend P's consistency if he is to maintain its near-universal acceptance; but really his consistency-'proof' is, tactically speaking, no use to him. He virtually admits that P looks inconsistent, and to show its supposed consistency he has to resort to a recherché argument which could hardly be among the intellectual possessions of 'the unthinking and un-philosophical part of mankind'. So Hume's consistency-proof, even if it were valid, would not achieve his purpose; for it could still be objected that since P *seems* to be a 'palpable contradiction' the vulgar are extremely unlikely to accept it.

Tactical motives aside, Hume gives reasons for saying that P is false but not logically so. Assuming for the moment that P is contingent, why should Hume say that it is false? He may well say that we have no cogent evidence for it, and that we accept it only to hide our fumblings with the concept of identity; but he goes further, maintaining that P is false. Why?

The answer lies in Hume's sketch of 'a few of those experiments, which convince us, that our perceptions are not possest of any independent existence' or, *a fortiori*, of any continuous existence.[55] Some of these 'experiments', e.g. those involving the effect of distance upon apparent size, merely remind us that facts about sensory states do not correlate one-for-one with statements we make about the objective realm: the visual sense-datum pertaining to the tree occupies less of my visual field than it did, but I do not say that the tree has shrunk. What such 'experiments' show is not 'that our perceptions are not possest of any independent existence', but only that our perceptions are not possessed of *all* the properties we customarily attribute to 'objects'. Hume may say that the 'experiments' refute The Belief in the naive form in which he thinks we hold it, but this is (1) false and (2) irrelevant. (1) What the 'experiments' really show is that Hume is wrong about the form in which we hold The Belief. Just because we do not say that the tree has shrunk, even though the

---

[54] See J. Cook, 'Hume's Scepticism with Regard to the Senses'.
[55] *Treatise*, paragraph on pp. 210–11.

relevant visual sense-datum now occupies less of the visual field, it is wrong to say that we take our objects to be our perceptions. (2) Even if these 'experiments' did refute The Belief, Hume could not argue from that to the falsity of P. For he says repeatedly that The Belief is false *because* P is false, i.e. because there are in fact no unowned perceptions; and so he needs an argument against P which does not have the denial of The Belief as a lemma.

Hume's first and most fully expounded 'experiment' is this:

When we press one eye with a finger, we immediately perceive all the objects to become double, and one half of them to be remov'd from their common and natural position. But as we do not attribute a continu'd existence to both these perceptions, and as they are both of the same nature, we clearly perceive, that all our perceptions are dependent on our organs, and the disposition of our nerves and animal spirits.

This could be just the argument I have been criticizing, but it could be something else. Hume may here be arguing that since I can modify my perceptions by modifying myself, my perceptions are therefore dependent upon myself. Unlike the other argument, this at least seems to head in the desired direction; but it too is quite worthless. Waiving several difficulties, we might concede that the argument shows that what perceptions *are had* depends upon the states of those who have them; but what has that to do with the thesis P that perceptions exist which *are not had*?[56]

Clearly, nothing could refute P once it is granted to be contingent. If P is not logically false there are no grounds for calling it false at all—or, of course, for calling it true. Some philosophers in our century, assuming that there could be unowned perceptions, have debated whether there are any; but this tiresome stretch of the literature confirms that the question is empty.

Hume's argument for P's contingency, which is much more interesting, rests on two premises. (1) There is Hume's analysis of the concept of mental identity. Although the details of this reflect Hume's general failure with the concept of identity, its main drift is clear. Against the view, which seems to be Berkeley's, that a mind consists of a naked substratum in which mental qualities inhere, Hume opposes his own claim that a mind is 'nothing but a heap or collection of different perceptions, united

[56] See Price, pp. 114–15; and Cook, op. cit. pp. 12–14.

together by certain relations'.[57] (2) The other premiss is Hume's
thesis, discussed in § 62 above, that all perceptions are distinct—
or, as Hume here says, that 'Every perception is distinguishable
from [every] other, and may be consider'd as separately existent.'
From (1) and (2) together, 'It evidently follows, that there is no
absurdity in separating any particular perception from the mind;
that is, in breaking off all its relations, with that connected mass
of perceptions, which constitute a thinking being.'[58] Whether it
does 'evidently follow' depends upon how we construe the premisses. For the argument to go through, I think we must understand its premisses thus:

(1) For some R: *x is owned by a mind↔x has R to some other
perceptions.*

(2) For no R: *x exists→x has R to some other perceptions.*

From these two it really does follow that

It is not the case that: *x exists→x is owned by a mind,*

which is just to say that there can be unowned perceptions.

When we demand (2)'s credentials, however, we find that it has
none. The nearest thing to it that Hume has so far introduced is
the much weaker principle:

(2') No partial description of a mind entails the rest of the
description of it

—this being what underlies Hume's anti-rationalist view that
what I have observed so far cannot entail what I shall observe
next. I here by-pass the problem, discussed in §§ 59–62, of how to
prevent (2') from slithering into triviality. My present point is
that (2'), however charitably interpreted, does not imply that
there could be unowned perceptions. What it says of any perception *x* which is had by some mind is that *x* might not have
been had—its being had was not entailed by the set of previous
facts about the mind in question—and this does not imply that
x might have existed without being had. If Hume has tried to
infer P's consistency from (2'), he has in effect moved from 'Every
perception is possibly-unowned' to 'Possibly there are perceptions

[57] *Treatise*, p. 207.   [58] Ibid.

which are unowned'—a non-sequitur with the same structure as the 'perceived'/'perceivable' argument of Berkeley's discussed in § 32 above. If on the other hand Hume has sought to infer P's consistency from (2), then he owes us a defence of the premiss.

78. *The despairing conclusion*

In the closing pages of Hume's section he reaps the harvest he has sown.[59] Having argued that The Belief of the vulgar—as he understands it—is untenable, Hume assails what he thinks to be the only other form The Belief could take, namely the 'philosophical hypothesis' that there are independent and continuous objects which are not perceptions. He rejects this as another worthless fiction, and thence concludes that in neither of its possible forms is The Belief intellectually defensible.

Minute exposition is not needed: once the fundamental mistake in these pages is understood, their details fall into place. I want only to display the basic mistake—to exhibit its structure and its roots in the deeper levels of Hume's thought.

For brevity, I shall use 'Objects are [not] . . .' to mean 'There are independent and continuous items which are [not] . . .'

Hume, we have seen, credits the vulgar with holding the Berkeleian view that objects are perceptions, and all his criticisms of the vulgar form of The Belief depend upon this interpretation of it. If one is to avoid the Berkeleian position without denying that there are objects, one must say that objects are not perceptions: this is the 'philosophical hypothesis' which Hume also rejects—because he equates it with Locke's view. That is, he assumes that if objects are not perceptions they must be Lockean 'real things' which are never themselves perceived and which have to be conjectured to exist behind the veil of perception.

The Lockean position is wrong, of course, and Hume has some sharp and relevant things to say about it. For example, sensory facts cannot be explained by the hypothesis that unperceivable objects are acting upon us, because:

As no beings are ever present to the mind but perceptions; it follows that we may observe a conjunction or a relation of cause and effect between different perceptions, but can never observe it between perceptions and [Lockean] objects. 'Tis impossible, therefore, that from

[59] *Treatise*, pp. 211–18 ('The natural consequence . . .' to the end).

the existence or any of the qualities of the former, we can ever form any conclusion concerning the existence of the latter.[60]

Although in its details this reflects inadequacies in Hume's theory of causality, it is a sound, Berkeleian move in the right direction.

Hume insists that the Lockean position, although it looks more sophisticated than the Berkeleian one, is really its inferior: it 'has no primary recommendation, either to reason or the imagination', while the Berkeleian position at least appeals to the imagination.[61] No one would have countenanced the Lockean view for a moment, Hume argues, if we were not first seduced by the imagination into the Berkeleian view and then pulled up short by reason or 'reflection':

The imagination tells us, that our resembling perceptions have a continu'd and uninterrupted existence . . . Reflection tells us, that even our resembling perceptions are interrupted in their existence . . . The contradiction betwixt these opinions we elude by a new fiction, . . . by ascribing these contrary qualities to different existences; the *interruption* to perceptions, and the *continuance* to objects.[62]

Our 'new fiction' is the Lockean view. It meets the original objection to the Berkeleian view, but falls foul of reason in other ways: we could not have evidence that there are any Lockean objects, we cannot even mean anything by the relevant expressions, and so on. Furthermore, in manoeuvring to meet a difficulty in the Berkeleian position we have thrown out just that element in it which was attractive to the imagination—namely the fiction of an unowned *perception* which would restore continuity, and thus identity, to a pair of 'resembling perceptions'. So we have flouted the imagination without properly placating reason, and our last state is thus worse than our first. In one place, after sketching the case against 'our popular system' as he understands it, Hume proceeds: 'And as to our philosophical one, 'tis liable to the same difficulties; and is over-and-above loaded with this absurdity, that it at once denies and establishes the vulgar supposition.'[63] This, though unhappily expressed, clearly makes the general point that Locke is a step backwards from Berkeley. The energy and elaborateness of Hume's arguments on this point show irritation with Lockeans who condescend to Berkeley.

Who are these annoying Lockeans? Most of us, much of the time; or so Hume must think. He does not introduce either Locke's name or Berkeley's, but he credits the vulgar with a view which is in fact Berkeley's, and assumes that the only alternative to it—other than denying that there are objects—is a certain position which is in fact Locke's. If these options exhaust the possibilities, then the case against Locke tells also against anyone who says: 'It would indeed be wrong to postulate unowned perceptions, but the objects to which we attribute continuity are not perceptions.' Given Hume's basic picture, just as the vulgar are 'all of us at one time or other', so the adherents of the 'philosophical system' must include nearly everyone at such times as he thinks about continuity. Hume attacks the 'philosophical system' with such persistence, I think, partly because he thinks that it is pretty common property—at least as common as the disposition to say '. . . but the objects to which we attribute continuity are not perceptions'.

That brings us to the important question: why does Hume think that he has to choose between Berkeley's position and Locke's? In answering this I shall replace the generic 'perception' by the specific 'impression', just to avoid a certain possibility of verbal confusion.

One answer, which is correct as far as it goes, is this: Hume thinks that *only impressions can be perceived*. Combine this with the Berkeley-rejecting thesis that *objects are not impressions*, and you get the conclusion that *objects cannot be perceived*, i.e. that there are independent and continuous items but we cannot perceive them. This conclusion contains the essential error in Locke's view.

The question 'Why does Hume identify the vulgar form of The Belief with Berkeley's position?' admits of the same answer: because he thinks that *only impressions can be perceived*. Combine this with the characteristically 'vulgar' view that *objects are perceived*, and you get the conclusion that *objects are impressions*. This conclusion is Berkeley's.

So, when we make the harmless statement which rejects Berkeley we are thought to embrace Locke; and when we make the harmless statement which rejects Locke and brands us as 'vulgar' we are thought to embrace Berkeley; and in each case the mediating mistake is 'Only impressions are perceived'. Once this is deleted, we can make both the innocuous statements at once: objects are not impressions, yet we do perceive objects. Rather than jostling for occupancy of our minds, with only one holding sway at a time, they can now be seen to be two elements in the single form of The Belief which we all hold all the time.

Those explanations do not go very deep, however. Suppose we put it to Hume that what we perceive are not impressions but objects, properly so-called. If he accepts this, what will it commit him to? It implies that he ought initially to have used only the notion of being in a sensory state, or of having an impression, and to have introduced 'perceive' and its relatives only after explaining what an independent and continuous object is. But Hume might cheerfully countenance this. He could say that this revised procedure would still allow him to get on with the job, merely requiring a systematic replacement of 'perceiving an impression' by 'having an impression' and so on. The revised strategy might look like making a real difference in connexion with 'Objects are the very things we feel and see', for now there would at least be a *question* as to whether this vulgar belief entails that objects are impressions. Still, Hume could answer the question wrongly. The concession that what we perceive are not impressions but objects is not enough in itself to get Hume back onto the rails; for, having made that concession, he can still say something like this:

Perhaps I have too hastily construed the vulgar view as entailing that objects are impressions, but have I construed it wrongly? Perhaps 'perceive an impression' is deviant English, but does it represent or generate any fundamental conceptual mistake? The answer is 'No' both times. When someone perceives an object, all that happens is that he has an impression; that's all there is to say about the situation. And so, given any statement about the perceiving of an object, there is an equivalent statement about the having of an impression. For the rest of my argument in the section to go through, perhaps slightly reworded, isn't that all I need?

Obviously we cannot rebut this just by saying again that what we perceive are not impressions but objects. We must go deeper.

I have supposed Hume to say '. . . isn't that all I need?' The right answer to that is: 'It may be all you need, but it is more than you are entitled to.' Hume's basic empiricist insight that there is nothing more to object-perceiving than impression-having does not imply that '*x* perceives O' is equivalent to something of the form '*x* has I' where 'I' names an impression. If '*x* perceives O' is to be expressed in the language of 'impressions', it must be equated with '*x* has I and . . .' followed by a long conjunction, or disjunction of conjunctions, many of whose constituent propositions will be of the form 'If . . . had been the case, *x* would have had I*'. That is to say, object-perceiving is a logical construction out of impression-having; or, more briefly, objects are logical constructions out of impressions.

Hume, like Berkeley, failed to entertain this phenomenalist alternative because his theory of meaning would not let him do so. According to phenomenalism, the only way to elucidate 'object' in terms of 'impression' is by spelling out whole statements about objects as complex statements about impressions; it does not allow one to complete 'An object is . . .' or 'Perceiving is . . .' in the language of 'impressions'. But Hume's atomistic word-by-word theory of meaning demands just such a completion, and so he has to say that an object is an impression and that perceiving is impression-having.

Consider the 'sea and continent' passage discussed in § 71 above. Hume there comes close to a true account of how objectivity-concepts, and beliefs involving them, help us in the intellectual management of our impressions. In that account, the making of an objectivity-judgement is presented as something like the application of rule: it is an intellectual performance which involves one in generalizing, connnecting, predicting. But it leaves no room for a purely phenomenal answer to the question 'What *is* the object which is being said to exist when I do not perceive it?' All it answers is the question 'What am I doing when I make a specific statement about an object's existing when I do not perceive it?'

That is why Hume has to desert his true account in favour of the untruth that the concept of a continuous object does no useful work. He cannot develop the correct account explicitly and in detail, for that would require him to deny something which he holds too deeply, and uses too often, to be able to subject it to critical scrutiny. It would require him to acknowledge that a concept or word-meaning is nothing like a quasi-sensory mental episode and is something very like a rule.

BIBLIOGRAPHY

COLLECTIONS

In the rest of the Bibliography and in footnotes each of these is referred to by the surname of its editor or first-named editor. Most of the material in Chappell, Engle, Martin and Sesonske is reprinted from books and journals.

V. C. CHAPPELL (ed.), *Hume: a Collection of Critical Essays* (New York, 1966).

GALE W. ENGLE and GABRIELE TAYLOR (eds.), *Berkeley's Principles of Human Knowledge: Critical Studies* (Belmont, Calif., 1968).

C. B. MARTIN and D. M. ARMSTRONG (eds.), *Locke and Berkeley: a Collection of Critical Essays* (New York, 1968).

D. F. PEARS (ed.), *David Hume: a Symposium* (London, 1963).

S. C. PEPPER et al. (eds.), *George Berkeley: Lectures Delivered before the Philosophical Union of the University of California* (Berkeley, 1957).

ALEXANDER SESONSKE and NOEL FLEMING (eds.), *Human Understanding: Studies in the Philosophy of David Hume* (Belmont, Calif., 1965).

WARREN E. STEINKRAUS (ed.), *New Studies in Berkeley's Philosophy* (New York, 1966).

BOOKS AND ARTICLES

A list of all the works I have referred to, or even of those which have helped me, would be so long as to be useless for most purposes. For students who want a basic reading-course relating to the main topics of this book, I by-pass a vast amount of good material and suggest the following two dozen:

C. D. BROAD, 'Berkeley's Denial of Material Substance', Martin, pp. 255–83 (from *Philosophical Review*, vol. 63, 1954).

JOHN W. COOK, 'Hume's Scepticism with Regard to the Senses', *American Philosophical Quarterly*, vol. 5 (1968), pp. 1–17.

E. J. CRAIG, 'Berkeley's Attack on Abstract Ideas', *Philosophical Review*, vol. 77 (1968), pp. 425–37.

J. W. DAVIS, 'Berkeley and Phenomenalism', *Dialogue*, vol. 1 (1962–3), pp. 67–80.

J. P. DE C. DAY, 'George Berkeley, 1685–1753', *Review of Metaphysics*, vol. 6 (1952–3), pp. 83–113, 265–86, 447–69, 583–96.

ANTONY FLEW, *Hume's Philosophy of Belief* (London, 1961).

JAMES GIBSON, *Locke's Theory of Knowledge and its Historical Relations* (Cambridge, 1960).

S. A. GRAVE, 'The Mind and its Ideas', Martin, pp. 296–313 (from *Australasian Journal of Philosophy*, vol. 42, 1964; also in Engle).

REGINALD JACKSON, 'Locke's Distinction between Primary and Secondary Qualities', Martin, pp. 53–77 (from *Mind*, vol. 38, 1929).

NORMAN KEMP SMITH, *The Philosophy of David Hume* (London, 1949).

NORMAN KRETZMANN, 'The Main Thesis of Locke's Semantic Theory', *Philosophical Review*, vol. 77 (1968), pp. 175–96.

J. A. PASSMORE, *Hume's Intentions* (Cambridge, 1952).

GEORGE PITCHER, 'Minds and Ideas in Berkeley', *American Philosophical Quarterly*, vol. 6 (1969), pp. 198–207.

KARL POPPER, 'A Note on Berkeley as Precursor of Mach and Einstein', Martin, pp. 436–49 (from *British Journal for the Philosophy of Science*, vol. 4, 1953; also in Engle, and in the author's *Conjectures and Refutations*, London, 1965).

H. H. PRICE, *Hume's Theory of the External World* (Oxford, 1940).

H. H. PRICE, 'The Permanent Significance of Hume's Philosophy', Sesonske, pp. 5–33 (from *Philosophy*, vol. 15, 1940).

ARTHUR N. PRIOR, 'Berkeley in Logical Form', *Theoria*, vol. 21 (1955), pp. 117–22.

GILBERT RYLE, 'John Locke on the Human Understanding', Martin, pp. 14–39 (from J. L. Stocks (ed.), *Tercentenary Addresses on John Locke*, Oxford, 1933).

JAMES WARD SMITH, 'Concerning Hume's Intentions', *Philosophical Review*, vol. 69 (1960), pp. 63–77.

J. F. THOMSON, 'G. J. Warnock's *Berkeley*', Martin, pp. 426–35 (from *Mind*, vol. 65, 1956).

I. C. TIPTON, 'Berkeley's View of Spirit', Steinkraus, pp. 59–71.

G. J. WARNOCK, *Berkeley* (Pelican Books, 1953).

ROBERT PAUL WOLFF, 'Hume's Theory of Mental Activity', Chappell, pp. 99–128 (from *Philosophical Review*, vol. 69, 1960).

FARHANG ZABEEH, *Hume: Precursor of Modern Empiricism* (The Hague, 1960).

ORIGINAL TEXTS

In quoting from Locke, Berkeley and Hume I have followed the texts of the least modernized of the readily-available editions, namely:

A. A. LUCE and T. E. JESSOP (eds.), *The Works of George Berkeley*, published by Nelson in nine volumes between 1949 and 1958.

A. C. FRASER (ed.), John Locke, *An Essay Concerning Human Understanding*, two volumes re-issued by Dover in 1959. John W. Yolton's edition, published by Everyman, is in many ways better.

L. A. SELBY-BIGGE (ed.), David Hume, *A Treatise of Human Nature*, Oxford University Press.

L. A. SELBY-BIGGE (ed.), David Hume, *An Enquiry Concerning Human Understanding*, Oxford University Press.

References to Locke and to Berkeley's *Principles* are given in a form which is valid for any edition. References to Hume's *Treatise* are to pages in the Selby-Bigge edition, which is the one most students will own. References to Hume's *Enquiry* are to Selby-Bigge's marginal numbers in his edition. The following correspondences should enable these references to be applied fairly easily to other editions (e.g. the excellent one by C. W. Hendel, published by the Library of Liberal Arts):

HUME'S SECTION-NUMBERS	SELBY-BIGGE'S MARGINAL NUMBERS
I	1–10
II	11–17
III	18–19
IV	20–33
V	34–45
VI	46–7
VII	48–61
VIII	62–81
IX	82–5
X	86–101
XI	102–115
XII	116–132

References to Berkeley's *Three Dialogues Between Hylas and Philonous* pose more of a problem, since each Dialogue is quite long and there are no agreed sub-divisions. My references are to pages in the standard edition by Jessop, listed above. Other editions would be much more useful if they would indicate in their own texts where the page-turns occur in the Jessop edition. Since this has not been done, other measures are necessary. For selected pages in Jessop, here are the most nearly matching pages in two popular editions in which the *Dialogues* are published along with other work of Berkeley's:

JESSOP	TURBAYNE (LIBRARY OF LIBERAL ARTS)	ARMSTRONG (COLLIER)
174	111–12	138
177	115	141
182	120–1	146
188	127–8	152
192	131–2	156
194	133–4	157–8
196	135–6	159–60
200	140–1	163–4
205	146–7	168–9
213	154–5	176
216	158	179
218	160–1	181
222	165	185
224	167–8	187
230	174–5	192–3
232	176–7	194–5
235	180	197
238	183–4	200–1
242	188	204
245	191–2	207
247	193–4	209–10
249	195–6	211–12
252	199–200	214–15
261	209–10	223–4

SUBJECT INDEX

INDEX OF NAMES